The Iraq WAR

Hidden Agendas and
Babylonian Intrigue

*The Regional
Impact on
Shi'ites, Kurds,
Sunnis and
Arabs*

"Writer Raphael Israeli combines the qualities of the historian, the expert of Islam, the remarkable linguist and connoisseur of American politics which make him the right man to write the chronicle of the 2003 war against Iraq. The Iraq War is a true chronicle in the original sense of the word: close to its resources and written from the perspective of an eyewitness. It is dramatic history, well written and the writer is always aware of weaknesses within greatness. The US/UK operation was disliked by the majority of the public opinion, the actors often confused and the outcome still uncertain. However, the writer convincingly argues that the rationale behind the war was right and US/UK policy-makers were driven by a staunch belief that often characterizes great historical moments. Israeli's most impressive chapter is the last one. It is an eye-opener for a liberal Western audience that often has an impressionistic and romantic image of the Middle East whereas the Middle East is a trap for all those who cannot read the mind of its rulers." *Marc Cogen, Professor of International Law, University of Ghent*

"In lucid language, *The Iraq War* presents the detailed drama of the American-British campaign, examining the complex tribal, religious, and ethnic components of this varied country. Written with insight and sympathy, this book should be a basic source for all readers and students interested in a New Middle East within which Iraq, in seeking cohesion and stability, is a primary player on the political chessboard." *Dr. Mordechai Nisan, Hebrew University of Jerusalem*

"Raphael Israeli's book provides significant insights for understanding the multifaceted aspects of the war in Iraq. Utilizing his wide knowledge of Middle Eastern societies and politics, Professor Israeli throws new light on the realities of the war, and offers valuable analysis of the impact of the war in terms of the future of Iraq (including ethnic divisions and religious–sectarian diversities), the evolution of the strategic situation in the Middle East – including Iran, Saudi Arabia, Syria and Turkey – as well as the role and influence of the United States in the region. This in-depth study depicts the present crisis Iraq finds itself in, set against the background of its historical setting. *The Iraq War* represents an important tool in understanding the recent events that have taken place at the heart of the most sensitive region in the world today." *David Menashri, Parviz and Pouran Nazarian Chair for Modern Iranian Studies, Tel Aviv University*

The Iraq WAR

The Regional Impact on Shi'ites, Kurds, Sunnis and Arabs

Hidden Agendas and Babylonian Intrigue

RAPHAEL ISRAELI

sussex
ACADEMIC
PRESS

Brighton • Portland • Toronto

2 4 6 8 10 9 7 5 3

First published 2004, reprinted 2011, in Great Britain by
SUSSEX ACADEMIC PRESS
PO Box 139, Eastbourne BN24 9BP

and in the United States of America by
SUSSEX ACADEMIC PRESS
920 NE 58th Ave   Suite 300
Portland, Oregon 97213-3786

and in Canada by
SUSSEX ACADEMIC PRESS (CANADA)
90 Arnold Avenue, Thornhill, Ontario L4J 1B5

British Library Cataloguing in Publication Data
A CIP catalogue record for this book is available from the British Library.

Library of Congress Cataloging-in-Publication Data
Israeli, Raphael.
    The Iraq war : hidden agendas and Babylonian intrigue : the regional impact on Shi'ites, Kurds, Sunnis and Arabs / Raphael Israeli.
    p. cm.
    Includes bibliographical references and index.
    ISBN 1-903900-89-1 (h/c, alk. paper) —
    ISBN 1-903900-90-5 (p/b, alk. paper)
    1. Iraq War, 2003. 2. Iraq—Ethnic relations. 3. Iraq—Politics and government—1991- I. Title.
    DS79.76.I87 2004
    956.7044'3—dc22
                                              2004000503
                                              CIP

Typeset and designed by Sussex Academic Press, Brighton and Eastbourne.
Printed and bound in Great Britain by TJ International, Padstow, Cornwall.
This book is printed on acid-free paper.

Contents

Preface

As this volume is going to press, while the predictions concerning the aftermath of the war and the difficulties of "Ruling from Horseback" have proved painfully precise, the controversies surrounding the weapons of mass destruction (WMD) in Iraq, the very *raison d'être* of the war, have continued to dominate the political and media arenas, raising doubts in the minds of many as to the justification of the war. The Kay Report in the US, and the results of the Hutton Inquiry in the UK, have placed the question of WMD in the public spotlight. Those who opposed military intervention prior to the Iraq War feel themselves vindicated by the embarrassing lack of WMD discoveries in Iraq. As a result, President George W. Bush and British Prime Minister Tony Blair, who pressed the case for war in the United Nations based on the assumption that Saddam did indeed have WMD stockpiles, now find themselves dogged by the controversy. The most vocal criticism comes from the Arab countries, more concerned with perceived Anglo-American "aggression" than the overthrow and capture of a brutal dictator. The discovery of mass graves across Iraq (some dating back more than a quarter of a century) has exposed the horrific acts and methods of one of the most cruel governments in living memory.

Though public inquiries in both the US and Britain have revealed embarrassing data about Western Intelligence shortcomings in information-gathering and analysis, thereby strengthening the hands of the Democrat candidates in the US, and the Conservative opposition in the UK, several incontrovertible facts remain:

1   The American search for stockpiles of WMD did *not* conclude that there were no such weapons. The conclusion reached thus far is that WMD have not yet been found; what happened to them during the months leading to the war remains a mystery.

2   There is no doubt in anybody's mind that Iraq did manufacture and use biological and chemical weapons, using them in the wars against Iranians and Kurds, and threatening to use them against Israel. Saddam has even boasted of utilizing such weapons. Iraq's Osirak nuclear reactor, destroyed by Israeli aircraft in 1981, demonstrated Saddam's nuclear intentions.

3   Hidden chemical materials have been found in Iraq, along with secret locations throughout the country that have been recently vacated, suggesting WMD development.

4   Rolf Ekeus, Former Head of the UN Inspections Effort in Iraq, knew better than anyone else the misleading and hide-and-seek tactics employed by Saddam and his regime. He had no doubt that WMD were being built in secret, though the UN inspectors had failed to discover them.

5   Recently, a MiG-29 was uncovered buried in the sands of western Iraq. Many weapons and stockpiles smaller than a Russian fighter plane could have been easily dissimulated in the vast Iraqi desert. Although these will be difficult to find, eventually they will be stumbled across. Absence of evidence is not evidence of absence.

6   Syria and other Arab nations collaborated (for a price) with Saddam, hiding Iraq's incriminating materials and weapons. Recently the list of recipients of oil vouchers, by the millions of barrels, were found in Iraq's state archives, detailing the beneficiaries, Arab and European, who assisted Saddam.

7   Military analysts and Middle East experts agree that the threat of a dictator like Saddam possessing WMD, now or in the future, justified pre-emptive action.

8   There is mounting evidence of the collaboration between Saddam and terrorist organizations, including Hamas, al-Qa'ida and Ansar al-Islam, some of whom are known to be searching for WMD in their battle against the West and Israel. Such cooperation could produce terrorist attacks that would dwarf even the horror of 9/11.

When the crisis between the US and Iraq was building up toward war, the main accusation leveled against Saddam was that he was amassing WMD that threatened his neighbors and American interests, and contravened UN sanctions and limitations; therefore he had to be removed from power. Though the US persisted in its accusations regarding the WMD issue, and throughout the crisis provided data to back its claims, it became evident as the crisis escalated that the US wanted to go to war regardless of the discovery of WMD; Saddam was, in the Pentagon's eyes, reason enough to go to war. However, while the advertised war aim remained those unconventional weapons that Washington felt it had to neutralize, two other problems presented themselves to policymakers: terrorism and oil. Importantly, though, neither aim was ever made a declared goal of the war.

There is no doubt that the future will unravel some of the questions that remain unanswered today. Equally, there is already sufficient evidence for the existence of the "smoking gun" in Iraq, even if the actual physical proof has yet to be located. But we have the bodies, the spent cartridges, the manufacturing materials, the specialists who spent decades manufacturing those weapons and then hiding them, and the testimonies of inspectors, and Iraqi military and scientific personnel, to justify the removal of Saddam Hussein. As for the tyrant himself, his fate remains undecided; his guilt, however, is not in doubt.

Acknowledgments

Like any book, this volume is the fruit of circumstance. I was on sabbatical leave at Wesleyan University in Connecticut (Winter and Spring 2003) when the clouds of the Third Gulf War began to gather, the hostilities broke out and victory was announced in Washington. The psyche of war enveloped America. The impressive patriotic spirit evinced by common Americans, coupled with intensive on-line, minute-by-minute coverage of the war by "embedded" war reporters and daily Pentagon briefings, provided an unprecedented flow of information, commentary and analyses by military, political, diplomatic, Arab affairs and other experts on virtually all aspects of the war. The major newspapers of the US were awash with written and photographic materials about the war, and published a daily supplement on the unfolding war. The electronic media followed the events continuously and provided frentic reports in harrowing detail every minute of the day and the night.

It became irresistible for a student of the Middle East, which I have been for years, to capture some of that flood of information, to make some sense of it, to contextualize it in the Middle Eastern, Arab and Islamic flow of events, and to take advantage of my proximity to the major centers of scholarship and decision-making during the war to discuss matters with people who knew something about the war and its background, who understood its worldwide ramifications and consequences, or who could offer insight into new developments. I handily availed myself of those opportunities and launched the project. At an early stage I contacted Anthony Grahame, Editorial Director of Sussex Academic Press, who immediately saw the worth of such an undertaking and encouraged me to bring it to a rapid completion.

I owe gratitude to a whole series of institutions and friends and colleagues who allowed me the luxury of devoting a full-time, worry-free isolation and intensive period of writing: first, at Wesleyan University, whose excellent library facilities and serene environment afforded me the possibility to draft the first chapters of the book; then, my friend and colleague, Tudor Parfitt of SOAS, who hosted my wife and me graciously in his splendid villa at Monlaur in southern France, where much of the writing was done; and finally my long-time friends, the Littmans, who once again have put at our disposal their magnificient Maison du Lac on the Lake of Geneva, which permitted the completion of the first draft of the volume.

The final polishing was done in my home base, The Harry Truman Institute for the Promotion of Peace at the Hebrew University, Jerusalem, which alone of all places provides a unique combination of peace of mind, amidst the madness of Middle Eastern events, with a sense of engaged field-work on the very spot where things happen, amounting at one and the same time to a full-fledged involvement with a total detachment. I am grateful for the office space, secretarial and library facilities, the host of colleagues one can consult with and the never-failing assistance one can get at this institution.

And then came the vast editorial work, expertly and enthusiastically undertaken by Sussex Academic Press. The Milken Library has also gener-ously contributed to make publication of this volume possible. I am grateful to both.

I shoulder alone, however, the responsibility for any error of fact or inter-pretation that may have befallen the text. If a mistake has survived all the screenings, proofreadings and suggestions of change, it will have been due to my failure to see it or understand it. For this I deeply apologize to whoever takes the time to read this story – the outcome of which will rever-berate throughout the Middle East for a long time to come.

RAPHAEL ISRAELI
The Hebrew University of Jerusalem
New Year 2004

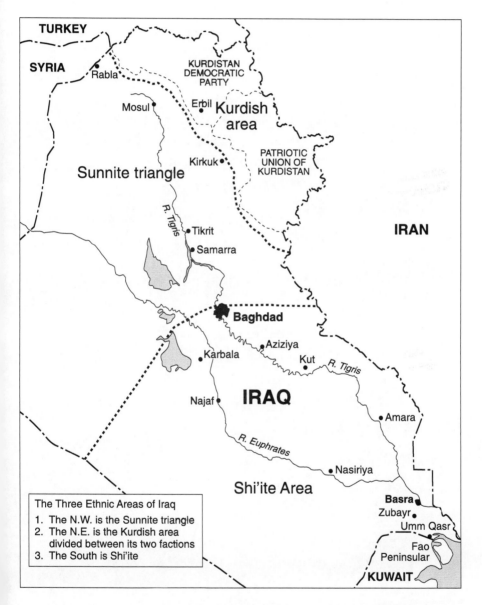

A map of Iraq showing the three regional/ethno-religious major divisions of Iraq (Shi'ites, Kurds and Sunnis), as well as the Capital Baghdad, the major cities where the battles took place, and the Tigris and Euphrates Rivers which delineate ancient Mesopotamia and modern Iraq.

To the Memory of the Allied G.I.s
Who Gave their Lives
To Remove the Tyrant
and Deter his Likes

Iraq under Saddam

In 1975, as a young deputy to President Takriti, Saddam Hussein was already considered by many as the strong man of the Iraqi regime. Equipped with an extraordinary ability to concentrate on his goals and take away a long-term view of events, he was intent on attaining grandeur, commensurate with his view of himself, of his environment and of the world. Saddam set out, step by step, to build up his image and his political strategy. With considerable political savvy and personal charm, he won the backing of both friends and foes – cajoling, promising, threatening and arm-twisting, never losing sight of his strategic goals which were dictated not only by personal ambition, but also by the constraints of his geo-politics.

Saddam's first goal was to unify his country around him by pacifying internal strife and providing national symbols attractive enough to rally the people behind his personal leadership. In 1975, at a great political "sacrifice," he signed an "agreement" with the Shah of Iran, recognizing Teheran's rights in the eastern half of the vast Shatt-al-Arab waterway, the confluent of the Tigris and the Euphrates, which for many years had been the center of a dispute between the two local powers, with Iran claiming sovereignty to half of the course (as is customary in the laws of nations which lay on either side of a waterway), and Iraq imposing its sovereignty over the whole body of water. The waterway was part of the Arab–Iranian rivalry in the Gulf area: the Iranians regard the Gulf area as Persian, hence their geographical and historical right to a share of the waters; while for the Iraqis and the rest of the Arabs, the Gulf region belongs to them, hence their right to total control over it. The matter was of vital importance to Iraq, not only because of the enormous quantities of water that flow through that semi-arid and steamy climate, but mainly because, compared with the long coastline that Iran enjoys, Iraq's access to the Gulf depended on unhindered and safe navigation along the lower reaches of the Shatt-al-Arab river, from Basra downstream to the Gulf. The "sacrifice" that Saddam cunningly made was to seemingly acquiesce in that "painful concession" of sharing the waterway.

The *quid pro quo* that Saddam cashed in on was the Iranian pledge to cease its support, logistical and political, to the restive Iraqi Kurds who on occasion sought refuge in Iranian territory from the Iraqi military. In fact, the Kurdish uprisings were a symptom of a much wider and ongoing rebellion in the area of Kurdistan which had been simmering for decades. The Kurds are one of the most severely oppressed peoples, historically, in the Middle East. Half of today's Kurdish population, which totals 25 million, are located in Turkey which refused, during Saddam's early years of power, to so much as acknowledge their separate identity as Kurds, insisting that they were "Mountain Turks," without culture, history or a language of their own. Although desperate to enter the European Market and the EU, Turkey's adamant and oppressive stance toward the Kurds perpetuated the Western view of Turkey as a Third World country of intolerance and bigotry. Hence Turkey's continued direct interest and involvement with Kurds in general, including the half that dwells beyond its borders, for fear of any bid for independence or autonomy that might find favor with Turkey's Kurds.

Another 10 million Kurds are equally distributed between Iran and Iraq, with the rest in Syria and various diasporas. Since Iran and Iraq both perennially sought to weaken each other in their contention for hegemony in the Gulf, the Shah had allowed the Iraqi Kurds not only to find shelter in his territory but also to use Iran as a launching pad for their subversive activities against the Iraqi regime. Saddam's ploy was to lure the Shah into the "historic agreement" and therefore strengthen his grip on the oil-rich Kurdish north by "pacifying" it, thereby denying the rebels any refuge or outside assistance. Saddam also secured the pledge of the Shah to desist from any trans-border deals between Iranians and Iraqi Kurds, in order to isolate and suffocate any Kurdish efforts at autonomy. For this he was surprisingly "ready" to pay the price of inviting his Iranian rivals into Shatt al-Arab.

Saddam comes from the Sunnite minority in central Iraq which rules Iraq, including the Kurds of the north; he was therefore, like other Sunnis, at odds with the majority Shi'ite community of the south, centered around the major port city of Basra, and sprawling into the holy cities of Karbalah and Najaf, where Imam Hussein and his father Caliph Ali, respectively, were buried, and a number of other towns such as Nasiriya, as well as significant districts of the capital of Baghdad, such as Sadr City. All in all, Shi'ites account for about 13–14 million, out of a total of 23–24 million people, or 60 percent of the population. Shi'ites look toward their religious leaders (the Mullah, headed and led by charismatic Ayatullah) for guidance. Shi'ites not only constitute the majority of the population but they also control the approaches to the Gulf where much of Iraq's agricultural and oil wealth is located, although they do not benefit from the country's natural resources and prosperity.

Bitterness toward Saddam and his oppressive policies against them were deeply rooted in the Shi'ite community. Saddam's regime is comprised of the Ba'ath Party, a socialist party that strongly advocates centralism and outlaws any real democracy. The Ba'ath appeared to the Shi'ites, and to other religious Muslims in the country, as unbefitting a deeply religious country. Saddam attempted to erase that hatred by co-opting more Shi'ites into the army, by opening to them some of the avenues of power, and by initiating economic development.

Saddam also created and maintained his own personality cult as the supreme commander and savior to whom all Iraqis should turn to and worship and adulate; this made it easier for them to accept any hardships that lay ahead for them, without Saddam himself being blamed. He always appeared in public in his military attire with a revolver at his side. Saddam's portraits were posted in public squares in towns and villages and along public roads, and his underlings organized massive demonstrations in support of him. A vast arch was erected in Baghdad (built by a British firm), on the shore of the Tigris, called the Arch of Triumph, made of two inter-crossing sabers held at their base by precise replicas of the two robust hands of Saddam. He also erected a series of lavish and expensive palaces built almost as if they were monuments to a great national figure – Saddam. This campaign of self-aggrandizement, repeated by Kim Jong-il in North Korea and Turkmenbashi in Turkmenistan, has culminated in the inference that likens Saddam to Hammurabi, the legendary ruler and legislator of Mesopotamia, who inspired awe throughout the ancient world. By culti-vating his own personality cult, Saddam was emulating his two political adversaries: Sadat of Egypt and the Shah of Iran. Sadat, prior to his peace treaty with Israel (1979), was regarded as the foremost leader of the Arab world, and therefore constituted the major threat to Saddam's drive to attain Iraqi regional hegemony. Sadat had posited himself as the successor of the Pharaohs, and boasted 6,000 years of Egyptian history and civiliza-tion, unrivalled throughout the world. Similarly, the Shah of Iran squandered untold amounts of money to revive Persepolis and the past glory of the ancient Persian Empire of which he wished to be viewed as its heir.

Saddam, an unknown quantity in inter-Arab politics, did not have to wait long to get his chance. First Sadat "faltered" when he launched his peace initiative with Israel, followed by the Camp David Accords (1978) and the peace treaty (1979). Saddam took the opportunity to call for two Baghdad Conferences, following the Camp David Accords and the peace treaty, where he announced the establishment of the Front of Rejection under his aegis, which ousted "treacherous" Egypt from the Arab League and made it forfeit its leadership role. At the two conferences, sponsored by twenty Arab states (all except Egypt and the Sudan), Saddam thought that he was close to attaining the Arab leadership position, but his war with

Iran would soon preoccupy him. The Shah's challenge also fell away with the eruption of the Islamic Revolution in Iran in 1979, which swept away the Shah and his regime, and ushered in a new threat in the form of an Islamic – and Shi'ite – fundamentalist regime on his border.

As part of his goal of regional hegemony and unchallenged, supreme domestic leadership, Saddam had set his sights on a formidable one million man army, the strongest in the Middle East, well equipped and well trained with the best weapons his oil money could buy. That meant building a hi-tech military industry that could produce missiles as well as nuclear, chemical and biological weapons. Saddam boasted at one point that he possessed a potent "binary" (combined chemical and biological) weapon which would enable him to oppose his neighbors and intimidate Israel. Those were the words that the Arab world, angry with Israel and the West, wished to hear, and those were the qualifications which won Saddam the coveted title of Saladin. Saddam achieved much of his weapons program objectives via collaboration with European and South American firms and governments, which elected to overlook his growing threat and instead channeled their industrial, military and technological expertise to him in return for oil. Saddam was building his power base unopposed while his two most formidable rivals languished on the sidelines.

The First Gulf War (1980–8)

Saddam needed to maintain the attributes of power he had labored to construct, as well as the enhanced stature that he enjoyed in the Arab world as a result. He realized that, in order to inspire credibility, he had to act, and that such actions were interpreted as being in the Arab interest, and not only in pursuance of his self-aggrandizement or for Iraq's primacy in the Gulf. The Khomeini Revolution in neighboring Iran in 1979 provided him with the perfect opportunity. Eighteen months after the new regime had settled down in Teheran, and fearing that the revolutionary passion of the Iranian Shi'ites might spill over into his own Shi'ite territory, Saddam decided to act. Ironically, it was under the terms of the agreement with the Shah regarding the Shatt al-Arab waterway that Saddam had consented to expel Khomeini from Najaf to Neauphle-le-Château in France; now he was called upon to destroy the threatening base that the returning exile had established in revolutionary Iran. Saddam's objectives were fourfold:

1   The adjoining Iranian province of Khuzistan which, although Iranian-dominated, was populated by Arabic-speaking tribes, was targeted as possible land to conquer. Saddam hoped that his coming, as an Arab "savior," would not only be welcomed by those Arabs, but by the entire Arab world which would rally around him in his struggle to

retrieve Arab lands from the Iranians, traditional foes of the Arabs. The rest of the world would refrain from protecting the revolutionary Iranians, who had provoked Western outrage following the capture of personnel from the American Embassy.

2   Any incursion into Khuzistan would amount to a relatively easy walkover, due to the purges of the cadres of the Shah's army in the new Iran which had left it decapitated and drained of experienced officers. Taking over Khuzistan would also demonstrate to Iraqi Shi'ites, who began agitating as a result of the Khomeini Revolution, that the new Iran could easily be overrun by Saddam's emerging Iraq. That, in turn, would imply to the Iraqi Shi'ites that they stood to benefit from supporting their new hero-leader, in contrast to the tragic defeats that Iraqi expeditionary forces had suffered in the past when sent to participate in wars against Israel.

3   Taking over Khuzistan would double Iraq's already fabulous wealth in oil production and reserves, allowing Saddam to outstrip even Saudi Arabia, and to take over the leadership of OPEC with its corollaries: a determining voice in oil prices, global political and economic clout, the rising stature of Iraq and of Saddam himself locally, regionally and internationally.

4   Invading Iran would also afford Saddam, for the first time since the inception of modern Iraq, a seashore of several hundred miles, which would allow the development and expansion of Iraqi naval power into the Gulf. Such a territorial acquisition would give Iraq a secure boundary away from the threatening Iranian lines; would ensure the growth of Basra into a formidable naval, commercial and industrial base; would give Saddam total and unrestricted control of the Shatt al-Arab waterway; and would enable him to build more deep-water ports on the Khuzistani coast.

The conditions seemed ripe for Saddam to achieve his goals. First, due to the perceived threat posed by the Iranian Revolution, few countries, least of all in the West, would rush to extricate the Islamist regime from its war plight. Second, the rich monarchies of the Gulf felt intimidated by the presence of Khomeini's Iran, especially due to their own restive Shi'ite populations. And third, while Iraq was well supplied by the Soviets and some Western countries, Iran was faced with a global arms embargo which incapacitated it in the long-run. All Saddam had to do was to tear up his 1975 agreement with the Shah, and reclaim Arab (i.e., Iraqi) sovereignty over the entire Shatt al-Arab, his only outlet to the Persian Gulf, now triumphantly re-baptized the "Arab Gulf."

Saddam launched his invasion in October 1980, quickly seizing control of much of Khuzistan within a few weeks of combat, to the point that the accomplishment of his war aims was very close to being realized in a short time. But Saddam had underestimated the ideological passion and the patriotic zeal of the Iranians. They fought back with a vengeance following the initial weeks of disarray. The heroic Iranian stand at Khurramshar, their own personal battle of Stalingrad, where Iraq's troops ground to a halt, marked the beginning of the end of Saddam's venture. Although Iran had neither the firepower nor the hardware to physically overpower Iraq, Saddam's forces were unable to engineer the *coup de grâce* that he had counted on. The war of attrition went on for eight years of classical trench warfare, where both parties bled profusely but made no gains. In the meantime Iraq field-tested its awesome arsenal of missiles and chemical weapons. Ultimately, Iraqi superior firepower was effectively cancelled out by Iran's territorial advantage and overwhelmingly hostile populace.

During the conflict, Saddam drew support from various foreign quarters: the Americans, the Soviets, the Europeans and much of the Arab world, most of whom were content to see Iraq contain the spread of the Iranian Islamic Revolution, all sponsored the Iraqi war effort. The Soviets and the Europeans sold Saddam weapons, facilitated economic credits, and came to regard him as a bulwark against radical Iran. The Arabs, especially the Gulf states, continued to pour billions in "loans" into Saddam's dwindling treasury, knowing that he would never be able, let alone be willing, to repay them. The Iraqi dictator declared that the war was a second Qadissiya battle, a modern-day enactment of a medieval campaign which saw the Arabs defeat the Sassanid Empire and install Islam in the Iranian Plateau. Saddam now symbolically stood at the forefront of Arab efforts to defeat the most dangerous long-term enemy of the Arab nation, and they, in turn, owed him their unconditional support: military, political, economic and financial.

Desperate to win support from the US, Saddam even re-established diplomatic relations with Cairo in a bid to repair relations with Egypt and edged closer to the Hashemite monarchy in Jordan. By repairing relations with the "moderates" of the Arab world, Saddam hoped both to isolate his arch-rival for the leadership of the Ba'ath – Syria – and to gain the approval of the US. He and his "allies" projected an image of a "moderate" Saddam who "really wanted peace," both in the Gulf and in the Arab–Israeli conflict. It was claimed that the Iraqi leader was in favor of a settlement between Israel and the Palestinians and that he was seeking to improve dialogue between the US and the USSR, his long-standing supporter. Other Arab states began echoing Saddam's accusations against Iran as the "aggressor," and praised Saddam as the "peace maker," arguing that he wanted regional stability; and overlooking the fact that Saddam was the aggressor, they argued that the Iranians were the intransigent party. The Arabs, along with the international community as a whole, conveniently elected to forget that Saddam had initiated the war in 1980, and had used chemical weapons on the battlefield. All those who aided the tyrant by keeping silent or looking the other way would live to see him turn against them.

When Saddam emerged from the war with Iran in August 1988, he claimed he was victorious; but the truth was that he had gained only some insignificant patches of Iranian territory at the horrendous price of hundreds of thousands of casualties, a crushed economy, huge debts and a country in dire need of reconstruction. His venture into Iran had also undermined his own – and his country's – credibility in the Arab world. However, Iraq still enjoyed widespread support and Saddam reveled in the new aura of victor, his stature intact and his credit in the West so high that even the barbarous gas attacks against Iraq's own Kurdish population in Halabja in late 1988, and his systematic destruction of hundreds of Kurdish villages and hamlets, went uncensored in the international community. If anything, he won praise for his "moderation" and his peace-making efforts.

Saddam immediately began the task of rebuilding his battered army and re-equipping it to meet the "million men" target, comprised of cadres of veterans of the war with Iran, and launched several vigorous diplomatic drives to promote his position in the Arab and Western worlds. His repression of the Iraqi Kurds, instead of being understood as part of his policy of *Lebensraum* (by repressing autonomous efforts that could threaten the solidarity of the Iraqi state, and extending his effective rule therein) was ignored because it came to be regarded as a purely "domestic affair." Having terrified his dissidents within Iraq, he now turned outward, threatening Israel with missiles and chemical weapons, playing up his role as the champion of the Arab and Palestinian cause. His huge army, which he continued to equip and train extensively, building a number of elite units called the Republican Guard, was enough of a guarantee to ensure the credibility of his menace and to turn him into a hero figure in Arab and inter-Arab politics.

Saddam also entered into a system of alliances in order to isolate Syria and render irrelevant its bid for "strategic parity" with Israel, which it had designed to ensure a role of leadership in the confrontation with Israel, now that Egypt had "defected." He wove together a Quadripartite Alliance, which included Egypt (which had signed peace with Israel a decade earlier), Jordan and the Yemen, which strengthened Saddam's diplomatic hand. He could thus not only weaken Syria's position *vis-à-vis* the Arab world, but also enhance his own image as a "moderate" and pragmatic Arab leader whose faith was in constructive inter-Arab diplomacy. His hatred of Syria was so great that he declared his support for the lost cause of Lebanese General Michel Aoun, who single-handedly battled against the Syrian occupation of Lebanon until the French mediated his exit from Beirut and his exile on the Riviera. It is difficult to understand how experienced leaders like Mubarak of Egypt and Jordan's King Hussein could have been so easily misled as to believe Saddam's propaganda. Ironically, Mubarak raised military forces against the tyrant when he united with the coalition forces in the Second Gulf War of 1991.

The Second Gulf War (1990–1)

Although Saddam had been severely bruised in his protracted war against Iran, he had emerged unscathed from it politically and psychologically. As the "victor" in that war, in which he allegedly defended the Arab cause, his profile was well-received. Presidential candidate Bob Dole, who visited him in the spring of 1990, returned to the US claiming that Saddam was "reasonable, moderate and pragmatic." Events in the disintegrating Soviet bloc, with which the West was preoccupied, reassured Saddam that any future military campaigns would not be subject to the scrutiny of the Western media and politics. His meeting with the American Ambassador to Baghdad, April Gillespie, left him with the impression that the US would not intervene in the foreseeable future in internal Middle Eastern disputes.

Saddam's ambition was twofold: control of the oil resources of his neighbors; and expansion of Iraqi territory, to take in shore areas for naval development. Kuwait was a small and weak country, easy to swallow and digest, and was wealthy in terms of both oil and coastline. What Saddam had failed to achieve during the First Gulf War on the Iranian shore, he would now attempt on the opposite side of the Gulf, in Kuwait. He created an artificial dispute with Kuwait over oil prices and the Rumeila oil fields in the buffer zone between the two countries. He then made public assurances that he had no aggressive intentions toward Kuwait, and vowed to his allies, including Mubarak, that he would seek a "peaceful solution" to the "conflict."

On 2 August 1990, at the height of the unbearable desert heat of the summer, Saddam launched attacks against Kuwait. His actions were condemned by most Arab countries, for different reasons, though it was clear that they were united in fear of Saddam's policy of war disguised as internal Arab arguments between "sister states." Syria was happy to engage in military action against Saddam. Mubarak, admitting that his alliance with Iraq and Saddam had been ill-advised, sought revenge. Saudi Arabia and the Emirates, the targets of Saddam's actions, hastened to embrace any means to check the Iraqi advance. The West, motivated by a desire to prevent the falling into the dictator's hand of a total of 20 percent of the world's oil reserves, decided to move, albeit with much hesitation, just as Saddam had calculated. Saddam correctly predicted that the US, the most likely interventionist power, would be initially stunned, distant and irresolute after the invasion of Kuwait. Unless it decided to act immediately with missiles and air-strikes, it would take many months to assemble a significant military force in the area – by which time Iraq would be entrenched in Kuwait. Besides, the Americans would find the desert conditions harsh: heat, dust, Islamic puritanism and a hostile Arab-Muslim environment.

While the US was building up its forces in Saudi Arabia, Saddam was confident that the Arab-Muslim countries would ultimately succumb to the pressures from their populations, who loathed the presence of Western troops in their lands, and especially their proximity to Muslim holy places. Saddam discounted the role of the Arabs who rushed to assist the Saudis, realizing full well that they were not there to help their American "allies," but to profit from the demise of the Kuwaiti and (possibly) Saudi royal houses. After all, he reasoned, had Syria truly wished to assist the coalition as it had declared, it could have done so much more easily and effectively by concentrating its troops on the Iraq–Syria border, forcing Saddam to fight a war on two fronts, rather than transporting them all the way via the Suez Canal to Saudi territory.

Intent on maintaining his presence on Kuwait soil, Saddam assumed his most moderate posture when he addressed the outside world: he wanted negotiations, he said, after he completed the occupation of Kuwait, not war; he would seek a peaceful settlement, he assured everyone, if the oil fields of Kuwait and the islands of Bubian and Warba were left in Iraqi hands; he was prepared to release all of his foreign hostages ("guests," he called them), if he was assured that no attacks would be mounted against him. His foreign minister traveled the world, reaffirming the peaceful intentions of the regime; his message was heeded in some quarters, to wit, the list of senior statesmen who approached Saddam to try to "save the peace" – Willy Brandt, Edward Heath and Yasuhiro Nakasone.

To his people and to the Arabs and Muslims in general, however, Saddam had another kind of message: the need for steadfastness against the "New Crusaders" who were scheming against the Arab homeland and the Islamic Holy Shrines of Mecca and Medina. He incited the people of Saudi Arabia to rise against their exploitative Royal House and the class of privileged princes and appealed to the people of Egypt and Syria to rebel against their rulers for having colluded with the West. Some of his agents were arrested in Egypt for plotting against the regime of his "trusted ally." Saddam's perceived "macho" defiance of the West, and the US in particular, won him tremendous popular support in the Arab and Islamic worlds. In Jordan, massive demonstrations were held in his favor by both Arab nationalists and Islamic fundamentalists. King Hussein, faced with such popular support for the dictator, could do nothing about these rallies. The Palestinians also heralded Saddam: The Mufti of Jerusalem delivered a sermon to the Believers, urging them to lend their hand to Saddam in his *Jihad* against American imperialism.

Saddam was, ultimately, defeated by the coalition forces, but his defeat was much less humiliating than it could have been, had the victors pursued the enemy to the gates of Baghdad. That they did not was due to the pressure exerted by the Arab coalition partners, who could not afford, politically or socially, to be seen as partaking in the defeat of an illustrious historical Arab and Muslim capital at the time of the Abbasid Dynasty (AD 750–1258). However, by failing to carry out that attack, Saddam was enabled to escape unscathed once again, and to prepare for the next phase of his long-term military campaign. For the moment President George Bush, Snr., fell short of delivering on his declared war aims: liberating Kuwait; removing Saddam; breaking Iraq's military backbone; eliminating Saddam's arsenals of dangerous weapons; and bringing about democratization in the Gulf. Kuwait was "liberated" from the Iraqis and given back to its Emir; but it was questionable as to whether Kuwait felt liberated when it fell back under his absolute rule.

As a result of his escape from heavy defeat, which allowed him to regather all his resources once more, Saddam returned to the development and proliferation of weapons and on cementing his absolute tyrannical regime. The sanctions imposed by the UN, had they succeeded, would have forced Saddam to comply with the requirements of disarmament. But the measures were not enforceable, and in a hide-and-seek game with UN supervisors that lasted the better part of the 1990s, he succeeded in circumventing the regime of sanctions and turned his country into a rogue state. In 1998 Saddam engineered a major crisis when expelling the team of international weapons inspectors from Iraq. The US, under President Clinton, was prepared to strike again at Iraq to make it comply, but UN Secretary-General Kofi Annan went to "mediate," and appeased the dictator with a deal that basically permitted him to pursue his programs without any outside supervision.

Constants in Iraq's Geo-politics and Strategies

Under a leader like Saddam, who has demonstrated an ability to both plan long-term and to survive, an Iraq that is constantly conscious of its geo-strategic position is bound to act on his policies. In the Arab arena Saddam resumed Iraq's activity in the Arab League; capitalizing on his vast popularity among the Arab masses, he pursued a course of blood and fire, supported terrorism and provided for the families of the "martyrs." He embraced the most abrasive Palestinian factions and emphasized his and Iraq's Arab character, thereby qualifying Saddam as the most deserving of the Arab leadership. His vilification by America helped boost his status among his Arab kin due to the widespread anti-American sentiment in the Middle East, which in turn enhanced his stature among his European business partners. The more turbulent the Israeli–Palestinian confrontation threatened to become, the more Saddam could benefit from the situation by pointing to Egypt and Jordan who had "betrayed" the Arabs and turned their backs on their own people. Saddam proposed the adoption of the most aggressive pro-Palestinian stance in the Councils of the Arab League.

There was no alliance of Arab and Islamic forces in the Middle East capable of threatening the might of Iraq that Saddam had built up, not only because inter-Arab conflicts are very unpopular in the region, but also because the Arab states lack either large armies (Kuwait, Saudi Arabia), do not want to harm relations with other Arabs or have inferior technology to Iraq (Syria, Iran). From Iraq's viewpoint, its army was strong and tenacious enough to absorb any Western or Arab attack and to survive it, even if it had to initially disband under the shock of defeat. But the cadres, their training, their patriotism and morale would remain; and their equipment could easily be replaced. Even if Iraq's industrial and technological base was demolished, it could be rebuilt with the oil income, and there was no dearth of advanced Western countries who would compete for such lucrative contracts.

In March 2003, Saddam's Iraq fell apart, when US and British forces invaded the country. Saddam's capture in December 2003 was the culmination of the coalition effort, and represented the end of the Ba'ath in Iraq. The aim of this book is to investigate the aftermath of the Third Gulf War, the War in Iraq, to analyze what kind of nation Saddam is bequeathing to his successors and to speculate on what kind of future awaits the new Iraq in the new Middle East.

2   *Iraqi and Coalition War Strategies*

Ever since his defeat in the 1991 Gulf War, Saddam had been planning further strikes to establish Iraqi regional hegemony, based on his relentless rebuilding of Iraq's military capacities, conventional and unconventional, reconstructing the country after the war and finding ways to circumvent UN sanctions. Although his war capacities had been severely curtailed following the war, he was able to adroitly exploit the rifts between UN members and America's own reluctance to engage in the day-to-day policing of the Iraqi state, under the Clinton administration. Saddam produced some remarkable achievements that enhanced his stature in the Arab world and the international domain:

1   In a relatively short time, the scars of war were removed: the destroyed bridges and bomb-struck roads were restored and such efforts quickly erased the trauma of the coalition attacks.
2   Following American permission for Saddam's military to use helicopters to quell the US-backed but ill-fated Shi'ite rebellion, Saddam soon regained control of the southern cities of Basra and Najaf;
3   The no-flight zone imposed by the Americans and the British in northern Iraq, although it succeeded in limiting Saddam's freedom of maneuver, failed to affect his capacity to deploy forces in Mosul, or the activation of his notorious security apparatuses to maintain his rule in the mixed Arab-Kurdish area.
4   UN sanctions were invalidated when countries – including Russia, Germany, France and China – continued to deal with Saddam and sold to him materials that enabled him to reconstruct Iraq's military industries and to manufacture unconventional weapons. Even "allies" of the US collaborated with him for their own benefit: Turkey and Jordan became his conduits for international trade and export of oil and the latter, along with Syria, became his sources of smuggled goods.
5   UN supervision of his weapons of mass destruction lasted from 1991 to 1998, but during that time the Iraqis developed an ability to cover up any evidence of WMD research, knowing when to evacuate sites

before their inspection, where to hide manufactured weapons and materials and how to hide documents or deny their existence. Saddam knew how to delay the inspectors without expelling them, citing "technical problems" and "misunderstandings" when supervision efforts were undermined.

6   Saddam's stature in the Arab and Islamic world was greatly enhanced when he championed the Palestinian cause and supported fully their *Intifada* against Israel. He paid the sum of $25,000 to each family of a deceased "martyr" – i.e., an Islamikaze[1] bomber.

7   Saddam succeeded in demonizing the US among the international community for the harsh sanctions which, he claimed, "deprived Iraqi children of food and medicine." Harrowing pictures of malnourished and sick children, exposed throughout the world's media, bought him sympathy; the plight of the "deprived innocent civilians" of Iraq, for many, eclipsed the serious breaches of UN sanctions Saddam had committed.

8   Saddam, who had a shared interest with Turkey against the emergence of a Kurdish state, enhanced good relations between the two countries, to the extent that Ankara, otherwise thought to be a close ally of the US and one of its main economic and military beneficiaries, was reluctant to allow American operations to launch from its territory prior to the 2003 war in Iraq.

9   Syria, his arch-enemy and rival for the leadership of the Ba'ath Party, was also reunited as an ally by Saddam, to the point that it acquired forbidden war materials for him, hid some of his WMD, and ultimately gave shelter to some of his family and other fugitives after the 2003 war.

10 Saddam's triumphant return to the Arab League and the participation of his envoys in its debates permitted him to address the Arab masses, thereby increasing his Arab leadership credentials.

11 Links with al-Qa'ida and other Islamic terrorist organizations portrayed an image of Saddam as a defender of the Islamic world against Western Judeo-Christian Zionist imperialism.

12 Saddam's grip on power in Iraq was strengthened post-1991. The liquidation of his rivals enhanced his reputation, in Iraq and across the world, as a real survivor, able to outwit and outfox any persons with designs on the Iraqi leadership. This supreme self-confidence increased throughout the period of his regime and was reflected in the attitudes and behavior of his senior military personnel.

This list of Saddam's most impressive achievements is crucial to understanding the upheaval the War in Iraq has caused to the Arab and Islamic worlds, when each of these structures, such as Iraq–Syrian relations and the absolute centralization of power under Saddam, collapsed entirely with the fall of his regime. The War in Iraq, it can be claimed, has altered the entire geo-strategic position of the US as a world power; new alliances will emerge; old allies will become enemies; and some countries in the region will have to revise their structures and policies to avoid becoming a future target. Furthermore, should the US succeed in establishing in Iraq some sort of representative government, there is no telling what kind of effect this will have on a region that has been traditionally ruled by autocracies: absolute monarchies, some of which parade as constitutional ones; republican authoritarianism, which hosts false, rigged elections; dictatorships; and, lately, republican monarchies where the power of the autocrat is bequeathed to the ruler's next of kin.

American War Objectives

The American objectives can be grouped in several categories: those relating to the conduct, or the vision, of the war; those calculated to improve the strategic position of the US after the war; those geared to improve America's image, both domestically and globally; and objectives related to the War on Terrorism. It is worth discussing each of these objectives because they will help explain the current situation in Iraq and contextualize the reactions of leaders in the Middle East and abroad. Acceptance of the necessity of the war hinged not only upon its quick and smooth success, but also upon the popularity of President Bush, who entered the war with high approval ratings sustained since he had declared his "crusade" against terrorism after 9/11, and who would be standing for re-election in the aftermath of the conflict.

The Vision of the War

The war planners, basing their philosophy around the necessity of winning the war rapidly, highlighted the imperative of decapitating the Iraqi regime at the onset of the war, on the assumption that, in a centralized dictatorship like Saddam's, the death of the tyrant would augur the collapse of the whole system and precipitate the surrender of Iraqi combatants and the end of hostilities. Therefore they produced special 21,000-lb MOAB (Massive Ordinance Air Blast) bombs, popularly known as "the mother of all bombs," designed to penetrate deep underground and rip apart reinforced concrete bunkers, a location Saddam was known to favor as a shelter. But Saddam was only the head of a leadership pyramid. Below him were his two sons Uday and Qusay Hussein, groomed to replace their father if he faltered or became incapacitated. Below them was a list of over 50 dignitaries, holders of the highest ranks and positions of responsibility in the

Ba'ath Party. Each of these figures, from Saddam down, was printed on a special deck of cards distributed among American combat troops, the infamous Iraqi "pack of cards." Saddam was the Ace of Spades.

Decapitation also meant targeting and destroying the symbols of power which lent respectability to the tyrant and his regime. That included their lavish palaces, their plush offices, their numerous hideouts and their wealth. The idea was that these objectives, if destroyed, far from raising the anger of the masses, would on the contrary elicit their jubilation. This was based on the assumption that many if not most Iraqis were, by definition, hostile toward Saddam. The contrast with the extra care that the invading forces would take to avoid hurting civilians, targeting civilian areas or unnecessarily disrupting the daily life of the average Iraqi, would be unmistakable. At the same time, however, the planners were aware that Saddam would have no compunction about positioning guns, missiles, ammunition dumps and dangerous intoxicants in schools, hospitals, mosques and in the midst of civilian population in order to attract American fire. Part of that inevitable complication could be averted by the surgical targeting of military objectives, by commandos undertaking covert military operations and also distributing from the air leaflets in Arabic across the targeted areas, warning the inhabitants of the impending attacks.

To attain the effect of "shock and awe" that the Pentagon counted on to expedite the pace of the war, the planners had in mind not only the massive use of airpower and firepower, but also launching attacks along several fronts simultaneously. Because the US forces were being assembled on land in Kuwait, Saudi Arabia and Qatar, and on the sea in the Gulf waters, the main thrust had to emanate from the south and northward toward Baghdad. And since the routes to be taken by the attacking forces in the south were limited, the attack would have to be a two-pronged onslaught through the desert toward Baghdad that would culminate in surrounding the Iraqi capital from the south-west and the south-east and in tandem with other forces descending from the Kurdish north. All this would necessitate the securing of the enormous supply lines of the coalition forces. That also meant that the troops had to beware not to engage in battles of attrition on the way to Baghdad, lest they be delayed in the desert, exposed to the elements and guerilla attacks by the Fedayeen Saddam and other loose elements of the Iraqi armed forces.

On paper, the Iraqi forces were a formidable enemy to be reckoned with. They included in their battle order about two dozen divisions, among them the much-touted Republican Guard, though they were under-armed, under-trained and not necessarily in high morale, since many of the recruits were Shi'ites who had suffered from Saddam's oppression. Ten years of UN sanctions had, in spite of the massive military industries and the large-scale smuggling of weapons and other war material into Iraq, greatly diminished the army's firepower, their will to fight and their ability to arm and mobilize large military formations that could arrest the American forces. Since the 1991 war, the Iraqis had been stripped of their air force, without which no modern warfare is possible. Much of their fighter aircraft had been destroyed by the Allies in 1991, and some of their remnants had been engaged and eroded when they occasionally challenged American and British planes during the decade of enforcement of the no-fly zone in northern Iraq. Nor had they under their command any advanced air-defense systems, such as ground-to-air missiles, that could launch air strikes against American fighter planes and provide land support to their ground troops. They did possess some stocks of short-range land-to-land missiles, which they began destroying under the scrutiny of the UN super-vision teams in their attempt to avert the war.

The war plan to take the coalition forces to the gates of Baghdad was conceived as a large-scale raid where technology, skill and rapidity would replace large ground formations according to conventional wisdom. It was a mammoth risk, but the planners trusted that, along with the concept of "shock and awe" designed to paralyse the Iraqis in the initial stages of the fighting, that it would succeed. In the previous Gulf War, 40 days of mas-sive bombardment had preceded the ground invasion, which prepared both the Americans and the Iraqis for the land attacks. This time, it was decided to run the two operations – bombing campaign and land invasion – simul-taneously. At the same time, it was absolutely imperative to urge the Iraqi people to rise against their own government, and therefore the policy of selective targeting was devised to destroy the infrastructure of the regime, but to preserve the infrastructure of society, so that civilian life in Baghdad and the rest of the country could be revived once the hostilities ceased.

Strategic Considerations

Strategically, the planners of the war had to confront the task of not only displacing the regime of Saddam, but also conceiving a new Iraq that would have to be helped back onto its feet in the aftermath of war. This task was assigned to former General Jay Garner, a veteran of the 1991 Gulf War who had assisted the Kurds then. The brief was to reconstruct Iraq as a successful, democratic and peaceful nation-state with an elected govern-ment and vibrant economy that would prove a model for other Arab countries to follow. However, this outcome was likely to cause friction in the Middle East. Indeed, the closest Arab allies of the US in the Arab world – Saudi Arabia, Egypt, Jordan, Qatar and Kuwait – were not exactly shining examples of democratic government that the Americans sought to install in Iraq. But they nevertheless also assisted America in toppling Saddam and establishing a democratic and anti-terrorist state in his place. That meant that these allied countries were asked to undermine their own regimes by supporting the demolition of a dictatorship which was to be replaced by an alternative form of government they themselves were opposed to. Therefore, while those countries supported America as a matter of their own survival, they remain uncertain of their own fate after the war, should American designs prove successful.

However, while those regimes who supported the US regarded themselves as immune to American intervention, in recognition of their assistance, the recalcitrant ones, such as Iran, Syria, Libya, the Palestinian Authority and others, were preoccupied by possible American strategic intentions in the post-war period, hoping all the while that US efforts in Iraq would fail. The Pentagon and the State Department, who initially seemed to share the same vision of a reformed Middle East after the Iraq War, were busy categorizing the major players of the Middle East into potential long-term friends and foes, distinguishing between sinister and unreliable regimes that ought to be removed from the list of the top allies, and those who emerged as the new allies who would need American protection in the aftermath of the war. If Saudi Arabia and Turkey were considered, before the war, as the key allies in the region, hosting American military bases, in practice it was Kuwait and Qatar who provided the military bases for assembling the coalition forces.

As the war preparations advanced, Turkey gradually found itself distanced from the US. Not only could it no longer be counted on for its staunch support (as in the days of Suleiman Demirel and Turgut Özal), when it served as the main airbase of the American Airforce in the 1991 Gulf War, but it was creating new difficulties for the American war planners, procrastinating when the issue of allowing US troops to launch attacks from Turkish soil was raised and even stating in no uncertain terms, its opposition to the American intention to topple Saddam by force. All this was in spite of the tremendous financial incentives that the US offered in return, around $30 billion, and exhaustive American diplomacy, which could not change the attitude of a stubborn Ankara government. Turkey's stance was a disappointment for the US, because for decades it had stood by the country, first as a key building bloc in the anti-Communist Northern Tier, then as a staunch NATO member and supporter (one of the very few countries which backed the US in the Korean and Vietnamese wars) Turkey had become a model of moderation in the turbulent Muslim world.

The emergence of the six Muslim Republics in Central Asia and the Caucasus after the collapse of the Soviet Union was an opportunity for the US to widen its sphere of influence there, using the Ankara model in these mostly Turkish-speaking countries to establish, reinforce and support their pro-Western orientation. The assumption was that, exactly as in Turkey, a pro-Western stance and a moderate regime would act as a bulwark against the rise of Islamic fundamentalism. As with Turkey, however, American assumptions were miscalculated. Developments emanating from the preparations for the Gulf War finally brought Washington's strategists to the realization that Islamic fundamentalism would not go away easily. The Turkish elections in 2002 saw the Islamists under Recep Tayyip Erdogan return to government by a crushing majority. Their predecessors, led by Necmettin Erbakan, had won the 1996 elections despite registering under 20 percent of the vote, much to the displeasure of the Turkish military. But in 1998 the prime minister was ousted by the military and his party banned, allowing Erdogan to run for office under a different party name and win the elections.

It remained to be seen whether the new government would abide by its promises to respect democracy, stick to its Western and NATO allegiances, and refrain from Islamizing its society; these pledges were intended to placate the military, regarded as the curators of the secular legacy of Kemal Ataturk. Erbakan had made the mistake of associating too closely with the Iranians, so Erdogan was wary not to upset that delicate Islamic–secular balance. Opting not to reject out of hand the American approaches and NATO allegiance, Erdogan decided to engage in a series of procrastinations, making any strategic decision on his part (which had been a matter of course with former prime ministers) contingent upon the approval of his reluctant Islamist Parliament. That ensured the prime minister the backing of a vast Turkish public equally sceptical about the war, in case Parliament approved the American move, at the same time signalling to the Americans that Erdogan could not act contrary to the democratic decisions of his Parliament. The decision also constituted a warning to the military, that while he heeded their support of the Americans by not rejecting them, he enjoyed the overwhelming backing of the public and the Parliament, and the military would have no interest in explicitly contradicting either support base.

In the eyes of the war planners, then, Turkey was no longer a reliable ally; the strategic future of the Middle East could no longer be predicated on it as a democratic example to the Arab and Islamic worlds. Already in the war in Afghanistan in late 2001, the US had concluded direct arrangements with some of the Muslim countries of Central Asia and used them as bases for attacks against the Taliban. No less disappointing, however, was Saudi Arabia's duplicity prior to, and after, the Iraqi crisis. For decades, the US had maintained the fallacy of its "alliance" and "friendship" with Saudi Arabia and was reluctant to heed the realities of the great hostility and anti-Western vitriol spreading throughout the Kingdom. The problem lay in the puritanical Islamic spirit of the country, which was run by a coalition of the Royal House of Sa'ud and the strict Wahhabi clerics. That coalition did not tolerate any non-Islamic values and believed that it could successfully modernize, importing the tools of the West in the military and technological fields, without "polluting" its Islamic environment with Western values. However, since the adoption of this policy in the 1950s, it became evident that the Saudi regime was fighting a losing battle against the forces of modernity and that the erosion of the monarchic-auto-cratic structure of the state was already underway.

The Americans and the Saudis soon settled into a pragmatic trade-off of American military aid and umbrella protection in times of need in return for the undisturbed flow of oil at fair prices. The Second Gulf War (1990–1), however, was a perfect illustration to the Saudis of their vulner-ability in the region. They lacked the advanced weapons and armies of Iraq; therefore they reluctantly called upon the US to repulse Saddam from Kuwait, even offering their territory for the massive deployment of American troops. When the Americans pushed the Iraqis out of Kuwait, the Saudis put pressure on America to withdraw its forces immediately, for fear of the continued presence of the Americans close to the holy shrines of Islam in Mecca and Medina. The Americans responded by removing most of their forces; their remaining troops were hidden from public view and their presence ignored. But radicals like Osama bin Laden and other Saudi clerics and nationalists kept protesting to the government to evacuate the Americans from the Peninsula in an effort to shield the country from "Westoxication." These radicals then resorted to violence, mounting several attacks against American targets, the most notorious of which was the Khobar towers incident in Dhahran, Saudi Arabia, on June 25, 1996, when 19 US airmen were killed in an explosion.

The overwhelming participation of Saudis (15 out of 19) in the 9/11 attacks, coupled with the barrage of criticism in the American media over the US "alliance" with Saudi Arabia, further strained relations between the parties. American publicists and columnists began to openly attack the feudal system of Arabia, its obscure rule by radical clerics, its pro-Arab, anti-Western system, oppression of Saudi women and refusal to permit any political reform that would usher in some form of participatory govern-ment. Saudi efforts to improve their image in the US were viewed as distasteful: a Saudi prince offered to donate $10 million to New York City following 9/11, but it was refused by Mayor Rudolph Giuliani because of the political strings attached to that bout of "generosity." So, when the crisis with Iraq began looming in the horizon, these "allies" found them-selves locked in an unusually strained relationship. Saudi Arabia disputed the US war aims because, unlike the 1990 Kuwait occupation, this time it was not itself directly threatened by Iraq; and it also had to support the Arab League policy that any attack against Iraq would constitute an act of aggression. On the other hand, the US was in dire need of its "low profile" bases in Saudi Arabia for the purposes of the war, something that the Saudis did not appreciate but could not reject since the Americans were there already.

The highly-visible re-positioning of large numbers of American troops in the Middle East would also serve to deter, if not intimidate, the other two main rogue regimes in the region: Iran and Syria. In defiance of American warnings, Syria had purchased military equipment and vital materials for the Iraqi regime, had itself developed weapons of mass destruction and sheltered international criminals and terrorists, including Alois Brunner, the Nazi escapee, the "political" heads of Hamas, Islamic Jihad and the two Palestinian Fronts (Popular and Democratic). More ominously, Syria continued to occupy Lebanon despite the mounting opposition to its "sponsorship" of the Lebanese government and its participation in the drug trade there. Syria had also continuously sponsored the Hizbullah in Lebanon, which had been created by Iran and supported by the Iranian and Syrian governments. Teheran was the source of funds and weapons and Damascus operated as the transfer station, directing these materials to Lebanese territory.

Hizbullah, a Shi'ite terrorist organization based around Iranian Islamic ideology and Syrian strategic manipulation, and deeply connected with international terrorism, had virtually taken over control of southern Lebanon since Israel's withdrawal in May 2000. Hizbullah had also hoarded thousands of *katyusha* missiles, to be used against Israel. The Americans also had reasons for wanting to undermine Hizbullah's influence. In 1983 President Ronald Reagan sent Marines on a peace mission to Lebanon; the Hizbullah committed the first major Islamikaze act of terror against the US when it used a truck-load of explosives to blow up the American barracks, killing 241 Marines in the process. The Pentagon did not forgive or forget that outrage, especially given that some of 2003 Iraq's War's key strategists, including Vice President Dick Cheney, Secretary of Defense Donald Rumsfeld and his Deputy Paul Wolfovitz, had all served under the Reagan administration and were aggrieved by the hurried American exit from Lebanon.

America also realized how the Iraq War could potentially affect the Iranian clerics' regime. The enmity of the Iranian Revolution toward the US, the "Great Satan" (compared to the "Small Satan" that was Israel), persisted throughout the lifetime of Ayatullah Khomeini against the bloody background of the First Gulf War (1980–8), where America showed favor to Saddam as the aggressor in the conflict at the cost of a million Iranian casualties. Iran had also continuously led, for several years, the Front of Rejection of the Islamic world against the peace deal between Sadat and Israel (until Saddam's Iraq took the title), and was instrumental in excluding Egypt from the Islamic Conference. Teheran had also become the venue of choice for all the major terrorist organizations, who convened annually with Khomeini to devise a common international terrorism strategy.

The planners of the 2003 war were faced with very serious dilemmas: they had to satisfy their Arab friends and their European allies on the

Palestinian issue in order to elicit their goodwill for the continued battle against terrorism worldwide; but giving in to Palestinian terrorism and rewarding it by yielding to their demands from Israel would amount to surrendering to terrorism. In view of the lessons of the second *Intifada*, which had broken out precisely after most of Arafat's demands had been met under the Clinton administration (2000), critics now called for the Palestinians to first renounce terrorism and put an effective end to it; but making any advance in Palestinian nationhood contingent upon an end to terrorism first would, *a priori*, block any achievement in the road map to peace, since it was evident that the Palestinian leadership would be unable, or unwilling, to arrest all the terrorists, shut down their organizations, collect the stockpiles of weapons and explosives in their possession and dismantle the infrastructure of terror. It was hoped that with Saddam gone, the source of financing to Palestinian terror would partly dry up, and the aims of the dictator, for so long a symbol of hope for victory amongst the Palestinians, would evaporate. The assumption was that the Palestinians would then be more amenable to dialogue and to eradicating terrorism as a prerequisite to achieving nationhood.

Image and Public Relations

The planners wanted decisive victory; but they also wanted to present America abroad as a benevolent and peaceful nation. Therefore, for them this was not a war of aggression, expansion or conquest; rather it was a war of liberation, to free the Iraqi people from the tyranny of Saddam, in order to afford the nation the values of freedom, democratic self-government, taking possession of its resources and to allocate funds to promote the well-being of its people. In contrast with the permanent war, misery, deprivation, strife, fear and threats that Saddam had brought to bear on his own people, America would usher in an era of plenty, peace and tranquillity, social harmony and hope. Instead of the weapons of mass destruction that Saddam had devoted his life to develop, and the terrorist networks that he set up, trained, financed and hailed as heroes, the New Iraq that was said to emerge under the American aegis was to erect a structure of civil society, a democratic life where all religious and social shades would participate, terrorists would be persecuted and good relations would be cemented with the rest of the world. It is difficult to gauge whether the Bush administration actually believed in these ideological goals, or if they were simply PR slogans designed to promote the causes of the war in the international community. Either way, the war planners began to sound like the great colonizers of the nineteenth and twentieth centuries who were eager to embark on their *mission civilisatrice* in order to save the "natives" from themselves and from their "backwardness" and "ignorance."

Great pains were taken by the Americans in the preparatory stages of the war to mobilize the UN majority behind them, because in order to truly legitimize the war the US would need the backing of the UN. When the US was still short of the necessary majority in the Security Council, in the face of vigorous French, German, Russian and Chinese objections, the war planners, backed by the British, the Spanish, the Poles and others, opted to proceed without UN authorization, all the while trumpeting their operation as a universally-supported mission, and describing the narrow field of active supporters as the "coalition." The decision was taken only to describe "coalition" deeds. American flags were not to be hoisted or waved since the operation would be the joint efforts of the "coalition." American civilian and military spokesmen, as well as the main field commanders, were briefed to report only in terms of the coalition, which they hoped would dilute the strong American character of the military forces mounting the invasion of Iraq.

The Pentagon was also worried about the mounting anti-war protests within American campuses and human rights organizations, who questioned the moral, economic and political validity of the war. These manifestations of public displeasure with the war not only tended to erode the public support prior to the outbreak of the war, but it was feared that it would also reflect on the negative public opinion in the Arab countries and Third World, as well as in Western Europe. The significant front of opposition to the war would, by default, be strengthened and energized by the emerging internal opposition in the US itself. Protests in Europe, including mass demonstrations in London, Paris and Berlin, encouraged anti-war feelings. Moreover, some Western "peace militants" went to Baghdad to serve as human shields for Saddam's regime, unwittingly allowing their propaganda exploitation by the regime.

The first major operational decision by the war planners to counter these trends was to "embed" reporters, including some big names in the American media, with the fighting troops and the main air and naval bases, including aircraft carriers. The rationale behind the decision was that, unlike the 1991 Gulf War, and the smaller skirmishes of Granada and the Falklands War, where the only news was the official versions of the hostilities given by the military HQs, this time reporters could join the advancing troops and witness for themselves the daily combat routine. The great advantage for the planners was that the journalists, though ostensibly "free" to form their own ideas and report on them, were in fact literally "in bed" with the troops they accompanied, sharing with them the exhilaration of combat, living in permanent danger, exposed to the elements, and the general horror of combat; that commonality of living and sharing would create a spirit of camaraderie and sympathy for the troops and their plan of action, which would be reflected in their reports. However, the presence of the reporters among the troops would pose an additional security burden and would expose civilian journalists to dangers that they were unprepared for.

Embedding also meant that the field commanders knew that their every step was monitored and discussed, which signified they would think twice before daring to act in a way that could be interpreted and viewed as abusive or uncivilized. The troops were repeatedly warned that their actions were being scrutinized, and therefore they had to refrain from shooting unless they were attacked; avoid the destruction of civilian neighbourhoods; circumvent populated cities rather than fight from house to house; prevent the destruction of holy places in Islam; take over the oil fields during the battles so as to avoid any major environmental disasters; attack only the regime and its symbols; and to show civility, forbearance and courtesy toward the civilian populations. The commanders repeated to journalists the mantra that they did not come as occupiers, but as liberators; that they had no intention to rule Iraq but to hand it over to the Iraqis; and that Iraqi resources belonged to the country and its people. The Americans further stated that they were intent on keeping public order, on reverting to normalcy as soon as feasible, and on supplying massive quantities of food, drugs and other crucial goods to the population at large, pending the return of the country to pre-war routine. All these declarations were to be recorded and transmitted to the world by the intermediary of the embedded reporters.

Millions of leaflets were also printed to be distributed on the ground or dropped by planes over major cities, communicating to the frightened civilians the American commitments regarding their welfare. As a gesture that the US did not intend to rule the country, no military government was designated beforehand. Unlike the military regime to which they had been accustomed under Saddam, Iraqi citizens were now promised that a civilian representative government would be elected as soon as possible, and in the meantime a former American general, Jay Garner, would undertake the mammoth task of repairing the damage to the Iraqi infrastructure and state. Democracy, an alien concept to the average Iraqi, was widely promoted by the coalition forces, and it was important for the Americans to be seen making institutional reforms, in order to highlight the differences, politically, in the new Iraq. Medical help to wounded Iraqis during the war was envisaged in the mobile American military health facilities pending the renewed functioning of the Iraqi healthcore network.

Iraq and the War on Terror

The war against international terrorism was the primary motivation behind President Bush's post-9/11 declaration and naming of an "Axis of Evil." The War in Afghanistan launched against the Taliban regime and the al-

Qa'ida terrorists who found refuge there was the first phase in the war against this axis. As in the case of Bin Laden, where Bush sought to destroy the terrorist network and the sympathetic regime, when Iraq's turn came, the American president was determined to eliminate both Saddam's regime and the terrorists that he had given refuge to and collaborated with. However, in the case of Iraq there was the additional problem of the unconventional weapons that Saddam himself had repeatedly boasted he was developing, and which to the post-9/11 US, represented a clear and present danger lest Saddam's rogue state hand them over to terrorist organizations. After years of complacency and of turning a blind eye to these developments, the issue of Iraq's weapons became urgent to the US now that it was a victim of terrorism, due to the deadly combination of a tyrannical regime armed with WMD and possible collaboration with terrorist organizations who were vying for such weapons.

So, the task of the war planners was not only to convince the world that it was imperative to discover what Saddam had accumulated during his four years of unrestricted development, but also to unveil that "smoking gun" that would justify the American invasion. The Pentagon therefore had to prepare technical teams equipped with the latest advanced technology and sensors to uncover the secret storage compounds of these materials and locate the roaming mobile laboratories. Unlike the UN teams who relied exclusively on what the Iraqis told them and on the ability of their detective technology, the Americans were counting on the human intelligence of apprehended Iraqi soldiers and scientists, to find the locations. Indeed, many of the 55 personalities featured on the card deck were those considered the key personnel in devising, planning, financing, manufacturing and stockpiling WMD. The Americans were quite confident that, even though their presentations of the evidence of Iraq's biological, chemical and nuclear threat in the Security Council remained inconclusive, once they were free to explore Iraq after the war they would be able to elicit enough information from defectors and POWs as to vindicate their stance.

Terrorism proper was also of some concern, because intelligence had allegedly unveiled secret links between al-Qa'ida and the Saddam regime, involving collaboration in the development of WMD. Two bases in Iraq were singled out: the Ansar al-Islam group, which had found refuge in northern Iraq after the Afghanistan War; and another training base for terrorism in the Baghdad area. The first had a reputation for experiments with deadly gases and chemical substances against animals, with the obvious intent to apply their results on human targets. Shocking clips were shown on Arab television featuring dogs, cats and birds, suffering agonizing deaths, and drove home a cruel message of what was likely to happen to human targets of terror should the same methods be used against them. The Americans were understandably interested in playing up the footage, not only to warn of the horrors terrorists wished to perpetrate against a civilian population, but also to gain credence for their determination to overwhelm Iraq as part of the war against terrorism. At the other base in Baghdad, footage was captured of a model jumbo aircraft serving as the training ground for hijacking operations. It was even insinuated that the perpetrators of 9/11 had been trained in that camp, which would assuredly link Iraq to al-Qa'ida and its field operations.

The Conduct of the War

The conduct of war is the supreme test for the leadership of the warring parties. Under the autocratic regime of Saddam Hussein, where the entire burden of leadership and responsibility rested on his shoulders, his cronies and advisors played a secondary, often subservient role in the major decisions of the war. Due to his position as the defending party who had to predict the American moves and respond to them, or counter them after they occurred, Saddam had much less room for maneuver than the attacking party. The Americans, who chose the course of the war, its timing and tactics, and *a priori* held the higher grounds of military power, were also under one supreme commander – the president of the United States. However, President Bush also had a vast chain of command, military and civil, which represented a distinct advantage in the battlefield. There were some disadvantages, however, including: settling contradictory interests between various branches of government and warring political personalities; being held to account by the public and the media; appeasing allies and foes; cajoling the United Nations and other international institutions; and heeding warnings of politicians and ex-generals.

Secretary of Defense Donald Rumsfeld, in his second term in office, exuded energy, resolve and a self-assured control of the data and the situation in his high-profile role during the war. Unlike the president, who trusted him fully and supported him in the face of criticism during the difficult moments of the war but personally maintained a low profile, Rumsfeld was the front-man of the war, its most prominent spokesman, its most committed leader and its most forceful advocate. He had personally reviewed and approved every detail of the war plan, and felt obliged to report to the public about its implementation, to respond to and refute the accusations that "his" untested doctrine had "resulted in the launching of the American offensive with *insufficient* forces."[2] Those concerns were raised when Washington was teeming with rumors that the Iraqi forces' willingness to fight had been underestimated, and in consequence the American troops assigned to the war were not thought to be up to the task. Rumsfeld, with the backing of the president and the main field commander, General Tommy Franks, the Head of Central Command, brushed aside such criticisms as either partisan or indicative of obsolete military thinking.

In the US, Rumsfeld was already under intense scrutiny not only by the anti war coalition in Congress, college campuses and the liberal press, but also by some Republican leaders who feared that the war might jeopardize George W. Bush's chances for a second presidential term. While his critics on the left blamed him for having ventured into the war in the first place, the right attacked Rumsfeld for not committing sufficient forces to a swift, decisive and ultimately triumphant conclusion. Unshaken in his convictions, Rumsfeld fended off the critics who called him and Paul Wolfowitz to task because their battle plans did not seem to be "panning out," sarcastically asking "where were the flowers thrown out at our troops?" [3] What the critics interpreted as the first signs of growing difficulties for the troops, the rational and determined defense secretary grasped as temporary difficulties that were bound to dissipate as the troops advanced. The critics included retired army generals who lectured to the media on the upcoming difficulties due to the insufficiency of the troops, and in consequence the undermining of the deterrent image of the US military.[4] But Rumsfeld would not budge.

Rumsfeld's strategy, which proposed to oppose the formidable Republican Guard units with a modest array of American troops, was also deemed unrealistic with regard to toppling Saddam. Baghdad alone was defended by six crack Republican Guard divisions, while the entire American expeditionary force comprised around four divisions, plus the British division operating independently in the Basra region. The Rumsfeld–Franks strategy called for a "rolling start" deployment of the troops, meaning that the attack began with what was available on the ground, pending the arrival of reinforcements, if and when needed. This approach caused some concern not only among retired generals and veterans of previous wars, but also by currently serving top brass of the Army. The Army, indeed, was considered the most recalcitrant in terms of resisting the streamlining military reforms that the secretary had devised, especially since his war plan did not lend primacy to conventional land forces. In his defense, Rumsfeld and his aides stressed the advantages of the plan, which enabled the US to take full advantage of its air superiority to shorten the time needed for deployment in the Gulf before the war. Some of his close supporters argued that:

> He accepts the idea that precision and information can combine to produce an increasingly effective military force . . . The plan is well conceived and the forces are appropriate for that plan. I do not believe it is too light. The force is vastly more productive and the systems are more productive. Under those circumstances you can lighten up. I am not aware of any engagement in which heavier forces would have been more effective . . . [5]

Understandably, the active generals who participated in the fighting were restrained in their reactions to the criticism voiced against Rumsfeld after the attack was launched. General William Wallace, for example, who commanded V Corps, leading the ground troops to Baghdad, when questioned about the sufficiency of his battle order, said that they were "adequate," [6] and his comments were frequently echoed by his commander, General Tommy Franks, who in all appearance maintained a good working relationship with the secretary. However, other former military commanders, like General Ronald Griffith, a divisional commander in the 1991 Gulf War, or General Barry MacCaffrey, did not lend much credence to the "shock and awe" air-strikes that were to stun the Iraqi Government; they were in favor of dispatching more artillery and armor units. They identified various needs on the ground that the soldiers would have to attend: to hold the cities; to protect the prolonged logistic lines; to fight paramilitary forces along the way; and to search for weapons of mass destruction. These factors, they anticipated, would require many more troops than were dispatched at the onset of the war. They also claimed that the light forces that Rumsfeld assigned to the task of conquering Iraq were not as agile as they were led to believe because, while they could be deployed rapidly, the forces did not possess enough manpower to proceed into Baghdad, which might compel them to advance more slowly, and so defeat the notion of the swift war.[7]

While the widest coverage of the war originated from the embedded Western media attached to the ground troops, the other heroes of the war, the US Air Force (USAF) fighters, remained for the most part anonymous. Although every carrier and air base had its embedded reporters, none of them could accompany the pilots on their sorties, making it difficult to report on their encounters with the enemy. Therefore, rather than the air pilots, it was the USAF equipment which won exposure; as with the navy units it was their firepower, gunnery, missiles and brands of aircraft which were perceived in their collective anonymity by both journalists and public and reported accordingly. This war, which reporters and military spokesmen could not help compare to other wars, leaned so much on technology and air-strikes that, it can be argued, its real heroes were advanced weapon systems and other sophisticated equipment, though not all the equipment was state-of-the-art.

For example, the A-10 Thunderbolt (also known as the Warthog), an Air Force aircraft designed to provide close air support to the advancing troops, was a veteran of the 1991 Gulf War, where it flew thousands of sorties and proved lethal against Iraqi tanks. The A-10 played a highly important role in the Third Gulf War, in spite of the absence of an effective laser targeting system on board the plane. Its cockpit has titanium plate armor to shield against anti-aircraft fire, and also comes with a high-speed front-mounted gun that fires depleted uranium and armor-piercing rounds. The A-10 Thunderbolt is equipped with air-to-ground missiles, anti-armor missiles, cluster bombs, laser-guided bombs and other bombs weighing up to 3,000 lb. Its devastating effect was noticeable throughout the war.

The main hopes for decimating the redoubtable Republican Guard, however, were placed on the Longbow Apache, an advanced version of the Apache, the Army's main attack helicopter. With its new radar and targeting devices the Longbow can track over 120 targets simultaneously, identify the 16 most dangerous among them and share the information with other aircraft and ground forces. Its infrared sensors and night vision enable it for all-weather and round-the-clock combat, and its radar can lock on to targets from a safe distance. Nevertheless, because of its massive, continuous and significant involvement in the battlefield, and its audacious pursuits of Iraqi tanks and Republican Guard units around Baghdad, it also suffered the most losses. On 24 March only a few days into the war, the first Apache was downed by Iraqi fire. Others were damaged near Karbalah or struck by light gunfire; still others fell, apparently intact, into enemy hands when they were forced to land due to technical failures, vulnerability to the extensive small-arms anti-aircraft fire, or the sand-storms that rendered them difficult to fly.[8] Its impressive array of guns, anti-tank missiles and rockets are partly operated by the co-pilot who also doubles up as a gunner. Its proven capacity in Afghanistan a year earlier, especially in surprising the enemy by flying low at night, made it, despite its relative vulnerability, into a crucial weapon in the war.[9]

From the decks of the aircraft carriers, led by the 97,000-ton, 4.5-acre flight deck *Abraham Lincoln*,[10] where President Bush would later stand to announce the end of the war, hundreds of FA-18 Hornets maintained an undisputed air supremacy throughout the war. Defying the storms that in normal times would have grounded fighting aircraft, the intrepid pilots kept on flying the sorties on which the ground troops depended. The *Abraham Lincoln* alone hosted on its deck and hangars one air wing, consisting of nine squadrons. On 26 March a storm engulfed the carrier, forcing the *Abraham Lincoln* to reduce the number of flights.[11] F-16 fighter-bombers battered Republican Guard positions and their T-72 tank formations with their 500 lb laser-guided bombs, careful not to hurt civil-ians and double-checking that no unnecessary collateral damage was caused to adjoining buildings.[12] The F-16 CG, a versatile all-weather fighter-bomber equipped with infrared targeting, carries two one-ton satel-lite-guided bombs or four 500 lb. laser-guided bombs. To prolong their range of action from their ground bases in the Gulf area, notably Saudi Arabia, they are equipped with mid-air refuelling ability, which they used when over Iraqi territory.

Remotely-piloted aircraft also played their role in the war, albeit with a much lower profile than the conventional fighters or helicopters. Predator drones, known as RQ-1s, accomplished secret missions such as exposing Baghdad air defenses which were then destroyed by fighter-bombers, or collecting intelligence and providing a bird's-eye view of the battlefield. The Predator is a slow propeller-driven and long-range pilot-less aircraft guided by an operator many miles away, thus avoiding any unnecessary exposure of American pilots. It is equipped with laser-detection devices to locate targets and Hellfire laser-guided missiles. The Predator's high-resolution cameras and cloud-piercing radar can take photos in real-time of minute details of the enemy's activities. The more than 100 missions undertaken by 15 aircraft in Iraq (a third of the total in US arsenals) have remained a closely guarded secret. The Marines operated their own Dragon-Eye drones, while the Army used their Hunter drones, which together with the Global Hawks can provide all-weather pictures of a vast area for 24 hours, assuring both tactical and strategic coverage of the entire battle theater. This large variety of pilot-less vehicles was certainly one of the ground-breaking features of the war, according to General Richard Myers, the Chair of the Joint Chiefs of Staff.[13]

The bombing offensive began on 19 March when three dozen Tomahawk cruise missiles were launched against Iraqi targets from four Navy ships and two submarines operating in the Gulf and in the adjoining Red Sea. This attack was part of the "shock and awe" policy of the war, calculated not only to stun the enemy but specifically to decapitate their leadership by targeting Saddam, his sons and their cronies. To that end, two F-117A stealth bombers, each carrying two one-ton satellite-guided bombs, were dispatched to bust the bunkers belonging to the leadership. The next day, as the British troops marched toward Basra, other forces seized Iraq's only port – Umm Qasr – and the Fao Peninsula where it is located, while Allied warplanes struck Iraqi artillery and missile positions in the south to pre-empt any danger they might pose to the invading forces. The main American thrust toward Baghdad was also launched on two fronts, along the river beds of the Euphrates and Tigris rivers. Cruise missiles were fired against several government and military targets in Baghdad, *inter alia* rein-forcing the idea of political and military decapitation: the presidential office compound, the ministries of planning and foreign affairs and the Rashid Air base.

Air attacks led by Apache helicopters were launched against the garrison in Nasiriya, the first major town northwest of Basra on the Euphrates, and against the air defenses at the Talil air base. One Apache carrying 12 American and British troops from Kuwait crashed, killing all on board. Even areas beyond the reach of US ground forces in northern Iraq, where American plans to invade from Turkish territory were undone by Ankara's procrastination, were brought into the circle of fighting when American cruise missiles were fired toward the elite Nebuchadnezzar Republican Guard division stationed just south of Kirkuk. By the end of the second day of combat on 20 March most of the vast territory of Iraq, which approximates an area the size of France, California or Japan, was involved in the war. Western Iraq, which borders with Jordan, was the exception to this, and here US commandoes had already taken position in the days preceding the outbreak of the war. Their goal was to prevent any missiles being launched against Israel at any cost, fearing that the Israelis would then seek to retaliate, a situation that America wanted to avoid.

On 21 March the H2 and H3 air bases were seized in western Iraq, at the same time that the war intensified on all fronts. Some 2,000 air sorties were ordered on the entire battle arena, focusing on 1,500 targets and involving 1,000 bombing missions. Under intense pressure, the Iraqi division which defended Basra collapsed, while the Umm Qasr port and the Fao Peninsula came under siege. In that sector alone, around 600 Iraqis surrendered and were taken prisoner, freeing Allied commandoes to take over, intact, two major gas and oil terminals. Concurrently, Apaches pursued their onslaught of the Iraqi army in Nasiriya, while the forward forces were already within 100 miles of Baghdad. The heavy bombing began to focus on Baghdad, where 1300 bombs and cruise missiles fell and created the first major impact on Baghdad's infrastructure. Missiles and bombs also rained down on the northern cities of Mosul and Kirkuk, gnawing at the dwindling power of the Republican Guard and the Jalawla air base there. On the next day, 22 March the rate of bombings diminished; "only" 1,500 bombs were dropped (compared to 2,000 the preceding day), attacking 500 targets (as against 1,500 the day before). While the Americans scrambled to control the fires that had been set at around 30 wells in the Rumeila oil fields on the Kuwaiti border, a helicopter collision over the Gulf resulted in more casualties. In the central war theater, where the 3rd Infantry Division was thrusting toward Baghdad, heavy resistance was encountered near Samawa, a small town northwest of Nasiriya. Four Americans perished when two of their personal armored carriers, or "Humvees," were struck by rocket-propelled grenades (RPGs). The advancing troops captured a bridge on the Euphrates north of Nasiriya and continued their race to Baghdad.

The relentless bombing of Baghdad continued unabated. Fuel trenches in the approaches to the city were ignited by the Iraqis, raising immense smoke screens that were to blanket the targets from American attacks. But except for the air pollution they created, the screens proved useless against the Americans, since their electronic systems and precise weaponry easily overcame this obstacle. The bombings spread to the northern areas of Iraq, where Ansar al-Islam, reputedly connected to al-Qa'ida, had found refuge and allegedly maintained a training base. If seized, that base could constitute the "smoking gun" that the Americans needed to justify *post factum* their invasion of Iraq. Mosul, the mixed Arab-Kurdish city in the north which lay at the heart of the oil-producing area in that region, and had been targeted as one of the war aims (along with Jalawla, now indentified as the HQ of the Iraqi 2nd Corps which commanded the divisions of northern

Iraq), once again underwent intense bombings, though the oil fields and civilian population were mainly avoided. In Kirkuk, a Kurdish enclave which had grown during the preceding decade, Republican Guard bases were now hit in air attacks, clearing the way for the Kurds to link up with American forces whenever their presence in the north became possible.

The smooth advance into Iraqi territory, which had initially heightened the morale among the American Command, soon dissipated as the war took a heavier toll on American lives. The mood quickly turned, with President Bush talking about the "difficult and long road ahead," warning against the illusions of a quick victory. Indeed, from the fifth day of the war on (23 March) a series of mishaps and setbacks presented the Americans with the harsh realities of war. A bombing raid on Basra accidentally killed around 70 Iraqi civilians, forcing the Americans to realize that collateral damage and civilian casualties, although unintentional, could fatally undermine the campaign and dampen the enthusiasm for bringing freedom and democracy to the Iraqi people. The unrelenting bombing of Baghdad and other population centers inevitably generated more civilian casualties and with it more criticism of the war, both within the US and outside of it.

The fifth day of combat operations was also a day of accidents and fatal errors which duly affected morale to a significant degree; it was clear that the Bush administration was unprepared for the incidents. First, the news came from Kuwait that an American G.I., Sgt Asan Akbar, of Muslim descent and conviction, launched a grenade at his fellow-servicemen of the 101st Airborne Division, killing one and injuring 15 others. (Just prior to the war against the Taliban in Afghanistan in 2001, the question of the participation of Muslim soldiers serving in the US military had came up for public debate, and the near-consensus among Muslim scholars was that no Muslim should fight against other Muslims.) There was genuine shock and bemusement at all levels of the military, from Asan's fellow soldiers to the high command, who could ill comprehend how there could exist an "enemy from within," who could act with such fanatic hatred against his own comrades-in-arms after he swore allegiance to the US. Consternation and embarrassment followed. But although the whole affair was rapidly buried by both the media and the Pentagon, doubts persisted as to the motives of the perpetrator, who was lauded by Muslim fundamentalists.

No sooner had that news been digested than another pair of reports about American casualties came in: 11 soldiers killed in action and, worse (in terms of media exposure), American POWs. Ten marines lost their lives in the battle raging around Nasiriya when an Iraqi unit which pretended to surrender launched a surprise attack. Following this a detachment of 12 American maintenance servicemen was captured by the Iraqis when they took a wrong turn. Some of the captured were shown on *Al-Jazeera* Television, the Qatari TV station, the others were presumed dead. This incident had also occurred near Nasiriya while advance American troops were already at Najaf and the outskirts of Baghdad. These two incidents showed, not only that Iraqi resistance was stronger than anticipated and that advancing rapidly forward did not guarantee the fall of the enemy pockets that remained behind, but also that the lengthening logistical lines were exposed and vulnerable. That put an additional burden on the advancing troops and further subtracted from the fighting units that should have been spared for the capture of Baghdad. Gradually, the field commanders realized that Iraqi commando units, dubbed Fedayeen Saddam (those who sacrifice themselves for Saddam), who had been prepared in advance to act behind the lines of an invading enemy, now posed a real and immediate threat to American troops.

The lessons of these incidents were quickly learned: the troops no longer advanced as rapidly as before, with the whole operation slowing down to the point that many feared it "was bogged down," and there was once again talk of the need for reinforcements, for more care and patience before US troops marched on Baghdad. The first week of the war ended with Basra still in Iraqi hands, with the British unable to enter peacefully as they had anticipated. Therefore, they decided to launch an offensive into the city, aided by reports of an uprising against Saddam's loyalists in Basra.

The battle for Nasiriya, involving some 5,000 American marines, was finally showing signs of turning in America's favor; near Najaf, an American fighter-bomber mistakenly knocked out a Patriot missiles battery; on the outskirts of Baghdad, US troops exchanged heavy fire with the defending Republican Guard units, who also caused severe damage to several helicopters, one of which was downed and its crew taken prisoner; and bombing missions began against Tikrit, Saddam's hometown stronghold. Things continued to go awry when two British marines were reported missing in action, the two American crewmen of the downed Apache were confirmed POW; the Patriot battery was destroyed; sandstorms with winds gusting at 50 mph, cut visibility, slowed operations to a virtual standstill; and a bombing mission close to the Syrian border mistakenly targeted a civilian bus, killing and injuring civilians.

On a more positive note from the Allies' viewpoint, an Iraqi ammunition depot was seized north of Najaf, raising the first concrete suspicions about the presence of unconventional weapons in Iraq; the port city of Umm Qasr came under total British control, which opened new avenues for the arrival and distribution of relief to the Iraqi population; some heavy Iraqi casualties were reported in and around Nasiriya; and the bombing assaults on Baghdad increased and became more destructive, with entire neighborhoods reported abandoned. Rings of smoke surrounded the city as its defenders desperately attempted to conceal their positions using a smoke screen technique. In the northern front, Kurdish troops, closely guided by American special units, took over a few villages which brought them closer to engaging the Iraqi forces in that area.

The skirmishes that brought the American forces to the gates of the southern Iraqi cities along the course of the Euphrates by the end of the first week of combat, now essentially grew into a two-pronged effort: past Najaf, into Hindiyah and then Karbalah, the second Shi'ite holy city, the 20,000 men and women of the 3rd Infantry Division, together with the 15,000-strong 101st Airborne Division, headed to Baghdad along the river. The second advancing front, led by the 1st First Marine Division (20,000 soldiers), drove to Baghdad along the Tigris River. After the 3rd Infantry raided Hindiyah, a mere 50 miles south of the capital, it seized an important bridge which allowed the troops to cross the Euphrates into the outskirts of Baghdad, on its way engaging elements of the Iraqi Medina Republican Guard. The 101st stayed behind in Najaf to fight Iraqi irregulars, in preparation for continuing its way toward Karbalah. The Marines seized Shatra on their way to Kut, where they would attack Baghdad from the southeast, along the Tigris which flows in the heart of the city. At some point north of Nasiriya, the Marine Expeditionary Force had to split its advancing units, since the terrain was becoming too dense: the 5th and 7th Regiments took a middle course between the two rivers toward Hillah and Iskandariya due south to Baghdad, while the 1st Regiment pursued its trajectory toward Kut, southeast of Baghdad. The air force pursued its strategic bombings in and around Baghdad, and against Iraqi positions near Kalak in the north, giving close air support to the advancing Kurds. American troops opened fire on a civilian van near Najaf, killing Iraqi women and children apparently trying to escape the city, illustrating the deadly results arising from confusion and misunderstanding on the battlefield.

By the beginning of April after 10 days of fighting, the American forces were once again optimistic, as the first signs of the foundering of Saddam's regime became apparent. In northern Iraq, the 173rd Airborne Brigade landed in Kurdish territory, followed by the improvisation of an airstrip near the town of Harir, which would allow the landing and launching of aircraft in the battles against Baghdad and Tikrit. In another raid US fighter planes destroyed a location controlled by Ansar al-Islam Muslim fundamentalists near Kalak, and Special Forces captured a poison factory site believed to be operated by the terrorist group. Under Kurdish pressure backed up by American power, Iraqi troops withdrew from the Kirkuk area. On 3 April the offensive around Karbalah defeated the Iraqi defenders and brought the American advance within reach of the capital. The next day a brigade of the 3rd Infantry captured the Saddam International Airport southwest of the city, a mere 10 miles from its center, while another brigade from the same division headed east to attack the capital from the south. The Marines crossing the Tigris River near Numaniya also headed to Baghdad along its northern bank. In another major battle near Kut, Marines wiped out the Baghdad Division of the

Republican Guard, which had been already devastated by air-strikes. Baghdad was being gradually surrounded from the south by the 3rd Infantry, and from the south and the east by the 1st Marines, and the combination of those forces was assiduously gnawing at the capital's periphery. The Battle for Baghdad, culminating in its fall on 9 April and separate accounts of developments in the Kurdish north and the Shi'ite south, will be tackled separately in later chapters.

The balance of the war unfolded in rapid succession: chaos and looting would reign throughout Baghdad in the days ahead; oil-rich Kirkuk fell into joint American–Kurdish hands on 11 April after the Iraqi garrison gave in to the public uprising there; Mosul followed the same pattern thereafter. In the town of Khanaqin, northeast of Baghdad, Ba'ath and army officials vanished when the news about the fall of Baghdad became known; Special Forces took control of the Syrian border to prevent Iraqis on the wanted list escaping, or Syrian supporters of Saddam from entering Iraq; in the south, the British were restoring order to Basra; while the Americans in Najaf witnessed the murder of a Shi'ite cleric who had just returned from exile in Iran. The entire northern front collapsed as remnants of the Iraqi loyalists retreated south, and air-strikes intensified on and around Tikrit, Saddam's hometown. On 15 April American troops captured Tikrit, thus eliminating the last major challenge to their takeover of the country. The clearest possible sign that the war, and the Saddam regime, were over, was the fact that some high-level Iraqi officials, including General Tahaseen Rafan, one of the heads of the domestic intelligence apparatus, reported out of their "own volition" to the makeshift American HQ in Mosul and negotiated the terms of their surrender.

The Problems of POWs and Casualties

Although only a relatively small number of American POWs were captured by the Iraqis, the individual plight of each one mobilized the entire nation. The hardships suffered by every soldier in combat operations barely register in terms of real suffering with the public. It is only the graphic depiction of POWs or casualties that generates sympathy. Accordingly, when, in the early stages of the war, four American GIs, including a woman, belonging to the 507th Maintenance Company and another two from the 227th Aviation Regiment, were reported missing in combat, and then confirmed POWs, they drew the focus of attention, however briefly, from the ongoing battles to their own human stories.[14]

The media coverage encompassed everything from the Geneva Convention which governs the treatment of POWs, to mutual accusations between Americans and Iraqis regarding mistreatment of their POWs. The trauma of the families who endured harrowing periods of anxiety were captured on film, as were the vigils held in support of the families and the demands for their prompt release. The spontaneous rallying of every military base, hometown, circle of friends, close relatives, authorities of the county or the state where the POW originated, all the way up to the White House and the Pentagon, made the POWs names and pictures familiar in the public domain, to the point that they surpassed in fame the field commanders who had led them into battle. Americans were incensed when the Iraqis broadcasted images of dead and captured GIs on *al-Jazeera*, in contrast to the American networks which generally refrained from such exhibition. The Bush administration accused the Iraqis of violating the Geneva Convention by exposing the American POWs to public humiliation. The American media, however, did print pictures of unidentified Iraqi POWs.[15]

American concerns rose when news began to filter through from the battlefield claiming that the Iraqis had executed some of the captured GIs. That contention, picked up by the American administration as evidence of the tyranny of Saddam's regime, was based on the pictures of dead American soldiers shown on *al-Jazeera* broadcasts together with the images of captured POWs. Other accusations were levelled against the Iraqis by senior American officials, arguing that the Iraqis were feigning to surrender and then shooting at American forces, blocking the flow of food into Basra, or "fighting like terrorists, not soldiers." American legal experts, such as Ruth Wedgwood of Johns Hopkins, insisted that irrespective of whether the war was right or wrong, the rules of its conduct were still binding on all parties. Others, like Michael Ratner of the Center for Constitutional Rights, castigated the US government for its hypocrisy, questioning the right of the American leadership to incarcerate, in Guantanamo Bay, the POWs from Afghanistan indefinitely and without trial. Victoria Clarke of the Pentagon patently accused the Iraqis of perfidy and treachery for raising white flags by soldiers dressed as civilians to draw American troops, who respect the Geneva Convention, into lethal ambushes.[16]

As the stronger, more humane and powerful party, America also began to care for the multitudes of enemy POWs and casualties, especially the civilians. It was not only a matter of holding them under custody and feeding them, but also of treating them medically, especially as Iraqi medical facilities were in a state of disrepair. Iraqi POWs numbered several thousand, since many soldiers fled the battlefield to the safety of American custody, and were an important source of intelligence gathering for the Americans, especially about the morale of the Iraqis. Some of these escapees told how they were forced at gun-point to fight. Morale among US troops was raised when stories of such brutality and cruelty were related, as they served as reminders of the freedom, equality and liberty they, as American soldiers, enjoyed. An American 116-bed field hospital commanded by Navy Captain Pat Kelly, built in Spain in February to treat the casualties from Iraq, began to function at the end of March 2003 when C-141 transports ferried patients there.[17] Back home in the US, while relatives of the confirmed dead in combat mourned in private grief or in public and communal ceremonies, the families of the POWs and the MIAs were left waiting for news, fearing the worst. Their uncertainty was shared by the nation at large and made the families the temporary focus of national concern, pending the arrival of confirmed reports of their relative's fate, falling into enemy hands, or being shown on Arab television, confirming their captivity, or in some cases, the devastating news of the death of their loved ones.[18]

Refugees and Relief Work

In an operation of the scale of the Iraq War, and based on the experience of the 1991 Gulf War, the Americans anticipated a massive outflow of Iraqis into neighboring countries and a large-scale displacement of refugees from combat zones. They also took into account that large quantities of food, medicine and other emergency supplies would be needed to accommodate the large numbers of displaced people. They were also aware that, as in the War in Afghanistan in 2001, any American relief assistance would be treated with great suspicion by the Iraqi people. The demonization of the US in the Arab and Islamic worlds has overlooked the significant aid contribution made by America to the Middle East. American support for UNRWA, which has been taking care of the Palestinian refugees for half a century, is far larger than all Arab countries combined. This sort of contribution contradicts the Arab stereotype of the US as an evil, selfish power, so such generosity is ignored. Nonetheless, the Americans and their allies took the necessary precautions to deliver relief as soon as the hostilities began.

The US had also planned for a long stay in Iraq after the war, which meant that in order to achieve a degree of stability and quiet, it could not afford to leave large portions of the Iraqi population uncared for, who had, in any case, been deprived of many basics during the quarter-century of Saddam's rule. Refugee camps were established along the borders of Kuwait and Jordan in anticipation of a large influx of destitute Iraqis. However, what actually happened on the ground was that many Iraqis reasoned that, if the US is to stay for the foreseeable future, they would also be better off if they stayed put and received the assistance brought to them under American rule. But the delay in capturing Umm Qasr, the only navigable port for large ships in southern Iraq, by the British, meant that large-scale aid could not be unloaded and deployed in the field in time. There was a wide gap between President Bush's assurances that large amounts of aid would be flowing to southern Iraq, and the military realities on the war front which interfered with the plans of relief workers from the International Red Cross and others. Everyone understood that as long as sporadic fire continued in Umm Qasr, no serious relief work could begin. At around this time the first reports came in about the dire humanitarian situation in Basra, a city of 1.5 million people which had been assigned to the British. Kofi Annan, UN Secretary-General, who had previously failed to end the Iraq crisis, now warned of the impending humanitarian disaster in Basra if relief supplies did not reach their goal forthwith. The city had been cut off from water and electricity supplies for several days, and there was fear of an outbreak of cholera and other epidemics.[19]

The coalition forces soon discovered that the navigation channels around Umm Qasr had been infested by underwater mines that the Iraqis had laid in defense of their only deep-water port. The mine-sweeping exercise took much longer than expected. Heavy fighting in and around Basra, where American bombings had killed dozens of civilians according to the reports of the Iraqi Red Crescent, had also caused the destruction of a main city bridge. Nevertheless, General Tommy Franks remained upbeat and assured reporters that soon the inhabitants of Basra would "have a better access to food and water than they had had for decades." His promises were backed by the fact that the British transport ship, the *Sir Galahad*, was only six hours away from Umm Qasr and ready to sail into harbor. The UN had operated, for the past decade, a relief campaign under the "oil for food program" from the port of Umm Qasr and fed two-thirds of the Iraqi population by a steady supply of food rations. All that Tommy Franks had to do was to maintain those distribution centers open and keep the flow of supplies constant and safe.[20]

The situation in the north, the home of the Kurdish minority, was quite different to the south. The Kurds still remembered the chemical attacks of 1988, and immediately upon the launching of American attacks on Iraq they feared retaliation from Saddam. The north has a mixed population of Arabs and Kurds, but in the cities primarily inhabited by Kurds, an exodus began of thousands of Kurdish families to the mountain tops. The Kurds lived under the trauma of the previous war when they rebelled against Saddam – his response was to make two million of them homeless. Only later, after the no-fly zone was established and enforced by the Allies, could the Kurds, unlike their more unfortunate Shi'ite counterparts in the south, build their virtual areas of security and autonomy. And unlike the 1991 war, when they had to spend the ice-cold winter on the snowy mountain tops with hardly any supplies, this time some Kurds were better prepared to move to their mountain shelters with enough food and many of their belongings. Others, less lucky, crowded into caves, tents and the carcasses of old buses to seek refuge from the cold and to wait for American relief.[21]

Since the fast pace of the war did not allow Saddam to act against the

Kurds within the government-controlled areas before they fell into American hands, and certainly not against the Kurdish-controlled zone around Erbil and Sulaimaniya, some of the refugees, sensing the war turning in favor of the Americans, soon began returning to their homes. However, relief workers feared that if the war dragged on they might not be able to provide all the food and medical needs for the prospective numbers of refugees. In the meantime some relief finally arrived at the besieged city of Basra and other towns in the south and a large-scale humanitarian disaster was for the most part averted. The renewal of full water and electricity supplies to the city was still unresolved at this point. Many people in Basra were seen drinking from the waters of the polluted rivers, which in turn raised the specter of epidemics transmitted by mass bodies of people drinking non-potable water. In addition to the $2 billion that the UN earmarked for humanitarian aid to Iraq, President Bush also asked Congress for $2.4 billion for aid and reconstruction, and this seemed to guarantee a good start for continuous relief work. The main goal was undoubtedly to restart the water treatment plant at Basra that had been paralyzed by electricity shortages, and to improve the fortunes of the other cities of the south, about which no information was available as the first week of the war drew to a close.[22]

While UN Secretary-General Kofi Annan and Prime Minister Tony Blair conferred on the question of relief to the Iraqi population, and President Bush was battling to get his multi-billion dollar aid program approved, the Ambassador of Iraq to the UN, Mohammed Adouri, launched a verbal attack on the US accusing it of exterminating the Iraqi population. His accusations so disgusted US Ambassador John Negroponte that he walked out. Though the US dispatched a large delegation of aid experts to Iraq, many private relief organizations asked Bush to let the UN coordinate the relief effort. At the same time, the US military completed a fresh water pipeline from Kuwait to the Iraqi border in order to substitute for the antiquated and paralyzed water systems throughout southern Iraq. The UN calculated that they would have to provide aid to at least 350,000 refugees, adding that they were ready to provide funds from the oil-for-food program to acquire electricity generators.[23] Despite the arguments between the coalition and the UN, and between the allies and Russia, France and Germany, never before was an aid program so well-funded and so speedily executed as this one. It is not that the parties concerned suddenly became great philanthropists or that Iraqi oil supplied the funds for the relief campaign, but that the main players, the US and Britain, knew that without a successful aid and relief program, their hold on Iraq after the war might become untenable.

Logistics and Welfare

The constant media-based interaction between the American public and the troops, and the emotional engagement of Americans at large with all details of the unfolding battles due to the non-stop coverage of the war, *involved* all Americans, at all levels – individual, communal and governmental – in the military effort, and, by extension, the troops participating in that effort. Every community or military base throughout the nation which sent their sons to the war held farewell ceremonies for them, prayers after they were gone, memorial services if they were hurt and welcoming parties when they returned. Vigils took place for the POWs and MIAs; officials of the churches and of the local and national governments were ever-present on the screens; and the daily briefings coming from both Washington and Central Command in Qatar gave the feeling that the entire nation was mobilized behind its soldiers. Never before in the history of warfare had the home front been as constantly and as deeply witness to the war front as was the case in the Third Gulf War.

At the outset of the war the Pentagon made public its array of air and ground supply vehicles in order to assure the public that all precautions were being taken to make sure that the troops would lack nothing of the requisites of combat: fuel, water, food and ammunition, regardless of the long lines of supply from Kuwait or their vulnerability. The list of vehicles included: The 60-foot long Heavy Expanded Mobility Tactical Truck that could carry, on all terrains, 5,000 gallons of fuel or ten tons of supplies; the M-1093 Standard Cargo Truck, protected by an on-board machine gun against enemy ground troops, capable of carrying five tons of supplies; the High Mobility Multi-Purpose Wheeled Vehicle (MPWV), able to carry eight people or cargo, and equipped with a heavy machine gun plus a grenade launcher; and the M2 Bradley, an armored fighting vehicle that provides protection for the rest of the supply convoy. It is armed with a chain gun and a machine gun, and a TOW anti-tank missile system. Overhead, for rapidity and emergency, the huge dual-rotor CH-47 Chinook helicopter, was able to deliver supplies on call; and the OH-58 helicopters, which accompanied the supply convoys, provided air support and made sure that no trucks were lost to the convoys in the vast open desert spaces they spanned.[24]

The fact that the combat units were closely shadowed by the media should not obscure the vital role of the supply units, whose missions became increasingly hazardous after a maintenance unit was ambushed near Nasiriya during the first week of the war. That incident, which raised criticism about the inability of the limited ground forces to protect their 300-mile supply lines, also forced the American Command to slow down its rush to the capital and pay more heed to the task of first defeating the Fedayeen Saddam and other Iraqi irregulars who were putting the supply lines in jeopardy. The large fuel tankers, which were particularly vulnerable targets to attacks, and on whose uninhibited operation depended the daily supply of 15 million gallons to the ground and air units, were now accompanied by attack helicopters overhead and Bradleys on the ground. Iraqi POWs presented another logistical problem, and the troops also had to hand emergency supplies of food and water to the hungry and thirsty Iraqi civilians, which exposed them to the threat of attacks by pro-Saddam Iraqis. The more forces that were engaged in protecting the supply lines, aiding the civilians and guarding the POWs, the more forces had to be diverted from the main goal of getting rapidly and in full force to Baghdad.[25] In this regard, the sandstorms which grounded entire units for days were a mixed blessing to the logistics people, as they were able to catch up with refueling and re-supplying the combat units before they moved on.

A novel dimension of the logistics elements of the war was the art of information supply. Just prior to the war, the Air Force launched into orbit a one-ton communications satellite to join a fleet of other satellites that made this war so sophisticated not only in the field of communications, but also in terms of guidance, weather forecasting, missile warnings, reconnaissance, target acquisition, precise bombings and damage assessment. The newly-launched satellite, known as the Joint Tactical Ground Station, is a portable complex for battlefield commanders that receives early warnings of incoming missiles and improves the accuracy of anti-missile weapons. Unlike the ground supply lines, which are fragile and exposed to enemy attacks, the satellite-technology supply lines are invulnerable to conventional enemy attacks. Although all these systems were innovations tested for the first time in Iraq, and proved their worth to the military campaign, skeptics wondered whether space-aided warfare could subdue sandstorms, or prove effective in urban warfare.[26] Indeed, in spite of these technological constructs, like the satellites and warning systems, small groups of determined Iraqi fighters could still derail, or at least slow down, a major operation, and well-trained American Marines still had to engage in physical combat in oppressive desert heat. Combat, no matter how influential satellite systems could be, was still fought in the physical, human arena.[27]

Caring for the welfare of soldiers also included their psychological well-being. Not a few soldiers, most of whom were young and novices to the battlefield, were scared of combat or were paralyzed by the prospects of a chemical attack, against which they felt helpless. Every uniformed person who goes to war is concerned about his or her fate, but the *esprit de corps* of the fighting unit is supposed to, in many instances, help overcome the fears of individual soldiers. In cases of extreme terror that grow into paralyzing traumas, psychiatry steps in to assist the individual in overcoming his anxieties. This was the job of the 883rd Medical Company that was attached to V Army Corps leading the ground operation in Iraq. The

Company specialized in combat stress or "battle fatigue," and was supposed to "reframe" the fears of the soldiers, exploring and defeating their neurosis so that they could rejoin their unit for combat. The psychiatrists of the company, for the most part reserve officers recruited for the war, taught their patients ways to relax, to contain their fears, using techniques that they termed "semi-hypnotic" or "self-massage." In addition, every division had its own psychiatrist, psychologist and social worker assigned to it.[28]

Unlike civilian psychiatry, where the specialist is focused on resolving personal problems and the treatment of such problems through a course of anti-depressant drug therapy, in military psychiatry the aim is to send the patients back to their combat duties. For that reason, drugs are used only as a last resort in order to avoid giving the patients the impression that they are sick, even though their psychological traumas often manifest themselves in the form of physical symptoms such as stomach aches, twitching and high levels of emotional pressures. Rather, anxieties are treated as a temporary, but normal, human reaction to the vagaries of combat. This treatment works: Around 80 percent of soldiers, after several days of rest, comfort, hot food and plentiful sleep, are ready to go back to the front. Israeli experiences in dealing with combat stress were studied by American experts, due the situation of an almost permanent state of war that the Israeli soldiers, regular and reserve, are exposed to. Often, soldiers who are unable to cope are assigned to low-pressure jobs in the services at HQ, until they are ready to rejoin their combat units. Unlike the Vietnam experience, where anxious GIs were usually flown out of the combat zones and hospitalized, the new doctrine suggests that the temporary traumatized soldiers remain in close proximity to their units where they are re-integrated as soon as feasible. This solution avoids creating feelings of failure and loss of self-esteem in the trauma-stricken soldier. While in the past soldiers who needed psychiatrist treatment were often viewed as "slackers," the arrest of the Muslim soldier who threw a grenade on his fellow soldiers in the 101st Airborne, and the desire to understand his motives, has brought some attention to the world of military psychiatry. Counseling is no longer frowned upon, and indeed it can be argued that it provides an additional emotional support to the soldiers, who have come to regard it as part of the well-being they are entitled to.[29]

3 Shi'ites in the South

During the advance of American troops into Iraq, the Western public were confronted with names, places and terms that they had never heard before, or had heard of but failed to fathom their significance. Names like Najaf and Karbalah; the dazzling celebrations of Ashura Day; the charismatic Ayatullahs that emerged into the streets; the newly discovered mass-graves of Shi'ites murdered by Saddam's regime; the insistence of the "liberated" Shi'ites on implementing an Islamic state to replace Saddam's ousted dictatorship; and the emergence under American occupation of a new political awareness among the Shi'ite majority in Iraq (13 million out of a total of 24 million) – all these events demand explanation as a prerequisite to the understanding of the unfolding war in southern Iraq.

The Shi'ites, who dwell principally in the south, up from Basra to Baghdad, were the first Iraqis that the Allies encountered – the British in Basra and the Americans in Nasiriya, Najaf, Karbalah and Hilla, and other towns along the way. The downtrodden Shi'ites, who never had a voice proportionate to their numbers in modern Iraq, especially under Saddam, surprised the Allied invaders by remaining suspicious of the newcomers, contrary to the expectation that they would demonstrate their support for the Americans and rebel against Saddam. Their reluctance to throw in their lot with the occupiers will be examined in the context of the history of the Shi'ites in Iraq.

Who Are the Shi'ites?

Following the death of the Prophet Muhammad (AD 632), a contest developed between his Companions as to who was the worthiest successor. Among the contenders was Ali, the Prophet's cousin and son-in-law (he was married to the Prophet's daughter, Fatima), but he was overlooked for the first three Caliphs of Islam (who were, in order, Abu Bakr, 'Umar and 'Uthman), though he eventually became the fourth Caliph of Islam. Ali was killed in battle during his Caliphship, and his descendants were denied any claim to power. They subsequently withdrew the Shi'a (literally, faction) from the contest for political succession of the Prophet, transforming it into an elaborate spiritual transmission of the Divine Light from the joint fore-fathers of the Prophet and Ali through the latter's descendants by virtue of his union with Fatima. Thenceforth, worthiness of succession to the Caliphate was measured by family ties to Ali rather than by personal merit. As that doctrine later developed, an apostolic chain of twelve Imams (hence Imamiya or Twelver Shi'a, the two foremost definitions of this brand of Shi'ism), beginning with Ali himself, then his two sons, Hassan and Hussein, were recognized, the last of whom went into hiding in the tenth century, and who will ultimately return as the Mahdi who will rule the world and bring to it justice and plenty. In the meantime, the Ayatullahs, the highest authority in the Shi'ite hierarchical clergy, have the sole spiri-tual power to "contact" the "Hidden Imam," and receive their inspiration on matters that require decision directly from him. Hence the extraordi-nary authority that the mullahs in Iran have, compared with the 'ulama in the Sunnite world who are usually submissive to the secular ruler.

In the contemporary Middle East, due to the vicious Arab-Muslim opposition to Israel, and in view of the support the United States and to a lesser extent the rest of the West are perceived as extending to Israel, there has been a revival of the old notions of martyrdom that were for the most part identified with the Shi'ites. All the Arab casualties of the half-dozen wars fought between Israel and its neighbors over the second half of the twentieth century are traditionally considered as martyrs. But it was the Hizbullah in Lebanon, a Shi'ite group sponsored by Iran, the foremost Shi'ite regime in the Islamic world, which created the modern terrorist martyrdom phenomenon. The idea that a martyr was a Believer who acci-dentally died in battle, and martyrdom was automatically thrust upon him as a mechanic result thereof, was replaced with a new model of martyrdom – where the Believer defied death actively, and was ready, if not eager, to die in the process of destroying the enemy. This type of terrorist martydom is known as the Islamikaze terrorism. Since the Hizbullah is the direct product of Shi'ite Islam, the same brand of Islam that rules Iran, and constitutes the majority in Iraq, the doctrine of Islamikaze can only be understood in terms of Shi'ite history.

Central in Iran as well as in other Shi'ite communities is the re-living of the legendary suffering of Hussein, the son of Ali, in Karbalah in AD 680, just before he was annihilated along with his followers by Yazid, the son of rival Umayyad founder, Mu'awiyya. The re-enacting of that horror, dubbed *ta'zia*, a sort of passion play, is displayed on Ashura Day: proces-sions of the pious beat and hurt themselves in an orgy of supreme masochism, which is considered the apex of identification with the suffering of Hussein. Suffering as a theme unto itself, including self-inflicted bleeding and death, has become a way of life for the devout Shi'ite, a fashion of expressing selfless sacrifice in honor of the assassinated son of Ali, the first true Imam and successor of the Prophet, whose rights had been "usurped" by three "imposter" Caliphs before him. The bitterness of the Shi'ia, the most downtrodden and persecuted branch of Islam (in fact, a group of them in Lebanon called itself the "Downtrodden on Earth," as a sign of distinction, not complaint), is best expressed in the anger and rush for self-sacrifice on the one hand, and the posthumous glorification of the martyrs on the other. So, young Iranians were encouraged to clear minefields during the first Gulf War (1980–8), with "keys to Paradise" hanging on their innocent necks; their parents were congratulated, not consoled, by family friends for the martyrdom of their children; and all those horrendous sacrifices were immortalized in the memorial for the martyrs in Teheran, a water fountain colored in blood-red, which symbolizes and eternalizes the endless flow of suffering and blood.

Naturally, those groomed in such a culture cannot be expected to recoil from the ultimate act of suffering, that is, death. Quite the contrary: the river of Islamikaze has never dried up in Iran, and it flows freely in other lands of Islam. The attractive rationale reads : "The skies are shrouded in black, rivers of tears are flowing, Hussein arrives in Karbalah to sacrifice himself for Allah. This is the Ashura story, tend your ears to listen to its sadness, let your tears flow for the King of the Martyrs, because he will bring you to Paradise."[1] These are the lyrics to one of the "musical-passions" songs that are re-enacted to commemorate the martyrdom of Hussein. These re-enactments, and the generally militant demands by the Shi'ites, for their rights and for justice, went into abeyance or adopted a low profile for centuries (a state of *intidhar*, namely waiting and expectation), due to the principle of *Taqiyya* (dissimulation), which was adopted after the mysterious disappearance of the Twelveth Imam, as a method of self-preservation in a hostile environment. The state of expectation for the return of the absent Imam provided the entire rationalization and driving power behind Twelver Shi'ism, inasmuch as it encouraged the Believers to suffer and wait. The more they waited and suffered, the closer was deemed the Imam's return (like the "pangs of the Messiah" in Judaism).

The last decades of the twentieth century, however, saw an ideological and political shift effected by the Sh'ia, under the revolutionary impulse of Ayatullah Khomeini. The nature of the change, which has taken the Shi'a from passivity and expectation to activity and aggression, is indeed nothing short of revolutionary. This is inherent in Shi'ite theology which recognizes the head of the clerical hierarchy as the *marja' taqlid*, the supreme reference who commands the emulation of the Believers. In fact this major figure, who gains his superior status through his scholarship and religious authority, is the supreme *mujtahid*, the "striver" to interpret the will of the Hidden Imam who is the actual ruler of the world. The *mujtahid* thus acquires in the Shi'a the power of a legislator, and his rulings are the law.

This is the reason why Khomeini spoke about *wilayat faqih* (the rule of the jurist), for only such Heaven- and Imam-inspired jurists, who are the upper echelon of the mullahs, could be clairvoyant enough to detect the Truth and pass it on to others. Khomeini wrote that "only the mullahs are able to take people to the streets and motivate them to die for Islam, and bring them to beg that they be allowed to spill their blood for Islam."[2]

The new activism brought about by the Islamic Revolution in Iran has taken up the tragic death of Hussein, which used to be viewed as a murderous and cowardly act sustained by that greatest of martyrs, and rendered it into an active declaration of war against injustice. In this context, Hussein becomes not someone to be mourned, but a heroic leader in battle and a model worthy of emulation on the way to Paradise. Hussein, the paradigm of martyrdom, will intercede on behalf of his followers to ensure the admission to heaven of the new generations of martyrs. Hence the flocking of millions of adults and children to the mosques in Teheran when the war with Iraq broke out and a call for volunteers to the front was sounded by the government. The demand for martyrdom by far exceeded the needs of the military.

The eagerness for death through martyrdom in Shi'ite culture often prompts young Iranian demonstrators to join processions, covered in their death shrouds, so as to signify that not only do they defy death, but they are also ready for it. Iranians were swept under the magic rhetoric of Khomeini, whom some saw as the Hidden Imam. The activization of the martyrdom of Hussein, which in Iran has involved a real change in the *ta'zia* ceremonies on Ashura Day, has also transcended Iran's boundaries and been made a model for other Shi'ites. The Hizbullah in Lebanon and the general Amal Shi'ite populace, also preach martydom. The Hizbullah not only routinely uses violence on the Israeli–Lebanese border, but is known to aid terrorism across the world: attacks against the Jewish Community Center and the Israeli Embassy in Buenos Aires (1992 and 1994 respectively), and its close cooperation with the Palestinian *Intifada*, both in coordinating joint operations against Israel and in direct involvement in arms supplies, demonstrate Hizbullah's religious–military stance.

The Hizbullah have also promoted Islamikaze: its first acts were performed in the early 1980s against the American and Israeli presence in Lebanon. As the Israeli presence in the southern part of that country wore on, those terrorist operations were intensified until they became the routine trademark of the violent encounters between Israelis and the Hizbullah, usually initiated by the latter. It took another decade or so before that mode of action was emulated by other Muslim terrorist groups, most notoriously the Sunnite Hamas, and to a lesser extent Islamic Jihad. All it took for the transition to take place was for fundamentalist Sunnite scholars, such as Sheikh Qardawi, to provide the missing link between the "natural" vying for suffering that fundamentalist Shi'ism has inherited from the *ta'zia* tradition and practice, and which pushed martyrdom to the top of the individual's striving to emulate the slain Imam Hussein; and the general Islamic hallowed idea of martyrdom and its rewards, not with the goal of self-inflicted pain but aimed at inflicting damage onto the enemy, even at the cost of one's life.

The Sunnite fundamentalist groups adopted the Shi'ite ways not only by embracing the Iranian and Hizbullah modes of operation, something that has been evinced in the collaboration of Iran and the Hizbullah with the Hamas and the Islamic Jihad, and the latter with the al-Qa'ida network, but also by creating their own version of the supreme sacrifice and suffering inherent in the *ta'zia*, only in reverse. In the field of battle and terrorism for the sake of Allah, we have seen nineteen members of al-Qa'ida committing collective Islamikaze acts on September 11, 2001. Al-Qa'ida fighters in Afghanistan defied death in the face of American airpower, as do Hamas and Islamic Jihad operatives in the Palestinian Authority, the fanatic Gama'at in Egypt, the Abu Sayyaf group in the Philippines, or the Muslim terrorists in Kashmir and India Proper. This universalization of Sunni Muslim terrorism risks, through its levels of frequency and diffusion, of becoming ever more adventurous in order to retain its impact. The almost daily attacks in Israel against its civilians by Hamas and Islamic Jihad have rendered these harrowing acts routine, to the point that they risk becoming accepted as "part of life," as if they were God-ordained and impervious to human intervention.

Even more worrisome, however, is that the non-Shi'ite fundamentalist groups do not content themselves with getting closer to the Shi'ites in terms of audacity, sophistication and the spread of Islamikaze worldwide. They are able to capitalize on being Sunnis like most of their compatriots, in order to draw into the circle of self-sacrificing terrorists other groups, like the *Tanzim* or the Popular Front among the Palestinians, who are not avowedly fundamentalists or Muslim zealots. Members of the Marxist-oriented Popular Front realize the high status of the Islamikaze in their society, and since they act against the same enemy as the Hamas, they seem to have no compunction about gaining popularity through the usage of the fundamentalist vocabulary and discourse. The Sunni Islamikaze are edging toward their Iranian model not only ideologically, as we shall see below, but even in mores and patterns of behavior. For example, the headgear around the forefront of the Hamas people parading in the streets of the Palestinian Authority, under the permissive eyes of its security forces and often in collaboration with them; the video cassettes they leave behind as their will and parting speech from their loved ones, but are often used by their operators as a "patrimony" to preserve and as an "educational tool" to recruit others; and the slogans, citations from the Holy Scriptures, and words of praise about martyrdom and the martyrs, are all ominous imitations of the Shi'ite model.[3]

The Shi'a in Iraq[4]

The proximity of the large Shi'ite population in Iraq to the Iranian hub of the Twelver Shi'a, and the location in Iraq of the most sacred shrines of the faith – Najaf, the Tomb of Imam Ali, and Karbalah, the place where Imam Hussein had suffered and was martyred and buried – explain much of the interaction between the two Sh'ite communities, and the ongoing personal, political and religious contacts. For 15 years, between 1963 and 1978, the exiled Imam Khomeini, who fled the oppression of the Shah to whom he stood as a menacing opposition, dwelt in Najaf and wove a whole network of links with local Iraqi clerics, until he was expelled to Neauphle-le-Château in 1978 by virtue of the "agreement" that Saddam had reached with the Shah and was to tear to pieces two years later when he invaded Iran. As a matter of fact, that ill-conceived and ill-fated invasion, which would extend into a horrendous trench war for eight years, was the direct result of Saddam's concerns lest the Iranian Revolution initiated by Khomeini in 1979 spill over into his Shi'ite territory. Conversely, many Iraqi Shi'ias, along with some of their high-level mullahs, also fled to Iran during and after the slaughter of the Shi'ites by Saddam, which followed their abortive rebellion in 1991, and were not to return until his regime was toppled by the Americans.

The assertive role that the Shi'ites are now carving for themselves in post-Saddam Iraq follows a long story of discrimination against them, which relegated them to the bottom of the political, economic and social pyramid for decades. In the aftermath of World War I, the Shi'ites at first welcomed the British conquerors as liberators to free them from the Ottoman–Sunni yoke. However, when they realized that British rule was there to stay they began to oppose the British Government and issued *fatwas* (religious verdicts) negating the legitimacy of the British Governor, Sir Percy Cox, on the basis that he was not Muslim. The opposition was led, and the *fatwas* issued, by Shaykh Muhammad Taqi Shirazi and his colleague, Shaykh abu-al-Hasan Isfahani, the foremost religious authorities of the time. The unrest erupted into a violent rebellion in 1920 when the British formally received a mandate from the League of Nations to rule the country, although they withdrew the idea of appointing a British Governor and elected instead the kingship of Faysal the Hashemite, who was brought over from Arabia. The British assured the Iraqis that eventually their mandate would be conducive to independence from foreign rule.

As a consequence, Shi'ite mullahs issued *fatwas* prohibiting their followers from participating in the elections of 1922–3, followed by the expulsion of three mullahs from Iraq, whereupon the leading clerics of Najaf and Karbalah left for Iran to seek asylum there. The Americans should learn from this if they think that democratic elections will be welcomed by the religious leaders in Iraq, who have already stated that they want neither Saddam nor the Americans, but a Muslim state under their own supervision. In Iran, where the exiles made their home in Qum, which had become the most prominent center of Muslim studies in Iran, they were hosted by the foremost Iranian cleric of the time, Shaykh Yazdi. The exiles had in all probability miscalculated, because they had believed that their departure would foment unrest and the British would recall them on their terms, but nothing of the kind happened. Quite the contrary, the government of Iraq under the British was content that during the elections the troublemakers absented themselves, and they were not to be allowed to return until 1924. In the coming years the Shi'ite leadership was more quiescent inasmuch as it was taken over by politicians rather than mullahs, and when trouble was announced again in 1927, it was Shaykh al Kashif-al-Ghita who mediated between the Shi'ite tribes and the authorities. Moreover, most Iraqi governments thereafter included one or two Shi'ite members, and on two instances they even became prime ministers.

As Arab nationalism took the lead, Shi'ite politics receded and the mullahs, including the troublemakers of yesteryear, also adopted a low-profile, although they continued to be the dominant spiritual personalities in their communities, so much so that when the British re-occupied Iraq during World War II, very little stir was caused among the Shi'ite leadership. The 1958 Qassem Revolution, which overturned both the King and the pro-British government of Nuri Sa'id, increased the pace of secularization, as communists and socialists came into power, supported by the downtrodden Shi'is. Furthermore, when the Ba'ath Party, also of "socialist" conviction, took over in a coup in 1963, most of its membership were Shi'ites, reflecting their proportion in the population. However, the Sunnites gradually predominated the party, and by the time al-Bakr, Saddam's predecessor, took over in 1968, Shi'ites had again sunk to insignificant numbers in political participation. When Khomeini was exiled to Najaf in the mid-1960s, it was under the regime of 'Aref, who was hostile to Shi'ites and in consequence the Ayatullah's political activity was circumscribed. The recognized head cleric of Iraq at the time, Ayatullah al-Hakim, at first disapproved of Khomeini's activism, but eventually supported him. His successor as the chief *marja'* of Iraq, Ayatullah Khu'i, continued nevertheless to oppose Khomeini's political activity.

After Hasan al-Bakr took power in 1968, Ayatullah al-Hakim moved from Najaf to Baghdad, at the same time that, due to the worsening economic situation, the Shi'ites turned back to their clerics for political leadership, and the Da'wa (the Mission) Party was formed with the support of many mullahs. When Saddam gained power in the 1970s he at first showed favor to the exiled Khomeini, at a time when tension was growing between Iraq and Iran. Saddam used the presence in Iraq of the immensely popular Iranian cleric as a form of propaganda against the Shah, until the 1975 "agreement" whereby the Iranian Imam was exiled to France, in exchange for the cessation of Iranian aid to Iraqi Kurds. But as long as Khomeini was in Iraq and Iranian pilgrims were allowed into the Shi'ite holy places in Iraq, the Iranian Ayatullah smuggled through them recorded messages and sermons back into Iran, which would eventually trigger the Revolution in the streets of Teheran that would force the Shah to abdicate.

The radicalization of the Saddam regime was accompanied by a steady, if hesitant, political revival among Iraqi Shi'ites. They renewed their religious processions in the holy cities and used them for political protest. The backlash from the regime was not late in coming: leaders of the Da'wa Party were executed, triggering in turn more riots. The Iranian Revolution in 1979 posed a direct challenge to Saddam, inasmuch as his restive Shi'ites were seen as likely to follow the model of their Iranian coreligionists. He had Ayatullah Muhammad Baqir al-Sadr arrested, and Ayatullah Shirazi, together with Shaykh Radwani, expelled from Iraq. They found shelter in Khomeini's Iran and organized and led Shi'ite opposition to Saddam. In April 1980, after an aborted attempt to assassinate Saddam, Ayatullah Muhammad Baqir al-Sadr was executed, together with hundreds more Shi'ites who were suspected of association with the Da'wa Party. Thousands of others were expelled to Iran. These irreversible moves burned the bridges between the Iraqi Shi'ites and the Saddam regime, and probably played a determining role in his decision to invade Iran in October 1980 and throw the two countries in a bloodbath that was to last eight years.

Prior to the war, the Iranian government had tried to organize the three major factions among the Shi'ites of Iraq into a cohesive resistance, with a view of controlling them: the Da'wa Party already mentioned; a guerilla group, akin to the Iranian Mujtahidin, called Paykar; and the Jama'at al-'Ulama, a group of pro-Khomeini clerics. All three factions were brought together from within Iran by Hujjat-al-Islam (a lower level than Ayatullah) Muhammad Bakr al-Hakim, the son of the slain Ayatullah al-Hakim. Saddam reacted to the threat of the Shi'ite opposition by beginning to woo the Shi'ites in the south, as the deadly war against Iran was pursued for most of the 1980s. Saddam couched the war in terms of a national conflict between Arabs (of whom the Iraqi Shi'ites are part) and Persians, harking back to ancient disputes that had opposed the two contenders for hegemony in Islam. Further measures Saddam took included diverting resources to develop the poor south, recruiting Shi'ites into the armed forces and attempting to reinforce the Arab identity of Iraqi Shi'ites. He used the symbolic appellation "Battle of Qadisiyya," the stunning defeat of the Iranians by the Arab armies in AD 637, to refer to his war with Iran. Khomeini promoted the symbol of Karbalah, where Hussein suffered and died, as the key-link for identity between the Shi'ites of the two countries. While Ayatullah Khu'i remained non-committal *vis-à-vis* this battle of symbols, even as he was put under house arrest, Shaykh Ghita did support the Iraqi regime's endeavor. But the prolongation of the war had, in any case, turned all Shi'ites into suspects and potentially hostile to the regime; many of them were executed, notably some members from the al-Hakim family.

There is a saying: "The rich get richer, and the poor get more children." This is especially true of the Iraqi Shi'ites. Like other poor areas in the Middle East, e.g. Egypt, Algeria and the Palestinian Authority, their population doubles every 20 years and more than half of it is under the age of 15, with all the potentially explosive demographic growth inherent in those statistics. From the 7 million Iraqi Shi'ites in the early 1980s, out of a total population of 12 million,[5] they have grown to at least 13 million out of 24 million at the beginning of the twenty-first century. Their 60 percent majority, which has seen its impact soar after the removal of Saddam, is further accentuated by the deep divisions within the Sunnite minority of 40 percent, which is almost equally split between the Arabs of Central and Northern Iraq and the Kurds of the north. The Shi'ite majority is overwhelming in the South, and Baghdad is split between Shi'ite and Sunnite neighborhoods. Iraq's oil and water wealth is also evenly split between the Shi'ite south and the Arab-Kurdish north. Hence the recurring talks about possible Shi'ite autonomy/independence in the south (and similar Kurdish claims for the north), due to the concentration of the Shi'ites and the continuity of their pattern of settlement in that area, and the resources which could ensure the vitality of such enterprise.

Shi'ite Cities and Towns during the Iraq War

As the main thrust of the war took the Allies up from the southern tip of the country at Umm Qasr all the way to Baghdad, through almost exclusively Shi'ite territory until the battle for the Iraqi capital was launched, the public around the world became familiar at first with the Shi'ites, their cities where most of the major battles raged, their displacement, their holy places and their interaction with the troops. Saddam's garrisons were present, and feared, and after their defeat Saddam's fedayeen and agents continued to roam the countryside and threaten the population, and Ba'ath officials were omnipresent to ensure the political loyalty of the populace. It is also true, however, that Saddam was so abhorred by the people, most of all the Shi'ites (and the Kurds) who were his foremost victims, that the moment they could be sure that the tyrant and his redoubtable apparatus of oppression were gone, people could not contain their joy and disbelief – though they soon regained their composure lest the Americans should think they were welcome to stay. For the sake of introducing some order in the chaos of the war, we shall deal first with the Fao–Basra complex where the British operated, and then the other southern cities of Nasiriya,

Najaf, Karbalah and Hilla, as the American troops advanced toward Baghdad.

Fao–Basra Region

The Fao Peninsula protrudes into the Persian Gulf and constitutes Iraq's main deep water access necessary for the importation of goods and the exportation of oil. The port city of Umm al-Qasr on the Kuwaiti border provides the facilities through which Iraq connects with the rest of the world, especially since the no-fly zone restricted flights into the country's hinterland. Upstream the mighty Shatt al-Arab, which delineates the border between the Peninsula and Iran in the East, lies the second largest city of Iraq – Basra, an ancient and vibrant port city of 1.5 million people, accessible through the channel of the river, which can accommodate some sea-faring ships but not the largest tankers. That entire sector of the front, which lay out of the way of the main American invading expedition, was assigned to the British Division of the Allied Coalition, both for the purpose of taking it over and then maintaining peace in it, and in the process also opening the channels necessary to push into Iraq the immense quantities of military provisions and ordnance, as well as facilitating deliveries of the massive amounts of food, water, equipment and medicine to the large population of Iraq, in order to avert a humanitarian disaster. The assumption was that due to the suffering of the Shi'ites under Saddam, the population would not only surrender peacefully and turn against Saddam's military, but would also welcome the "liberating" troops and cooperate with them. But things were to turn out slightly differently.

While Umm Qasr is a modern town and port, Basra had been established as a garrison city (*misr*), at the height of Arab expansion under the second Caliph, 'Umar ibn-al-Khattab (AD 634–44), together with other *amsar* like Kufa in Iraq and Fustat (later Cairo) in Egypt, which were to become the nuclei for the future major cities of the emerging Arab empire. As a rule, the conquering Arab armies elected cities on the border of the desert to which they were accustomed over seaports, hence their choice to build Basra as their garrison city inland rather than on the Fao Peninsula. However, the expanding Arabs also chose, as a rule, to build their new cities on river banks, not only for the facility of water supply and transportation, but also for defense, until they crossed the rivers to continue their conquest. Basra, like other *amsar*, was built of the bank of Shatt-al-Arab closest to the Arabian Peninsula, which remained their home, but could not be relied on any longer for supplies as the large expanse of territory under their rule kept growing. Therefore, they built these cities, where they constantly maintained their Arab majority even when they later on opened up to the general population, and used them as launching pads for further expansion. Before Baghdad came into existence, Basra was the center and the converging point of all manner of religious and scientific ideas; it was a vibrant intellectual focus for sects, schools and aberrant trends. It is there that the eighth-century thinker and supreme intellectual, Hasan al-Basri (bearing the name of his city), lived, and it is there that the fateful debate on whether the Qur'an, the Word of God, was created, was led, which would help to crystallize Islamic dogma for the coming generations.[6]

Basra was also the major place where Iranians and Arabs lived side by side and jointly created the new Islamic culture, which would subsequently influence the heterogeneous culture of Iraq. For example, while the holy city of Najaf has preserved its Arab character, the other holy cities for the Shi'ites in Iraq – Karbalah and Kazimayn (now virtually a suburb of Baghdad) – possess a strong Iranian influence. Even when Baghdad was built as the capital of the Abbasids (750–1253), Basra remained for a time the recognized, mature and shining capital of cultural life of the emerging Islamic empire. It was not until the ninth century that the intellectual center would move to Baghdad where the splendor of the Imperial Court attracted the brightest, the most talented and recognition-seeking variety of intellectuals. Until the end of the ninth century, the sprawling city of Basra, which now connected with, and eventually swallowed, the ancient Iranian port city of Ubula, remained, together with Siraf on the Iranian coast, one of the main ports in the Persian Gulf (this in spite of the fact that the long access route to its port, via shallow waters, was not particularly attractive to sea-faring navigators). In those days, the mouth of Shatt-al-Arab was much further inland and ships had to wallow through the lowlands to reach the more easily navigable river. Since then, the huge quantities of silt carried by the flow of the waters have built up and enlarged the sea-coast of southern Iraq.[7]

Déjà Vu: *Return of the British to Basra*

Following World War I the British took over Iraq under the Mandate of the League of Nations. All public works were transferred to the authority of the nascent Iraqi government; however, the railway system and the port of Basra, which were considered strategic assets, remained under direct British control, and a joint British–Iraqi directorate was put in charge of the port trust. Britain landed its forces of occupation at Basra in 1916, and again in 1941 during the rebellion of Rashid Ali at the height of World War II.[8] So when the British showed up once again at the gates of Basra in March 2003, both sides had a sense of *déjà vu*. On 20 March British troops marched into Basra and Umm Qasr, while Allied planes were bombing Iraqi missile and artillery sites. The next day, the Fao Peninsula was under siege and 600 Iraqi soldiers surrendered. A firefight raged around Basra for several hours, ending with the collapse of an entire Iraqi division. At the same time, commandos seized two major gas and oil terminals. The fourth day of combat saw the spectacular burning of 30 oil wells in the Rumeila field just outside Basra, as Marines desperately tried to control some of the blazing wells. But, contrary to expectations, the resistance offered by Basra's defenders was persistent. Some Iraqi paramilitary personnel pretended to surrender, only to then attack British troops, causing some casualties. Much to the frustration of the army command, which had hoped to pacify the city rapidly and avoid hitting civilians, the harsh resistance continued in the days ahead, forcing the British to cautiously begin to gnaw at the city's periphery, amid reports of a rebellion by Shi'i opposition against the garrison loyal to Saddam. On the other hand, the troops took control of Umm Qasr on the seventh day of the war (25 March), thus allowing in shipments of equipment and supplies once the mine-sweeping operation was complete. In the coming days, British troops launched a series of commando raids and artillery attacks around Basra before they attempted to take control of the city from the thousand or so paramilitary forces and Fedayeen loyal to Saddam.

The resistance forced the Allies to neutralize the threat posed by southern cities before they proceeded northward: attacks were being launched by small Iraqi forces entrenched within those cities against the long and vulnerable supply lines connecting the front divisions to High Command. Lt Colonel Tim Collins, a battalion commander from the British Royal Irish Regiment which participated in the battle for Basra, urged his troops before they launched the battle, in terms that will probably be immortalized in military history, to disavow the *déjà vu*:

> We go to liberate, not conquer. We will not fly our flags in their country. We are entering Iraq to free a people, and the only flag that will be flown in that ancient land is their own. Show respect for them.
>
> There are some who are alive at this moment who will not be alive shortly. Those who do not wish to go on that journey, we will not send. As for the others, I expect you to rock their world. Wipe them out if that is what they choose. But if you are ferocious in battle, remember to be magnanimous in victory.
>
> Iraq is steeped in history, it is the site of the Garden of Eden, of the Great Flood and the birthplace of Abraham. Tread lightly there. You will see things that no man could pay to see and you will have to go a long way to find a more decent, generous and upright people as the Iraqis. You will be embarrassed by their hospitality even though they have nothing. Don't treat them as refugees, for they are in their own country. Their children will be poor. In years to come they will know that the light of liberation in their life was brought by you.
>
> If there are casualties of war then remember that when they woke up and got dressed in the morning they did not plan to die this day. Allow them dignity in death. Bury them properly and mark their graves.
>
> It is my foremost intention to bring every single one of you out alive, but there may be people among us who will not see the end of this campaign. We will put

them in their sleeping bags and send them back. There will be no time for sorrow.

The enemy should be in no doubt that we are his nemesis and that we are bringing about his rightful destruction. There are many regional commanders who have stains on their souls and they are stoking the fires of hell for Saddam. He and his forces will be destroyed by this coalition for what they have done. As they die they will know their deeds have brought them to this place. Show them no pity.

It is a big step to take another human life. It is not to be done lightly. I know of men who have taken life needlessly in other conflicts. I can assure you that they live with the mark of Cain upon them. If someone surrenders to you then remember they have that right in international law and ensure that one day they go free to their family.

The ones who wish to fight, well, we aim to please.

If you harm the Regiment or its history by overenthusiasm in killing or in cowardice, know it is your family who will suffer. You will be shunned unless your conduct is of the highest order, for your deeds will follow you down through history. We will bring shame on neither our uniform nor our nation.[9]

On 26 March the British reported a civilian uprising in the heart of Basra, after British bombers demolished the Ba'ath Party HQ, the symbol of Saddam's rule there. But there was also a tacit recognition among the British, officially understood by Prime Minister Tony Blair himself, that since the Shi'ite population of southern Iraq had been let down by the Americans in 1991, it was unfair to expect it to rise again if Allied backing was not guaranteed to it. In 1991, and with American encouragement, the Shi'ites defied Saddam's rule after the cessation of hostilities of the previous Gulf War, confident of US military backing. But not only did the Bush administration betray them, it even permitted Saddam the use of helicopters to "police" the south. The Iraqi forces took this as a license to turn the area into a killing field – tens of thousands of Shi'ites perished with the world looking on. The Shi'ites' suspicions against the Allies were thus very justified, and the British understood that. Therefore, they tried to get the Shi'ites of Basra to realize that this time it was different. If the British succeeded, and if the Shi'ites joined them, that would signal to the rest of the south that Saddam's grip was slipping, which would constitute a deadly psychological blow to the tyrant and a corresponding boost to Allied troops' morale. US Defense Secretary Donald Rumsfeld sounded a note of caution, urging not to encourage the Shi'ites of Basra to revolt before the Allies were effectively able to protect them.[10]

Iraqi loyalists stormed out of the city the morning of 26 March daringly attacking southward with tanks and armored vehicles in a surprise countermove against the British thrust. Air strikes quickly destroyed the Iraqi column and brought their move to a standstill. In the face of continued resistance by irregulars in the inner city, the Allies dropped leaflets with satellite phone numbers, encouraging the Basra authorities to call to negotiate surrender. When the local population rose in rebellion, Saddam loyalists fired mortar shells into the crowd. The British responded by firing their own artillery. Shaykh al-Hatami, an Iraqi opposition leader living in Canada, who had contacts in Basra, explained to the media that the Shi'ites had avoided massive rebellion, contrary to expectations, out of sheer fear of reprisals from the regime, and predicted that once the security apparatuses of Saddam were toppled one could expect a more enthusiastic participation in revolts. The American officials who heard this "original and insightful" analysis might have answered that, when Saddam and his apparatus were toppled, the rebellion would no longer be needed, and that if there were no fear, then what is the meaning of a "rebellion" in the first place? Al-Hatami also said that prior to the British invasion, the city was put under curfew, with Fedayeen loyalists threatening to execute anyone who broke the curfew. Either way, the British realized that they had to break into the city, because the siege of a well-supplied[11] bastion would not end the suffering of the population who would not rise unless it saw clear signs of the collapse of the regime. For the besieged population, the fact that the British were waiting was a sure sign that they had no intention of overwhelming the city, so why would they risk their necks, as they had done in 1991, only to pay a heavy price and in vain? Saddam had also engaged tribal chieftains in and around Basra, through bribery, pressures and propaganda, to fight on his behalf. It was now the task of the Allies to persuade them to switch sides, if and when they realized that Saddam's days were numbered.

On the first day of April the battle for Basra inched forward when a British force seized the town of Abul-Khasib, southeast of the city, cutting the road between Basra and the Fao Peninsula. To the west of Basra, another British force took over the town of Zubayr, now a suburb of the city, where a Ba'ath Party HQ was located. The HQ was destroyed by Britsh troops, and one of its top officials taken prisoner. British commanders moved to cut off Basra from any access by other Iraqi troops, using air power to destroy a bridge and repositioning their troops around the city. As the British encircled the city the horrors of Saddam's loyalists became apparent: A woman who waved to British troops in the outskirts of the city was found hanged the next day. On 3 April a Shi'ite cleric in white turban and flowing black robes came out of the besieged city of Basra and announced to an astounded British officer that the Ba'ath Party officials in town were so desperate that they were ready to surrender. The cleric also recounted that the Ba'ath loyalists needed clerical protection to give them safe passage when they decided to withdraw. He told reporters that, contrary to the political analysts who had expected the Shi'ites to rebel against the regime, his people did not trust the Americans. A British leaflet which was distributed in Basra promised the beleaguered inhabitants that "this time we won't abandon you," but their previous experience taught them otherwise.[12] It was not until 7 April that the First Armored Division, after two weeks of patient and methodical siege warfare and a gradual gnawing at its periphery, finally, thrust into the center of Basra, fulfilling their promise to the city's civilian population.[13]

Nasiriya

While British forces were preoccupied with Basra and the problems it posed, American troops were rushing toward other targets, first of all Nasiriya. The first American casualties of the war, POWs and MIAs, occurred here. In the 1920s, when the British had shown favoritism to the Sunni minority which they installed in government, the Shi'ites in Nasiriya rose in rebellion, precisely when the British were considering detaching the Shi'ite south from the rest of the country. In 1936, the Shi'ites rebelled again, when the Sunni-dominated government in Baghdad took secular measures such as abolishing the veil and banning certain aspects of the Ashura celebrations.[14] The coming of the Americans seventy years later only confirmed that the same concerns of the Shi'ites were still alive. From day 2 of the war, 20 March, 2003, Apache attack helicopters launched fierce assaults on a regular Iraqi division near the Talil Airbase in the vicinity of Nasiriya while the avant-garde of the troops was just 100 miles from Baghdad. It was near Nasiriya that the 12 maintenance servicemen were taken into Iraqi custody or killed, and another four GIs were killed when their Humvees were hit by rocket-propelled grenades. While the battle was going on around rebellious Nasiriya, 10 marines were killed, but their division seized a bridge over the Euphrates and made its way to Baghdad, while others pressed on toward Samawa on their way to Najaf. As they proceeded north, toward Najaf, the troops left behind a major battle between 5,000 marines who sought control of the city center of Nasiriya, and the Iraqi troops who were desperately attempting to defend it.

While the battle of Nasiriya wore on, causing heavy casualties to the Iraqi troops, and to some civilians, American commanders blamed the Iraqi military for having drawn the marines into the populated areas of the city. The blending of combatants into the civilian populace of the city made surgical blows by the Americans almost impossible and caused many casualties. Civilian casualties also had an impact on critics of Saddam who previously supported the American invasion, but then turned against it when they observed what seemed to be indiscriminate bombing of civilian targets. They asked: If the Americans want to topple Saddam, why didn't they go directly to Baghdad and cease fighting in Nasiriya and other cities on the way? According to reports, the defenders of the city were Fedayeen Saddam from the dictator's hometown of Tikrit. They identified the commander of that unit as Ali Hussein al-Majid, known as "Chemical Ali" for his role against the Kurds in 1988. He was sent by Saddam to organize the defenses of the south, and ordered shot any soldier who took off his uniform, refused to fight or deserted the battlefield. To secure their flanks as they were advancing in and around the city, marines raided private houses and confiscated arms, an act that increased hostility among the civilian population.[15]

Najaf

As the troops moved on, new battles commenced in the outskirts of Najaf. This ancient city was not like any other Shi'ite town: It stood at the focus of Shi'ite identity and was likely to draw strong resistance from its self-sacrificing Shi'is against any perceived foreign invaders. Special caution, consideration and briefing of the troops were necessary to keep things under control. Najaf is the site of the tomb of Imam Ali, the father of the Shi'a, who met his death in Kufa, just four miles from Najaf. According to Shi'ite tradition, it was Ali's will that his body be put on a camel and wherever it knelt became the burial place. That place was Najaf, which thereafter became one of the most important shrines for the Shi'ites worldwide. Another tradition relates that the famous Abbasid Caliph, Harun al-Rashid, accidentally ran into Najaf while on a hunting trip, and instinctively gauging its importance, ordered the construction of the Tomb on that spot. The first large mausoleum was built there in the tenth century but it was reconstructed many times over. Thereafter, Najaf, together with its twin, Karbalah, became one of the spiritual centers of the Shi'a, attracting many pilgrims and students from all over the Shi'ite world.

The 3rd Infantry Division got to the plateau north of Najaf three days after the opening of the offensive, on 24 March positioning itself for the onslaught of Baghdad. Iraqi ammunition depots were seized in that area, and Iraqi POWs were taken into captivity. One depot in particular, a plot of 5 x 2.5 miles, was suspected of storing chemical weapons; it was the hope of the coalition that the depot would prove to be one of the "smoking guns" that could justify the war. Two specially equipped vehicles from the 51st Chemical Unit cruised around the deserted compound, but they have detected nothing to date. The UN inspectors had also visited the area on several occasions since November 2002, but had found nothing incriminating. However, since bunkers, electrified fences, large caliber weapons and many trenches were abandoned there, one could only speculate upon possible activity. An Iraqi general who surrendered to the Americans was an invaluable source of information; he told his captors that while he personally was not involved with weapons of mass destruction, he knew of underground bunkers and tunnels that neither he nor other senior staff were permitted to enter. Triple-locked doors barred the entrance to some

100 bunkers,[16] which raised suspicions that the Iraqis had something top secret to hide, or at the very least they had stored secret materials until recently, and then removed them to an unknown destination.

Iraqi irregulars and snipers slowed down the movement of the 3rd Division, which had bypassed the city to rush to the depots, but the big battle of Najaf was yet to come, with Iraqi forces reportedly hiding in schools to escape American bombings. Many weapons and uniforms were found, indicating they had been left behind by either retreating or surrendering Iraqis, but most unsettling of all were the gas masks that were with the abandoned equipment, a sure sign the Iraqis were ready for chemical warfare.[17] On 26 March the Americans killed hundreds of Iraqi infantrymen in the desert north of Najaf, in a fierce battle where, due to swirling sandstorms, air support could not be called in by the attacking force. Sandstorms, a recurring force in southern and western Iraq, were a huge nuisance to the Americans. Only with the aid of Blue Force Tracker, a high-tech satellite system, could the troops navigate back to their camp during the storm. The troops had to stick to their camp in the central desert, because it was the base (dubbed Forward Operating Base Shell), for the helicopter gunships that accompanied the division on its way to Baghdad. There was great concern about Iraqi snipers lingering in the area, and there were fears of possible mortar fire that could devastate the helicopters and the troops. The soldiers bulldozed the sand into long berms and dug bunkers for refuge, or huddled into the back of trucks or Humvee carriers. When the storm quieted down, the landscape resembled the surface of Mars – a blinding bright aura colored the sky with amber. Veterans of the 1991 Gulf War came equipped with baby-wipes to overcome days of no-shower and no decent toilet, in a situation where every slight scratch can become a sore wound. Choking chemical suits had to be worn most of the time, adding to the soldiers' discomfort.[18]

So, instead of being enthusiastically hailed as liberators by the Iraqis in the south, as was anticipated by the Pentagon, they were welcomed by a series of those bitter storms, while most Shi'ites were sitting on the sidelines waiting for the war to unfold. American troops then realized that the war needed to be conducted more violently than desired or expected, while at the same time care had to be taken of the civilian populations. On 27 March the end of the first week of fighting, Nasiriya had fallen more or less into American hands, despite continuing pockets of resistance. Najaf was by now circled, American troops were on their way north, and a total of 4,000 Iraqi POWs had become captives, not counting the ragtag of irregulars that no one wanted to take prisoner. It seemed to the Americans that the closer they got to the capital, the tougher the battle grew. At dusk, American Marines engaged a group of some 1,000 Iraqis who were concentrated in a railway station just south of the Euphrates. They called in artillery, followed by a sustained five-hour battle causing 21 Marine casualties.

Frustrated by their inability to distinguish between Iraqi soldiers, irregulars or just civilians, the Marines started to arrest anyone who wore black, the color of the Fedayeen and other Saddam loyalists. Sometimes those fighters, dubbed "Saddam's Martyrs," wore civilian cloth over their black attire, and due to the positions they took in hospitals and schools, they could hardly be distinguished from the common citizenry.[19]

When units of the 101st Airborne approached Najaf in the first days of April they were greeted by thousands of jubilant residents who cheered and gave thumbs-up signs to soldiers. Compared to the scenes of resistance and hostility that the Americans had encountered before, this was a refreshing welcome, perhaps due to the relief that the Shi'ites felt from the long years of Saddam's oppression. But there was also another aspect to the battle of Najaf. Like in other cities, hundreds of die-hard irregulars had taken up positions in key buildings in order to slow down the American advance, if not stop it altogether. Several even holed up in the Ali Shrine, probably out of the belief that the Americans would not dare attack it. They were right, because in spite of the fire those Iraqi irregulars were showering at the Americans from the top of the shrine, the Americans abstained from returning the fire and resisted the temptation to fall into the trap of desecrating the place and raising against themselves the wrath of the entire Muslim world. The pathetically comic Iraqi Minister of Information, Muhammad al-Sahaf, had already advanced that accusation to the international press, which brought a staunch denial from Tony Blair and another vow on his part that the Allies were not out to battle against Islam or its holy places, only against Saddam's regime.[20]

On the other side of the four-lane avenue approaching the Tomb of Ali was a gigantic bronze statue of Saddam Hussein, which suggested to the Shi'ites that against their historical and spiritual Ali there was today a concrete and omnipresent ruler who wielded real power. They loathed that symbolism and it was therefore little wonder that, when the Americans entered Najaf, and at the behest of an Iraqi colonel, they placed explosives at the foot of the statue and blew it up, to the cheers of jubilation of the onlookers. To the Shi'ites, Saddam was not eternal nor unbeatable, and as a symbol he had just been toppled before their eyes. Ironically, it was a Sergeant Love who led the destruction operation.[21]

The impact of this act can be rightly gauged against the fact that this city of 400,000, like others throughout Iraq, was dominated by portraits of Saddam: All government buildings bore large mural paintings of Saddam depicting him in heroic poses, gazing into the distance or firing his gun. When the blast came, the crowds erupted into cheers. The horse and its rider, Saddam, came crumbling down from the pedestal; onlookers embraced the rebelling Iraqi soldiers, took pictures on top of the rubble and contemplated about the eventual collapse of the real Saddam in Baghdad. The dearth of water to the population in this scorched and thirsty land was partly replenished by the relief supplies of the troops, and inspection of public buildings was started. Of the 24 public schools examined, the 101st Airborne found that all had larges storages of weapons: mortar, ammunition, grenades and mines that turned school classrooms into armories. Najaf's chief cleric Ayatullah Ali al-Sistani, who had been under house arrest for a decade was liberated by the Americans, who sent his captors running for their lives.[22]

When American troops entered the city, the rank-and-file Shi'ites, fearing that the occupiers might have come too close to their sacred shrine and their adulated Ayatullah, formed a living human chain to defend against the approaching troops. Faced with this problem a wise American commander, Colonel Chris Hughes, backed down, turned his weapon upside down to signal that there was no hostile intention, ordered his soldiers to kneel down and direct the barrels of their guns toward the ground. A murmur of acknowledgment passed through the crowds, and smiles appeared on all faces, American and Iraqi. Colonel Hughes' actions calmed the tense atmosphere and permitted the troops to retreat orderly without any violent clash with the crowds.[23]

Hilla

After Najaf comes Hilla, part of the triangle of the Shi'ite holy cities, though this one is located east, rather than west, of the Euphrates. In medieval Iraq, the Shi'ite dynasty of Mazyadid emirs had made their capital in Hilla. The Mazyadids were recognized in the eleventh century by the Buyids who ruled Baghdad. Modern Hilla was built in 1101, under the Seljuks, by Sayfu-l-Dawla Sadaqa, when most southern Iraq came under his influence, and he turned his capital into a center of Shi'ite learning. The Mongol invasions which devastated Baghdad in the thirteenth century spared Hilla as the center of Shi'ites peacefully submitted to them. This produced the development of the Shi'ia at the expense of the defeated Sunna in Iraq, after the fall of the Abbasid dynasty.[24] During the Timurids (fourteenth and fifteenth centuries), Hilla retained its status as the most important center of Shi'ite learning, but after that it was looted and destroyed and lost its primacy during the Safavids to Najaf and Karbalah which had the holy shrines of Ali and Hussein, respectively, and which helped them to gain prominence by way of the pilgrimage of pious Shi'ites and the centers of learning which developed there. On the last day of March a fierce battle faced the 101st Airborne in the shape of Iraqi troops in the outskirts of Hilla, but the Americans chose not to enter the city. The battle of Hilla, further to the north, was what permitted Najaf to fall almost without resistance. As the commander of the First Brigade put it : "Hilla was the battle, Najaf was the cakewalk."[25]

On the northern edge of Hilla lies the ancient site of Babylon where one of Saddam's many palaces was constructed, as an expression of that megalomaniac's delusion of parity with Hammurabi. There, soldiers of the First Airborne discovered multiple caches of weapons and ammunition, but no soldiers to man them. The combination of arms and palace, both surrounded by squalid habitations for his people, was the summum of Saddam's regime: an insatiable appetite for luxury, protected by weapons at the hands of an oppressed people that lived in fear. The widespread looting wherever signs were clear of the collapsing regime was evidence that the social system too, held together by fear and terror, was coming unhinged. People were waving and cheering in the streets just south of Baghdad, where the defenders were simply not in evidence, and the most loquacious civilians explained to the American troops the characteristic oppression and torture of Saddam's regime; hence the jubilation of some Iraqi individuals at the sight of the American soldiers who freed them at a stroke. While they were overjoyed at the sight of Saddam's humiliation and rout, however, many Iraqis also wanted to see the Americans out; only thus could they befriend them. General David Petraeus, Commander of the 101st Airborne, which had driven the Iraqi troops out of Najaf and Karbalah, and was now mopping up Babylon and Hilla, had a telling sidewalk discussion with a local school teacher, Mr Razzaq, as he handed him a commemorative coin struck by the Division:

> Gen. Petraeus: This has nothing more but a symbolic value.
> Mr Razzaq: I cannot have anything of any value, unless I am sure you have come for the sake of our people.
> Gen. Petraeus: I would let the Army's actions speak for themselves over the next few days, and I would bring the coin again to you . . .
> Razzaq: You will find me again in Saddam Secondary School, named after him . . . [26]

It was not all looters and sycophants. Impressive and proud people with integrity were also in evidence, as was the decency of American generals who could level with common people and hold talks with them, without aggrandizing themselves as the victors or debasing the enemy as vanquished. General Benjamin Freakley, vanguard of all the forward attacks, nevertheless found the time to tend to a water plant that faltered in Babylon and called his engineers to straighten the access road to a local museum.[27] It is hard to imagine Iraqi generals in that role. In addition to the sprawling depot site near Najaf described earlier, inspectors explored another site near Muhawish not far from Hilla on the Euphrates. At this site, though sensors registered the presence of chemical agents, the Mobile Exploitation Team Alpha found that the chemicals were of the organophosphate kind used in pesticides. Nevertheless, the Iraqis went to great pains to hide eleven 20-gallon drums which contained a thin liquid, which might have been used for manufacturing chemical weapons, even if no physical evidence to this effect was found. Though the discovery of WMDs had to be postponed to another day, the teams of the 75th Exploitation Task Force could not help notice the improvisations that were taking the place of the dwindling Iraqi regime. When they got to a militia training school for inspection, they found Shi'ite clerics in charge, clad in their white turbans and black robes and refusing to be photographed, declaring that the Shi'ites did not need any American relief and that they had matters in hand.[28]

Hindiya

On the last day of March the troops were fighting around Hindiya, just outside Karbalah, the second holy city for the Shi'ites. In Hindiya, the Americans entered the local Ba'ath Party HQ, where they found large quantities of ammunition together with mortars and heavy machine guns. There too, irregulars affiliated to the Party were at hand to offer resistance to the invaders, while elements of the Nebuchadnezzar Republican Guards that had been pulled out of Baghdad to help defend the south were in retreat. The Third Infantry, which was carrying the burden of the fighting along that front, captured an Iraqi battalion commander from the retreating Republican Guards. At the same time, Marines raided and occupied the town of Shatra, just north of Nasiriya, where the Iraqi Southern Command, headed by Ali Hasan al-Majid, was located. Two weeks into the war, and ten hours after crossing the Karbalah Gap, the 3rd Infantry captured a damaged bridge on the Euphrates north of Karbalah, in a fierce battle lasting three hours. Having removed this last obstacle, the Americans were now less than 20 miles from Baghdad. The First Brigade of the Division, after spending a week north of Najaf, occasionally engaging scattered Iraqi irregulars, now swept across the plateau north of Karbalah and inched toward the capital. But Karbalah itself was still to be taken.

Karbalah

Karbalah, like Najaf, and to a lesser extent Hilla, is one of the most sensitive places in Shi'ite history, primarily due to its historical ties to Hussein's martyrdom (AD 680). His Tomb, also called *Masjid Hussein* (the Mosque of Hussein), has become the holiest shrine for Twelver Shi'ites worldwide. The first edifice was built, like Ali's in Najaf, by the Buwayhids in the tenth century, who were Shi'ites themselves, and was destroyed many times by Sunni rulers who feared the tensions created around the shrine during the Re-enactment of Hussein's Passion on Ashura Day each year. Now the Tomb is a domed shrine and probably the most frequented place of pilgrimage for Shi'ites after the Ka'ba in Mecca. The Shi'ites use clay from Karbalah, which has been sanctified by the blood of Hussein, to make cakes that the Believers use to rest their foreheads on during the prayer prostrations. Twelver Shi'ites also perceive the clay as having healing properties. According to tradition, while the body of Hussein is known to rest in the Tomb, his head, which had been brought to Caliph Yazid (who ordered Hussein's murder), is kept in the Hussein Mosque in Cairo. Before that it used to lay in the Ummayad Mosque in Damascus, and a sanctuary remains there in his memory. Both places have become points of pilgrimage for Shi'ites. In Shi'ite martyrology, Karbalah became the supreme theme and model, hence its centrality in Shi'ite worship and its sensitivity *vis-à-vis* anyone who dares to interfere in its celebrations and commemorative festivals, like the Ashura that Saddam Hussein banned. The Khomeini Revolution in Iran had posited the Shah as Yazid, murderer of Hussein,[29] and Saddam himself could easily have slipped into that role in Iraq if it were not for the fear of driving a sharper wedge between the Shi'ites and the ruling minority Sunnites for whom Yazid and the Ummayads are held in high respect. Instead, the Iraqi Shi'ites used the metaphor of Nimrod to dub Saddam, something that all pious Muslims could agree with, since that figure was known in Islamic tradition as someone who had challenged the authority of Allah.[30] Conversely, exactly as Khomeini had been identified with Hussein the martyr, so could the Iraqi Shi'ites easily identify their martyred leaders, now or in the future, as worthy of that comparison, with all the attraction, love and disposition for sacrifice that this symbolism evokes.

This inspiration from the powerful and perennial Karbalah model may have a significant impact in Iraq as well if the Americans come to be perceived as a new Yazid and the downtrodden Shi'ites once again perceive themselves in the role of Hussein, the eternal and paradigmatic martyr. In that case, anyone killed in an eventual clash with the Americans, like thousands killed by Saddam during the Shi'ite rebellion in 1991, would be counted among the ranks of the martyrs who died with and for Imam Hussein. In pre-Revolution Iran, Khomeini, who was the remote instigator of the upheaval from his exile near Paris, was perceived as some sort of a Hidden Imam, who would come back to install justice on earth, hence his powerful hold on the minds of the people even in his absence.[31]

No one could imagine an October Revolution in Russia or a Communist Revolution in China without the presence on the ground of the charismatic leadership of Lenin and Mao; but in Iran it became possible for the exiled leader to smuggle in his recorded tapes, which were played in mosques and emboldened people to go out to the streets and defy the powerful armies of the Shah. The absence of the leader, far from demeaning from his impact, can on the contrary increase it as he is viewed as the messianic actor playing the Hidden Imam. Any exiled or otherwise absent popular Shi'ite leader of the Iraqis could wield that kind of aura too, under what Momen called the "Karbalah Factor." In other words, when a Hidden Imam is expected to return, then no sacrifice is too great to realize that dream. And even though Shi'ite messianism is predicated on the waiting to the return of the Imam (hence the "Awaited Imam"), and therefore anyone who has ever claimed to be him was discarded as a heretic, popular demand for such a figure to restore peace, justice and plenty is so intense in times of distress that it might prevail over doctrinal considerations which do not permit such a development.

On 5 April the Americans entered Karbalah and found a considerable number of tanks abandoned by the withdrawing Iraqi forces. Pockets of resistance persisted from among Republican Guard, Army or irregular forces who still sporadically fired on the 101st Airborne. But the fate of the city was sealed. The attackers pushed the defenders beyond a park to a school and then a Ba'ath HQ, both of which were turned into reinforced military positions. In some parts of the city, as elsewhere, the crowds welcomed the Americans with enthusiasm; in others the obstinate resistance was continued from Syrian paramilitary volunteers who had been recruited to serve the faltering regime's Fedayeen with hefty financial remunerations. Karbalah, a holy city of over half a million people, was only one-tenth the size of Baghdad, and the battle over it was seen as a rehearsal for the major fight for the capital. During the battle, the GIs were once again fighting the weather as well as the Iraqi military, with scorching 105 degrees (fahrenheit) and swift desert winds that sent the fighters seeking patches of shade under their Humvees and helicopters. They tried to satisfy their intense dehydration with the supplies of soda they had taken at Kifi to the south, because their bottles of water were so hot as to be undrinkable.[32]

After much of the Shi'ite south fell into Allied hands, and as the Americans were inching toward the outskirts of Baghdad, the attention of the world was turned northward. Newspapers around the world announced on 10 April the capture of Baghdad and the virtual end of the war. But just as the war in the north was far from complete, so the war in the Shi'ite-dominated neighborhoods of Baghdad and down to Basra and Umm Qasr was also far from over. The capture of Karbalah meant that the Karbalah Gap, the narrow straights between the city and the Razaza Lake to the west, was wide open for armor right through the 60 miles separating it from Baghdad to the north. Hence the importance of the capture of Karbalah. Helicopters dropped infantry units on three sides of the city, while from the northwest, tanks which had circumvented the center on their rush to Baghdad advanced to the encircled city center. On Friday, 5 April scouts from the 3rd found 31 fully-loaded Iraqi tanks abandoned, which prompted one GI to quip that the parking lot of the tanks looked like a used car dealership.[33]

So close to Baghdad, but faced with so little fighting spirit among the much-feared Republican Guards, signaled to the Americans that the collapse of the entire Iraqi defense was close at hand. Some saw Iraqi surrender as a response to the American leaflets which had urged them to leave their vehicles and quit. Others saw abandonment as the result of over-powering American fire, which literally pulverized into smithereens any visible, actual or potential Iraqi military threat.[34]

The Aftermath of the Battles in the South

One week into the liberation of their historical and religious cities from Saddam's grip, and after the removal of his picture kneeling in prayer on the exterior of the gilded Tomb of Ali in Najaf, the Shi'ites were still fearful and uncertain of what came next. The Curator of the Tomb, who had appeared at the Shrine during the 1991 uprising, had been executed by Saddam, so the Shi'ite clerics who had been in exile, like Abd al-Majid al-Khu'i, and dared to return to the city after its capture/liberation, were still guarded. Khu'i, for example, preferred to wait to see what happened in Baghdad next before he committed himself to anything. As a majority population, the Shi'ites realized that the fortunes of any future government would largely depend on them, once the dictatorship was eradicated, and the one-man/one-vote equation would, they hoped, restore to them their long-lost political voice. In this situation, the Americans and their allies, who had expected to be welcomed as liberators, had instead endured fierce pitched battles for every Shi'ite city thus far – from Basra, through Nasiriya, Najaf, Hilla and Karbalah. This was due to resistance from Saddam's forces, regular and irregular, but the Shi'ites had done nothing to help tilt the balance in the Allies' way, signaling that they had internal-ized the lessons of the rebellion of a decade ago. The same attitude was expected in Baghdad where the largest concentration of Shi'ites dwelt. Moreover, while in 1991 the Iranians extended some help to the Shi'ite rebels by allowing some of their deserters from the First Gulf War (1980–8) to rampage back into Iraq, now the US warned that such marauders across the border would be dealt with militarily as adversaries. The Shi'ites inside Iraq now found themselves alone once again and vulnerable should Saddam return to power.[35]

The Head of the Iraqi opposition group in Iran, Muhammad Bakr al-Hakim, who had fled into exile in 1980, had warned of the armed resistance of the Iraqi Shi'ites if the Americans stayed beyond the requisite time to remove Saddam Hussein. In other words, the Shi'ites did not wish to be allies of the US, much less its protected subjects, and their attitude was purely utilitarian: get the dictator out and get out yourselves, or face armed rebellion. Consequently, the war cry of the Shi'ites since March has been "neither Saddam nor Americans," and on a more "positive" note some of them did not hide their ambition to set up a Muslim, i.e. Shi'ite, state in Iraq. These ambitions have been encouraged, if not by the Iranians, who fear American retribution, then by their Hizbullah surrogates in Lebanon. In this vein, the spiritual mentor of the Hizbullah, Sheikh Fadlallah, issued a *fatwa* (religious verdict) at the outset of the conflict, banning any Muslim from aiding the Americans. There was a possibility that, as in Lebanon, where he pitted the Hizbullah against Israel, he might move to sanction similar acts of Islamikaze against the US should it drag its feet in Mesopotamia. With Iran (and Syria) inherently interested in undermining any American-client state on their borders, they might very well attempt to cultivate any militant Shi'ite group that is willing to serve their agenda. But the Iraqi Shi'ites, who are themselves divided, are not guaranteed to adopt the same political program featuring the deep involvement of clerics in politics as instituted in Iran by Khomeini. Indeed, they may be much more interested in reviving the Iraqi/Arab centers of the Shi'a, in Najaf, Karbalah and Hilla, at the expense of Iran's Qum.[36]

On 10 April Sheikh Abd al-Majid al-Khu'i, the London-based Head of the Khu'i Foundation and son of the legendary Grand Ayatullah Abul-Qassem al-Khu'i (the towering Shi'ite cleric of his generation who died under house arrest in 1992), was killed by a rival Shi'ite mob in the Ali Tomb in Najaf just one week after his return home from exile. The murder of Khu'i, who was collaborating with the US and Britain, did not augur well for the American plans to restore peace and order in tandem with the Shi'ite majority of the country. The fact that he was grabbed within the Holy Mosque, stabbed and then shot, left many question marks as to who was responsible for the murder. Speculation was rife that Iran or Saddam loyalists, who resented his predilection to act under the Allied occupiers, were behind the slaying. A second question was: Why was he so damnable in the eyes of his killers as to justify a murder on the premises of that most holy of places? In any case, the revival of murder as political statement in Shi'ite circles after the many decades of Saddam's tightly-enforced restrictions left much to be reflected upon by those responsible for planning the future of Iraq.

A rumor also circulated in Iraq regarding the identity of the second cleric killed in the mêlée. Some argued the cleric was one of Khu'i's aides; others claimed it was the cleric appointed by Saddam to oversee the site. In any case, the murder seemed not only to signal that in the post-Saddam era the battle for control of the Imam's Mosque was already raging, but that any heavy-handed interference from outside would be of no avail until the contending Shi'ite groups either settled their accounts or came to some consensus. It is significant that Khu'i went to the Mosque that day to attend a meeting of clerics who were to appoint a new Curator for the Shrine. Khu'i's assassins must have resented the influence he was building up in the affairs of the city, and moved to eliminate him before he became too powerful.[37]

Any new curator would have to re-establish the pilgrimage to Najaf (and Karbalah) that was banned by Saddam over fears that celebrations imbued with the Karbalah Spirit might get out of hand. The younger Khu'i, who repeatedly voiced his support to moderation, the rule of law and democracy, was considered fit for such a job by both the Allies and some moderate Shi'ites, and that was perhaps the reason for his elimination. But Ayatullah Ali al-Sistani was also a moderate, having been under house arrest during Saddam's regime; he was released only when the Americans approached the city. In the face of the deep tribal, ethnic, personal, local, regional, political and religious divisions among the Shi'ites in particular and Iraqis in general, it is hard to see how one can stem the eruptions of hatred and retribution, and bring them all under one authority. After the murder of Khu'i at the hands of his fellow Shi'ites, another poignant case in point was Basra, where once the Ba'ath cadres had retreated or surrendered, vengeance became the order of the day. Chilling vows to kill rivals "by hands and bare teeth" were voiced in public. Even after the British completed the takeover of the city and began policing its streets, many armed people roamed its alleys and fired upon whoever was not to their liking. People in the streets were dragging behind their vehicles statues of Saddam, kicking and stoning them on passage, but commoners were longing for the restoration of order at the sight of lawless armed thieves and robbers who made the law by defying it. Many remembered the horrors committed by Saddam's regime and cronies during and after the quelling of the 1991 Shi'ite Rebellion, but religious sheikhs, many Shi'ites among them, were also accused by the populace of collaborating with Saddam in return for the hefty payments he handed to them. In this atmosphere of suspicion, accusation and lack of trust in any local leadership, Basra had to, for now, remain under direct rule of the British.[38]

But Basra, like other parts of the Shi'ite south, had undergone some changes for the better as well. For the first time in decades, Believers went to the mosques without fearing the presence of Saddam's agents. People huddled for prayer, this time without looking suspiciously over their shoulder, and hugged each other in disbelief, reveling in the rediscovery of freedom of expression and of faith. Their gratitude to their liberators was also evident, for after 30 years of secret prayers at home, now was the time to re-embrace communal worship in the open. The scars of religious oppression were plain to see. Much of the Jami' Imam al-Siddiq Mosque, named after one of the Twelve Imams, where the Believers had assembled for Friday prayer, bore the scars of its destruction during the Uprising of 1991. Shi'ites who had tried to visit Najaf or Karbalah had been stopped in roadblocks and turned back, and their revered mullahs were confined to their homes, if not killed or exiled. Even when the al-Siddiq Mosque had been reopened in Basra, Saddam's agents occupied an adjacent building, ready to interfere when things threatened to get out of control. Now a young mullah, who filled in for the departed ones, exhorted his flock to unite in the rebuilding of the country and to shun the un-Islamic act of looting, and gave a hint as to his preferences for a future government: "not a religious or a tribal leader, but an educated person."[39]

Despite a general mood of relief at being released from the regime of Saddam, there are people, especially the privileged Ba'ath Party members, who evidently miss his regime, which supposedly provided plenty and looked out for its members; these same people fear the uncertainty and chaos of post-war Iraq. The Ba'ath Party, which had been founded in the 1940s by the Syrian Michel Aflaq on a platform of socialism and Arab nationalism, underwent a drastic transformation under Saddam. It became a Communist-style centralized organization that held its membership together through a cocktail of fear and reward. The legacy of Saddam's Ba'ath Party is that people live in expectation of a new regime, any regime, that can bring back predictability to the vagaries of daily life.[40]

In other parts of the Iraqi south, such as the holy Shi'ite cities, other concerns began to emerge. In Karbalah, Shi'ite clerics attempted to take control of a bombed-out weapon plant in the aftermath of the fall of Baghdad, following other cases of clerics who staked a claim at other public grounds such as militia training camps. The clerics claimed that they wanted the facilities as schools for their community, though in all instances in question the grounds were infested with unexploded ammunition that would have made those locations dangerous. The real reason may be the fact that some of those clerics seemed to be representing Iranian interests; they were insistent that the Americans vacate those places forthwith. The clerics seemed so eager to see the Americans go that they were ready to forego the aid and relief that the Americans were promising, well before General Garner's Office of Reconstruction had the chance to implement his program of food distribution. There was concern that the clerics' desire to take over those tracts of land before any relief plan was installed might enable them to entrench themselves there and hoard ammunition for days to come. The American experts who searched those grounds for WMD found equipment originating from various countries buried in trailers and covered with gravel and dirt, which could be used for both civilian and military purposes. Particularly worrisome were crates that carried labels indicating the presence of ovens on the site; ovens, possibly incubators, made in Germany or the UK, could be used for culturing germs and viruses for biological warfare. Apparently, the ovens had been looted and carted off before the American investigators got there. In any case, the impression was that nuclear and biological laboratories were there, hence the clerics' eagerness to take possession of them.[41]

In the holy city of Najaf, intrigue was simmering following the unsolved mystery of the murder of Khu'i, and there was talk around the turquoise Tomb of the Imam of more murders. Khu'i had been flown in by the Americans a week before his murder, hoping to win over Najaf to the new *Pax Americana*. The identity of the second murdered man was revealed as Haidar al-Rifa'i, the hereditary Custodian of the Mosque. Al-Rifa'i was seen as a collaborator of Saddam Hussein and was said to have been the real target of the murder, while Khu'i, together with four other men who were also killed, were apparently caught up in the mêlée. Other observers suspected that the murder was, in fact, premeditated, and that it was all part of the power struggle for the control of the Holy City, with outside powers meddling, notably the US and Iran, which have a strong influence on the Iraqi Shi'ites. Iran's geographic proximity, the fact that it had hosted many Shi'ite notables who fled Saddam, and Khomeini's personal association with Najaf, meant that it commanded the most numerous following there. A spiral of killings and reprisals, attempts and vengeance was feared in the Holy City. Already one could sense the tensions stemming out of the many webs of loyalty: while some swore by the name of Bakr al-Hakim, the Teheran-based leader of the Supreme Council of Islamic Revolution in Iraq (an organization's name that sends chills down the spines of anyone fearing a duplication of the Iranian Revolution in Baghdad), others dubbed the murdered Khu'i, the son of the great adulated Ayatullah Abul-Qassem al-Khu'i, as an "infidel," an indication that he was not killed "spontaneously" after all but had been the target of a justified premeditated assassination.[42]

Khu'i's murder, soon to be followed by the assassination of al-Hakim, led to a spate of stories and conspiracy theories that flew around. His long exile in London and his association with the Allies made him a *prima facie* suspect of Islamic betrayal. Khu'i was posthumously accused of having stolen the funds of a religious seminary in Najaf to set up his charitable foundation in London; another rumor suggested that when he was stabbed by the angry mob, thousands of dollars were found hiding under his robe. The story, which carried little credence, did not explain why the body of a murdered man would be searched for dollars. It gradually transpired that American Special Forces, who brought Khu'i to Najaf, had hoped to use his pro-Western stance and influence to swing the Shi'ite Holy City of Najaf to their side, in their bid to establish some sort of representative government in post-war Iraq, and thus pre-empt the pro-Iranian faction of Hakim. But the murder undid those plans. When the Americans entered the city, and as they waged a five-hour-long battle to dislodge the Iraqi soldiers who had taken shelter in the Mosque, they attempted to negotiate with Ayatullah Sistani, who had been held under house arrest by the Saddam regime, expecting him to issue a *fatwa* in support of their presence. Sistani apparently rebuffed their request, claiming that he would not meet them before they flew in Khu'i into town. On 5 April the meeting was to take place between Khu'i, who was riding in a Special Forces Humvee, and Sistani, at the latter's home. However, crowds concerned that foreign troops were heading to the Mosque blocked Khu'i's way, and the Americans backed down to avoid an inflammation. Another meeting was later scheduled and did take place.[43]

Khu'i, with active American support, had begun building his power base in Najaf. He hired bodyguards who proved woefully ineffective at protecting him – which raises further questions about their loyalty in the first place and perhaps their complicity in the murder. But immediately upon his arrival, other clerics who envied how Khu'i had lived in relative peace in London while they were suffering under Saddam, moved to bar his way. Chief among them was Muftadah al-Sadr, the son of Muhammad al-Sadr, who had been assassinated in 1999. During Ayatullah Sistani's long house arrest, the young Sadr grew in influence, and some suspected that he maintained a close relationship with Iran. He opposed the American invasion of Iraq and certainly their appointed "puppet" – Khu'i. Khu'i, under American instigation and discreet protection, attempted to take over the Ali Tomb and Mosque, the symbolic focus of power and influence in the Holy City. Rifa'i, the Custodian of the Mosque, who had been accused of collaboration with the regime, was particularly resented by the Shi'ites – he had left the Shrine unattended during the fighting. When Khu'i wanted to bring Rifa'i back to the Mosque under the *Pax Americana* as a sign of reconciliation, he was met by the angry crowd who stabbed both men to death, along with four others in the ensuing fighting. Reports emerged that an even greater tragedy was averted when a man pulled out a hand grenade, but the mob suppressed him. What most eye-witnesses agreed about, however, was that it was the two warning shots fired by a desperate and frightened Khu'i, one of which apparently hit the crowd and caused one death, which further enraged the people and resulted in the tragic death of Khu'i and his protégé. Following his murder, Khu'i was buried beside his father and grandfather on the premises of the Mosque.[44]

A measure of the growing self-confidence and in consequence the newly-found political assertion of the Shi'ites in the post-Saddam era, has been their rediscovery of the freedom of travel to all parts of the country, especially their holy cities, where, without restraint or discretion, they give vent to their religious celebrations such as Ashura. During Saddam's era, they journeyed furtively on the pilgrimage trail to Karbalah or Najaf, under the threat of arrest and torture, but now they can, and do, in their thousands, journeying all the way from Basra, through Najaf, Kufa and northwards to Karbalah, or from Saddam City southwards to the same destination, passing on their way scorched military barracks abandoned by the routed Iraqi troops or Allied checkpoints on the main highways. On 22 April Ashura Day, Karbalah commemorated the killing of Hussein. The Spirit of Karbalah, the symbol of the supreme sacrifice, sent hundreds of thousands on the road from all parts of the country to converge on Karbalah in preparation for Ashura. The journey thither was in itself so exhilarating that some of the travelers expressed the hope to die making the pilgrimage. The masses converging on Karbalah carried either green flags of Islam, red flags representing the flow of blood, or black flags with inscriptions in tribute to Hussein: "Hussein, my Love, the Knight!" or "Apple of my Eye, Hussein!" While in the procession, people would occasionally stop, beat their chests and chat "We will never forget you, Hussein!"[45]

The awesome processions of Shi'ites converging on Karbalah from all over Iraq was only a tame prelude to what was to come on Ashura Day. Now the Believers, in an orgy of masochistic self-inflicted suffering, would flagellate themselves to bleeding point, in a vain and perennial attempt to relive, on the fortieth day of the commemorative mourning, the imagined atrocities that Hussein and his retinue had undergone. Women shrouded in black, disabled Believers in wheelchairs or using crutches, all had only one wish in mind during that sinister ceremony: to die, like Hussein, as a Martyr. They bought lambs on the way for the symbolic sacrifice to Hussein and made their way in a mood of elation and suffering. They proclaimed their jubilation over the new freedom from Saddam Hussein, and remembered that they were free, at long last, to suffer publicly once again. They were delighted that no more Ba'ath laws could be imposed on them, but were saddened by the sights of devastation and the ravages of war they observed along the way. They could not help recognize their debt to the Americans who had rid them of the tyrant and his apparatus of oppression, but they also could not contain their anger at the scorched land they had left behind. Suspicions were aroused among the marchers in the procession that the Americans were only interested in oil, not the Iraqi people, as evidence of the presence of American guards in oil fields, not in hospitals, museums or public facilities suggested.[46]

The range of Shi'ite reactions to the suppressed sense of grievance they had contained for decades was considerably widened when Saddam City in Baghdad, the largest concentration of Shi'ites in Iraq, also fell to the Americans. Saddam City had been built on the northeastern part of the capital in 1958 as Revolution City, after the toppling of the Hashemites by the Qassem Revolution. But since Saddam came to power and renamed it after himself, it had deteriorated into a slum. Signs pointing to the city were corrected to "Sadr City," a reference to Muhammad al-Sadr. While ware-houses, schools, hospitals and other public institutions were burning, the firemen were sitting indolently waiting for replacements to their stolen equipment and unpaid monies due to them. Saddam City is located on the east side of Baghdad and is characterized by misery and devastation: its leaders had been arrested and tortured by Saddam, its mosques closed and its residents oppressed, and in the aftermath of the defeat of Saddam, the city was still licking its wounds and subjected to arson, murder, looting and robbery in the lawlessness that swept and followed its fall. Now that the Believers felt they were free from the exactions of the departed regime, their chiefs vowed to actively spread their Islamic message. A sliver of revenge also runs through Saddam City. One of the mosques in the neighborhood had been shattered by Qusay Hussein in 1998 while secret police slaughtered 400 worshippers as they knelt in prayer, and left their bodies to rot on the prayer mats. Now the worshippers stalk the streets at night, searching for the remaining Fedayeen. They resent American troops preventing them from pursuing their rampage. The same Shi'ites who welcomed the Americans into the gates of Baghdad, wearing the stars and stripes, were now warning that if the Americans did not leave forthwith, "Bush will become another Saddam," and be dealt with accordingly.[47]

The sight in the heart of Baghdad of a Shi'ite mullah handling an automatic weapon is in itself an indication of the special status that Shi'ite clerics have won for themselves in their embattled country. On 15 April a few days after the fall of Baghdad, a cleric was spotted in the courtyard of a hospital in Saddam City, pointing his gun at the body of what he described as a "Syrian suicide bomber" who had come to destabilize the liberated city of Baghdad. He wanted American engineers to check and defuse a bomb he suspected was hidden inside the body before anyone could come close to it. A third man at the scene was beaten out of his van and identified by the mullah as the "second Syrian" bomber, and although he ran away was later caught. When a Marine squad arrived some hours later to defuse the bomb, the body had vanished, and another, more senior, mullah denied that there were any Syrians in the neighborhood. That incident was typical of the contradictory and nebulous reports that were flowering around town. Claims and counter-claims of shootings and motives clouded the atmosphere of the city. One week after the American conquest of Saddam City, gunfire could still be heard all around, sometimes erupting into fierce battles into the thick of the night. A mullah complained that cars without number plates were simply shooting at people in the streets and throwing the blame on the Sunnites, who wished to take revenge on the Shi'ites for not having fought against the American invasion. The Sunnites were already envious of the new political and religious stature the Shi'ites seemed to be acquiring in post-war Iraq. Others claimed that Saddam loyalists were trying to make Baghdad ungovernable for the Americans. Still others thought that the mayhem was due to a Ba'athist desire to impute the chaos to the Americans. It was speculated that disorder would prevail as soon as the rank and file of Saddam's loyalists were free to act after the leadership had been decapitated.[48]

Marines positioned at the edge of the city said that many non-combatant individuals, including Syrians and Jordanians, were surrendered to them by local inhabitants. They believed that much of the shooting emanated from nervous Shi'ites who were either warding off real or imagined attackers, or taking advantage of the chaos to settle their accounts with old rivals. The marines decided to let the population sort its problems out by itself. It was at least encouraging to see that with all the lawlessness, no adversaries were willing to shoot at the Americans: when the latter ventured out with tanks or personal carriers into some network of dark and remote alleys, the exchanges of fire usually fell silent. Even when American patrols ran at night through the streets of the city, at a time that they might be vulnerable to attack, the local residents usually appeared on balconies waving to the soldiers. But as soon as the Americans departed, the fire erupted once again. Horror reigned throughout the night in the entire 80-block long Shi'ite neighborhood. Some mullahs attributed it to "Wahhabi mercenaries" paid and sent by the Saudis, so it was claimed, to frighten and humiliate the Shi'ites and create instability for the American rulers. Common Shi'ites blamed the gun violence on the Shi'ite and Wahhabi clergies, who were positioning themselves for future power struggles on the backs of the uneducated Believers. These rumors prompted some Shi'ites from Saddam City to demonstrate in downtown Baghdad against the security situation and to vow that, since their lives and those of their families were worthless, then they might have to blow themselves up alongside American troops in order to make their protest heard.[49]

The main southern cities of Iraq, from Basra through Nasiriya, Najaf, Hindiya and Karbalah, right into Baghdad, are situated along the axis of the Euphrates River, and their fall signaled that all of the western valley of Mesopotamia had come under American control. But from Basra northwards, the eastern valley of the Tigris also had to be conquered along the towns of Amara, Kut and Azizya before Baghdad could be taken from the south and the southeast. This was the responsibility of the 24th Marine Expeditionary Unit, upon whom it fell to uproot Saddam's military from one position to another. Kut, a city of 300,000, remained the major holdout in southeastern Iraq after the fall of the Euphrates Valley and Baghdad into American hands. The planners of the war had expected the battle around Kut to be prolonged and difficult, following reports that foreign Mujahideen had flocked into the city to make it a last stand before Baghdad, in addition to Ba'ath and Saddam loyalists who were holed up there. The rapid advance of the 3rd Infantry and the 101st Airborne farther to the west along the Tigris River, and the early fall of Baghdad, however, had turned Kut into an isolated and surrounded holdout that could not stand alone for long. As a result, when the Marines got to its gate, expecting a duplication of the pitched battle they had in Nasiriya before they split northward to the Tigris in late March the irregulars had either quietly left town or gotten rid of their fatigues and replaced them with civilian clothes to mask their presence. Failing to distinguish who was who, all the Marines could do was to let the hundreds, and then the thousands, flock out of the city after their weapons were confiscated. Among the laundry, the goats and the bags of worthless money that the refugees were carrying, the marines found grenades, rifles, uniforms and shells which were also confiscated before the people were set free after some interrogation. In a nearby ditch a tank was found stuck in the sand. In another scene, an Iraqi armored car carrying seven men on board was searched for weapons and turned out to belong to the Ba'ath. Its hapless passengers pleaded to the Marines: "Brothers! We are all brothers!" and were released.[50]

The Americans were very wary of Islamikaze bombings, following an incident at Nasiriya a few days earlier, where two Iraqi women blew themselves up, killing four unsuspecting Marines who had let them come close to the their checkpoint. Now everyone was checked at the Kut checkpoint, women included, much to the displeasure of their husbands. Iraqi vehicles were stopped 100 yards before the checkpoint, and all the occupants were made to get out and squat. Sad and humiliating as this was, it was preferable to further security breaches. The American occupiers also had to deal with Sayed Abbas, a Shi'ite preacher, who declared himself the mayor of Kut the day it fell, and took up residence in the plush city hall, surrounded by his underlings. The Americans dismissed him as a false prophet, a clown and an imposter, but the more they slandered him the stronger he seemed to become. He spoke at huge rallies of his followers, vowing "sacrifice," the key concept of the Shi'a, and promising to unite the people in self-government. Despite the American pretense to rule the city, Abbas' people set up roadblocks at the approaches to the city from the south originating from Nasiriya. Abbas has grown so popular that returning exiles from Iran stop by to pay homage to him, and a slogan at the entrance to his office proclaims: "Freedom – Yes, Occupation – No!" On 19 April a gathering of 5,000 followers assembled at the Grand Mosque as an expression of the freedom to gather publicly that was strictly prohibited under Saddam. However, rather than showing gratitude toward the Americans who made this gathering possible in the first place, Abbas called upon his flock to "resist the dividers," much to the embarrassment and dismay of the Americans who were helplessly looking on.[51]

Embarrassment apart, this phenomenon of Shi'ite clerics taking over local rule not only poses a challenge to the American presence and presumed rule of the cities of Iraq; by simply walking into city halls and declaring themselves plenipotentiaries to govern their people, without any due process of election, nomination or appointment, these clerics pre-empt American intentions to democratize Iraqi society by attempting to impose on it their own political system. What is more, as the tremendous popularity Abbas possesses increases, clerics are still much more desirable to the populace than any imposed or "elected" leader, and the Americans will have a hard time convincing the crowds that they know what is best for the Shi'ites ahead of their adulated clerics. Not incidentally, Abbas is a local leader of the Supreme Council for the Islamic Revolution in Iraq, a political party that was outlawed under Saddam and has ties to Iran. The Council's leader, Ayatullah Muhammad Bakr al-Hakim, was said to be planning a visit to Kut to encourage support for Abbas. It is also telling that among the throng of supporters of Abbas in the City Hall Compound, which has become his stronghold, there are members of Hizbullah and radical Shi'ite militants like the Badr Corps and the al-Da'wa Party. Against this background of groundswell support for the local leader, who apparently draws financing and religious support from the outside, it is hard to see what the Americans can do to usurp the self-proclaimed mayor.[52]

The politically inexperienced and historically ignorant American troops tried to react to the Abbas crisis the way armies react: with unsubtle brutality. They stormed the City Hall compound in mid-April 2003 and seized a cache of automatic weapons, but followers inside the compound vowed to be better prepared for the next raid and threatened in future to use themselves as human bombs. Special Forces spent their days in a local hotel lobby performing observations and monitoring Abbas' movements, after plans to terminate his rule were shelved. While the American Civil Administration in Baghdad, first under Jay Garner and then under Ambassador Paul Bremer, is occupied with the large problems of recon-structing Iraq and putting it back on its feet, it is in towns like Kut, left to the discretion of Marine colonels who are trained to fight but not to construct civil society, that the fate of *Pax Americana* will be decided. As in other cities, the Americans have convened meetings of local tribes, clerics and notables of Kut, in an attempt to come up with some consensual agree-ment on how to govern the city. But in view of the strongly entrenched Abbas, it is hard to see how the Americans can unseat him without provoking further mayhem. In the meantime, while Abbas speaks in favor of an "Islamic democracy," whatever that means, some intellectuals are vying for a form of pro-Western democracy under the aegis of Ahmad Chalabi, the Shi'ite moderate cultivated by the Americans and the British as the head of his Iraqi National Congress. He was flown to Iraq to build for himself a power base of support after the Shi'ite south was conquered. Abbas evidently regards himself as the choice of Allah and of all his many qualities, modesty is certainly not the most salient. He praises himself effu-sively and arguably commands the respect of his townsmen, even though the American command in Kut insists that his fans are paid actors and his cronies are backed by the Iranians.[53]

When the main battles of the official war in Iraq were declared over by mid-April after about four weeks of combat, the center of gravity moved to politics and to the political hub of Iraq where all problems of the country are reflected and dealt with. In politics, the Shi'ites, having tasted freedom once again, have rediscovered their true weight, based on their vast majority in the south. They are currently in the process of readying them-

selves for the struggle for Iraq. The trends that have been described above
– some leaning toward the Iranian model under the leadership of clerics,
others promoting modernization, democratization and secularization
under the aegis of a mixture of clerics, intellectuals and expatriates who
were groomed in the West and are finding their way back home – have
barely begun to crystallize and manifest themselves. Although the Shi'ites
dominate the South, where they possess their numerous constituencies, oil
wealth, holy cities and local leadership, the issues will be decided, in all
probability, by the Americans, in tandem with returning expatriates like
Chalabi and moderate clerics who would opt for a gradual weaning of Iraqi
society from the shackles of autocracy and centralization. Throughout that
process, however, the various local authorities, religious or otherwise, will
have to be consulted if any political/progressive process is to be successful.
The political hub of Baghdad is not only the seat of government and residence of some senior clerics and the intelligentsia – who will all have a say
in the process of transformation that Iraq will be undergoing in the coming
months and years – but also the center from which Ambassador Bremer
will direct his activities. Add to that the fact that Saddam City, the Shi'ite
part of Baghdad, has the highest concentration of Shi'ites in the country,
and is also the place where their misery is the most pronounced and their
grievances the most loudly heard, and one can begin to comprehend the
daunting task that the new government in Baghdad faces.

Kurds in the North

4

Just as the south is characterized by the widespread pattern of Shi'ite settlement all the way from Basra up to Baghdad, the extreme north of Iraq is Kurdish country, with some salient differences from its Shi'ite counterpart:

1   Unlike the barren south, many of whose towns and villages are located in the great valleys of the Tigris and the Euphrates, the north is much more mountainous and green. In military terms, while the south is wide open to quick and multi-track movement of armored formations, mobility in the north is limited to specific mountain passes. Therefore, the Kurdish areas are much better suited to infantry and special forces.
2   Though the Shi'ites in the south are sub-divided into tribes and a multitude of religious, personal, tribal and local allegiances, their combined Arab and Shi'ite identity unites them in a similitude of a more or less uniform religious and ethnic group which shares much in common. Moreover, they have always held their Arabism in common with the Arab Sunnite elite which has been ruling the country since its inception. By contrast, the Kurds in the north, while they share their Sunni Islam with the rest of non-Shi'ite Iraqis, their ethnic identity, which they hold in common with their kin across the borders of Iran, Turkey and Syria, by far outclasses their religious affiliation. In short, being a Kurd is far more important than any affiliation with their fellow Sunni Iraqis.
3   The Kurds in northern Iraq are divided between tribal loyalties, mainly the Talabanis and the Barazanis. Ostensibly this division is based on political grounds, following two different political parties, but is in fact in line with clan divisions in the footsteps of dominant tribal chieftains.
4   Unlike the Shi'ites who constitute the majority among the Iraqis (some 13 million out of 24 million), the Kurds are smaller in numbers, numbering close to 20 percent (or 5 million, of the total population), and they feel doubly marginalized: once as the members of the overall Sunnite minority, and again as the subjugated Kurdish minority

within the Sunni group. They would rather form coalitions with other Kurds outside Iraq than rally to the Sunnite elite that has ruled modern Iraq since its inception, and certainly rather than submit to the majority rule of the Shi'ites.

5   Unlike the Shi'ites in the south, who seek assistance from coreligionists in adjoining countries only, such as Iran, the minority Kurds would accept aid, protection and guidance from any outside power willing to extend their hand to them. Unlike the xenophobic and suspicious Shi'ites who would shun any domination that is not their own, the Kurds would embrace any government that guarantees their rights or defends their autonomy.

6   Unlike other Shi'ite majority groups who have achieved independence in countries such as Iran and Bahrain, the Kurds cannot boast any independent existence beyond a very few ephemeral and ultimately aborted attempts.

7   While the Shi'ites are for the most part predominant in the cities and towns of the south and in parts of Baghdad, many of the Kurds share the northern cities of Mosul and Kirkuk with the Sunnite Arabs. So, even in mountainous Kurdistan where they live in isolation and constitute the overwhelming majority, they still must live side-by-side with large Arab populations, many of whom were settled there during the Saddam regime.

8   While the Shi'ites have always struggled for their part of the government cake and resources, shunning any separatism, the Kurds have always entertained a strong motivation for autonomy, even independence, often backed by violence against what they perceive as oppressive regimes.

9   The Shi'ites, even those who welcomed the Americans initially, have refrained from taking an active part in the hostilities, and were quick to demand their departure, while the Kurds have actively allied themselves in combat with the invading forces and are not eager to distance themselves from the occupiers once the war is declared over.

It is essential to understand the Kurds' social and political ambitions in order to gauge their role in the making and unmaking of Iraq and to evaluate the chances of success in rebuilding a new Iraq in the post-Saddam era, based on both the territorial integrity of its present-day boundaries and on the impossible and contradictory social and ethnic composition contained therein. It is also important to remember that northern Iraq as a whole is not the Kurds' exclusive domain the way the south is for the Shi'ites. In addition to the mixed cities of Mosul, Kirkuk and Sulaimaniya, where Arabs and Kurds dwell together, there are many purely Arab cities, such as Tikrit, Haditha and Faluja, where the ruling Sunnite minority constitutes a local majority and renders these cities local bastions of the regime. In consequence, while the Americans left the purely Sunni Arab towns in the north until the very end of the operation in Iraq, out of the belief that these strongholds would be subdued when besieged and isolated on all fronts, in the Kurdish north they did not have to fight at all. Quite the contrary: they parachuted into friendly territory and immediately joined forces with their eager Kurdish allies to march toward Baghdad. American rallying of the Kurds had become essential especially after their attempts to launch an attack on Baghdad from Turkey was abolished after the Turkish Muslim government rejected the US plans.

Who Are the Kurds?

The Kurds are an ancient people, supposedly descendants of the Medes, an Indo-European people similar in ethnology to the Persians, and whose empire existed around the sixth century BC. The Kurds do not appear in modern Arabic writings until the ninth century AD. They have since times immemorial lived in the mountainous areas west of the Caspian Sea, on both sides of the Zagros mountain range, through lower Anatolia to the mountainous areas of northern Iraq and Syria. Unlike the Semitic languages of the Middle East, the Kurdish language belongs to the Iranian group of the Indo-European tongues, and it is spoken in a multitude of local dialects and written in various scripts: Arabic in Iran and Iraq, Roman in Turkey and Cyrillic in the former Soviet Union. Due to the centrality of the Kurdish language in Kurdish nationalism and identity, the countries which partitioned among themselves the territory of Kurdistan (the Land of the Kurds) have made attempts to forbid or discourage its use, except for the Iraqis who have, on the contrary, tolerated the use of Kurdish in schools and in public life. And so, paradoxically, while in Turkey, supposedly the most democratic and Western-oriented country in the Islamic world, historically the Kurds were not even acknowledged as a people (they were usually referred to as the "Mountain Turks"), their nationalism suppressed and their language banned for decades, Iraq under the gruesome dictatorship of the Ba'ath party did tolerate Kurdish iden-tity, even though other manifestations of Kurdish nationalism were cruelly quelled.[1]

Since the Kurds, now numbering around 30 million, have never been unified politically, their diffusion among five different nation-states has greatly impacted on their local identities, cultures and languages and contributed to great differentiations among them, which at times grew into veritable yawning gaps. The greatest bloc among them, about half the total, constitutes a quarter of the Turkish population of 60 million; in Iran they number 7 million out of 60 million (12%); in Iraq they are 5 million out 24 million (over 20%); in Syria, 1.5 million out of 15 million (10%); and the rest (another million or so) exist in the former Soviet Union – mainly Armenia and Azerbaijan – and in Western diasporas. In Iraq, while the Kurds are conscious of their individual Kurdish identity, which they zealously maintain in their mountains of the north, they have been part and parcel of Iraqi national life, participating in national government and refraining from outright separatism beyond cultural autonomy in their towns and villages. Though some Kurds in Iran are Shi'ite, and in Turkey, Alewis, the great majority are Sunni Muslims. Most Kurds are organized in rural tribes, but about one-third of them have lately been urbanized. In Iraq, they reside pricipally in the four Kurdish provinces of Sulaimaniya, Erbil, Kirkuk and Dohuk. In another three towns – Khanaqin, Mandali and Sinjar – they constitute the majority of the population, and have considerable minorities in other towns and cities, such as Mosul. Under the Ottoman Empire, Kurdistan – a geographic but not political notion – lay in its entirety on its border area; but during World War I the British and the French conquered Iraq and Syria, and the new interstate boundaries left Kurdistan divided into five different sections. The discovery of oil in Kurdish territory, in addition to its strategic position as the seamline between Iraq, Syria, Turkey and Iran, added impetus to Great Power interest in that remote part of the Middle East.[2]

The rise of Kurdish nationalism under the Ottomans had resulted in uprisings among the restive Kurds beginning in the 1840s, but most of that unrest focused on local affairs and did not give rise to an outright demand for independence and statehood. However, after the promulgation of Wilson's Fourteen Points, which recognized the right of self-determination to national groups, the Kurds became one of the prominent voices of the minority groups and occupied nations that demanded independence. Indeed, after World War I there was much talk of affording independence and statehood to the Kurds. Under articles 62–64 of the Treaty of Sèvres (1920), autonomy was promised to the Kurds of the Ottoman Empire, to be transformed into independence one year later following a referendum. But those promises were reneged upon by the Powers, especially after the integration of the Kurdish part of Anatolia into the new Turkey established by Mustafa Kemal Ataturk. As Turkey laid claim to the old Mosul Vilayet of the Empire, which included most of Iraqi Kurdistan, the British were compelled to support the Iraqis, especially after oil discoveries in the Mosul area. The exclusion of Turkish and then Iraqi Kurdistan from the pledged autonomy rendered the idea of Kurdish independence irrelevant. Even when the Commission of the League of Nations mandated to settle the conflicting claims of Turkey and Iraq, recommending that Kurdish interests in Mosul, where they constituted the majority, should be "taken into consideration," the British ignored the League. The *fait accompli* of a divided Kurdistan was thereby established. *Sic Transit Gloria Mundi.* The Kurds, who had struggled for recognition for years, and whose history, culture and numbers certainly made them worthy of autonomy and independence, disappeared from the political scene and became footnotes in the histories of other nations, just as the Palestinians and Jews, who were fewer in numbers, gained world recognition for their national struggles.[3]

In accordance with the San Remo Conference, Iraq became a state in 1920. After the Anglo-Iraqi Treaty of 1930, which guaranteed Iraq independence, the Kurds remained unsatisfied; their demands had not been met and the pledges to them were not fulfilled. They mounted a large demonstration in Sulaimaniya on 6 September, 1930 that was violently quelled by the Iraqi–British authorities: "The Black Day" Massacre saw 30 Kurdish killed or wounded. Kurdish appeals to the League of Nations for independence having fallen on deaf ears, centers of resistance to the Iraqi government emerged in Sulaimaniya and Barazan in the north, though there were Kurdish intellectuals in the urban areas who elected to work via the Iraqi central government. The movement of Kurdish resentment culminated in the 1943–5 uprising of Mulla Mustafa Barazani, which was crushed with the assistance of the British Royal Air Force, and saw Barazani's forces retreat into Iranian territory. The Qassem coup in 1958 proclaimed Iraq a republic as part of the Arab nation, and declared the Arabs and Kurds as equal partners in the state constitution. That statement was designed to neutralize the separatist aspirations of the Kurds rather than to recognize their national rights in Iraq. *Prima facie*, Qassem's ambition was to forge a new Iraqi identity from all the various components of Iraqi society. Quickly, however, Qassem's partner in the coup, abd-al-Salam 'Aref, began pulling republican Iraq toward the fashionable Pan-Arabism of which Nasser's Egypt was the recognized champion. That tension resulted in the Shawwaf anti-Qassem coup in Mosul, with the Kurds and the Leftists (Communists and Ba'athists) supporting Qassem and the Pan-Arabists standing behind Colonel Shawwaf. The result was all-out conflict, with Kurds and Yazidis opposing Arabs, Christians against Muslims, Kurds against Arabs, and the soldiers of the Kurdish 5th Brigade fighting their Arab officers.[4]

Qassem had the upper hand, but the Leftist ideology of the regime did not penetrate the Kurdish (and Shi'ite) areas. For though the Leftist parties were active in the urban centers of Sulaimaniya and Mosul, and had members among the Kurdish intellectual circles, they could not influence the traditional relationships between the peasants and their chieftains, or between tribal leaders. Animosities persisted between the Kurds, who were employed in the growing Kirkuk oil industry, and other minorities such as the Muslim Turkomans, who were artisans and merchants, and the Christian Assyrians. Not even Qassem, who sought to placate the Kurds, could accept the proposal for a culturally and politically autonomous Kurdistan. Ultimately, Qassem's inability to cope with the aspirations of the Kurds (and other minorities) brought about the renewal of their repression by the government, showing up the difficulties over the perennial issue of the identity, autonomy, self-rule and loyalty of the Kurds in Iraq. This problem continued under the Ba'ath regime in the 1970s, especially under Saddam since 1979, with the Sunnites maintaining their near-monopoly on power, the Shi'tes refusing to incorporate modernity and secularism into their religious thinking and the Kurds holding on to their separatist dream. The identity problem of Iraq was far from resolved; the Saddam era of centralization, terror and conflict saw the rekindling of violence between the Kurds and the regime, which culminated in the massive bombings and annihilation of hundreds of Kurdish villages in the 1980s. The move against the Kurds had been premeditated by Saddam during his tenure as Vice-President to Takriti, when he signed the agreement of 1975 with the Shah. This agreement saw Saddam recognize Iranian sovereignty in Shatt al-Arab; Saddam also expelled Ayatullah Khomeini from Najaf, who threatened the Shah throne. In return Saddam obtained the closure of Iranian borders to Iraqi Kurdish rebels. The chemical bombing of the village of Halabja in 1988 briefly brought the Kurdish people's plight to the world stage, with horrific human suffering broadcast onto televisions around the world.[5]

Those chilling scenes were engraved in the Kurds' collective memory to such an extent that, when Operation Desert Storm was launched (1991) as a response to Saddam's invasion of Kuwait (August 1990), the Kurds, who together with the Shi'ites were encouraged to rebel against the regime, took to the mountains, knowing full well what awaited them when the Americans withdrew. The latter, recognizing their responsibility for stirring the Kurds and then abandoning them, appointed General Jay Garner to oversee the humanitarian relief to the Kurds, a job he undertook with humanity and sensitivity. Garner's efforts explain why, on his return to Kurdish territory in April 2003 after the Iraq war, he was greeted warmly and with thanks. The interval between the 1991 and 2003 wars was perhaps the best period the Kurds have experienced in recent memory. Under the protection of the no-fly zone imposed by the British and the Americans during the 12 years of UN sanctions against Iraq (1991–2003), the Kurds were virtually immune to any air attacks by Saddam's air force which had attacked them in Halabja in 1988, destroyed their villages all through the 1970s and 1980s, and terrorized the Shi'ites in the south. With the Iraqis unable to dislodge them from their mountain bastions, the Kurds in fact exercised a degree of economic, cultural and political autonomy, experiencing an unprecedented level of prosperity, peace, recognition and freedom. For the Kurds of Iraq to support the Third Gulf War, therefore, they had to be persuaded that removing Saddam either improved their prospects for secession and independence, or at the very least preserved the status quo which has been much to their liking. Saddam being the greatest obstacle to their emancipation, they did not need much persuading. The

Kurds hoped that their full commitment to the anti-Saddam coalition would automatically raise their fortunes and improve their stakes in the post-war arrangements. Such a hope, however, may eventually be tempered by the harsh practical reality of a post-Saddam Iraq.

The Opening of the Northern Front

When the Americans were in the planning stage of the war, their strategy was that, simultaneously with the invasion of Iraq from the south, they would thrust from the Turkish border southward to Baghdad, thus compelling Saddam to split his forces and fight on two fronts. However, the Islamist government of Erdogan in Ankara, which enjoyed a massive majority in the House and among the public, and was therefore less open to outside pressures or financial inducement, resorted to a tactic of dragging their feet, under all manner of procedural pretexts. Eventually the Americans, who had 30,000 troops on board ships off the Turkish coast waiting to land, were compelled to call that plan off, instead using the soldiers to reinforce their bases of attack in Kuwait. That not only altered the war plans and dictated a slower pace in the rush northward to Baghdad, but also enhanced the importance of the Kurdish allies in the north, who were originally to be kept out of the combat zone; now they became key allies by default. America was initially ready to disregard the Kurds once again, because placating the Turks was thought to be more expedient and wiser in the long run, for the latter had conditioned their support on the total Kurdish exclusion from the war plan. Moreover, to make sure that the Kurds of Iraq would not gain independence in the mayhem of the war, thereby kindling the fire of nationalism among the Turkish Kurds once again, the Turks made sure to obtain American consent to advance their troops into northern Iraq and block the way of the Kurds in both directions: Turkish Kurds from aiding their kin across the Iraqi border, and Iraqi Kurds from inciting their brethren in Anatolia to rise against Turkish oppression.

The Turks' opposition to any plan granting passage to American troops, or air bases for the Allied bombers on their territory, scuppered these conditions. Their concern was not only that they could not collaborate with a Western power against an Islamic sister state, but that if Iraq should be dismantled as a result of the war, the rise of secessionism among the Kurds in Iraq might be fatal to their own interests in Anatolia. Ironically, by not letting the Americans through, the Turks turned the Kurds into crucial allies of the US; the latter would therefore not feel obliged to preserve any Turkish interests post-war, in view of their unexpected and destructive recalcitrance in the pre-war stages (which stood in sharp contrast with the super-collaboration of Özal government for the previous Gulf War). The

Kurds were savvy enough to capitalize on the American strategic needs in the war and on Washington's frustration with Turkish "allies" it had so blindly counted on. Thus from the onset of the war the Kurds became vital partners in the opening of the northern front, in tandem with the airborne brigade and Special Forces that US transports landed in the north in airfields previously secured by the Kurds.

At the very outset of the war, when the American–British onslaught was launched in southern Iraq, General Henry Osman was appointed to run the northern Iraq operation, on a much more limited scale than the original plan. Worse, while previously the Americans had consented to the movement of Turkish troops into Iraqi Kurdistan, now the US turned round and became wary of letting the Turks into Iraq lest they clash with the Kurds. The Turks responded by stating that they would need their forces to guard the border and prevent a refugee problem from developing, but the American commander made it clear that his troops would shoulder many of the responsibilities that had been assigned to the Turks had they joined the coalition forces. European Union suggestions that Turkish incursions into Iraq might hurt its bid to join the EU, finally persuaded Ankara to stay out of the unfolding conflict. But while the Turks did not hide their mistrust of the Kurds in Iraq, Kurdish generals gave their soldiers orders to shoot at any Turkish troops trying to cross the border into Iraq (though the light arms of the Kurds were no match for Turkish armor). On 23 March American cargo planes ferried Special Forces and equipment into northern Iraq at the same time that combat jets were bombing Iraqi positions in and around Kirkuk and Mosul. Until the build-up of forces would develop into a full-fledged war, General Osman played the diplomat, shuttling between Dohuk on the northern tip of Iraqi Kurdistan, where the Kurdish forces were headquartered, and the Turkish Command in Ankara, trying to appease the moods and avert a military clash between the two bitter rivals.[6]

Thereafter, General Osman made his way to Salahuddin, the mountain resort northeast of Erbil, named after the illustrious medieval Saladin, himself of Kurdish extraction, who distinguished himself as the victor over the Crusaders and the liberator of Jerusalem from the Christians. Salahuddin is now the HQ of the Kurdistan Democratic Party (KDP) that controls the northwestern half of Iraqi Kurdistan which borders on Turkey. The southeastern half of the territory is under the Patriotic Union of Kurdistan, and in its extreme south, a group of Islamic militants, the Ansar al-Islam (Supporters of Islam) in all probability connected with al-Qa'ida, found refuge on the border with Iran. As in Afghanistan and the Yemen, these radical groups of Muslims seek bases on the seam-lines between provinces or countries, preferably in inaccessible mountainous areas, from where they can move across borders when they are hunted down. The Americans were trying to coordinate a joint operation with the Kurds against that Islamic stronghold, and in preparation they bombarded it from the air from the opening of hostilities. The Americans also dispatched cruise missiles against another Islamic group, known as *Komali Islami Kurdistan*, under Mullah Ali Bapir, who travels freely in the region under the protection of his gunmen and controls Khurmal, a town adjacent to the enclave of the Ansar. Some 64 Komali fighters were killed in the bombardment and tension rose in Khurmal where Ansar and Komali fighters mingled. In effect, after the American attack, the Komalis, who had been neutral over the Iraqi conflict previously, added their power to the Ansar to make up a force of over 1,000 fighters. Iranians were meddling with those two groups, but the Kurds wanted them out of their territory so that they could concentrate their fighting force against Saddam.[7]

Across the border in Turkey, the local capital of the Kurds – the city of Diyarbakir (population 600,000) – was seething with furtive activity; talk in broad daylight was too risky under the tight scrutiny of the suspicious Turkish troops. This teeming center, which is considered the spiritual capital of all Kurds, was awash with rumors of the forthcoming American moves that were likely to bring succor to the Kurds, but there was also a realization that the Turks were keeping a close eye on the events and would not allow the situation to get out of hand. Detachments of Turkish Kurds were patrolling the border with Iraq, occasionally penetrating at places to monitor the movements of the Iraqi Kurds, for fear that the freedom the Iraqi Kurds had enjoyed since 1991 might percolate into Turkish territory and cause turmoil. The Kurds inside Turkey envied the relative freedom of their Iraqi kinsmen. Younger Turkish Kurds swore that should troops from Turkey invade Iraqi territory, they would volunteer to assist their people against their country. In any case, the Kurds trusted neither the Americans nor the Turks and were certain both powers were together concocting the demise of Iraqi Kurdistan.[8] Kurds on the front in Iraq, fearing reprisals from Saddam, took to the mountains for refuge. Only a succession of American victories and Iraqi failures would convince the refugees to return home and restore life in the cities of Sulaimaniya and Arbil (Erbil), the two largest towns in the Kurdish zone.[9]

Small squads of the American Special Forces that had landed in Iraqi territory started operating behind the lines, guided by Kurdish scouts, while units of the Kurdish fighting force began taking up positions around Kirkuk and Mosul in anticipation of an upcoming attack, both to open the much talked-about Northern Front and to decimate the Ansar al-Islam base. On 24 March Ansar fighters attacked a Kurdish outpost in the village of Anab next door to Halabja, killing a Kurdish fighter and wounding others. Three of the attackers were killed, one of them a Kurd from a rival faction and the others Arabs from Jordan and Syria who were apparently connected to al-Qaida and the Taliban and had fled from Afghanistan following the American offensive.[10]

On the night of 26–7 March 1,000 American troopers from the 173rd

Airborne Brigade were dropped over the Kurdish part of Iraq, adding substantially to the otherwise extremely thin deployment of forces in that region after the Turkish refusal to allow the Northern Front to be triggered from their territory by the forces of the 4th Infantry Division that was now diverted as reinforcement to southern Iraq.[11] The force, dubbed one of the "largest airborne operations since World War II," secured the Harir airfield in Kurdish territory allowing heavy equipment, including M-1 Abrams tanks and Bradley fighting vehicles, 105mm mortars and Humvees armed with missiles, along with additional troops to safeguard the rich oil fields of the north, to launch the joint attack with the Kurds against the Islamist enclave and to ensure that Turkish and Kurdish troops did not collide. The Kurds set up roadblocks on all routes approaching the airfield to secure its perimeter.[12]

In the meantime, realizing that the Americans were intent on circumventing the Turkish "embargo" which had prevented them from marching into Iraq from the north, Ankara declared that it did not intend to send forces into Iraq "beyond those who were already posted there" as a *cordon sanitaire* against any subversive activities of Iraqi Kurds in Turkish territory. The Kurds for their part were adamant that they would not let any Turkish troops into their territory, as they were concerned that the coming of the Turks would also signify the end of the autonomy that they had been enjoying since 1991.[13]

Under the heavy pressure of American bombings, Iraqi troops near the towns of Chamchamal and Qarahanjir just east of Kirkuk began to buckle, in spite of the fact that they vastly outnumbered the ill-equipped Kurds that faced them. Jubilant Kurds marched right into the positions vacated by retreating Iraqi troops, and it was feared that, in the absence of a large American presence, horrific acts of inter-ethnic vengeance between Arab and Kurdish Iraqis might occur. The Kurdish Pesh Merga fighters tried to restrict the movement of journalists lest the looting by unruly Kurds be reported worldwide, but to no avail. It was simply impossible to stop the reports of the steady stream of Kurdish looters, who carted away anything they could lay their hands on in full view of the television cameras and in spite of the presence of a flabbergasted foreign press. Free vent was given to the feelings of resentment and bitterness against the Iraqis, borne out of years of torture, killings, arrests and decimation. Unlike the Shi'ites in the south, who were non-committal in the beginning and then asked the Americans to leave, the Kurds hailed their new allies as liberators who delivered them from the claws of the dictator. Jalal Talabani, the Chief of the Patriotic Union who controlled the southeastern part of Iraqi Kurdistan and led the Kurdish operations there, presided over the takeover of Bani Maqan, a Kurdish town where Iraqi troops had been posted. For Talabani, the victory was not only a symbolic transfer of power, but also a milestone in the demise of Saddam. Already, the Kurds, under the cover of continued American bombings, were heading on the road to Kirkuk.[14]

The American paratroopers who had dropped on the Harir (ironically, for a military base, meaning "silk") airstrip northeast of Erbil in the Kurdish Democratic Party territory of the northwest, were busy digging in, in preparation for an Iraqi counter-attack that never came. Unlike their counterparts further south, who were enduring wretched, desert conditions, the paratroopers in the alpine north were trying to dig their defenses around a rain-soaked valley, where their airstrip had been paved, mended and secured by Kurds eagerly awaiting their arrival, and were now surrounded by the high and treacherous mountains of Kurdistan. Now it was evident, as American forces continued to amass, that joint attacks would be mounted against the Iraqis in the days ahead, in an attempt to penetrate down to the northern reaches of Baghdad, for what was expected to be the apex of the war. Another airstrip in Kurdish territory near Sulaimaniya was already absorbing American cargoes loaded with heavy equipment for the coming attack, while Special Forces operating in the north near Mosul were preparing the grounds for the offensive in that sector by taking over the Akre airstrip.[15]

Sarget, a suspected al-Qa'ida enclave on the Iranian border, and reported to be a center for the manufacture and testing of poisons to be used by terrorists, was blasted into the stone age by intensive American bombings and PGMs (precision-guided missiles/weapons). American Special Forces, together with Kurdish fighters, launched a ground attack during the last three days in March killing some 250 Muslim terrorists who manned the facilities or trained in them. The Ansar al-Islam bunkers have yielded large amounts of intelligence, including laptops and masses of documents, that may lead to future operations against world terrorism. Evidence was reportedly found of the manufacturing of the ricin gas made from castor beans, and of Arabs (Moroccans, Syrians, Palestinians, British and Jordanians), who were either in the camp or linked to al-Qa'ida worldwide. However, some 300 members of the Ansar al-Islam, including four senior leaders, succeeded in escaping to neighboring Iran, thus vindicating their premise of personal safety in seam-line regions. These terrorists will certainly resurface elsewhere, unless the Iranians arrested them when they crossed its border, which is unlikely.[16] By 1 April some 2,000 paratroopers and several hundred Special Forces had amassed in their consolidated positions in the north, so as to make the prospects of a northern front more palpable. While waiting for their next mission, the American soldiers were basking in the hospitality and friendliness of the Kurds, against a backdrop of lush green cornfields and mountain slopes, freezing night temperatures and deep mud, a far cry from what they expected or what their fellow GIs encountered in the south. Humvees had been landed in the airstrip, to allow for mobile patrols, and large trucks were at hand to ferry people and equipment around the growing base.[17]

By the beginning of April the result of the constant American bombings and pressure from the north on the one hand, and the growing hopelessness of the Iraqi troops in and around Baghdad, on the other, engendered retreats by Iraqi forces first around Kirkuk and then Mosul, without any major battles being fought. Kurds who had lived under Iraqi repression were seen looting abandoned Iraqi positions and bunkers. The accumulating American troops in the north gradually saw the prospects of taking part in the war dimming; but their relatively small number would not even suffice to police the large cities of the north if the Iraqi forces unilaterally left. The Turks watched with growing concern the increasing power of the Kurds, for lack of any substantial force to rein them in. They feared that if they got control of the major cities of the north with their tremendous oil wealth, their bargaining position might engender new demands for autonomy or even secession, which would in turn create turmoil in Turkish Kurdistan. Baradash, and then Kalak east of Mosul, and then Mosul itself, were abandoned by the devastated and demoralized Iraqis, and there were only Kurds in the vicinity to move in. Similarly, in the southern sector east of Kirkuk, Kifri and Karez were deserted by the Iraqis and the Kurds moved in.[18]

It turned out that while all Republican Guard units had been withdrawn to help defend Baghdad, only the unmotivated conscripts were left behind to defend in the north, and that quickened the collapse of the lines once many of them deserted, despite the threat of punishment by death squads. That was the picture that reproduced itself quite frequently in northern Iraq and contributed to the foundering of the defenses of that region far quicker and easier than ever expected.[19]

Kirkuk was in sight of the Kurds. The oil-rich city of 600,000 has been claimed by Arabs, Kurds and members of the Turkoman minority as theirs. Even though Talabani's fighters, fresh from their victory over the Ansar al-Islam, were the only viable military power to contend it, once the Iraqis had retreated, they were under pressure from the Americans, fearful of a Turkish backlash, to show restraint. American Special Forces were busy conducting reconnaissance and guiding air-strikes to the areas in conjunction with their Kurdish allies. Kirkuk, due to its strategic and economic importance, had been defended by rings of trenches and bunkers, but the devastation of American bombings had caused the Iraqis to retreat inwardly and abandon the outer belt of positions. Aware of the events of 1991, when the rebelling Pesh Merga briefly controlled Kirkuk and engaged in massive looting, the Americans were wary of letting the Kurds in. Nevertheless, as the Kurdish fighters gnawed at the periphery of Kirkuk, at the pace of American bombings and Iraqi withdrawals, desertions and surrenders, the Kurds were strengthening their hand for a final assault, even as they were declaring that they had no intention to attack, lest their Turkish neighbors be infuriated.[20] Much the same pattern recurred around Mosul, but remaining Iraqi troops there fought vigorously and counter-attacked combinations of Kurds and Americans until they were overwhelmed by a far superior American firepower in general and airpower in particular.

The Americans, who depended on the Kurds for much of the manpower for such assaults, had another problem on their hands: the two rivaling Kurdish parties, headed by the Talabani and Barazani clans, needed to be coordinated in action, and the American commanders in the region often had to resort to diplomacy in that endeavor. They succeeded in assembling a force of 400 Kurds, together with 10 American Special Forces (those were the proportions in the north between American troops and their allies) to attack an Iraqi force of 2,000 soldiers in the town of Khazir on the road to Mosul, the third largest city of Iraq. The town changed hands several times: the retreating Iraqis counter-attacked with courage and determination, and then American air-strikes dislodged them from their hard-won positions, thus permitting Special Forces and their intrepid Kurdish companions to hold their ground and then advance. It took two days of bitter combat (3–4 April) between the heavily-equipped Iraqis and the light-armed, but air-supported Americans and Kurds before the battle was finally decided.[21]

The Special Operations forces, otherwise known as Green Berets, who operated in northern Iraq, were part of a larger war effort that embraced the entire Iraqi war front and encompassed many thousands of troops. Some of them penetrated the streets of Baghdad, others attacked some of Saddam's palaces and a squad from their midst rescued Jessica Lynch from captivity. Small detachments of those forces, in unison with their British, Polish and Australian counterparts (some say also Israelis), acted covertly in western Iraq to search and destroy missiles and missile launchers that could reach Israel. This complex array of secret operations has won the Special Forces' activities the epithet of the "Invisible Campaign." Those forces were directly linked to a network of intelligence that included informants, satellites, surveillance planes and an intelligence-gathering agency, and enabled them to respond in real time to the warnings or the targets to which they were assigned.[22]

Limited bands of Green Berets, amounting to six teams of 12 men each, who operated in squads of six, had showed up in northern Iraq before the hostilities started. Their small numbers notwithstanding, they were able to wield so much advanced technology as to make a genuine difference, especially in areas where massive troops could not deploy. In the north, Task Force Viking rallied the Kurds in the pre-war days and was able to call in air attacks against both suspected terrorists or bases of weapons of mass destruction, or Iraqi military targets. After the war began, Special Forces cleared the way for the 173rd Brigade's paratroopers, but until the latter's arrival, they had to bear the brunt, together with the Kurds, of defending American interests. After the arrival of the paratroopers, the Special Forces continued their reconnaissance and cleared minefields, but their main tasks remained to work hand-in-hand with the Pesh Merga, to unify the Kurdish command, and train the Kurdish fighters in the use of more sophisticated weaponry and combat tactics.[23]

But tragedies also developed from that intimate collaboration. On 6 April an American Special Forces officer traveling with a convoy of Kurdish troops on its way to cut off the main highway between Mosul and Kirkuk, mistakenly called down an air-strike on the column; a bomb exploded, killing 18 and wounding 45, most of them Kurdish fighters. Among the seriously wounded was Wajih, the younger brother of Massoud Barazani, the leader of the northwestern part of Iraqi Kurdistan and rival to the Talabani clan to the southeast. The wounded were flown out, in critical condition, to Germany for medical treatment. Massoud's son, Mansour Barazani, was only slightly injured. The Kurds, including some of those who were wounded in the mishap, unlike their compatriots in Iraq and the Arab world, took the incident in good spirit and regarded it as an error caused by the highly technological nature of the war. They vowed to continue collaborating with the US and were not the least bitter over the incident. They were deeply grateful for the removal of Saddam, and they understood that the air-strike had to be called in to silence the Iraqi armor attack on the light-armed Kurdish convoy. The pilot had tragically confused the two convoys.[24]

The elimination of the Ansar al-Islam stronghold in the Kurdish area bordering with Iran did not put an end to the terrorist threat. A few days after their expulsion, scores upon scores of Ansar infiltrated back into Iraq, out of fear of the Iranians. Because of their determination to penetrate into American-conquered territory and harass the Allied forces; or, because of Jalal Talabani's request, they were extradited back to Kurdish forces. The terrorists were rooted out of their hideouts in the dozens by Kurdish fighters. Hundreds gave themselves up, adding to the many others who had been killed or surrendered during the joint American–Kurdish attack. Of the initial force of 650 terrorists who had gathered in the mountain refuge, about 25 percent of them were foreign nationals who had fled Afghanistan after the defeat of the Taliban. But concerns remained that those still at large constituted a clear and present danger to the Americans and their allies through assassinations, car bombs and other terrorist activities. While active in their remote border seam-line, the terrorists ruled the villages under their control in a Taliban-like fashion, with prohibitions against music, drinking, smoking and the exclusion of women from mainstream society.[25]

It was not until the fall of Baghdad that the US and its Kurdish allies could pay full attention and divert the necessary resources to focus on the oil cities of Kirkuk and Mosul, which the Americans wished to secure because of: (1) the strategic importance of the two cities; and (2) because the numbers of troops at their disposal were not enough to decisively achieve victory. The Kurds, who were restlessly gnawing at the periphery of these major cities, were not permitted to attempt the final assault on their own, lest they provoke the Turks or take over the oil wealth. The Kurds had prepared in both cities an infrastructure of rebellion and had blueprints for taking control of those mixed centers where Kurds constituted a large portion of the population, even though they were not strictly included within the perimeters of the two Kurdish autonomous regions since 1991. On 9 April American and Kurdish troops took over the Maqlub Mountain Ridge, a strategic peak which dominates Mosul from the northeast; from that point, only 20 miles of flat terrain remained to be covered, and had the strategy gone according to plan, US armor would have quickly punctured the city's defenses. Some 2,000 Kurds, supported by American airpower and some Special Forces, were poised for the final assault. The Kurdish presence also prevented the Iranian-backed Badr Brigade of the Iraqi opposition from taking up positions which might have facilitated unilateral action on its part. The Badr Brigade, the military arm of the Supreme Council for the Islamic Revolution in Iraq, had a different agenda from that of the allies and would have conceivably opted for an Islamic republic in Iraq, backed by the mullahs of Teheran. With the beginning of hostilities, the Badr Brigade marched into northern Iraq from Iran. Its presence, coupled with a weak American force, further complicated the execution of the war in that territory as the subjugation of Baghdad approached its completion.[26]

The withdrawal of the Iraqis from the Maqlub Ridge permitted American and Kurdish troops to roll through the gates of the St Matthew Monastery, one of the vestiges of Christian Assyrian presence in northern Iraq. The monastery, which was declared liberated by the Allies, had been named after a fifth-century monk who lived in a cave on top of that mountain, and whose body is said to be watched over by the monks to this day. The Assyrians, who make up 4 percent of the Iraqi population, belong to the list of faiths and ethnicities that were persecuted by Saddam, together with the Shi'ite majority (60%) of the south and the Kurdish minority (15–20%) of the north – the others are the Turkoman and the Yazidis – while the Sunnite minority (around 20%) of Baghdad and central Iraq occupied the top level of the social hierarchy. Upon the fall of Baghdad and the proclamation of the removal of Saddam's regime, there were outbursts of jubilation in the Kurdish areas, repeated among the Shi'ites, but uncertainty prevailed in the midst of the oppressed Assyrians. On the one hand, some Assyrians, like Tariq Aziz, the Vice-Prime Minister and the "sweet voice" of "moderation" of Saddam in the West and in the Vatican, were elevated by the regime to the highest positions, but conversely, common Assyrians were grateful for Saddam's demise. In one corner of the St Matthew monastery lies a metal collar for people who want to make a wish.

If the person wraps the collar around one's neck and it opens, the wish is granted; if it remained closed, the wish is denied. Judging from the uncertainties that the aftermath of the war is plunging Iraq into, it may be a long time before the collar opens around the necks of those who wish for peace and tranquility.[27]

In Sulaimaniya, the capital of the southeastern part of Iraqi Kurdistan, in the heart of the Talabani region, the war-toughened Kurds who had fought Saddam since he came to power, could hardly contain their elation. Suddenly, it seemed that all the years of persecution, torture, sacrifice, massacres (including chemical weapon attacks) and oppression were removed at one stroke. Even the much-feared biological or chemical warfare against them by a desperate Saddam, as some observers predicted, failed to materialize. The Kurds had every reason to chant, dance, celebrate in the streets and shoot firecrackers, in what one reporter called an "unashamedly pro-American rally," with shouts of thanks to Bush, to America, and hugs and kisses to American soldiers who were looking on with unveiled astonishment, or to any foreigner who happened to roam around town. Similar scenes were seen in the streets of Erbil, the capital of the northwestern Barazani part of Kurdistan. The continued presence of Iraqi forces in nearby Kirkuk and Mosul did nothing to dampen their enthusiasm and sense of celebration. A happy Kurdish father, who witnessed the birth of his new son that morning, announced that he was calling him "Azores," after the island where George W. Bush and Tony Blair had met to finalize the war plans. He announced that it was in gratitude to them.[28]

The next day, 10 April swiftly and unexpectedly, Kirkuk fell. The light American–Kurdish attack which was merely intended to tighten the grip on the city by occupying its major intersections, rapidly combined with the pressure of a civilian uprising to send the Iraqi troops fleeing, sucking the allied forces inward. Kirkuk's main asset is oil, and the Americans quickly took control of the oil fields before they could be damaged. The American presence averted any inter-ethnic killings that might have occurred between the Arabs and the Kurds. However, the Kurds did loot homes, businesses and government offices that were predominantly Arab and identified with the now defunct regime. The highways to both Sulaimaniya and Erbil, the capital cities of the two halves of Iraqi Kurdistan, were crowded with thousands of cars laden with looted items. The Turks expressed their concerns over the Kurdish conquest of a city which, by its wealth, could provide the financial underpinnings of a Kurdish state, and did not calm down until the Americans reassured them that it was they who occupied the city, not the Kurds. The almost unintentional capture of Kirkuk had far-reaching strategic ramifications: its domination of the major road junction of northern Iraq meant that the remaining Iraqi garrisons in the next two major cities north of Baghdad – Tikrit and Mosul – would become isolated, together with a ring of lesser towns and villages around them, and would fall like ripe figs into the American lap. In practical terms it signified that the front lines were shrinking, which heralded the end of the main battles for the conquest of Iraq in its entirety.[29]

The triumphant entrance of Kurdish fighters accompanied by journalists to the city was anti-climactic, since after the fierce exchanges of fire in the morning, the city fell silent by noon. The citizens, mainly the Kurds among them, were ecstatic to meet the incoming troops. The remaining Iraqi troops and Saddam loyalists slipped out quietly toward Tikrit, the last holdout of the regime, with Kurdish troops and American Special Forces on their heels. Pursued and bombed by the American Air Force, the Iraqi troops and officials were followed out of the city by the infuriated, vengeful and relieved citizens who were looting offices and setting them aflame. A long convoy of 75 Iraqi vehicles headed south but was not attacked from the air, for fear that civilians might have sought refuge in it. But all along their flight the Iraqi soldiers left a trail of cartridge belts, helmets and uniforms, indications that they opted to slip out of the city in civilian cloth. Every so often there were tanks, armored carriers and other vehicles, doors open, undamaged: all pointed to an enemy in retreat, an enemy that did not want to fight. So swift, uncalled for and unexpected was the retreat, that one might speculate that some mysterious plan was being put into practice of saving the forces for some ultimate battle elsewhere instead of letting the forces erode into submission. For otherwise, judging from the crates of ammunitions, supplies and food that were left behind untouched, one would think that a centralized effort had been deployed for a last stand against any attack in Baghdad.[30]

In the streets of Kirkuk, fresh evidence of violence against the remaining officials of Saddam could be seen: prison wardens were shot or hacked to pieces with axes; the giant statue of Saddam in Central Square was scaled by Kurds and beaten with the furor of a long-suffering people who were giving vent to their sudden deliverance. As the statue was finally toppled, symbolizing the demise of the tyrant, other onlookers were holding signs welcoming and blessing the Americans. There were civilian casualties too: shot by the retreating soldiers, caught in minefields or accidentally struck by celebratory gunfire. Immediately after the Kurdish fighters swept the city streets, civilians ransacked military and government facilities, shops and offices: furniture, appliances, even fire extinguishers, anything that seemed to hold any value was lifted. Even the Kurdish fighters participated in the orgy of looting. A group of Kurdish soldiers were seen driving off with a forklift carrying a load of stolen tires and towing a stolen pickup. Only with the arrival of troops of the 173rd and the installation of a Kurdish civil government (and probably also when little was left to loot), did the ransacking subside.[31]

The Arab population of the city, for its part, either fled in fear of revenge, or stood by and helplessly observed the delirious Kurds celebrating and scavenging. Surprisingly, except for a few acts of vengeance against remaining officials of the regime, there was no mass killing of Arabs; surprising, considering that some 100,000 Kurds had been expelled from the city by the Saddam rule in the preceding decade, and were replaced by Arabs, within the policy of diluting the Kurdish grip on the north and lessening their threat to the regime. That policy has created a whole system of contradictory claims to homes, property and entire cities, and the Kurds, who now wanted to sort things out, immediately differentiated between the original Arab inhabitants of the city and those willing "settlers" whom they saw as collaborators with Saddam.[32]

In spite of American assurances and the apparent moderation with which the Kurds behaved toward the Arab population, however, the Turks, alarmed at the inroads made by the Kurds in Kirkuk, decided to send in "military observers" to monitor the situation in Kirkuk. Ankara wanted American reassurances that the Kurdish fighters were under US control. The State Department issued renewed pledges that American troops would soon have the situation under control once reinforcements arrived at the city. Turkey was not satisfied with the American response, and even insinuated that it was still considering sending troops to northern Iraq should the Kurds take possession of the city.[33] To allay their fears, Jalal Talabani, the leader of the southeastern region of Kurdistan, was made by the Americans to pledge that his forces would vacate Kirkuk as soon as an American garrison arrived. Talabani reiterated his conviction that the city would be open to all in the new Iraq.

After Kirkuk, Iraqi troops stationed in Mosul also began to show signs of surrender. The process seemed more orderly than in Kirkuk, amidst continued American bombings against the Iraqi garrison and an attempt to destroy a building occupied by Barazan Ibrahim al-Tikriti, Saddam's half-brother, who was in charge of hiding his money.[34] After Iraqi troops pulled out of the city, a convoy of a dozen Special Forces, with several hundred Kurdish fighters, drove into Mosul, once again raising suspicions as to the existence of some master plan for a strategic withdrawal. Though Iraqi snipers shot at American forces and their vehicles, forcing them to retreat for a while, no serious and sustained effort was made by the Iraqis to fight a rearguard battle of withdrawal, or even to harass the Americans long enough to halt their advance, despite their decisively overwhelming numbers. At any rate, the withdrawal signaled freedom for the locals to indulge in plundering the local university, clinics and hospitals, government offices, hotels and the central bank, though on a lesser scale than seen in Kirkuk.[35]

While waiting for the forces that had conquered Baghdad to complete their takeover and then turn to Tikrit and its surroundings, supposedly the last holdouts of the Ba'ath regime, it was essential to secure the peace in the northern cities, and substantial American troops were dispatched there in order to allay Turkish fears and prevent further violence. Once the Ba'ath infrastructure had broken down, a power vacuum had opened up, and the Americans well understood that if they did not fill it forthwith, the Kurds might, with the attending Pandora's Box of uncertainties and chaos that might be opened as a result. Kurdish officials who rushed to the newly-liberated cities to establish some modicum of order and rule, hoping to strengthen their foothold there, criticized the Americans for "not thinking about the next day" when they let the looters and other troublemakers take over the streets, destroy government buildings and plunder their contents.[36]

Rather than preparing a force to police the conquered cities before they were taken over, in order to impose order immediately and prevent the uncontrollable spoiling of all working government mechanisms, the Americans instead opted to allow the people to let off their accumulated steam. Only when the orgies of looting, burning and killing subsided, did they try to take over and install a new civilian order. But the second part of that process was much harder, and this is what the Kurds resented. Not only was it difficult for them to re-establish order after the immediate chaos of post-Saddam Iraq, but when the Americans arrived in force to impose some peace and civility, they marginalized the Kurds, and tried to inde-pendently, and without sufficient experience, re-create a workable system of government. A suspicion has penetrated some circles that the Americans wished to hand the cities over to the exiled Iraqis of the Chalabi camp, and an orderly civilian system under the Kurds was not compatible with that proposed handover process.

In Mosul, the Arabs make up 60 percent of the population, hence their emphasis on an "Arab President," not a Kurdish one. They had benefited from Saddam's rule while the Kurds suffered. The looting in the city was blamed by the Arabs on the Kurds and vice versa: brawls broke out over stacks of cash at the plundered central bank, before the building, like half a dozen others in the city, was set ablaze. The Nineveh International Hotel, the finest in town, was looted with frenzy, its mattresses, rugs and any other movable fixtures hurled out of doors and windows, using sheets as makeshift ropes to lower down more fragile items such as chandeliers. The same cleaning-up operations were carried out on the university campus and technical labs, the hospital and even its ambulances. The Americans were nowhere to be seen. It was reported that, because the Americans had insisted on an unconditional surrender by the Iraqi officers and officials, their passage into the city had taken longer than anticipated, allowing looters to strip many institutions clean. It is more likely, however, that the Americans did not have any available troops to enter the city and police it, and while they were waiting for reinforcement, the people of Mosul felt they had the opportunity to take their multitude of private vengeances for all they had suffered under Saddam. The only other available force to impose order, as in Kirkuk, i.e. the Kurds, were not be permitted by the Americans to set up their *Pax Kurdana* in the city.[37]

Outside the big cities there were also many villages, like Maryam Bak, south of Kirkuk, many of which are populated by Arabs, most of whom did not share the Kurdish enthusiasm for the war. The villages are ideal nondescript neighborhoods for Saddam's supporters to change cloth and melt into the population, either to prepare guerilla attacks against the American occupiers and their Kurdish collaborators, or to lay in abeyance until circumstances permit their emergence from hiding. In the nearby village of Hawija, half way between Kirkuk and Tikrit, for example, a gun skirmish erupted on 12 April as if to exemplify the fragility of the situation between the rival ethnic groups. Kurds returning from Arab villages were seen driving loaded trucks with spoils of war. Officially the Pesh Merga roaming the countryside were to avoid any contact or friction with their rivals, but local skirmishes were unavoidable. In Kirkuk itself, until the promised fresh American troops arrived to police the city, it was the Pesh Merga who imposed the rule. Looting continued throughout the second day of its conquest/liberation. The main cotton plant of the city and the offices of the North Oil Company, which manages the oil wealth of northern Iraq, were ablaze, and tension reigned among the city's Kurdish and Turkoman minorities. To negate the possibility of violence, the American commanders in the field assembled Kurdish, Turkoman and Arab officials in an attempt to clear the air and form a council of notables that might help govern the city. But because of their thin ranks, there was little the Americans could impose, so they had to put up with the continuation of plunder taking place before their eyes.[38]

It was not until April 12, when the troopers of the 173rd Brigade were ordered into the city, that the Americans began to make a show of force and tighten their grip. They discovered a large depot of warheads, but were not certain whether they were of the prohibited kind. At the same time, the thousands of Kurdish fighters who had been roaming the streets and sleeping in commandeered buildings finally began evacuating the city at American instigation, in trucks and buses and in good order, back to their Kurdish enclave in northern Iraq, though a Kurdish official remained in charge of the administration until a new city government could be put in place. Significantly, 500 traffic and security officers also remained to help police the streets, a task now under the command of the 173rd Brigade. Finally, the combined force was stopping all cars and forcing looters to leave their spoils curbside. The combined American and Kurdish police force, supplemented by a skeleton Kurdish administration, were able to restore order to the city. The Kurds were also gaining kudos, showing that they knew not only how to fight, but also how to be disciplined, to withdraw their irregulars when the order came, and to help manage the city when called upon to do so. With the violence, arson and looting reduced, people returned to the streets. American civil affairs officers also arrived and were prioritizing with the Kurdish temporary administration about how to put the city back on its feet and reactivate public services. Their commander, Major Sarracino of the 96th Civil Affairs Battalion, declared that soldiers from his unit would move in soon to repair the damaged facilities of the city, and first of all to restore power so that water was running once again. Relief teams were also at work assessing damage and cleaning minefields and destroying ordnance depots lest they find their way to local opposition groups or to international terrorists.[39]

In Mosul, the third largest city in Iraq (after Baghdad and Basra) and the largest in the north, Colonel Robert Waltemeyer of the Special Forces assembled 30 religious, tribal and community leaders to lecture to them about the freedom he had come with his troops to install in Iraq, and asked for their help. On the third day after the capture of the city, reinforcements finally arrived from the 10th Mountain Division and the Marines to help the Special Forces to stabilize the city. Some inhabitants waved at them in greetings, others spat at them or made obscene gestures. The population was evidently angry at the slow pace of the American takeover, which came after the looting had decimated much of the city's infrastructure and services. To build a door after the horse had run away from the stable is no consolation to those who need the horse alive now. Unlike Kirkuk, itself a sprawling city of 600,000, and half populated by Kurds and other minorities that are not inimical to the US, Mosul has a population of 1.5 million, mostly Arabs, and is considered a center of Sunni Arab nationalism in northern Iraq, somewhat the counterpart of Basra or of the holy cities of the Shi'a in the south. It is also teeming with minorities, most of all Kurds, whose hostile relations with the Arabs mean the city is on the brink of violence at any time. Memories are still strong over the inter-communal riots that had racked the city in 1959, and the present war situation, which was accompanied by Arab and Kurdish looting, did not ease tensions in the least.[40]

From his HQ at Mosul Airport, Waltemeyer, with few troops and a hostile population, was caught short in his confrontation with the task at hand, because he had to function not only as a commander, but also as a mayor, a diplomat, police chief and director of public works. When the looting first started, Waltemeyer tried to block thousands of Kurds from entering Mosul, out of fear that the sight of Kurds inundating the capital of northern Iraq, in close proximity to the Turkish border, might prompt the Turks to intervene militarily. The Turks had already expressed their anxiety over events in Kirkuk; any duplication of that situation in Mosul, closer to Turkey than Kirkuk, might force Ankara to send troops into Iraq – a situation the US did not want to arise. Waltemeyer personally stood on the road, according to one report, threatening to shoot any Kurds who crossed the line into Mosul. He faced not only the problem of the tensions between the Arab majority and Kurdish minority (20%), but also a string of Arab tribes around Mosul, divided among themselves. He also tried to harness local Imams to preach against looting and violence, and to convince former policemen to maintain civil order. The colonel's difficulty was in bridging the cultural chasm that separated him from his new subjects. The perceived arrogance with which he acted did not endear him to the audience he was trying to serve. A local Arab attending the pep meeting with the colonel aptly remarked: "He has beaten Saddam, not the Iraqi people." [41]

Whether because they were robbed of their victory in Kirkuk by the Americans, or just due to a sense of ethnic vendetta, the Kurds picked on Arabs in neighboring villages and expelled them from their homes, creating a humanitarian problem crisis. Some remarked of the Kurds that, having suffered repression and expulsion under Saddam, they were now resorting to the same inhuman measures. This conduct by America's most enthusiastic allies in the war has not only cast a long shadow over the chances of rebuilding post-war Iraq peacefully, but also impacted on US–Arab relations. The Kurdish leadership, who from the start wished to present an image of humanity, collaboration with America, civilized behavior in the war and limited ambitions within their autonomous regions, were embarrassed by these eruptions of violence. Some of them even feared that the Kurdish mobs were repeating the mistakes of the Saddam regime which had cost him his alienation from his people. However, military leaders among the Kurds insinuated that the expulsion of the Arabs had the tacit approval of the US, which was concerned about future stability in the oil-rich region. Predictably, America denied that accusation. Political leaders of the Kurds also refuted those claims, insisting that Jalal Talabani was committed to multi-ethnic tolerance and coexistence.[42] If that was indeed Talabani's stated position, it certainly ran against the bitter memories of recent history, which the Kurds do not forget or forgive.

Under Saddam Hussein, Kurds had been systematically "relocated" from Kirkuk and the surrounding villages and replaced by Arab immigrants who were either forced by the Ba'ath Party to move or were lured by subsidized housing so as to help turn the demographic balance around. Decades later, the victorious Kurds now found that Arabs were living in previously Kurdish houses; part of the Kurdish resistance to the tyrant was their commitment to redeem the property from which they had been exiled. For the record, Kurdish leaders say that in post-war Iraq, where the rule of law should prevail, they would pursue legal channels to regain their property, not violence or dispossession of the Arabs. Be that as it May in five villages south of Kirkuk, Arab inhabitants were notified by Kurds to vacate their dwellings within days. Human rights organizations who monitored the situation claimed that 2,000 Arabs had already been displaced by this rather callous process. Some reporters said that they had witnessed a similar state of affairs in Arab villages northwest of Kirkuk. Some Bedouins who were themselves victims of uprooting, could not understand why the US did not move fast enough to prevent entire Arab villages from being looted or vandalized, even after American tanks had reached Kirkuk itself. They felt betrayed by American talk of freedom, which in fact amounted to trading one prison with another. The ransacked villages left an impression of desolation and vandalism: furniture lay smashed and house animals wandered around empty houses in ghost villages. Several houses were repainted and apparently prepared by the new occupiers who lay historical claim to them.[43]

On 14 April Lieutenant-General Tahaseen Rafan, who ran an Iraqi intelligence network in Kurdistan under Saddam, together with some of his underlings, came to the American HQ in Mosul to discuss the terms of their surrender, hinting that others would follow if the agreed terms were favorable. The offer was attractive to the Americans, because Mosul was the hometown of many senior officers and officials of the Ba'ath, whose surrender might contribute considerable intelligence to the occupiers and also widen the base of collaborators for the reconstruction of post-war Iraq, precisely because this city was considered a center of Sunni-Arab nationalism in northern Iraq. Among famous Mosulians were Izzat Ibrahim, the Vice-Chairman of Saddam's Revolutionary Council and the overall commander of northern Iraq, and General Sultan Hashim Ahmed, the Iraqi Defense Minister. There were rumors during the war that both might have been hiding in their native city, and both were on the list of wanted war criminals. The six Iraqi officers who negotiated their surrender sat with Colonel Waltemeyer in the desolate airline office that stood in as his HQ in the city. He said to his prospective captives that he was mostly interested in information on weapons of mass destruction (WMD), on terrorism and on wanted senior officials. They denied knowledge of those matters. The colonel also wanted to know the fate of the Iraqi V Corps, composed of tens of thousands of soldiers, which had mysteriously melted away upon the withdrawal of the Iraqi troops in the north. There was concern that the "disappearance" of that large military body had been concerted from above, to fool the Americans into believing that the war was over, and that they might re-emerge in the form of guerillas or fedayeen to disrupt the reconstruction process.[44]

Another Iraqi officer among the six who surrendered was Nashwan Fateh Isma'il, responsible for security at the University of Mosul. His task was to infiltrate staff and student bodies, spying on them, arresting the dubious among them and nipping in the bud any subversive campaign. He tracked all political activity among the 5,000 students and repressed any non-Ba'ath activity. He had some 50 agents throughout the campus, including some professors and several "students" who worked for him full-time. His payroll also included some professors at the University of Erbil, the capital of the northern Kurdish autonomous region. Internet access was strictly monitored by a professor who checked on each web page visited by the students, and anyone who received messages from the US was expected to report on them. He said that his own work was also under tight supervision by other officials he refused to talk about.

Lieutenant-General Rafan, a domestic intelligence official, disclosed that he had repeatedly gone as a security officer on Iraqi Airlines, that each flight carried some 18 agents to protect the plane from hijackers, but that none of them engaged in espionage. His latest assignment had been to control many agents in Kurdish areas, some of whom he had never met personally. General Rafan was himself an ethnic Kurd who had thrown in his lot with Saddam, but now he felt threatened by the families of the victims of the Halabja chemical attack in 1988. He insisted that he now had no choice but to remain loyal to Saddam because if he defected he would risk the lives of his family members. He warned that if the Americans did not come forward to protect former Iraqi officers and officials, they might be forced to remain in hiding or even take up arms.[45]

A measure of the troubles to come, even as the city had apparently surrendered, was given on 15 April when at least 10 Iraqi men were killed and 16 wounded in Mosul in a confrontation between Marines and protesters. It began when some 130 marines tried to take control of a downtown government building and were encountered by an angry crowd of thousands of Iraqis. Special Forces had attempted to take over that same building a few days earlier but were repulsed by heavy fire. The considerably larger unit of Marines who made the second attempt at capture in order to turn the building into a center of civilian activity, faced a large, unhappy crowd. When one of the protesters shot in the direction of the building, the Marines fired into the crowd which dispersed only when American planes began roving overhead. (The Iraqi version of the story was quite different: they were pelting rocks on an unpopular exiled Iraqi leader, Misha'an al-Jabouri, who returned from Syria and hailed the coming of the Americans in his attempt to effect a political comeback, claiming that he had been appointed governor of Mosul.) The Marines then opened fire into the crowd, killing several and wounding many more. The American Administration, quick to issue statements about "excessive force," "violation of human rights," and "trigger-happy" troops when commenting on other, similar situations in the Middle East, now understood the situation of frightened teenage soldiers, who feel threatened by thousands of furious and violent attackers, and for whom shooting remains the only way of avoiding a cruel death by lynching. In this violent encounter, the Iraqis accused the Americans of terrorism and inhuman attitudes toward children and the sick, while the American soldiers could not understand the ingratitude of the Iraqis whom they had come to protect. Yet another case of Babylonian lack of communications, easy to criticize when it happens to others (see the reporters' attitudes during and after the war), and to dismiss when your own forces are involved.[46]

The next day, auguring ill for how the days ahead were to unfold, another gun battle occurred on a roadblock in Mosul. When the skirmish was over, four Iraqis were killed and 10 wounded, with the Marines again claiming self-defense and the Iraqis talking about the second day of wanton "massacre." This was the second lesson in two days for the Americans: the Arabs relish and play upon a "victim complex." What they do is always right, everything done to them is wrong. They are the poor, intimidated, humiliated and needy, therefore the world always owes them everything. They feel humiliated by the very fact that someone is stronger, better, more developed, richer, more advanced than them, because all those qualities expose their own incompetence and insufficiency. They cannot make peace with the idea that while they were once the glory of the world and nations trembled before them, their fortunes have changed, and now the Arabs are far behind the rest of the world. Hence their tendency to blame all their troubles on the others, all the while believing that they are peaceful, honest, cultured people who do no harm to others. The others are always the aggressors, the barbarians, the arrogant, regardless of what they do to redeem themselves. In this instance, the Americans are expected to supply food and medicine, to keep the order, to liberate the Iraqis from tyranny etc., but they must be also attacked and harassed, expelled from Iraq, accused of interfering in Iraqi affairs and blamed for the war, for the disorder, chaos and looting that their own people caused. Their world is a Kafkaesque one, where there is no connection between cause and effect, reason and consequence, trigger and result. Therefore, no discussion, persuasion, debate or reasoning is often possible, no resolution workable.

Through the "victim complex" prism no interrogated witness ever heard any Iraqi shooting, only Americans firing to kill without reason. American witnesses meanwhile maintained that they had come under sustained fire to which they had to respond. In all, within two days, right in front of the Governor's office in downtown Mosul, which was occupied by American troops, Iraqi casualties had risen to 17 killed and 39 wounded, an intolerable toll for both the occupiers and the occupied. Some Iraqis explained that while policemen had fired warning shots toward looters, the edgy American troops felt they were being shot at. However, despite this unsavoury incident, American officers in Mosul still believed that at that point they were welcome among the majority of the population, despite the fact that the city remained insecure and basic utilities such as water and electricity were still cut off. The electric supply came from Kirkuk, 110 miles away, a city that was also under American occupation and had its own problems with services. Colonel Waltemeyer had convinced some policemen to resume their duties for the sake of peace and order, but after the last incident, in which several policemen were caught in the shooting and wounding, there was little incentive for others to join the force. The colonel, who was trying to establish a council of elders to help run the city, encountered grievances among the population, who also complained about symbolic matters, such as the hoisted American flags, the flights of combat aircraft which reminded the inhabitants their status as the occupied and subjugated, or the roaming, thieving Kurds. This was the perceived heavy-handedness of the military occupation for them.[47] Had they known the cruelty and murderous behavior of their national army when it occupied "sister" Kuwait over a decade earlier, they would certainly have counted their blessings to be under American occupation.

As the occupation in northern Iraq was entering into its routine, and a semblance of order and security set in, Iraqis began to unearth the past, literally and figuratively. Around Kirkuk, in mounds that stretched in rows across the hard and cracked land, hundreds of unmarked graves were dug up by the families of relatives arrested by Saddam's gruesome security apparatus. Many of the graves seem to belong to Kurds who had been hurriedly buried under those mounds after they were tortured and executed. Human rights groups, as well as many Iraqi families, had waited for the collapse of Saddam's regime, to begin the long and chilling process of identifying and registering the dead, and to return the identified remains to the bereaved families. Some thought the remains, just behind a bottling plant outside Kirkuk, might belong to civilians seized and killed randomly during the 1991 Kurdish uprising; others suspected that they were areas of the burial places of the "Anfal Operation" of 1988 (the year of the chilling chemical gas operation against Halabja), in which Saddam waged all-out assaults against Kurdish villages, accounting for the disappearance of some 180,000 Kurds; still others contended that the graves were the burial grounds of thousands of soldiers who had been killed during the Iran–Iraq war (1980–8). Some Iraqis recalled convoys of trucks loaded with coffins arriving at that spot in 1988: they were told to bury the dead quietly because those were the corpses of "hanged convicts." Years of investigation will be necessary in post-war Iraq to gauge the horrendous scope of those massacres that may surpass, in terms of ratio and horror, the worst of Stalin's purges, which lasted as long and were directed by as sick a mega-lomaniac and paranoid dictator as Saddam.[48]

Baghdad in the Center

5

It would be impossible to grasp the extent and depth of the trauma of the Baghdadis, the Iraqis, the Arabs and Muslims at the sight of American troops roaming the streets of the Iraqi capital, if one does not comprehend first the powerful symbol that Baghdad has constituted throughout history. So much so, that it was this symbolism which prompted the Saudis to press the Americans to arrest their advance toward the Iraqi capital during the 1991 Gulf War, for fear of being associated in the Arab and Islamic historical consciousness with collaborating with the "new Tartars" who descended upon that epitome of glory and humiliated it to the ground. True, transient emotions registered on all screens at the sight of Saddam's dominant statues, cast in bronze to last for eternity, being toppled and trampled with rage and vengeance; but the anger was directed at the tyrant, whose suffocating and overwhelming omnipresence could not be tolerated by those who suffered under his boot: Shi'ites, Kurds, other minorities, conscripts who were shipped to the front to die in vain, families of the missing and killed, and basically anyone who was not directly nurtured by the Ba'ath, the security apparatus or the Saddam family. But that should not obscure the fact that, after all is said and done, the deep pride of the Iraqis and Arabs in their ancient historical capital will backlash on the American occupiers and force them to leave sooner than they anticipated. It was not for nothing that except for Kuwait, whose very existence has been the most challenged and threatened by the Iraqis, no Arab state wished to be seen as siding with the war against Iraq, let alone with occupying its capital.

Baghdad is not only history, glory, culture and pride; it is also a living demographic and political reality, the beating heart of a large and wealthy Arab country that under normal circumstances of civilized rule and realistic policies, could be the envy of much of the world. Nowhere is the damage done to Iraq by its tyrant as evident as in this sprawling city of over five million, where ethnic and religious loyalties collide, where the struggle for power unfolds, where new ideas are emitted and suffocated, where the obscenities and excesses of power are committed on a grand scale, and where the prominence, nonchalance, arrogance and opulence of the wealthy and the cronies of the regime stands in such a sharp contrast to the grinding insignificance, oppression, exploitation and poverty of the masses. Yet, there is a prevalent mood of superiority among the Baghdadis for their ability to partake of the glorious historical experience of their city, similar to the way Parisians speak with disdain about the rest of France ("la province"). And, like Paris, Baghdad has been not only the focus of power, but also the breathing heart and mind of the country, the place where standards of taste, literature, theatre, cinema, dress, learning and culture are made. All the roads, canals and railways go to Baghdad or from it to accommodate its multifarious population which constitutes a quarter of the total. The fact that it has been built on the Tigris River, one of the two that make up Mesopotamia, adds much charm and attraction to a city that over the past 50 years has more than doubled its population.

Baghdad in History

When the Abbasids, who drew their support from Khorasan in eastern Iran, established their new dynasty (750–1258) inherited from the Umayyads (AD 661–750) based in Damascus, they sought to build a capital close enough to their Iranian power base. But since the main city of Iraq in those days, Kufa, was the bastion of Ali's family, who was killed and posthumously became the spiritual Imam-founder of the Shi'a, the second Abbasid Caliph, al-Mansur (AD 754–75) toured several sites and decided upon Baghdad, in close and symbolic proximity to the ruins of the ancient capital of the Iranian Sassanids, Ctesiphon, otherwise know as *al-Mada'in* (literally, "the towns" of Ctesiphon and Seleuceia), 60 miles on from Babylon. The village of Baghdad had the advantage not only of being perched on the western bank of the Tigris, but also of being located at the closest point between the Tigris and the Euphrates – a canal connects between them. Palm plantations and water supplies were at hand, Egyptian and Syrian trade caravans passed by via the desert, while upriver from the Gulf, at Shatt al-Arab and Basra, Chinese goods could be shipped inland. In terms of defense, Baghdad's positioning by the rivers meant it could only be accessed by ship or across a bridge. It is here that al-Mansur decided to build his capital, which he baptized as *Dar-al-Salam* (the House of Peace).[1]

Baghdad was a circular city in the Sassanid tradition, with four concentric walls pierced at the four cardinal directions by gates opening toward Basra, Kufa, Syria and Khorasan and surrounded by a moat. An extravagant Caliphal palace, with a large throne room modeled on the Sassanids, and a grand mosque, constituted the city center surrounded by vast lush gardens. Its glory, approximated in Western Islam only by Cordova, was reflected in the classic and immortal *One Thousand and One Nights* under

Caliph Harun al-Rashid (AD 786–809). Unlike the relatively pristine life in the court of the Ummayads in Damascus, which kept the Caliph in touch with his subjects and with other members of the Arab aristocracy, life in al-Mansur's new "Round Capital" was planned as a bastion for the Caliph and his harem, his Imperial Guards and retinue, and the major Imperial offices of the realm, while the commoners lived in the poor and simple neighborhoods. In other words, the Dynasty's power was not based on voluntary support of the Arab aristocracy, but on the servants/slaves and groups of the protégés of the Caliph. Within his court and palaces, the Caliph lived in great luxury, disregarding the strictures of the Holy Law, such as drinking wine, which he scrupulously enforced on his subjects. Access to the Caliph was extremely difficult and depended on the role of the *Hajib* (the Gate Keeper). When he appeared in front of his subjects on rare occasions of public festivities or victory processions, he was clad in such glamor as to make him appear remote and idolized.[2]

All these manners, which had many Sassanian elements inherent in them, must have been studied scrupulously by Saddam, who restored them with great pomp and at great public expense. Baghdad knew sieges during the battles for power between Harun al-Rashid's children, Amin and Ma'mun, as a result of which Ma'mun, the victor, for a while neglected his capital before he regained it in AD 819. After that, he favored the descendants of Ali for a few years (something that the Shi'ites today would credit him for), until the Black Flags of the Abbasids took over the green colors of the House of Ali. Baghdad, and other Arab-Islamic towns of the Middle Ages, were much larger and much more numerous than their European equivalents, and they owe their growth primarily to military bases where the conquering armies were concentrated before their campaigns and after their victories, which later developed into sprawling and vibrant urban agglomerations. Baghdad, like Fez in Merinid Morocco, Cairo in Fatimid Egypt or Cordova in Muslim Spain, grew not only into the political and administrative capitals of the reigning dynasties, but also became cultural and economic centers. The growth of Baghdad liquidated Ctesiphon, exactly as Kairouan in North Africa eliminated Carthage, and in both the descendants of Bedouin conquerors turned urban while the rural areas were left to the occupied natives. According to estimates, hundreds of thousands lived in Baghdad then, as in great Islamic cities, while Europe of that time seldom knew towns that surpassed 10,000 in population.[3]

There were more previous mentors that Saddam may have learned from. Caliph Mu'tasam (AD 833–42) decided to leave Baghdad and establish a new capital in nearby Samara, up river from Baghdad, though the latter remained the commercial and social center of the Empire. Little by little the Caliph became dependent on his army of professional Turkish soldiers, whose influence became so great they even determined who would inherit the throne in the Imperial family. Only in AD 892 did Caliph Mu'tamad

(AD 870–892) return the capital to Baghdad, but the squabbles between various contenders for nominal rule continued, while the actual power was in the hands of military men. In 1055 Tüghril Beg the Seljuk marched into Baghdad after Iran had fallen to his armies, and received from the Caliph (who had nothing beyond his title) the actual powers of a Sultan, with a mission to wipe out the Shi'ites. The Mongol invasion destroyed Baghdad and put an end to the nominal rule of the Abbasids. Due to Mongol law which prohibited the spilling of royal blood, the last Abbasid Caliph was rolled up in carpets and trodden to death by horses. The Ilkhanid dynasty moved its capital to Tabriz, but a contender for their crown returned to Baghdad and made it his capital in 1340. That encouraged Timur to sack Baghdad in 1390 which, together with the shifting away of trade routes made the once glorious city's demise inevitable. Under the Ottomans, Baghdad regained something of its former status administratively, though not commercially. The slow recovery of Baghdad began with the British takeover during World War I, and the institution of an Iraqi government under the British Mandate in the 1920s.[4]

The British placed a member of the Hashemite family, Faysal ibn Hussein, on the throne as King Faysal I in 1921. Oil reserves began to be developed in the 1930s under an agreement signed by the Iraqi government and a number of international oil companies. Full independence was achieved in 1932 when the British Mandate was officially terminated. Iraq remained a constitutional monarchy until 1958 when a group of army officers headed by Abd-al-Karim Qassem overthrew the government. In 1963, the Ba'ath Party (the Arab Socialist Resurrection) seized power in Baghdad. The oil boom of the 1970s brought new wealth to Baghdad and the regime promptly abused its oil income on extravagant expenditure and the enrichment of Saddam's cronies, and on a military program, including the acquisition of non-conventional weaponry to forge a new Front of Rejection following the Sadat Initiative and Egypt's peace with Israel. In addition to the famous religious sites connected with great Muslim spiritual leaders, Baghdad is also replete with many presidential sites; the eight largest of them were included in the agreement signed between UN Secretary-General Kofi Annan and Saddam in 1998, under which the palaces were searched for unconventional weapons. Originally, the innermost wall of the city contained the Imperial Palace of the Emperor, the second wall defined the quarters of the soldiers and the outer enclosure contained the homes of ordinary people. The merchants' quarters and bazaars were located outside the city walls. Then the city began to expand across the river to the east of the Tigris, which later became the center of the city.[5]

Baghdad also has acquired a major religious importance to the Shi'ites, perhaps second only to Najaf and Karbalah, when the Seventh and the Ninth Imams in the apostolic chain of the Twelve were buried at Kazimayn, now a suburb north of Baghdad. The place still draws many Shi'ite pilgrims. Other saints, like Jilani or Abu-Hanifa, the founder of the Hanafi School of Islam, which predominates in the Middle East and Central Asia, are also found in Baghdad. Jews boast the presence in Baghdad of the tombs of Ezra the Scribe and Ezekiel the Prophet. Until 1451 Baghdad was the seat of the Exilarch (the Head of the Jewish Exile in Babylonia). Though the Jews moved to Israel in 1950, there are other minority communities in Baghdad which help it maintain its ties with the past, such as Nestorian Christians. Despite this rich background, Ba'athist Saddam lent more prominence to Hammurabi of ancient Mesopotamia and projected himself as his successor. However, since the First Gulf War, when he first needed the Arabs to side with him against Iran, and then during the Second Gulf War (1991), when he needed to attract all Muslims to his *Jihad* against the US, Saddam judiciously utilized symbols of Arab patrimony and Islamic heritage.[6]

Baghdad in the War

With a population of more than five million, or about one-quarter of the total population of Iraq, and as the seat of government and much of the intelligentsia and the arts, Baghdad was and remains the beating heart of Iraq, not only due to its past glory but also its economic and political centrality. Even the wealth of the country which is not centered on Baghdad – the oil – is administered from there. Its factories produce leather goods, furniture, wood products, chemicals, electrical equipment, textiles, bricks, cement, tobacco and processed foods and beverages, not to speak of the oil refineries which provide the city's consumption and beyond. Its rapidly growing population has grown almost 20-fold in three generations since independence, from 360,000 in 1932, a phenomenon repeated in many Third World countries and in other major cities of the Middle East such as Cairo, Damascus and Amman, as part of the process of modernization and unrestricted urbanization. Three major universities have been created in Baghdad in modern times, over 1,000 primary schools and hundreds of secondary-schooling institutions. Before it came under siege over the course of the three Gulf Wars, Baghdad was also one of the main centers of Arab culture, not only due to its glorious past, but also as home to a new generation of talented artists, writers, intellectuals, professionals and poets, when they were not stifled or otherwise mobilized by the regime. The roads of modern Baghdad are wide, especially in the west side where government offices lie.[7]

No wonder then, that in view of its glory and its present-day dense population, holy shrines, diversity of religions, culture and ethnic groups, and patterns of neighborhoods on both sides of the river, much thought was given to Baghdad in the war plan, and much care was devoted to handling its sensitive nature.

The planners had also remembered that a decade earlier, when the American troops were edging toward Baghdad in the 1991 Gulf War, the advance was aborted due to Saudi pressures and threats. Those presumed "allies" of the US could not afford to be seen to contribute, or even condone, the American occupation of the old capital of Islam. Their protests and threats forced America to withdraw; the advance could have saved another war and more casualties a decade later. This time, when the Americans realized that they could count no more on their "allies," they adopted a unilateral approach to the war plan, and focused all assaults toward the final objective: Baghdad. The capture of Baghdad was not only crucial to bringing about the end of Saddam's rule – an essential component of the war aims – but its capture was to be symbolic of the demise of the entire regime, and would allow the occupiers to overhaul the entire system that was based in Baghdad, eliminate the power base of the regime and take a firm grip on the city's power structure. That was why, from the outset of planning, and then at the outbreak of war, Baghdad came to be regarded as the major prize of the war.

The entire war operation had been predicated upon the assumption that Baghdad would be the target, and the forces which had been deployed in the field were directed and structured accordingly. The three divisions that advanced steadily on three parallel axes from Kuwait northward, were equipped to move rapidly through the Iraqi desert and reach the capital early on. The forces were instructed to circumvent the cities along the way, as they were only accessory to the main and real target. And to the extent that they lingered at Nasiriya, Najaf or Karbalah allowing themselves to become embroiled in low-level skirmishes and sieges, it was only when the Americans realized that they had to reinforce their rearguard in order to secure their long logistical lines extending back into Kuwait. Moreover, since according to the Command's expectations the real and costly battles would be pitched in and around Baghdad, they had every interest in reserving their energies for that purpose rather than being drained in smaller battles. The Americans had also planned for a northern invasion from the Turkish border that would have forced the Iraqis to split their forces and facilitate the conquest of Baghdad in a pincer move from the north and south simultaneously. As it turned out, since the northern front ended up *sans* Turkish support and dependent on the Kurds, emphasis had to be shifted to the southern troops, and therefore, together with the conquest of the southern cities they never relented on their advance north.

The American planners also understood that the fall of Baghdad would not only signal the end of the Saddam regime, which would necessarily bring down with it all pockets of resistance elsewhere; but as a moral and symbolic gesture, Iraqi soldiers would surrender, so demoralized would they be by the fall of legendary, and unbeatable in recent memory, Baghdad. Furthermore, being the hub of business, government, transportation and national life, no one could hope to master the rest of the country and its administration unless one had a full control of the capital beforehand. From day one of the war, with the idea of entering Baghdad seeming remote, reports of the approaching assault on the capital took center stage. The war began with the abortive bombing of the bunkers where Saddam and his family were suspected to be hiding, and the end of the war came with the toppling of Saddam's statue in the heart of Baghdad; an act seen, rehearsed and projected in slow motion ad nauseam, as if to compensate for the fact that Saddam himself remained at large. In the eyes of the occupiers, his humiliation in the heart of his conquered capital was to be the epitome of his demise, and so it proved.

From the initial stages of the war the newspaper headlines proclaimed "The Goal is Baghdad,"[8] a mantra repeated daily until Baghdad was captured and the tyrant's statue was toppled on 10 April at the end of the third week of the war. Even as American tanks were speeding through the desert 300 miles to the south, the Air Force was relentlessly knocking out strategic targets in and around Baghdad: command posts, leadership bunkers, missile and cannon batteries, military installations, government offices and TV and radio stations, all designed to weaken the Ba'ath grip on the city and to sow confusion and demoralize the troops and the fanatics who still supported Saddam. Specifically targeted were (1) Republican Guard units who defended the approaches to the capital, (2) the system of communications that might help them to coordinate attacks and request reinforcements, and (3) the anti-aircraft gunnery and missile systems that were barring the American pilots' way. The plan was to immobilize these elements, and disrupt Iraqi preparations for urban warfare when the Americans reached Baghdad. To this end, as early as 25 March the 11th Attack Helicopter Regiment began to launch attacks on a brigade of the Medina Republican Guard near Baghdad, after the Air Force hammered Iraqi radars and tried to eliminate surface-to-air missile launchers. The Iraqis defended themselves with significant numbers of irregulars armed with light weapons. The helicopters flew low over the ground to avoid radar screens, but that made them vulnerable to light arms, so much so that in one single attack, 32 Apaches were damaged in light-combat encounters, and one Apache was shot down.[9]

The two-man crew of the downed Apache was captured; military chiefs were so concerned that their advanced technology might fall into Iraqi hands that the next day two ATACMS (Advanced Target Acquisition Counterfire Missiles) destroyed the downed helicopter. The Apache attack had resulted in the destruction of just 15 armored vehicles, partly because of bad weather, but partly also because that was the first combat experience of the pilots, and tactics had to be adapted to the ground situation. In the coming days they would perform much better. At any rate, the American commanders were determined not to rush their way into the city, content to collect intelligence data before they pinpointed their strikes in the city so as to avoid unnecessary large-scale civilian casualties. The commanders also chose early on a strategy of infiltrating or thrusting at key centers of the city and overwhelming them (rather than fighting from house to house) with engineers preceding them to remove obstacles, followed by tanks guarded by infantry against grenades and anti-tank missiles. Apaches would be called in by spotters overhead to launch Hellfire missiles when necessary. General William Wallace, the Commander of V Corps who headed the ground operations, made it clear that by "forming joint combined arms teams that include the Air Force, Army aviation, light infantry, armored forces, engineers forces," he would be able to go after any specific target for any specific purpose.[10]

As the forces were edging toward Baghdad, there was concern that the Iraqi Command might, in despair, activate its non-conventional weapons against the invading troops. To limit the danger, it was decided that the attack on Baghdad would be led from two directions along both the Euphrates from the southwest and the Tigris from the southeast, to replace the idea of a coordinated attack on the capital from the north and the south. But Saddam Hussein, who had escaped the American bombing against his bunker with most of the leadership intact, resurfaced in Baghdad, and in a speech to his people he claimed that the Allies were "in real trouble."[11] Similarly, Tariq Aziz, the Deputy Prime Minister and Muhammad Saeed al-Sahaf, the Minister of Information (an Arab euphemism for the official propaganda machine), still argued that the war was going Iraq's way, mocking the Allies and promising them defeat and humiliation. It is difficult to know whether these men were indeed persuaded of their own delusions or were just attempting to slow down the pace of the collapse and allow themselves time to escape.

The American 3rd Division, after having swooped past Najaf and Karbalah, was heading toward the Medina Division of the Republican Guard in order to confront them head on. According to a war plan laid out by Tariq Aziz to foreign journalists, however, Iraqi troops would engage the invaders through irregulars. The leadership of the Party was convinced that in open battles, and against American air superiority, the elite Iraqi troops would be pulverized. The Iraqis thought that they could merge their troops into the general population, and begin to engage the Americans using guerilla warfare, forcing the US forces to leave through random attacks and explosions, and allowing the underground Iraqi Command to regain control of the country. This is a plausible explanation to the repeated American contention that they did not encounter the resistance they expected in the defense of Baghdad. The battles for Basra, Umm Qasr and Nasiriya, which the Allies had dismissed as "pockets of resistance," alerted the Iraqi Command that the Americans were not free to move, unrestrained by pace or terrain. For the Iraqi Command, the Iraqis would have to wage their battles by pursuing their presence within the enemy and in his rear and to inflict upon him maximum casualties. The Iraqi Command was hoping to instill in the hearts of their people the model of resistance of the southern cities, to use them as templates for the decisive Battle for Baghdad.[12]

The Iraqi al-Medina Republican Guard Division was only one of three divisions defending the approaches to Baghdad, but it was supposedly the toughest. It was dug in with state-of-the-art T-72 tanks facing south of the Iraqi capital, i. e. the direction of the three advancing American divisions. It was assumed by the Americans that the elite units would fight well because they were not recruited from conscripts but are volunteer units who receive bonuses for their loyalty and special training. These units, which had been founded by Saddam during the First Gulf War (1980–8), were also expected to distinguish themselves in battle during the Second Gulf War (1991), but after 38 days of air-strikes and artillery barrages, they elected to withdraw from Kuwait into the Iraqi hinterland. This time, the Americans calculated that since the Iraqis would be fighting on their home turf in Baghdad, they would be more valiant in battle though their weapons might have been compromised following 10 years of UN sanctions. There was even a possibility that as a last desperate measure, the Iraqis might resort to chemical or biological weapons. However, well before the Americans got to Baghdad, the air attacks took their toll both on the heavy weapons[13] of the Guards and on their will to fight. Nevertheless, the attacking forces took the positioning of the Guards very seriously and over-estimated the weight and validity of their reputation. The Americans perceived the Iraqi defenses as consisting of two formidable rings outside Baghdad: an outer ring 50 miles from the capital and another anchored to the outskirts of the city. In addition to Medina in the south, the Nida Division was positioned to the east and the Hammurabi to the west, while the Adnan, usually deployed north of the city, was advanced to Tikrit, Saddam's power base.[14]

Up against the Guard divisions was the 3rd Division, which made it north but stalled to wait for reinforcements, better intelligence, or for a strategy to attack the Guards and their double ring of defenses on the periphery of Baghdad.[15]

It did not occur to the war planners that, as in the previous Gulf War, the Guards or their command would elect to dissipate into the population and preserve their force, rather than squander it in a war of attrition against the superior American forces. Typically, each division of Guards would comprise 10,000 men, about 200 T-72 tanks, some 200 BMP-2 personnel carriers, 50 GH N-45 Howitzers with a range of 25 miles, and several units of anti-tank and anti-aircraft mobile gunnery.[16] Much of the Guards' military capacity was destroyed in the grinding air war, so one can only speculate on the Guards' actions had their fighting strength not been paralyzed. Motivation of the Guards is difficult to measure; in siege conditions, the besieged are often broken in the end. A more pertinent question is, why didn't the soldiers surrender to the Americans, knowing that they were much safer and better fed in American captivity than roaming the streets? Add to that the repetitive pattern of the waning of troops in Nasiriya, Najaf, Mosul and the subsequent ambushing of American troops by small squads of Iraqis, and you have perhaps the answer to one of the puzzling quandaries of the war.

While the Americans were knocking on Baghdad's door, the cumulative effects of the bombings were being felt. Those who hoped for Saddam's final elimination were taken aback every time he reappeared to make a statement. Despite this presence, Saddam had lost control of the state apparatus. Iraq, which was closest to a centralized, coercive and controlling Stalinist regime (along with North Korea), suddenly found itself without a government at all, with the citizens left to fend for themselves. Government offices had been reduced to ashes, senior officials were in hiding or on the run, and all services were inoperational. To the extent that Saddam retained a degree of intimidation and authority even as his regime was collapsing, years of tyranny meant that his people, unless absolutely assured that Saddam was gone for good, would not dare challenge him; second, the informal apparatuses of security and the Ba'ath continued to function somehow. The skies were full with smoke from burning fuel, very few people were still going to their shifts in the bombed government buildings, and apartment buildings were emptying with their tenants fleeing to relatives in the suburbs or in adjoining towns and villages.[17] Squads of Fedayeen, Party loyalists and other remnants of the security machinery were taking the law into their hands, since few formal militias or regular army were in sight. In this eerie atmosphere of a ghost town, where the only people to be seen were journalists and scavengers, this vibrant city was bracing itself for attack.

On 27 March two violent blasts killed 17 people and wounded dozens of others. Initial indications suggest a US bomb, by mistake or by design, but there are also rumors suggesting that Saddam's agents provocateurs were behind the blast. An Iraqi soldier, disguised in American uniform, was seized attempting to blow himself up in the middle of a crowd; it was clear that Saddam's soldiers were willing to massacre civilians and blame the Americans. Evidence pointed to a stray missile as responsible for the attack, much like the Amariya incident of 12 years earlier when an American projectile obliterated a bunker with 400 civilians inside. This latest attack gave rich material to Saddam's propaganda machine. Next, Iraqi Radio and Television buildings, on the west bank of the Tigris, as well as a nearby main telephone exchange, were also knocked out.[18] Nearby Saddam Tower, the tallest structure in Iraq at 700 ft, was also hit. Saddam

Tower had been hit by the Americans in 1991, but Saddam defiantly rebuilt it with his statue at its base. The platform supporting the statue featured a scattering of American missile fragments, and bronze likenesses of George Bush Snr. and Margaret Thatcher are embedded at the statue's feet. It seems that this time the Americans may have won the contest of re-building and re-hitting.[19]

The standard of living in the city receded further on 28 March: many telephone lines were damaged, with no one available to repair them. Within a week, American troops had come to within 50 miles of the city, poised to take it, in the meantime showering destruction and death upon its frightened inhabitants. While the Americans saw their camping on the outskirts of Baghdad as proof that the day of reckoning was near, the Iraqis boasted about their exploits harassing the invading troops and inflicting casualties on them. The Iraqis did not ask themselves what would happen when the Americans reached the city. Who would stop the American advance then? The Iraqi Minister of Defense, General Sultan Hashim Ahmed, who at that critical juncture briefed foreign correspondents about his troops' achievements and America's impending defeat, was either totally delusional or was never at the receiving end of accurate war reports from the field; both cases reflect the tradition of Arab war-reporting. For example, Arab war reports during the 1967 War, when their armies were lying in tatters, still boasted of their victories. The Americans, on the other hand, in order to convince the Baghdadis to collaborate with them, spread widely the news about the assistance and relief brought by the Allies to the people of Basra.[20]

In any case, the fact that the Allies had to fight their way north from town to town delayed the assault on Baghdad, even though the war effect on the capital was becoming more marked by the day. Instead of shaping up to attack the Medina Division, the 3rd Infantry was getting bogged down in battles around Najaf. Similarly, the Marine column which was trying to catch up with the right flank found themselves three days late in launching their attack on Baghdad.[21] On the last day of March Allied missiles struck a presidential compound on the Tigris River in central Baghdad, while other missiles and bombs rocked the southern limits of the city, hitting a Fedayeen training camp, an intelligence compound and a missile site. By 1 April it was estimated that the two Republican Guard divisions which defended southern Baghdad – al-Medina and Baghdad – had 50 percent of their fighting effectiveness wiped out by American bombardments, as was the fate of the other two divisions that came in as reinforcements – the Hammurabi and Nebuchadnezzar. Although the American Command confirmed that it would put in whatever it took in terms of casualties to fulfill its mission, it was very circumspect regarding the pace of the battle for Baghdad.[22]

On 2 April Army and Marine units crossed into the Red Zone, namely the outer perimeters of Baghdad where the great battle was expected to break out. It was decided that the attack would not be a dash into Baghdad, but a step-by-step advance that was to destroy first the remnants of the main units that were deployed in its defense, in the process gnawing at the periphery of the capital. Only once this phase was complete would the Americans take over dominant points within the city, and then the entire urban area on both sides of the Tigris. To try to persuade the Iraqis not to use chemical weapons, the American military broadcast radio warnings that any soldier who followed orders to use such weapons would be held accountable.[23]

On the outskirts of Baghdad the 1st Marine swung eastward on 1 April sending thousands of its troops to the southeastern city approaches, readying themselves for their push into the urban area. They reached the Tigris at the point where it dissects the city. The plan that was now taking shape, following the war of attrition against the Republican Guard, called for a two-pronged assault: The Third Infantry would attack from the southwest, while the Marines who had taken the swing eastward, were now positioned to attack around Highway 1. In the maze of villages and hamlets that shielded the capital from the south and the southeast, common people seemed to welcome the Americans. Official Iraqi propaganda tried to drive a wedge between the American invaders and the Iraqis, urging the crowds not to accept American food that "might be poisoned."[24]

As the American forces were pouring into Baghdad from two directions, their slogan, which reflected the overall strategy of the war, was rehearsed once again: Destroy Saddam's forces; avoid civilian casualties and damage to the infrastructure; provide relief. The American Command was still worried that the conquest could develop into a costly hand-to-hand battle, therefore it still prescribed caution and patience and planned to infiltrate special units into the city for both reconnaissance and ground attack purposes by commando raids and strikes against sensitive targets, in order to avoid protracted and costly urban warfare. For now, American bombers, using smart bombs and other heavy ordinance, were systematically destroying the Command and Control system of the Iraqi military, to sever the link between the supreme command and the field commanders.[25]

According to the American plan, the pounded Republican Guard divisions were to be brought to the brink of annihilation, to allow a hole in their front line for Allied troops to penetrate through. Intelligence tipped that the Guards had been ordered by their Command to withdraw to the inner perimeter of the city, in order to consolidate the rest of their forces for their last stand. But when the Americans intercepted those orders, they decided to move in swiftly and trap two Guard divisions before they had had the chance to retreat to their new defensive positions and to finish them off. A new tactical choice presented itself, as a consequence, to the American Command: either (1) push ahead to Baghdad via the defeated and scattered Guard divisions before they had time to reorganize; (2) destroy first the other Guard divisions on the flanks of the advancing Americans lest they counter-attacked and stymied the American advance; or (3) simply wait until the long-awaited and fresh 4th Infantry Division could be added to the existing troops to launch the final assault. That last option was no longer valid; while the ships were still unloading in Kuwait the troops and equipment of the 21,000 man newly-arrived division, the momentum to take Baghdad became unstoppable and irreversible. At that point, however, fears still reigned in the American Command, based on the sobering experiences of Basra and Nasiriya, that the combination of irregulars, the Iraqi Special Forces and the rest of the Republican Guard might turn Baghdad into an awesome battlefield that would necessitate the presence of the additional infantry division.[26]

And yet, as the Marines were pouring over the Tigris on their way to the "big bang," they were wondering where those famous and awesome Republican Guards had gone to. For, except for small skirmishes, the Guards were nowhere to be seen; one Marine captain even boasted: "It is the same thing everywhere; the Iraqis fire a few shots, we train our guns on them, and it's over in five minutes." Were these the legendary Guards that were so feared and necessitated pushing forward to the front the 4th Infantry Division to overcome the expected resistance? There was a dissonance between the battle that everyone anticipated in the fight for Baghdad, and this long series of skirmishes, which was not qualitatively different from the other encounters in Nasiriya, Basra or Karbalah, where the Guards had not been involved. Was then the Republican Guard fighting ability just another myth cultivated by Saddam? Or were the American air-strikes so devastating that those elite units were destroyed even before they engaged in serious combat? Or did Saddam's forces choose to avoid combat and spare their forces? For when? What were they made for if not to stand up and fight in the crucial moments presaging the fall of the capital of the Ba'ath regime and Islam's history? As the Americans were advancing evidence of fighting was widespread: ammunition depots blown up, damage to buildings, bullet-riddled cars, burnt-out tanks and armored carriers and countless numbers of dead bodies of Iraqi soldiers lying around, some amassed in piles under a scorching sun.[27]

As the Marines were heading toward what they still thought would be a difficult showdown with the Nida Republican Guard Division southeast of Baghdad, they encountered little resistance when they took over the bridge over the Tigris which channeled them to Baghdad. They also seized the bridgeheads which allowed them to add pontoons to ferry the thousands of vehicles across. Appropriately, that surreal scene of a massive American advance and a crumbling Iraqi defense was described by an embedded American reporter as "the lack of fighting, broken only by short bursts of shooting." Iraqi soldiers, presumably not Guards, were walking up and down the roads waving white banners for surrender. Civilians who suffered under Saddam were not enthusiastic about an American occupation either, all they wanted was for the Americans to leave Iraq as soon as it had been liberated from Saddam.[28]

Now it seemed that most of the Guards were concentrated in the heart of Baghdad, once the Baghdad Division was pulled up northward from Kut due to the American advance, and the Adnan and Nebuchadnezzar Divisions were withdrawn southward from the Kurdish region once it became evident that the US could not deploy substantial forces from Turkish territory. In addition, there was the Special Republican Guard, the only unit Saddam had originally entrusted with the defense of the capital, while the other Republican Guard divisions were bottled up within the besieged city. It remained to be seen whether, and to what extent, these divisions would be able to join forces with all the retreating troops to form a coherent line of defense and a coordinated defense system.[29]

On 4 April elements of the 3rd Infantry took partial control of Saddam International Airport southwest of Baghdad. Once again, the expected harsh resistance was not there. The vanguard of the Marines along Highway 6 in the southeast, likewise, were literally cruising into Baghdad, with only hordes of disgruntled, disorientated and some visibly jubilant civilians streaming out of the city southward, apparently also in anticipation of the coming battle. Unlike the reserved reception the Americans got in the southern cities of Iraq (which may be attributed to the uncertain fate of Saddam's regime at that point, as well as the Shi'ite hostility to the US), now everyone knew that the end of the tyrant was fast approaching and people felt free to express their anger and relief.[30] Sophisticated execution of the operation continued apace: a four-engine turboprop MC-130 Combat Transport landed on the highway between Karbalah and Baghdad prior to midnight, Thursday 3 April. It unloaded two armed Humvees, communications and a team of Special Operations to help win the battle for Baghdad from within. They were to move covertly on foot or in vehicle, to report on movements of Iraqi forces, to connect with and coordinate between Iraqi opposition groups, direct fire to specified targets, neutralize Ba'ath officials and Fedayeen guerillas and to assist in searching, locating and capturing Iraqi leaders.[31]

Having taken over the airport and secured its runways in the west, and having encountered no serious resistance in the East, the 3rd Infantry and the Marines now felt free to rush into Baghdad and "go as far as they could." However, in the suburb of Aziziya, the Marines encountered a tough element of the Nida Guard with dug-in tanks deployed in a defensive pattern. The Air Force was called in to undermine the Iraqi positions, which were either wiped out or damaged. In the process many civilians were killed, with some claiming they were avoidable deaths. Discarded military uniforms were left on the roadside, a sign that Iraqi soldiers had run away and melted into the civilian population. Some soldiers were captured by the

Marines and put in POW camps.[32] The 3rd was advancing faster than the Marines, and it reached the outskirts of urban Baghdad on 4 April while the eastern prong of the move was still making its way along the Tigris of which the 1st Marine had control. All the while Information Minister al-Sahaf was still assuring the foreign reporters that the Americans were failing and remained like a "snake in the desert."[33]

As he was taking advantage of his last opportunity to boast, the American forces were bent on studying the city streets, the various ethnic and religious groups in the city and dealing with the "left-behinds," – isolated pockets of Iraqi troops who might still pose a threat to American supply lines. The takeover of Saddam International Airport had brought the American Command considerably closer to the completion of its mission. As a presage to the coming end of the tyrant, it was decided to re-baptize the new acquisition, Baghdad International Airport.[34]

The wide vistas of the Iraqi desert that became familiar sights for the Americans over two weeks of fighting, with cities and towns in the fertile valleys adjoining the large two rivers, now narrowed down into one river valley. This valley led into a city densely built-up on both banks of the Tigris, housing a variety of ethnic and religious groups, military installations, palaces of untold wealth and shacks of extreme poverty: Baghdad. Combat here would have to be different – there were no longer wide plains to sweep and conquer, no military installations to assault and subjugate. Nor were there the open spaces vulnerable to intense air assaults. The density of the population allowed for the defenders to hide among innocent civilians and take shelter among them. Now the names of streets and contours of neighborhoods, major buildings and main road junctions were the territorial details the troops needed to know. They learned that Baghdad, which housed close to 25 percent of the total population of Iraq, was divided into nine major neighborhoods, and the modalities of fighting in each would depend on: the nature of the population; the extent of its welcoming or resisting the Americans; what sorts of weapons were deployed or stored there; proximity to major religious and humanitarian institutions; and the fortunes of the war itself when it came to hand-to-hand combat. That meant that no blanket bombing was possible, and even surgical bombings had to be careful not to harm civilians. Especially important was that civilian relief on a massive scale had to be prepared and dispensed as hostilities began.

The nine neighborhoods of the city revolve around Liberation Square at the heart of the Old City, the historical pride of Baghdad and of the Arab and Islamic worlds, which lay mainly east of the Tigris. The main financial district and the old bazaar, as well as 10-story buildings, are lined up on both sides of the main streets. Immediately to the northeast of the Old City, across the Army Canal, lies the very densely populated Shi'ite slum, Saddam City, where about one-third of the city dwellers live in a congested maze of alleys and concrete buildings. Immediately to the north of the Old City and adjoining Saddam City's western limits is Waziriya, a middle-class Shi'ite neighborhood. Northwest of there, on the west side of the Tigris, is Kazimiya, another slightly older, Shi'ite middle-class area. At its heart the Kazimiya Mosque, one of the most important in Shi'ite Islam, being the burial grounds of Musa al-Kazim and Muhammad al-Taqi, the Seventh and Ninth Imams (hence it is also known as the Kazimayn – the two Kazims). Further south, but still west of the Tigris, is the Tashri/Karadat Maryam Quarter, where the downtown government offices and vast monuments are concentrated. The National Assembly and ministries as well as many of the presidential palaces are located there, with a wide array of tunnels and bunkers to shelter the leadership. Among the objectives targeted for American bombings were the Ministries of Information, Industry and Planning, the State TV and Radio buildings, the Ba'ath HQ, the Council of Ministers and various presidential facilities.[35]

Further west are the new upscale, less dense suburbs of Mansur, Ma'mun, Yarmuk and Amariya, where professionals and upper-level Ba'ath officials made their homes. What used to be the horse-racing track was replaced by the Grand Mosque, ominously located not far from the Intelligence Service HQ. At the edge of Amariya are the Abu Ghraib Presidential Palace, one of Saddam's largest, as well as the runways of the previously-named Saddam International Airport. In the southern part of the city, in the peninsula delineated by the great loop of the Tigris, lay the Karada suburb, an affluent and fashionable residential area, replete with cafés, shops and restaurants, which borders with Wahda to the east, the favorite area of foreign embassies and the National Theater on Fatah Square. To the southeast, and parallel to Saddam Airport in the southwest, lies the major Rashid Military Airport.[36]

The coalition air campaign, which was continuously waged upon Baghdad since Day One, had to differentiate between those various neighborhoods. If, for example, bunkers of the leadership, presidential palaces, military bases, government buildings and communications centers were attacked, the residential areas, certainly those inhabited by Shi'ites whom the Americans didn't wish to antagonize, were largely spared. Civilian casualties were usually as a result of stray bombs or because of their proximity to major Allied targets. Where major religious sites were concerned, especially the Shi'ite shrines in Kazimayn, great care was taken to avoid their destruction, even at times when it was known that important military or government targets lay in their vicinity.

It was that policy of selective and careful targeting that allowed citizens to carry on their daily life in Baghdad while bombs were falling on government buildings. A reporter noticed that "life under the bombing has continued to roll forward with an everyday nonchalance that, in its own way, has been as hard to adjust to as the bombing." People went about their business selling expensive luxury items to the rich, shopping in the markets, the bazaars and the trendy shops, washing their cars, or gazing at the blazing presidential palaces that were being bombed. In other words, though the American raids were devastating to the machinery of the ruler, and in the long-term would unhinge the centers of power, they were not perceived by individuals throughout the city as directly threatening to one's daily routine. The American take over of the airport and the Abu Ghraib Junction that leads west to the Jordanian border, a move that completed the encirclement of Baghdad from the west and the south, did not seem to affect the lives of its residents, especially those on the east bank of the Tigris furthest from the heavily-bombed downtown area. The fact that no blanket-bombings were inflicted on the city seemed to reassure people that they would be safe. By 4 April after almost three weeks of intensive air-strikes, only 250 civilians had been killed in Baghdad, and less than 2,000 injured (across the whole of Iraq, the numbers stood at 700 dead and 5,000 wounded). This is in itself an indication of the great care taken by the planners over civilian casualties, stray projectiles and predicted collateral damage. For example, a 48-hour warning ahead of the bombing of the Ministry of Information gave its occupants time to flee; the rest was done by using PGMs (Precision Guided Missiles), so accurate it was akin to using a sniper rifle.[37]

The overall American strategy had been to cut Baghdad off from the countryside, so that in General Myers' words it becomes "almost irrelevant." The idea was that the fewer civilian casualties among its defenders, the greater the chances of large-scale surrenders among the population, which would render street fighting unnecessary. On the other hand, in an urban setting it is easier for the defenders, who know the terrain well and can operate among a friendly population, to harass invading troops. Guerilla warfare can be carried out with few resources against a better-equipped army. Before the invasion began, Tariq Aziz, when asked how his troops could stop the Americans without the swamps and the jungles that the Vietnamese had, retorted: "Let our cities be our swamps and our buildings be our jungles." Unlike other cities in the south, however, that were avoided in order to keep pushing northward, and unlike the swathes of unimportant jungle and swamps that cost America in Vietnam, Baghdad was the very target of war.[38]

Hence America could pool all its resources into that one major battle. In a briefing at the Pentagon, Defense Secretary Donald Rumsfeld made the point that America was a protector of civilians in Baghdad, not an enemy: "While coalition forces have taken extraordinary measures to protect innocent civilians in this war, Saddam Hussein has sent death squads to massacre innocent Iraqi Muslims. Saddam has killed more Muslims than perhaps any living person on earth."[39]

The relative ease with which the airport was taken without any fierce gun battles, foreshadowed the rest of the battle of Baghdad. The Iraqi response to the assault of the First Brigade of the 3rd Infantry was to send three T-72 tanks from Baghdad's center to repulse them, but two of them were destroyed by shoulder-fired Javelin missiles. Aircraft destroyed another dozen armored vehicles northwest of the airport, while other planes hit other targets within the city perimeter. Fifty Iraqis, some soldiers and some airport employees, were captured. Within hours, the engineers were at work clearing the runways and reviewing the airport installations, including the control tower, hangars, six jet-liners belonging to Iraqi Airlines and terminal buildings which escaped largely unscathed. Caches of weapons were discovered in bunkers and depots, and blown up.[40]

At the other end of Baghdad the Marines of the 1st Marine were pouring in their thousands into the southeast reaches of the city, firing artillery for cover as they spread in a broad arc to the east and thence to the northeast, so as to surround the city on three sides. The Americans believed that after the backbone of the Guards had been systematically pulverized by air and artillery attacks, individual fighters simply retreated into the civilian population. Suddenly, all the talk about waiting the Guards out by way of a siege until the reinforcements of the 4th Infantry arrived from Kuwait, were reversed as a new strategy was adopted of keeping moving, exploiting "windows of opportunity." A more sophisticated and fine-tuned mode of gradual and cautious advance was skillfully adopted.[41]

Marines also ran into foreigners who had volunteered to fight for Saddam; they shot suspected "suicide bombers" ready to blow themselves up with the advancing American troops. Along with the burnt carcasses of Iraqi vehicles, civilian and military, one could see uniforms that deserters had stripped and left behind, and smoke billowing over the remnants of the bombed and shelled Iraqi positions, which became no more than holes in the ground. Apparently in this fashion the Medina and Nida Republican Guard had been decimated early on. Cluster bombs descended on the withdrawing Iraqis, also hitting civilians. So much so that the entry of the Marines into the city was a pretty "bloodless affair," as one reporter had it.[42]

It gradually transpired that the American assumption was correct that, under the weight of continuous bombing and shelling, the defending Iraqi units would be so depleted of equipment and ammunition that they would crumble. In which case Special Forces from inside the city and Marines from the outside would perform a clean-up operation. Saddam's Special Republican Guard, reinforced by foreign Arab volunteers from Egypt and Jordan, would be patrolling the streets, trying to assert their control, and convincing the common people that Saddam was still in charge. While 3rd Infantry and 101st Airborne were pitched on the southwest, with much of the 101st still policing Karbalah and Najaf, there remained relatively little strength in the available one-and-a-half divisions in the south, and the less-than-one 1st Marine Division in the southeast, to deliver the *coup de grâce* to a once proud and rebellious capital city that was now frightened, humiliated and on the brink.[43]

A measure of the newfound American confidence that the battle of Baghdad was drawing to its end were the speculations about the "day after," the pressing questions by reporters and the media in general about the future government in Iraq, and the plans for reconstruction that began to take shape.[44] The focus on Baghdad was somewhat interrupted for a time when a suicide bomber killed three American Special Operations troops about 120 miles northwest of the capital near the Haditha Dam on the Euphrates. The dam had been captured to prevent Iraqi forces from blowing it up and flooding the American advance toward Baghdad along the Euphrates Valley. The suicide bomber, a pregnant woman, approached the roadblock in her vehicle. When the soldiers went to question her credentials, she blew herself up. She and her fellow female Islamikaze ("suicide bomber") were later glorified in the Arabic press in much the way Palestinian women and children "suicide bombers" were posthumously put on the pedestal and presented as models of self-sacrifice throughout the Arab and Islamic worlds. The Haditha Dam incident (4 April), just as American troops were penetrating the city of Baghdad, was feared could become the precedent for Iraqi or foreign lone Islamikaze attackers – one of the very few arrows left, in addition to WMD, in the Iraqi quiver, especially after senior Iraqi officials hinted at such acts.[45]

On 5 April the forward American forces sent a battalion of 60 tanks and other armored vehicles into the city from the south in a lightning raid, killing an estimated 1,000 Iraqis in the process. Many civilians were caught in the cross fire, though the anticipated mass massacre did not occur. The 64th Armored Regiment of the 3rd Infantry's Second Brigade returned to its base in south Baghdad from its raid to the center through the Karada suburb via a route that avoided the densely populated areas and was clear of hostiles. As Iraqi leaders still enjoyed some degree of control, and enjoined their people to fight the Americans and harass them, all the while denying coalition announcements of advances into Baghdad, one could detect in their tones indications that they no longer believed their own propaganda. The raid had proved that the Americans could move at will through Baghdad whenever they wished, until they established a firm and permanent foothold in the heart of the city. Even after the swift retreat of the American raiding unit, Special Forces remained within Baghdad to enhance targeting information and intelligence on the whereabouts of the hiding leaders.[46]

The massive destruction of Iraqi tanks and armored vehicles, and the killing of hundreds of Iraqi soldiers, had thrown the remaining defenders off balance, making the American task of taking the city over much more tangible.[47] This was confirmed by al-Sahaf, who called upon all the people in Baghdad to fulfill their duty and use their weapons, claiming that those who did not would be "cursed." High prizes were promised to any Iraqi who destroyed an American tank or other item of heavy equipment, and instructions were issued publicly to Iraqi soldiers who lost contact with their units to join any others they could find. These are definitely not instructions conveyed to a winning army.[48]

On 7 April Iraqi mortar fire was directed at an American armor unit that had made a parking lot of Saddam's Republican Palace. When an M1 Abrams tank can position itself under the portico of the palace, while soldiers moved around the ornate rooms and gilded baths and marveled at the luxurious balustrades, that was the best possible sign that Saddam's reign was coming to its end. His humiliation before his subjects, who were watching with disbelief the descent of their dictator to his lowest ebb, also meant the humiliation of Baghdad, of Iraq, of Iraqis, whatever their opinion of their demoted absolute ruler, who was well on his way to demise. The Abu Ghraib or Fao Palace, located at the edge of Saddam International Airport, probably with safety and escape in mind, was now also firmly in American hands. Snipers and Syrian "volunteers" who guarded it were captured (though one of them tried to hide in a refrigerator).

Simultaneously, a squad of the Special Operations Forces attacked the Ministry of Information building in a raid geared to undermine the last bastion of Saddam's propaganda machine. It was from there that al-Sahaf conducted his relentless campaigns of denial and disinformation. In one particularly surreal moment, as an American column of 100 armored vehicles rolled across the capital parade grounds, under the mammoth gate made by the exact replicas of Saddam's robust hands holding two huge crossing sabers, al-Sahaf was assuring foreign correspondents at the Palestine Hotel that Americans were being massacred and defeated at the gates of the city, and that "the Infidels were committing suicide by the hundreds at the gates of Baghdad."[49]

American forces also surrounded another landmark in Baghdad, the Rashid Hotel, whose basements were said to be packed with a communications and command center linked by tunnels to the Foreign Ministry and Intelligence building. Though that building was considered a highly strategic spot, even a potential hideout for Saddam, it was removed from the list of targets because of the many foreign reporters, visiting dignitaries and aid groups that were headquartered there. A commando operation was necessary to seize the building and its treasures without inflicting too many casualties on foreign onlookers, though they had been warned to evacuate Baghdad before the start of the war. The Army and Marines were now advancing on many fronts, shooting their way through the streets and razing buildings used by snipers. Many civilians were caught in the gunfire, either when trying to find shelter amidst the chaos, running away in total confusion and disorientation, or ignoring the warning shots that the advancing troops fired over their heads. Leaflets that had been distributed and appealed to them to remain indoors had not been heeded. In any case, the battle for Baghdad was on.[50]

After the collapse of the Iraqi elite units, even the Special Republican Guard, which had been kept in Baghdad to protect the leadership, was in an advanced state of dissolution. The Special Security Organization, a ruthless paramilitary force responsible for enforcing the government's rule, was also disintegrating. Last-ditch efforts by the leadership to retain some sort of command structure were hampered by the utter destruction of the communications and command centers by precision bombings and shellings since the onset of the war. The battle of Baghdad, which never took the shape of a well-conceived and integrated operation but occurred as a series of scattered, opportunistic raids, was coming to an end for Saddam. The question vexing the American command was: where was Saddam? Without confirmation of his death, his shadow would linger on and possibly undermine the plans for reconstruction. Taking advantage of the general mood, the American troops raided the camp of Salman Pak, south of Baghdad, long suspected as the hub of Iraq's development of unconventional weapons, and a training ground for international terrorism. But WMDs or "smoking guns" have not yet been found.[51]

Emboldened by their successes, thousands of American troops were now penetrating deep into Baghdad. They liberated prisoners who were being interrogated and tortured in city prisons, shook hands with citizens, distributed sweets to children and helped distribute food and relief in the streets. In the Shi'ite neighborhoods of east Baghdad, people were elated to see Saddam removed but they were also skeptical of the Americans' intentions and of their long-term plans in Iraq. The Marines were already on their way for the final push to clear the center of the city from the last pockets of resistance, possibly to link-up with the Army troops coming from the west and the southwest. The Americans were cognizant, and issued orders to the troops accordingly, that they had to minimize civilian casualties if they wanted collaboration from the population after conquest was completed.[52]

Some collateral damage was inevitable: in a heavy bombing of a bunker suspected of sheltering Saddam, 14 civilians in the adjoining buildings were killed. The American advance proceeded through street battles, using tanks and armored vehicles, moving and fighting carefully and slowly, contrary to the earlier vision evinced by the American military that use of armor would be avoided. A foothold on Saddam's main presidential palace on the Tigris soon grew into a beachhead of several square miles, and from there expanded to other areas of the city. The streets looked deserted, except for wild dogs running up and down aimlessly, and winds sweeping noisily through the streets like the echo of a ghost. Only hospitals were beehives of activity, as cars of all sorts rushed the many patients and wounded to the emergency rooms. A lone A-10 Warthog in the sky dived repeatedly, busting Iraqi tanks. Black smoke billowed from the burning fuel that the Iraqis had set ablaze to hamper the Americans. Another lone A-10 was shot down by an Iraqi missile over the international airport. On the eastern side of the city, Marines supported by Apaches seized the al-Rashid military base some three miles from the Republican Palace to the west.[53]

As American troops were also advancing to the north of Baghdad, this enabled the attackers to develop a pincer movement that would give them control on both sides of the Tigris in central Baghdad, much sooner and at a much lower cost to both the troops and the civilian population, than the original plan called for. The fall of the city center in American hands three weeks after the war was launched would officially signal the defeat of Saddam and lead the Pentagon to announce the end of main combat operations in the war. The Americans also now controlled the four main bridges on the Tigris which connected the Government offices in the west and the business and residential areas east of the river, where most of the city's population lived (mostly Shi'ites lived here). Reports from the hospitals confirmed that in the battle for the control of the Government quarter in the west alone, there had been some 300 civilian casualties with about 10 percent of this number, or around 30, dead. The Al-Sa'ah restaurant, on Ramadan St 14 on the West Side, said to be the favorite of the Iraqi elite, was destroyed in the bombings, leaving the crowds and American intelligence guessing who might have been there when it crumbled and buried its customers. Apparently the only road still open for escape was the northeastern one toward the Iranian border. Toward the end of 9 April two American fighter bombers launched their missiles against a high-rise east of the Tigris which had snipers perched on its rooftop. That was the Board of Sports and Youth building, the stronghold of Uday Hussein, Saddam's older son. Uday had abused his position of power to torture anyone who dared criticize or otherwise antagonize him (such as the Iraqi national soccer team, whose players had their feet lashed if they dared lose a game).[54]

The plan for the final assault on the city, which was well-thought out, consisted of three large task forces from the 3rd Infantry which would attack the city from three directions. The Second Brigade, having punched its way through to the city center the night before, stayed there, instead of fighting its way back and forth, using the Saddam Government Center as its base to strike out at the remaining Iraqi troops. The Third Brigade had maneuvered meanwhile around the north of the city and was driving south. And the First Brigade was attacking from another direction. Parallel to this large-scale but precise maneuver, the Marines were proceeding from the east while the Special Operations forces were already acting from within the city. This combination of conventional, air force, Marines and Special Forces had been experimented in Afghanistan and then in the southern cities of Iraq, notably Nasiriya, Najaf and Karbalah, to unhinge the enemy and throw him off balance, and it worked again in Baghdad. Limited intelligence on buildings, organizations and enemy deployment, and the very real risk of friendly fire at a time when so many forces were converging on the city center from all sides, presented the American fighters with some immediate challenges. Add to that the risks of Fedayeen and Islamikaze bombers and one understands why it was necessary to divide the city into sectors, to identify which of them had fallen to American control and which were still under enemy grip. Contrary to the initial expectation of the Americans that their advance would be cautious and slow, they now capitalized on their rapid success and administered a multi-arm, multi-dimensional, swift and mighty punishment to the Iraqis. The Americans wanted a quick and decisive strike and they got it: after three days of fighting Baghdad lay at their feet, vanquished and humiliated.[55]

The troops of the 101st Airborne were not idle either. One battalion from their ranks joined the 1st Brigade of the 3rd Infantry while it was fighting its way through the capital, and assaulted the fortified HQ of the Special Republican Guard on Black Hill, not far from Saddam (now Baghdad) International Airport, turning the structure into carcasses and debris and its defenders into heinously dismembered bodies.[56]

Since there was no one to surrender or call the war off, Baghdad did not officially "fall," but the day of 9 April when the Americans entered unopposed into the heart of Baghdad with Iraqis cheering, was essentially the day Baghdad fell. There was no sign of any government or authority in the city at all. The ordinary civilians did not mind. They took to the streets, cheering, their celebrations veering between jubilation and rage. After a column of American armored vehicles paraded into the city without any resistance, a crowd gathered at the foot of an enormous statue of Saddam, and with the help on an American vehicle, they pulled it to the ground, beat it with their sandals victoriously and danced on it. That early celebration, which shocked some and elated others throughout the world, became the symbol of the war aims and of the war débâcle. It was still early days because skirmishes would continue in the alleys along the Tigris and forces loyal to Saddam would harass the invading troops. But nothing could hide the comprehensive defeat suffered by the Iraqis, the most devastating rout any Arab army had experienced in modern times since the 1967 Six Day War. "There is no Government left!" exclaimed General Buford Blount, the commander of the 3rd Infantry, at the sight of that 20-ft statue being dragged and beaten on the ground.[57] That was the end of the battle for Baghdad, and the beginning of other concerns.

After the Fall of Baghdad

No sooner had the celebrations quieted down than the concerns about paci-fying the city and completing the liberation of all Iraq jumped to the forefront of American concerns. In Baghdad, the chaos was so total that the first question was: how does one restore order before beginning to reflect upon the successor government to Saddam. Jay Garner, a former American general who had served during the previous Gulf War as the coordinator of Kurdish affairs in northern Iraq, was now considered as the man best suited to constructing the new administration and putting the country back on its feet. But in the meantime more pressing issues were on the agenda of the American military, who had to administer the city until a new permanent government could move in. While those connected with the Ba'ath regime were either trying to dissolve into the populace or run away to locations where they could live in anonymity, those who opposed the regime and were its victims came forward as alternative prospective leaders, or simply tried to eke out a living feeding their families amid the prevailing chaos and insecurity. The state of shock at the speed with which the situation had been reversed, and the celebrations which gave vent to popular joviality over the change, soon ran their course and it was now necessary to go back to routine. But no return to routine was possible as long as there was no security in the streets and no authority was in sight.

The most threatening danger to the rule of law was the spontaneous wave of looting that erupted in Baghdad, far beyond anything the war planners had ever imagined or predicted. All public institutions of the previous regime immediately became free prey for all. An irresistible wave of looting swept across the entire Baghdad community. In wars, tradition dictates that the victors may collect their booty from their vanquished enemy, as part of the price the latter is made to pay. In Baghdad, the horrendous and unstoppable orgy of thievery and robbery, was exercised against their own country, their own institutions and to the detriment of common interest and the public. The only plausible explanation for what, in effect, amounts to self-looting, is that Saddam's regime was so hated and the people so massively and desperately suffered under him, that it must have seemed almost "natural" and "vengeful," to take from the tyrant and his cronies what they had illicitly stolen from the people. All those hordes of looters believed the regime owed them a debt for its cruelty, corruption and exploitation. They did not feel that they were stealing *per se*. The looters were persuaded that they were re-appropriating what was duly theirs. At any rate, the systematic frenzy of looting that embraced Baghdad during the first week of the coalition takeover stripped all government offices, party HQ, military installations and presidential palaces as well as hospi-tals, laboratories, schools, even museums; all were stripped bare, erasing their ability to function under the new administration.

When, on the day Baghdad fell, an Abrams tank with the Marines breached the wall surrounding the compound of the Directorate of General Security (the HQ of the national secret police), they encountered an other-worldly scene. Looters were already hard at work, like a cloud of locusts, descending on anything that was not fastened down and taking it away. Hundreds of men were scampering about and literally cleaning up the HQ. Whether the lifted items were useful or not didn't matter; it seemed that what mattered was the self-appropriation of public property to every individual looter: police cars, horses, foam mattresses, desks, typewriters, chairs, office supplies, air conditioners or parts thereof, blades of a disassembled ceiling fan, complete fans, tires, refrigerators, sofas and anything that could be carried away by hand, in cars (themselves often stolen), or wheeled away on office chairs. It resembled a huge popular celebration that no one dared to interrupt, and whose progress lasted but a few days until there was nothing more to loot. Entire families pulled up in their cars and went on the rampage. Often the car itself was stolen from some collapsing institution. Others enlisted trucks and pick-ups and loaded them with various items while stunned American soldiers looked on. As part of that huge spontaneous celebration money bills featuring Saddam's face were ripped up, a further example of rage and relief. The same scenes occurred in practically all public offices. Some government offices were set ablaze after the looting, while the looters returned home, trophy in hand, a sign of their participation in the final stages of the dumping and obliterating of Saddam's trappings of rule and power.[58]

American participation in the looting, apart from being passive observers, consisted of seizing large quantities of documents for intelligence purposes. Those were needed not only to provide answers about the whereabouts of Saddam and his family, but mainly to locate the famous "smoking gun" – the Iraqi weapons of mass destruction which were the ultimate trigger of the war itself. Research teams from the CIA and other agencies scoured government, financial, educational and research institutions searching for evidence. Intelligence officials estimated that the rapid collapse of the Government in Baghdad was the fruition of rumors that Saddam had been killed. Others saw in the rapid withdrawal of Saddam's elite forces and their merger into the population part of a design to keep as many of them intact to effect a later comeback, as with the surprise return of Napoleon from Elba. Cautious analysts evoked the frustrating experience of Afghanistan and Pakistan where protracted efforts to locate Osama bin Laden failed, and counseled patience and a long-haul effort to find Saddam. The fact that Saddam and his cronies had prepared a sophisticated network of tunnels and bunkers for long-term survival meant that the search for them may be drawn-out and laborious. Many Iraqi citizens approached the American military and offered information which might lead intelligence officials to answer some of the quandaries regarding

Saddam's disappearance and his arsenal of unconventional weapons. The Pentagon also made efforts to lure former Iraqi officials into collaborating with the Americans, promising significant rewards.[59]

Scenes in the streets of Baghdad also featured the overflowing of emotions, reflections on the future, bewilderment at the almost miraculous removal of Saddam, who had become a fixture in the lives of the over-40s for the past 30 years. There was disbelief at how so revolutionary an act could occur in such a short span of time. A man, tears streaming down his face, was yelling in the streets: "Touch me, tell me this is true, tell me the nightmare is over!" When Baghdad awoke to the reality that the Americans had taken over the city, all the compressed fear that had been ingrained in their souls for so many years suddenly evaporated. All the expressions of anger, frustration, protest and criticism that had been suppressed suddenly erupted into the open in an almost hysterical fashion. Clusters of Iraqis of all ages and from all walks of life were converging on foreigners and American troops, shouting at the top of their voices blessings for Bush and America and curses on Saddam. On the western side of the Tigris, dominated by Sunnites and government offices, the mood was divided. In some neighborhoods of the northwestern part of the city, angry Fedayeen were still freely roaming; people voiced their anger and contempt for the Americans. These mixed manifestations of pro- and anti-American attitudes reflected a situation where, instead of overall American control with pockets of resistance scattered about, Baghdad had American pockets of control surrounded by a hostile and suspicious environment. The general sense of control that the Americans exhibited was generated by their feeling that they had the upper hand, and not because of their omnipresence in the city that was limited by their thinly spread troops.[60]

The predominant mood, nonetheless, in most of the city suburbs, was one of celebration and joy. Citizens gave flowers to the American troops, hugging and kissing them and riding their armored vehicles in an élan of gratitude and joy. Others beat statues of Saddam in fits of disgust and vengeance. Some people, especially the veterans of previous uprisings, were already asking what would happen the day after the cheers and the jubilation. For all the feasts and celebrations, the fate of Saddam remained a mystery. Rumors circulated about his whereabouts on a daily basis. Others stated that any Iraqi government, with or without Saddam, would be preferable to American rule. And there was still the issue of the unexpected evaporation of those Guard and Special Guard units who were supposed to make the capital impervious to invaders. What had happened to them? The highways in Baghdad, littered with abandoned Iraqi tanks and other vehicles, only told part of the story. Where were all the thousands of troops that had attended to them? An indication of the answer lay in the many uniforms and boots strewn near abandoned tanks, and the deserted security offices, police stations and Ba'ath Party facilities. Deserted buildings had made significant portions of Baghdad easy to conquer, but these abandoned posts and weapons left behind them a series of sinister questions.[61]

In southeastern Baghdad the same question marks arose. The 1st Marine awoke on the morning the capital fell with a plan to fan out through the city and capture the remaining Iraqi positions. It was supposed to be a costly and bloody operation. As their first battalion attacked before dawn, through the urban neighborhoods of the south, they found nothing and they encountered nobody. By noon the Marines had rolled throughout the marked territory without firing a shot. Instead they found the UN compound being looted, trashed and stripped bare. Hundreds of Iraqis descended on it, ripping computers off the walls and stalls and loading all appliances on their trucks before they made off with their booty. The colonel of 1st Marine, having found no one to fight against, ordered his men to stop the frenzy of looting. Outside the compound another endless convoy of looters were pushing supermarket carts full of goods they could still find on the shelves. In other parts of the city the Marines made attempts to stop the looting, but to no avail. They could not understand how a few hours earlier they were shot at by the Iraqis, yet now they were greeted by liberated civilians expressing their thanks as they carried away their booty.[62] Were some of these "civilians" secretly soldiers hiding from the Marines? Why had a supposedly resilient enemy disappeared off the face of the earth?

The most recent answer, which became conventional wisdom in Pentagon circles, was that the Iraqis could not stand the relentless air attacks, precise bombings and other ground artillery devastations. According to this concept, the ground battles were only the final phase of the inevitable vanishing of Iraq as a fighting force. This is certainly plausible as providing part of the explanation, but it does not answer the most pressing query with regard to the sudden volte-face of the elite Iraqi troops. Another piece of information perhaps sheds some light on what happened. When tanks from the 3rd Infantry were making their first thrust into Baghdad, US soldiers captured a senior Republican Guard officer; he admitted that his troops were fatally disorganized, inasmuch as they lacked any intelligence indicating that the Americans had reached the city and were entering in force. Maybe, then, when al-Sahaf was making statements about slaughtering the Americans while they were already in the heart of Baghdad, such statements were not symptoms of a form of delusion, but were in fact based on poor intelligence and ignorance among the leadership figures. The American commanders, who had prepared for Baghdad becoming a major killing ground, sensed that the situation had changed, and that if they pushed relentlessly, the Iraqis might fold. Therefore, they scrapped the original plan to cautiously probe the city and instead launched bold thrusts toward its center. The gamble paid off when, instead of facing chemical warfare and a maze of guerilla forces, US troops encountered only sporadic machine-gun fire and small bands of defenders. Defense analysts attribute the vindication of the war plan to the flexibility of the commanders in the field, who could take the initiative and alter it according to what they identified as "windows of opportunity." One analyst summed the situation up by saying that "the US military is great at seeing opportunities and seizing them." The capture of a disoriented Iraqi colonel, who blundered when he blindly led his column into the American troops without realizing they were there, is therefore credited with the sudden shift in the winds of the war.[63]

It is evident that the American commanders in the field not only showed a remarkable degree of flexibility and stamina, of foresightedness and courage, but also demonstrated flair in the battlefield. In a combat situation, both sides suffer casualties, exhaustion (or combat fatigue) and frustration. They have rehearsed various battle scenarios and are poised to implement them. The defending party (be that in terms of terrain or fighting cause), also has an advantage. However, final victory goes to the side that can mobilize the extra physical and emotional strength and determination to go one step further, to adapt to changing circumstances, to improvise a new plan on the go and to keep urging the troops to victory. In this regard, and in light of the lessons learned from other wars where Arab commanders were involved, there is no doubt that the Americans had the edge in the final analysis. Speed of attack is also crucial in combat scenarios. The Americans moved so rapidly and simultaneously through so many parts of Baghdad that they simply overwhelmed the Iraqis who failed to understand what was going on around them and were unable to regroup and alter their defense plans.[64] For the American command, the fall of Baghdad did not mean the end of combat operations. As long as the stores of unconventional weapons and the leaders listed on the deck of cards were not located, the fighting would continue. The CIA was ready to use a cash reward system to track down thousands of Saddam loyalists, senior Iraqi officers, intelligence networks and senior Ba'ath cadres.[65]

The symbolic toppling of the statue of Saddam, however, was seen in many US circles as an epoch-making event comparable to the fall of the Berlin Wall. While the West Germans were capable, because of their stable democratic government, of incorporating East Germany, it is less certain that the powers-that-be are able to concoct for the Iraqis the regime and the government they need or can submit to, while the regimes in the rest of the Arab world watch frightened of what the prospects of democracy might signify in terms of their own survival. The Arab media made much of the fact that it was the Marines, using a cable attached to a US tank-recovery vehicle, who actually brought down the statue of Saddam in Central Square. The unfurling of the American flag was a clumsy political statement and it was abruptly stowed away. But the immediate question was: How could the American occupiers perpetuate the collaboration of the

populace once they began to arrest the looters and other criminals, intro-
duce law and order in a country that knows neither, and prevent revenge
killings? Even disregarding their imposition of law and order on the streets
of Baghdad, the Iraqis, like other Arabs and Muslims, had no reason to
applaud American policies toward the Middle East, especially toward the
Palestinian issue, which had been one of Saddam's Arab policy priorities.
It became conventional wisdom in Washington that the war to win the
hearts of the Iraqis and to re-order the structure of the regime would be
much harder than the battle of Baghdad.[66]

For the American troops taking hold in Baghdad there were some ironic
moments. The German Embassy and the French Cultural Center, both in
east Baghdad, were hit by the wave of looting. Germany and France, along
with Russia, had defended Iraq prior to the war against American war
designs, leading international efforts to force President Bush to accept an
extension of UN weapons inspections, and delaying US military action.
But these two nations' embassies were now stripped of all their furnishings,
even curtains and decorations. At the French Center the looters burst water
pipes and flooded the ground floor, books were left floating in the reading
rooms and a photograph of French President Chirac was smashed. The
French Embassy building, also in east Baghdad, was spared only because
of the French guards who defended it, but the German Embassy, which
thought it was shielded behind its "friendship" with the Iraqi regime, was
also rampaged. On the same day, looters attacked and stripped the
UNICEF building, which had provided relief to Iraqi children. There was
speculation that people directed their anger at the agency because it had
plied to Saddam's manipulations of the theme of the UN sanctions, which
he accused of causing untold suffering to the children. Al-Kindi Hospital,
a major shelter for the hundreds of Iraqi civilian wounded, did not escape
the looting either, as beds and electrical equipment were lifted away,
making the already dire situation in Baghdad's hospitals even worse.[67]

The Iraqi leadership did not escape the wrath of the crowds either. As
well as the looting of Saddam's many palaces, there were more personal
attacks and focused acts of resentment. Tariq Aziz's mansion, for example,
was completely depleted of its furnishings, but the looters left intact his
library, containing the complete works of Saddam, a book by President
Nixon and the novels of Mario Puzo, author of *The Godfather*. Ali Hassan
al-Majid, Saddam's cousin, also known as Chemical Ali for his massacre
of the Kurds in Halabja in 1988, was in the process of building a new house
in Baghdad, but in his storage area behind the house, many Western ameni-
ties were carried away by the looters, including a model of a Ferrari, a
Japanese water scooter, a parachute for free-jumping, a video library that
encompassed dozens of Hollywood movies, more than 100 racing-car
wheels and the complete fittings for a luxury European kitchen. One looter
made the point: "Everything in this place belongs to the Iraqi people, not

to Chemical Ali." The anger vented against Saddam loyalists was repeated throughout Baghdad; it was feared that the anger might escalate into revenge killings. Reporters witnessed a group of young people catching and beating up a man in central Baghdad they claimed was a Ba'ath official, but he succeeded in running away, throwing himself, ironically, at the feet of American soldiers. The soldiers later explained that the man had surrendered deserters from Saddam's army to the authorities for a price, hence the hatred directed toward him. The victim started kissing the boots of the soldiers, pitifully shouting that he detested Saddam. The soldiers let him go after his persecutors left.[68]

The Americans were primarily interested in the big names of the regime, most of all the Hussein family itself. Having failed with an attack on the restaurant where Saddam and/or his cronies were supposed to be on the opening day of the assault on Baghdad, the search for the top brass of the regime was now on, given that access to all parts of the city was available. On 10 April the Americans attacked a mosque and later bombed it but still missed the opportunity to kill the Iraqi leaders who were there. Saddam was rumored to have been at the Imam al-Adham Mosque in the Adhamiya neighborhood, where he sought shelter after he was injured. Later the Marines advanced on the mosque in a pitched battle that lasted several hours, at the end of which seven fighters, believed to be Syrians, were taken prisoner, but three cars, presumably carrying Saddam or people close to him, escaped. A bomb was dropped on the mosque, ripping the main dome – an act based on information that a group of the leadership was convening there. People in the neighborhood said that Saddam had visited the mosque a few days earlier and greeted a throng of his supporters from the roof of his car. Iraqis angry that the Americans had attacked a place of worship, chased an American reporter with rocks. Adhamiya was a likely hiding place because the Americans had not fanned out into it; Iraqis had assumed that their places of worship remained immune to attacks, as the Americans had previously reported.[69] One could imagine Secretary of State Colin Powell lecturing about the "unacceptability of harming a mosque," had it occurred elsewhere and had it not involved Americans.

The mayhem did not recede in the next few days, with looting and disorder continuing and the Iraqis getting more and more impatient about the American inability to restore order, though most of the core of the city was quiet and the main five bridges connecting the two parts of the city were opened to traffic. At the Rashid Hotel, American troops were assigned the unusual task of breaking up a tile mosaic of President George Bush, Snr. on the floor of the lobby, where everyone could step on it at will. A combination of two Arab cultural elements are at play here. First, the sole of one's shoes is considered by the Arabs the dirtiest surface anywhere, hence their insistence on leaving shoes outdoors when they step into mosques and often, but not always, into private homes. In popular parlance, one has to apologize for mentioning shoes even in a neutral and innocent context (e.g. "I bought shoes for my son, may the curse be far from you!"); therefore, trampling upon someone with one's shoes on is about the most contemptuous gesture imaginable. Hence the trampling over the statues of Saddam all over Iraq, and the recurring sight of ladies who removed their shoes to beat with fury the toppled statues of Saddam in Baghdad's streets. Second, part of the concept of Arab bravado is the symbolic act that can often substitute for the real thing. If you cannot bring America to its knees or beat it, then burn its flag; if you are helpless facing its leaders, then trample upon their likenesses or burn their effigies; if you cannot emulate American democracy, then carry it to its "burial" in a coffin and proclaim its death; if you are intimidated by America, proclaim that you are stronger and that you will beat it in any confrontation; and if you are defeated and retreating, declare, like al-Sahaf, that it is America (or any other enemy for that matter) that is withdrawing and licking its wounds.[70]

The mobs continued to set ablaze government offices and other public institutions: they wished to obliterate the memories of Saddam and his rule, even as they were policing the streets and chasing away Fedayeen loyalists who were still lingering in certain neighborhoods. The Sajida Presidential Place was ransacked, as was the gaudy Rashid Hotel. Entire families carted away beds and tableware. The looters were no longer only the poor of the Shi'ite neighborhoods, but also professionals. A pharmacist came with her husband, an obstetrician, and their two children, to help themselves to brocade sofas and heaps of fine porcelain, declaring that they did not feel guilty in the least because they had "paid a thousand times" for their booty. When the greedy crowds banged on the door of a hospital in their bid to ransack it, a doctor had to discharge his rifle in the air to disband the mob. Only when a gang of looters began carting away rocket-propelled grenades from an armory at the Ministry of Planning did American troops intervene and disperse the crowds. The American presence was so sparse throughout the city that they were unable to control the looters even if they wanted to. In the final analysis it seemed that the matter of allowing or prohibiting looting was left to the discretion of the local commanders, who sometimes acted when they were sensitive to the ransacking of entire buildings, or to grave violations of public order in general, and had troops available to deploy; and at other times they let the crowds celebrate and enjoy themselves, when their attitude was nonchalant toward disorder in a foreign country, or they did not have the requisite troops to impose civility. The more cultured Iraqis who cared about peace and order in their neighborhoods and did not take part in the looting, criticized America, accusing it of having wreaked havoc in Baghdad and then failing to re-install public order. It was the repeated complaints lodged by Iraqi civilians, and the realization among the Americans that they were causing long-term damage to their reputation and to their ability to impose order if they did not bring a halt to the chaos immediately, that caused them to put an end to that mayhem. Or perhaps there was simply nothing left to rob, strip and cart away.

Nothing left, except for the National Museum in Baghdad, the repository of treasures that have no equal anywhere else in the world, home to ancient Mesopotamian cultural artifacts. Fortunately, some of the Museum's priceless gold, silver and copper antiquities, and some fabled bronze- and gold-overlaid ivory artifacts had been removed for safekeeping elsewhere, or seized by Saddam for display in his palaces. Enough else was stolen and destroyed to make any civilized person mourn the irretrievable losses to art and culture. The 28 galleries and vaults of the museum, protected by steel doors and descending several floors underground, were ransacked by thousands of looters for two days in a row, with hardly any intervention from the American troops. Unique artifacts from the Sumerian period (3360–2000 BC) were ransacked, smashed and stolen. Worse, the looters left behind a trail of smashed ceramics, torn books and burned-out torches – rags soaked in gasoline – which were used by the scavengers to light their way through the Museum's corridors. The scavengers included men, women and children, some armed with pistols, rifles, axes and knives. They stormed out of the building carrying their precious antiquities on carts, bicycles or wheelbarrows, or else in hand-carried boxes. Smaller items were stuffed in the pockets of the looters. When the crew of an American tank was alerted by phone by the Museum's employees, they rushed to the scene and fired rounds into the air. The marauders were taken aback and retreated, but after the crew left 30 minutes later, the looters were back in earnest. American troops were powerless to prevent the cultural disaster that was unfolding before their eyes.[71]

Was this barbaric vandalism yet another manifestation of anti-Saddam wrath? One could claim that since Saddam had forged links with the provinces of Hammurabi, it was only natural to expect the populace to shun ancient Iraq as they associated it in their minds with Saddam. The more cultured and rational people of Iraq, including its intellectuals and artists, would certainly refute such an argument, and indeed many did, most of all archaeologists and museum curators who understood the cultural value of the lost artifacts, and felt keenly the outrage committed by the pillagers. It is more likely that the type of people who loot public property in the first place do not differentiate between historical items of value and modern implements, such as chairs and air-conditioners. The lust to gain materially from either was probably the driving force behind the looters, who took advantage of the disorder to increase the stock of their belongings. Rebelling against Saddam or his regime was only a post-factum rationalization for those who felt some remorse about their deeds. At any rate, Museum employees were horrified to see looters use sledgehammers to smash locked glass display cases and rifles and pistols to break the locks.

While most of the looters appeared to be from the impoverished areas of the capital, and therefore, it could be argued, acted out of ignorance, others were visibly middle class, educated people who appeared to know exactly what they were looking for, and headed precisely to the most valuable items. An Iraqi archaeologist, witness to this cultural tragedy, directed his invective against President Bush:

> A country's identity, its value and civilization resides in its history ... If a country's civilization is looted, as ours has been here, its history ends. Please tell this to President Bush. Please remind him that he promised to liberate the Iraqi people, but that is not a liberation, this is a humiliation ... [72]

While world art experts were lamenting the loss, they also drew attention to other national museums, like the one in Mosul that holds many Assyrian artifacts from the Nineveh ruins. International archaeologists urged the American government to protect Iraq's treasures and precious archaeological sites, and to act to retrieve some of the stolen artifacts. Concerned scholars in the field had warned the Pentagon prior to the war of such dangers, and cited the 1991 case, during the previous Gulf War, when nine (out of thirteen) Iraqi regional museums had been plundered. Baghdad was spared on that occasion because the Government had remained intact. Even under Saddam's rule armies of illegal diggers, financed by foreign entrepreneurs and driven by the overseas black market of antiquities, had been hard at work stealing artifacts and smuggling them across the border. There is little doubt that the looting of the Museum has been at least in part motivated by the illicit trade of antiquities. The Museum of Art of New York City (MANY), and other well-wishers throughout the Western world, announced their mobilization to help retrieve and restore the stolen treasures and urged the American administration not to shirk from its duty to maintain order in Baghdad and prevent further damage. More than 230 scholars of ancient Mesopotamian history from 25 countries, headed by Oxford and Yale Universities' specialists, signed a petition to the UN, appealing to the Americans to safeguard the artifacts. As these protests were raised around the globe, news came through that Iraqi antiquities officials and researchers had barricaded themselves inside the Museum in order to protect some of its valuable collections.[73]

Tikrit and the Last Stand

After Baghdad fell, with Saddam and his family nowhere to be found, speculation mounted that he may have escaped to his native town of Tikrit, over 100 miles north of the capital, to make his last stand. However, self-preservation was always Saddam's modus operandi, not glorious defeat, and the Iraqi leader instead slipped into the shadows, his voice occasionally broadcast across Iraq, urging patriotic Iraqis to attack the American "imperialists." The precedent of Vietnam had been repeatedly evoked by the Palestinians and other Arabs, and it is evident, judging from the remarks made by Tariq Aziz on the eve of the war, that the Iraqi Command had considered subversive guerilla warfare tactics. Although the Iraqi desert cannot give the same kind of shelter to guerillas as the jungles of Vietnam, there is evidence (and some of it was seen during the battles for the cities of the south and in Baghdad itself) that the dense pattern of settlement in the cities was seen by Iraqi planners as an acceptable substitute terrain to conduct a guerilla campaign from. At any rate, no sooner had the American troops settled in Baghdad than some of them were told to prepare to move north to eliminate the last putative shelter of Saddam in Tikrit. Many of the Iraqi military leaders as well as some top political leaders were thought to have retreated to Tikrit. The first encounters with the Iraqi military would, it was assumed, take place as soon as the Americans crossed the Tigris to the north into Saddam's region.[74]

The Marines attacked Tikrit after they destroyed a column of Iraqi tanks, killing some Iraqi soldiers and gaining a foothold in the city. There was resistance, again much less than anticipated for a last stand and for the ancestral city of Saddam himself. Mosul and Kirkuk having also fallen to American hands, the battle of Tikrit was to be the last of the war. Several thousand Marines and hundreds of armored vehicles were amassed for this last stand of the war, the city having been heavily bombed for several days. A repetition of the Baghdad tactic: i.e. speed and overwhelming force on selected key-targets, was to be utilized, though on a much smaller scale than in the capital. When Tikrit fell, not one single important town could be said to still be in Saddam's hands. The battle of Tikrit was expected to be a fight to the bitter end, but when the Marines stormed the city on 14 April five days after the fall of Baghdad, they found empty streets and buildings, much as they encountered in Baghdad. The troops broke into a lavish presidential palace, something they had rehearsed many times before, but the grandeur of this Xanadu stunned Americans and Iraqis alike. It consisted of two miles of lush river front, with about 90 buildings, all off-limits to ordinary Iraqis. Looters now ransacked the palace until only mortar remained. Outside the palace, the Marines tightened their grip on the city, again wondering what had happened to those elite units of Iraqi soldiers. As in Baghdad, the question remained: were they ordered to retreat and re-engage later, or were they afraid to engage in battle and elected to make off and dissolve into the population?[75]

The city the Marines found was a monument to Saddam's vast ego. It seemed that his deepest psychological need was to demonstrate before his townspeople how a boy of theirs, from a modest background, could make it to the top of the hierarchy. For many Iraqis, he was and remained anonymous in extraction and social status, but for Tikritis, Saddam was the personification of the miracle of the Ba'ath Party, which could push one from poverty to riches. Now Saddam's palaces were empty, his regime decimated. No wonder then, that he chose to be absent when the supreme act of humiliation, his un-ceremonial demise, unfolded. How could he stand the shame and the loss of face in front of the people who watched him grow to absolute power? The early onlookers preceding the looters were amazed at some of Saddam's extravagance: homes, offices, servant quarters, lakes, swans, ducks and rare birds. Before venturing into the city, the Marines dropped leaflets warning the population to stay indoors. The Iraqi forces that were supposed to make a last stand must have also heeded the notice. Individual Iraqi soldiers who had deserted Baghdad under the menace of American air-strikes admitted that there was no way they could win the war; surrender was the only option.

Nevertheless, while defending themselves against any suspicion of cowardice, they sang the praise of their deposed leader, who was good to his Tikrit, but particularly, they said, because "he was the only Arab leader who fired missiles against Israel," and that alone made him, in Arab eyes, a great man.[76]

6

The Hidden Agenda: Oil, Terror and WMD

When the crisis between the US and Iraq was building up toward war, the main accusation leveled against Saddam was that he was building weapons of mass destruction (WMD) which threatened his neighbors and American interests, and contravened UN sanctions and limitations; therefore he had to be removed from power. Though the US persisted in its accusations regarding the WMD issue, and throughout the crisis provided data to back its claims, it became evident as the crisis escalated that the US wanted to go to war regardless of the discovery of WMD; Saddam was, in the Pentagon's eyes, reason to go to war alone. However, while the only advertised war aim remained those unconventional weapons that Washington felt it had to neutralize, two other problems presented themselves to policymakers: terrorism and oil. Importantly, though, neither aim was ever made a declared goal of the war.

Ever since 9/11 and President Bush's vow to pursue the terrorists and the states that sustained them, listing Iraq as a member of the Axis of Evil, a general mood of expectation reigned that after Afghanistan and the removal of the Taliban, Saddam's turn would come soon (though no one could tell whether Baghdad would precede Teheran and Pyongyang or succeed them). The timing of the Iraqi crisis coincided with the converging of the separate issues of terrorism and oil in a way that served the interests of the US, or so the Americans believed.

For 12 years Saddam had resisted UN sanctions and defied the US. In 1998 UN teams of inspectors were expelled from Iraq, contravening an "arrangement" worked out under Kofi Annan's mediation. Iran and North Korea, along with Iraq, were also not accountable for their schemes, but there was no official regime of sanctions against either of them, and to set in motion such a procedure would have been costly, protracted and controversial. The State Department succeeded in persuading President Bush, against the best advice of the Pentagon, that a procedure was already in place in Iraq, and it would be quicker, less divisive and more consensual to mobilize the UN Security Council behind it so as to lend to it international legitimacy. A UN-sponsored resolution would attract a large coalition of allies who would, at least, not oppose the operation, even if they did not wish to actively support it through military, logistical, financial and diplomatic channels. But problems transpired when it became clear that the US had less support in the UN than it had counted on. Its international isolation meant that the US would have to act without UN legitimacy. At that stage, the war preparations were so advanced, with troops pouring into the Gulf region, and President Bush so committed, on the record, to Saddam's removal, that war became inevitable. In the absence of international legitimacy, a "smoking gun" scenario was constructed, which dictated that, if the US and its allies did nothing, Iraq's tyrant would be in a position to activate the many large-scale arms at his disposal and damage US and international interests. The evidence was based not only on the data collected by the teams of inspectors over the years (and especially on the fact that the teams were prevented from collecting or even accessing to certain data), but principally on intelligence services – the CIA, and some of its allied counterparts across the world such as MI5. This intelligence, the Americans believed, was enough of a smoking gun to proceed.

President Bush's War against Terror, which began in Afghanistan, gradually became tied in with WMD. Not only were there terrorist training bases in Iraq, but it was evident that Saddam was openly endorsing Palestinian terrorists, including Islamikaze martyrs, by paying their families $25,000 each. Bush's fear was that WMD, in the hands of terrorists, could wreak havoc on the world order and pose a level of threat to the West that would dwarf 9/11. When al-Qa'ida acted against America, it did not possess WMD. Saddam, however, was thought to own advanced apparatuses of biological and chemical weapons, of which he had publicly boasted in the 1980s. Saddam had been close to achieving nuclear capability in 1981, though on that occasion an Israeli air-attack neutralized the threat. But the manufacturing of chemical and biological weapons, hard to monitor and easy to hide, was not confirmed as being discontinued. Saddam, one of the only dictators in history to have used chemical and biological warfare, along with his links with terrorism, made it incumbent upon the US to act immediately.

The exposure of Saddam's twin evils became one of the main targets of the war planners, and many efforts were made before, during and especially after the war to provide the "smoking gun" that America could not come up with convincingly enough prior to the war. In the thick of battle, specialized teams were sent to explore ammunition dumps and stores of weapons, barrels of suspected liquids and mobile laboratories, off-bounds compounds in military zones and all seized security forces HQ. Advancing troops also allocated land and air forces to eliminate suspected terrorist bases, even as military units were sorely needed on the battlefront elsewhere. At the end of hostilities, in the face of critics who continued to challenge America's right to wage war against Iraq, the US stepped up its efforts in Iraq to hunt for WMD. It is still widely expected that when all the available Intelligence, findings on the ground and the de-briefings of some senior POWs are pieced together, ample proof will be available to make America's case.

Administration communiqués did not mention anything about oil, though it was obvious that, as in the previous Gulf War, that oil was always in the background, hidden behind more acceptable slogans like liberty, terrorism and human rights. Therefore, to the extent that oil was mentioned in the war aims, it was always in the context of "saving the oil fields" from arson, "keeping the oilfields for the Iraqi people," or "averting major environmental disasters" by wrestling the oil fields from the "evil regime of Saddam." The oil stakes are high, for Iraq sits on the second or third largest reserve of oil in the world (after Saudi Arabia and perhaps also Iran), concentrated mainly in the Shi'ite area in the south and near the Kurdish area in the north. Iraq is capable of producing 2–2.5 million barrels of oil a day which, together with Kuwait and the Gulf states that are loyal to the US, can attain or even surpass Saudi Arabia's production of eight million per day. Since 9/11, Saudi Arabia has been ambivalent about its support for terrorism; only domestic attacks arouse a response. Saudi clerics and some of its state machinery continue to be critical of the US instead of the terrorists, resisting American pressure to reform its educational apparatus along western lines. America's impatience with Saudi Arabia, which gave rise to Bin Laden and his likes, came to a boiling point when, during preparations for the war, Riyadh asked that US forces adopt a low profile and not proclaim in the open the use they were making of Saudi air bases.

The war in Iraq brought new options for the Americans, inasmuch as they would no longer depend on Saudi Arabia either for oil or for military bases for their future operations in the Middle East. Turkey had also failed to prove its loyalty to the US, forcing the Americans to alter their war plans and practically eliminate their northern front; now Saudi Arabia had followed suit. As a result these two pillars of American policy in the Middle East for the past half-century became detached; significance shifted else-where along the Arab side of the Gulf, and above all Iraq. The new configuration of the Middle East, where the US shares a common border with Turkey, Iran, Syria and Saudi Arabia, means that each one of those powers would be very attentive to American opprobrium and wary from any démarche that might upset Washington. Blackmail by terrorism, oil or weapons of mass destruction would be much more difficult to exercise with impunity. Hence the inter-connection between those three elements and the adroit American use of all three during the war, though some of them (terrorism) were more prominent in public discourse than others (oil, for example). Examining these elements will shed some light on the relative weight of each of them, and of all three combined.

The Oil Issue

A major element in the hidden agenda of the US – the oil issue – underscores the tensions that have reigned between the US and Saudi Arabia, as the major consumer and the major exporter, respectively, in the world oil market. Saudi Arabia is the most influential member in the world cartel, OPEC, and it is concerned lest the re-entrance of Iraq into an already-saturated market might drive market price beneath the convenient $30 per barrel. Iraq's proven reserves stand at over 100 billion barrels, or over 10 percent of the world total; Saudi reserves are double that. However, while Saudi Arabia's oil fields have been explored, developed and exploited, Iraq's have stagnated since the 1991 Gulf War. In the past few years, the US has imported from the Arab world close to 1 billion barrels annually, representing close to one-third of total US imports. More than half of American-imported Arab oil came from Saudi Arabia (close to 600,000 million barrels), followed by Iraq with one-third (300,000 million barrels). Saudi columnist Saleh al-Namla wrote well before the Third Gulf War that the American invasion of Iraq meant, on the economic level, the rebuilding of the modern petroleum facilities of Iraq and the enormous exporting power attached thereto suggested that America "would not only become a major mover in the international oil market, but a principal player in it. This would mean not only control of the quantity and price of oil but also the ability to exercise arbitrariness by striking at petroleum countries and causing their bankruptcy."[1]

OPEC's decision on 11 June 2003 to keep its current production quota, indicates its belief that Iraqi oil will not enter the world picture before late 2004 at the earliest. Paul Bremer, the American overseer of Iraq's reconstruction after the war, while admitting that Iraq's recovery of oil production was slower that originally projected, was optimistic that it could attain 2.5 million b/d by the end of 2003. Iraqi officials, who know something about their country's oil production, are far less optimistic. Immediately after the war the production rate in Iraq was about one-third the projected amount – some 800,000 b/d, 500,000 of which came from the old Kirkuk oil fields and the balance from the richer Rumeila fields in the south. The major reasons for this sluggish production have been UN sanctions which for over a decade have permitted a limited amount of export under the UN oil-for-food program, though illicit export was pursued via Jordan, Syria and Turkey. As a result of the curtailed export, production had to be cut down. Equipment fell into disrepair. During the war itself many facilities were looted and it will take time to replace the missing equipment. And the American bombing of the K-3 pumping station, which provided petrol from northwestern Iraq to the Ceyhan pipeline in Turkey, disrupted that export route. Finally, it would take time for the Iraqis to repair their main pipeline linking northern and southern fields.[2]

Saudi oil experts who voiced their concerns before the war about oil becoming "the first casualty after the American invasion of Iraq" were accused of not defending their "sister Arab country," as much as they were concerned about the economic losses that they might incur as a result of the war. One article complained about the "naked American freedom in the oil market and the militarization of this strategic item in order to lower prices by divorcing them from the markets' instruments of supply and demand."[3] Such blinkered and crude anti-capitalist comments were echoed by a paranoid economist from King Abdul Aziz University, who voiced his concern with regard to the damage that American control of the Iraqi wealth might cause to OPEC: "as it is known, the Western world is trying to destroy OPEC, because they prefer to see oil prices decline but only to the level that would not cause harm to their Western oil companies."[4]

Following the success of the War in Iraq and the American occupation, as the prospects of a long-term American presence became concrete, Saudi Arabia's concerns increased. They feared that the US would make Iraq leave OPEC; this would "cause mortal competition among all the producers" and bring about a drastic drop in oil prices, with the concomitant ruinous elimination of large parts of the oil producers' high income that the OPEC cartel assures them today. Demands had been voiced by various quarters in the past that Arab oil be taken over by the West and its proceeds distributed more fairly to the population rather than among corrupt sheikhs or tyrants, but the question of legitimacy had always stood in the way of such a take over. In the context of war, however, legitimacy is discarded in favor of a pragmatic approach of plying to the rules established by the conquering power. Indeed, even though the Americans have been making efforts to give the Iraqis some form of "democratic" government, they have announced that Paul Bremer would act as a *czar*, able to veto and overturn any decision of the "Provisional Council."

Saudi concerns over the future of OPEC, with the consequent balance shifting between OPEC and non-OPEC members of the oil-producing community, were not unfounded; after all, the takeover of Arab oil by a Western power, the unimaginable scenario, was not so unlikely anymore. That meant that the Arabs understood that they could no longer blackmail politically through threats to increase oil prices, but, no less importantly, they also became aware of the following "dangers": first, that the US might privatize the Iraqi oil industry for the benefit of the American oil companies, followed by British and Australian ones (excluding French, Russian and German companies who opposed the war); second, that those oil companies would manipulate the prices and drive them down; and third, that the price competition might push the prices down to the $22–$28 per barrel in the immediate future, with further reduction down to $15–$18 in the longer term.[5]

This would return oil prices to the post-1973 crisis level of the "oil shock," when prices quadrupled literally overnight, from $3–$4 to $12–$16. For the oil-producing countries, who have developed a heavy reliance on oil production and export, and who have cut drastically on their outlays since prices have fallen, further cuts in their income might generate bankruptcies in their economies. A Saudi expert, Dr al-Sani'i, writing for a London-based Arabic paper, concluded that American intervention in Iraq was wholly driven by oil considerations, because post-9/11 US macroeconomic indicators were showing a deteriorating trend: budget deficits, national debts, unemployment and so forth, which, if unchecked, might bring about "the collapse of the largest economy in the world."[6]

The conspiracy theories did not stop there. Another Saudi writer expressed the concern that "Zionists are planning to enter the petrochemical industry in Iraq, and even in the Gulf countries, under the cover of globalization and unilateral economic complementarities. We have nothing to offer but tears and denunciations about our wealth being stolen under our nose." Jeanne Kirkpatrick, known for her support to Israel, urged the withdrawal of Iraq from OPEC.[7] Another commentator, writing for London-based Arabic paper *Al-Hayat*, claimed that OPEC was now entering a defensive period with the return of Iraq to the oil market, which had heftily profited from its absence for a decade. An Iranian official was quoted as warning that if Iraq produced more than its OPEC quota, a price war would become inevitable.[8]

With a projected output that can reach its zenith some 6–8 years hence, Iraq's oil industry, which by then will have restored the pre-1991 level of production and developed new fields, could undermine Saudi Arabia's primacy and reduce it to a secondary role. As things stand now, every $1 drop in the value of a barrel of oil means a loss of close to $3 billion annually. One can only imagine what a decline of $8 or $10 a barrel might do in the long run to an already strained and deficit-ridden economy which relies for 85 percent of its income on oil. To fulfill that overall strategy, the Americans have been hard at work since the end of the combat, both on cracking down on disturbances to peace and order, without which no stability and no full-fledged resumption of oil production can proceed, and also on the diplomatic level, to lend as much international legitimacy as possible to those designs. At the end of May 2003, the American civil administration could pay the first salary to Iraqi officials, ironically in dinars bearing Saddam's face. And according to Mr Ghadhban, the Director-General of the Ministry of Oil, the acting Minister under the Americans pending the election of a permanent government, the oil industry could, shortly, not only supply the entire domestic consumption, but would also begin to export.

The American military gave Iraqis three weeks beginning in May to hand in automatic and heavy weapons in order to facilitate the restoration of normalcy. On 15 June 2003, the amnesty period ended; from then on, individuals caught with unauthorized weapons would be detained and would face criminal charges. During the looting spree after 9 April many weapons – from pistols to automatic arms and anti-tank grenades – were stolen and sold on the market at low prices, probably purchased by people and organizations who intended to launch a guerilla war against the US, or to engage in criminal activity that would jeopardize American ability to rule the country and rescue its oil industry. The latter, with 40,000 workers in electric production, received top priority in regaining their posts. The UN Security Council approved a US-drafted resolution on 20 May 2003, giving America and Britain broad powers to use Iraq's oil resources to finance its reconstruction, paving the way to resume Iraq's oil export industry, and ending 13 years of UN sanctions.[9]

Pro-Saddam or otherwise anti-American opposition forces are working to help undo what they regard as US schemes. The main opposition groups are the Sunnites in central and northwestern Iraq, Saddam's heartland. The strategic oil pipelines that are supposed to sustain the resumption of oil export all cross this area. As long as Saddam Hussein was at large, issuing orders to his people to fight the Americans, no one could say that oil exporting was guaranteed. Moreover, since the Americans wish to repatriate some of their combatant troops who bore the brunt of the war for months since their early deployment in September 2002, troops from allied countries, including Poland, Spain and the Ukraine, might be called to replace them, which could have an effect on the security, and hence oil export, situation. These imponderables are further aggravated by the putative links between Iraqi oil and terrorism. According to one source, two shadowy banking networks close to al-Qa'ida, and a pro-Taliban Saudi oil company, were involved in buying oil from Saddam under the UN's oil-for-food program. Although oil sales took place under UN permission and supervision, the system was plagued by kickbacks that allowed Saddam to buy political support to finance his intelligence activities, his purchases of weapons and even terrorist organizations.[10]

Among Iraq's customers was a Lichtenstein-based firm, Galp International Trading Establishment, a subsidiary of Portugal's Oil Company, who chose as its legal representative Asat Trust. Asat was targeted by the US and the UN as a financier of al-Qa'ida through its links to al-Taqwa, a cluster of financial groups spanning the world from the Bahamas to Europe and controlled by the Muslim Brotherhood. Iraq therefore funneled money to al-Qa'ida via an oil company that worked with one of the terrorist groups' financial backers. Another company contracted to Iraq was the Geneva-based Delta Services, a subsidiary of Delta Oil, the Saudi company which maintained a close relationship with the Taliban when they were harboring Bin Laden. It is believed that Delta Services landed a contract to export from Iraq 13 million barrels, and in the process $7 million were paid as kickbacks. On 7 November, 2001, President Bush named the al-

Taqwa network as the group responsible for distributing money to al-Qa'ida under the guise of legitimate banking activity. Bush subsequently froze the assets of several companies linked to the bank, including the Asat Trust. The two heads of al-Taqwa, Youssef Nada and Ali Ghaleb Himmat, are members of the Egyptian Muslim Brothers, who acquired Italian nationality and live near Lugano. On their board is a Swiss convert to Islam with pro-Nazi views who claimed that al-Taqwa only funneled money from rich people in the Gulf to poor Muslims in the Third World. But according to American officials, Hamas had transferred $60 million to al-Taqwa in 1997, and after 9/11, al-Qa'ida received financial assistance from Nada.[11]

Back in 1996, Italian Intelligence had claimed that al-Taqwa and a wealthy Kuwaiti, Nasreddin, were financial backers of Islamic groups such as Hamas, Algeria's FIS and Gama'at, the Egyptian group that eventually merged with al-Qa'ida in 1998. Intelligence referred to the Egyptian Islamic Jihad, headed by Ayman al-Zawahiri, who became Bin Laden's deputy and the brains behind al-Qa'ida and its 9/11 attacks. Their merger proceeded through suspicious business activities and several Islamic charities and centers worldwide. Italy could not verify those suspicions at the time because it could not investigate the Swiss bank accounts of those companies. However, after Bush targeted al-Taqwa, Switzerland opened its own investigation of the group. Al-Taqwa's Bahamas branch was shut down in April 2002 under American pressure. Nada was shut down at the end of 2002.

Saddam Hussein was well known for setting up shell companies in tax havens to channel resources and had been doing so since the 1980s. The Swiss Muslim convert Ahmed Huber was quoted in a Swiss weekly as saying that Nada enjoyed friendly relations with numerous Muslim leaders, including Saddam. Nimir Petroleum, another Saudi company, controlled by the Saudi millionaire Khalid bin Mahfouz, was accused in several lawsuits of backing Bin Laden, but Mahfouz consistently denied the charges. The Delta Service Swiss subsidiary was liquidated in 2001.[12] These cases demonstrate how the international oil business, when left unchecked by international watchdogs, can become involved with terrorist activities, especially when the majority of terrorists come from the nations with the greatest oil wealth.

When the war broke out and it seemed that Iraq's oil production would grind to a halt, Kirkuk's massive fields continued to pump oil into the pipeline to Ceyhan, Turkey. Some analysts believed then that as the oil stocks were low and the prices volatile, the continued flow of Iraqi oil would help calm the oil markets. A dispute then broke out at the UN Security Council regarding the future of Iraq's oil wealth. Britain and the US, the main Allies in the war, took sides against Russia and Syria, who opposed the war in the first place and had their own interests in Iraq and its future. The UN Secretary-General Kofi Annan moved to re-authorize the seven-year old oil-for-food program but the Russians, the Syrians, the French and others opposed the move, arguing that authorization would amount to a recognition of the legitimacy of the war. The Americans, with British support, were pushing the idea that the revenues from the oil sales be made available to the Allies to address humanitarian problems within Iraq. The sum of $8 billion had already accumulated in the UN escrow account, because Saddam was not spending the available money for food and medicine, despite his propaganda presenting the UN and the US as evils who did not allow "starving Iraqi children to enjoy the wealth of their country." A failure to agree within the Security Council would have produced the suspension of the oil-for-food deal, which in turn would have brought oil production in Iraq to a standstill.[13]

Before the war Ceyhan drew some 700,000 b/d from Kirkuk, but since the storage tanks there could hold only up to 10 million barrels in total, the producers in Kirkuk had to lower their quota of daily output. Oil traders claimed that banks would no longer provide letters of credit to buyers of Iraqi oil, apparently because of confusion over the future of the oil-for-food program and the apparent dispute in the UN. The delay also witnessed some saber-rattling in the Security Council, with the American delegate accusing the Russians of procrastination and unnecessarily prolonging the suffering of Iraqi children by preventing the oil-for-food program from continuing, while the Russians counter-attacked, claiming that American bombs created the suffering of the Iraqi children. The Russians and the Syrians disagreed with the text of the authorization, stating that the UN would coordinate with the "relevant authorities," meaning America. Echoing the Cold War, the Russians even insisted at the Security Council that the Americans should pay themselves according to the clause in international law which obliged the "occupying belligerents" to make reparations for the damage they caused in the conflict. They opposed the proposition that Iraqi money from the oil-for-food program should pay reparations to the US. Recriminations apart, the humanitarian problem was not resolved.[14]

As the war progressed, however, the immediate problem of extinguishing burning oil wells came to the fore. The billowing black smoke hampered the American bombers and visibility, which was already limited by the sand storms and was a prerequisite for rapid maneuvering in the anticipated armor battles with the Republican Guard. But also important for the Pentagon was putting Iraq back on its feet on the morning after the war, which was based upon the full resumption of the oil production and the gradual increase of that capacity thereafter. Retreating Iraqis, especially in the south, succeeded in lighting up several wells to destroy Iraqi oil-producing ability. In the Rumeila area, gushing oil fields sabotaged by the Iraqis destroyed water wells on which the nomads in the area depended. The Americans brought in men from Texas, experts in restoring sabotaged oil wells, anticipating that Saddam's strategy was to leave behind a scorched earth. As a result the Allies succeeded in taking control of all 600 wells, the infrastructure of pipelines and pumping stations; only nine were sabotaged, and just five of them – a remarkable few – continued to burn by the end of the first week of the war. This was a far cry from the 741 wells that the Iraqis torched in Kuwait during the previous Gulf War, and has helped keep the oil prices at $30 a barrel after rising to close to $40 on the eve of the war.[15]

Boots and Coots was the Texas company responsible for capping the burning wells. The 13 men from the company were told that after the fires were extinguished and production resumed to the full capacity of 2 million b/d, foreign companies would arrive with the purpose of developing new resources and reaching the level of 6 million b/d within 10 years. That level of production would bring Iraq almost on par with Saudi Arabia. Their job was to come close enough to the inferno to set off an explosive charge to starve it momentarily of the oxygen it needs for combustion. The oil is still flowing, but with the ignition turned off the well becomes approachable and is capped. The job is hazardous, because oil burns at 2,000 degrees Fahrenheit, turning the sand to glass. It blisters and sears the flesh of the technicians, while the air around them clogs the respiratory system and settles in the lungs. But the job went on valiantly until the wells were extinguished one by one.[16]

To hint at the future plans concocted by the Pentagon, Philip Carroll, a retired chief executive of Shell, was mentioned as a candidate to be nominated to take charge of the production of oil in post-war Iraq. His main job would be to retain the highly-skilled Iraqi professional cadres in order to upgrade the dilapidated equipment and facilities which were allowed to fall into disrepair during 13 years of embargoes. Concurrently, building companies like Bechtel and Fluor, the latter formerly headed by Carroll, were approached for participation on the reconstruction of post-war Iraq.[17]

As victory in Iraq began to loom in the horizon, legal issues were raised as to who would be entitled to produce, sell and spend the proceeds of the oil; who would decide the priorities; future development of oil fields; and who would control the anticipated income of tens of billions of dollars. Many contenders were lurking around the corner: from the American administration who would appoint its own people to direct the oil business and use the income to hire American companies to do the reconstruction work; to British firms, who in the name of the war alliance which had cost Blair politically, would now ask for economic rewards; to the UN which would strive to enhance its image in Iraq, and which is used by Russia, Germany and France to campaign for the need of the international community to reclaim Iraqi business from the exclusivity of the Anglo-Saxons. Experts predicted that these complications would take weeks to resolve, but the mere expectation of a solution already drove the prices 20 percent downward compared to the eve of the war, when the prospects seemed uncertain. Until the war broke out, it was clear that the UN was the sole trustee of Iraqi oil, including the reserves that had accumulated in Ceyhan and the escrow fund used for activating the oil-for-food deal. By the day Baghdad fell, on 9 April the Rumeila fields were completely secured by American engineers, from both the Army Corps of Engineers and the civilian company Kellogg Brown and Root, a unit of Halliburton, were already on the ground shutting down the wells to stop the pressure from building up in them.[18]

Disagreements over Iraqi oil only emerged after the ground war commenced. Prior to the war there was a UN office in Baghdad which had stewardship of the oil sales, approved prices and authorized sales contracts mandated by the Security Council. On 17 March just two days before the bombings began, the UN office was evacuated. Iraq's government agency, the State Oil Marketing Organization (SOMO), did the actual buying and selling of oil, but all under the authorization of the UN, and without the latter any SOMO dealings would be legally void. American conquest has changed the situation dramatically: oil buyers may be reluctant to purchase oil from America while the handover of authorization from the UN's office remains incomplete. Even if they bought, they might offer lower prices to compensate for the extra risk factor. Under those uncertain conditions many oil traders would rather wait for the debate over authority to be solved than venture into a purchase that may later turn out to be illegal. The escrow money remained the only legal repository for the income from oil, but SOMO, which collapsed along with the rest of the Saddam regime, must be transferred to another seller approved by the Allies and the Security Council. This was urgent, because the oil-for-food program was about to expire. Until a change was agreed upon, the UN would remain the sole authority to approve sales and to collect the proceeds into its escrow fund. Some legal experts have pointed out, moreover, that the Geneva Conventions restrain any occupying power from making long-term commitments, particularly commercial ones, with regard to the wealth of the occupied, something that by necessity puts shackles on America's hands in its dealing with the future of oil in Iraq.[19]

As long as the legal situation remained ambiguous, any American company would be reluctant to invest in modernizing and developing new oil fields in Iraq unless it is guaranteed significant mid-term returns. And the interim American administration would be challenged on legal grounds if it tried to authorize such a deed, by other companies who had previous contracts with Iraq (as was the case with various French and German corporations, for example). The US has been sensitive to these issues; beyond the bland statement that oil would be exploited "for the benefit of the Iraqi people," it does not want to shift attention from the stated war aim of removing Saddam and disarming Iraq. The US is, however, counting on oil income to finance reconstruction. Income from oil will be in the area of $15–$25 billion annually when production rises gradually to 2.5 and to 3.5 million b/d over the next few years. The cost of reconstruction in Iraq, including oil, is estimated at $20 billion annually, that is, the equivalent of the entire projected income from exported oil. Iraq not only has tremendous expenditures on food and imported goods, but it carries enormous foreign debts of $60 billion and faces reparation claims upward of $200 billion as a result of its invasion of Kuwait in 1990. All this means that even in the unlikely event that the income from oil doubles in the coming years with the development of new oil fields, Iraq's economy will have to be topped by heavy foreign investment, which would curtail any potential investor hoping for long-term profits. In addition, investment coming from American oil companies, like the management expertise and technologies needed to develop the fields, would generate resentment among Iraqis which could have recriminations in the business world.[20]

The fall of Kirkuk in the north, with its large oil production, added yet another element to the oil situation. When the city was captured the oil fields and facilities were surprisingly left intact. Before any solution presented itself to prospective investors, however, a scandal broke out involving the top echelon of the American administration. It turned out that the Halliburton subsidiary hired to extinguish the fire in the oil wells would make enormous profits under a preferential contract given to it by the administration. Vice-President Dick Cheney was the chief executive of the Kellogg Brown and Root between 1995 and 2000, before he retired to run for the vice presidency. He received compensation in the amount of $30 million from the company for his resignation. Since 9/11, the company had won significant business from the Pentagon, including contracts as the exclusive supplier of logistic services to the Navy and the Army. The Corps of Engineers who contracted Kellogg Brown and Root claimed that it was the only contractor capable of meeting the standards required by the military as well as their stringent timetable and worldwide capacities. That did not, however, remove the shadow of improper action from the Pentagon and its top brass.[21]

To end the legal confusion, the US advanced a proposal to the Security Council to lift the sanctions on Iraq. Ending the sanctions would eliminate the exclusive authority of the UN to export Iraqi oil and supervise the escrow fund, and the US, as the occupying power, would then be responsible for oil production and the distribution and allocation of oil income. *Prima facie* the proposal was simple, because the US and Britain, who had been the strictest and the most insistent of the Security Council members to impose and enforce the sanctions, which had given rise in 1995 to the oil-for-food program, were now the sponsors of the proposal to lift them. The other members, notably France and Russia, were not always keen on enforcing it, and logically they would be the most interested in abrogating the sanctions. Now the parties shamelessly reversed their positions. Times had changed: Saddam's government, dispensing contracts to those who "cared for the welfare of the Iraqi people," and opposed America in its war against Iraq, was no more. Once it became evident to the recalcitrant powers that the US wished to cancel the sanctions in order to push the UN out of the Iraqi oil picture, France, Russia, Germany and others sought ways to arrest American efforts to monopolize Iraqi oil. Therefore they opposed the lifting of sanctions.

When the oil-for-food program was established in 1995, it was precisely calculated to allow the sale of enough oil to pay for the food and the medicine needed by the people. Under this regime, every Iraqi was entitled to 2,280 calories daily, with additions to infants, pregnant women and those displaced from home, and some 60 percent of the Iraqis benefited from the program. Many of the recipients sold part of their rations which reappeared in the market at high prices. The Iraqi Government bought the rations in bulk for the total population, which were inspected by UN officials at ports of entry and then sent out to warehouses across the country, and from there to over 40,000 corner stores across the country, where people picked up their rations with coupons issued by the UN and the Government. In three northern areas which encompassed autonomous Kurdistan the UN distributed the coupons and the food while in the rest of the country it was the Iraqi Government's responsibility.[22]

The US moved in the aftermath of its victory in Iraq to shut down the pipeline that had provided Iraqi oil illegally to Syria, thus circumventing the UN embargo. The pipline's existence was no secret – even American companies bought some of that oil – having begun its operation in 2000, with the explicit intention of violating the sanctions. After the fall of Baghdad, Syria served notice to its customers that deliveries would be reduced by 200,000 b/d, exactly the amount that the pipeline could carry. Prior to the war, Security Council members pressed for explanations of that violation by their fellow member of the Council, but under the umbrella of Russia, France and China, Syria evaded the issue. The deal was beneficial to both Iraq – who received funds beyond what the UN sold – and Syria, which purchased illegal oil at a huge discount and then charged hefty fees for its transit and marketing as its own. But when the US established itself as the victor in Iraq, in order to exert pressure on Syria, which it called a "rogue state," Defense Secretary Donald Rumsfeld announced the cutting off of that pipeline. Iraqi interest in the Iraq–Syria pipeline stemmed from the fact that it brought Saddam an annual income of $1 billion. The pipeline had originally carried Kirkuk's oil to Tripoli via Syrian territory, but the line was closed in 1982 following the souring relations between the two nations. An investigative reporter for the Energy Intelligence Group, Axel Busch, uncovered the reactivation of the pipeline in the late 1990s. But the Syrians either continued to deny the whole affair, or said that they were selling their oil and using Iraq's for domestic consumption.[23] Damage to the southern fields of Rumeila was relatively small and soon American fire-fighters took control of the situation and began the process of restoring them. But in Kirkuk the takeover of the oil fields was slower and subsequent to the looting which robbed many oil facilities of their most rudimentary equipment, including toilets. In fact, when the managers of the Iraqi North Oil Company in Kirkuk regained their HQ after the American victory, they found that they had no offices, no cars, no computers and only a few employees who dared to come to work under American rule. If, up until the war, North Oil produced some 850,000 b/d, after the war the pumps fell silent: they were in such a state that company officials predicted that it would take weeks to produce oil for local consumption and months before resuming exports. Despite predictions that Saddam might order his troops to blow up the oil wells, they escaped unscathed until the looters came.

The night of 11 April the day after Baghdad had fallen, the buildings of North Oil, like many other public institutions, were stripped bare and set afire; doors and windows were broken; and everything in sight was taken away by Kurds, soldiers and civilians alike. Company cars were packed with fans, tires, bulbs, mattresses, porcelain, flower pots and even drop-ceilings to sell as scrap. They took the computers, the trucks, the forklifts, the cranes, the buses, the shelves, the desks, the chairs, the cabinets in the offices where all data were stored, and made off through Kurdish military roadblocks to Kurdish territory. No records were left behind. The result was that a company with 10,000 employees was no longer operational.[24]

Only after the rampage calmed down, when there was nothing left to steal, break or burn, did damage assessment begin and American aid helped rebuild the organization from the bottom up. North Oil's previous manager, Ali Hamid al-Tikriti, was a tribal member of Saddam's family and had fled for his life on the morning of the American–Kurdish ground attack. One of the major issues that the American civilian overseers – first retired General Jay Garner, and then Ambassador Paul Bremer – decided to tackle in post-Saddam Iraq, was the oil industry. Post-war reconstruction plans were focused around an economic revival sparked by the oil revenue. However, even though the Security Council has essentially determined to lift sanctions, and oil exports are expected to resume as soon as production once again exceeds domestic consumption, it is still far from certain by whom and how the exports will be channeled. Will a decision be made by the Iraqis themselves or will the Americans decide to pull out of OPEC? Who will allocate the spending of oil revenue? And what will happen to the escrow fund? It is likely that these issues will be sorted out only when the new Iraqi Council appointed by Paul Bremer begins to determine its working procedures, and a source of legitimacy is established to take possession of the oil revenue and to dispose of it.

The War against Terrorism

On 16 April as the main battles of the war dissipated, President Bush flew to St Louis, where he told a gathering of Boeing workers that Saddam's regime had come to its end and that it was time for the UN to lift the sanctions against Iraq. Abrogating the sanctions, Bush said, would make it easier to sell the oil and pay for the reconstruction of post-war Iraq. Unable to vindicate his belief that Saddam was amassing WMD, Bush switched the emphasis of his speech to the global war against terrorism. He said:

> By a combination of creative strategies and advanced technology, we are redefining war on our terms . . . Terrorists and tyrants have now been put on notice: they can no longer feel safe hiding behind innocent lives . . . [25]

This was the strongest justification yet of the war in terms of the global battle against terrorism, and represents a shift from disarmament to the targeting of terrorist states, organizations and individuals. This statement had long-term ramifications, inasmuch as it confirmed that after 9/11 the US was no longer only on the defensive against terrorism, but that it would seek aggressively to eradicate it from wherever it exists. The warning served notice to other regimes that sponsor terrorism, like Iran and Syria, that they too could expect to be ousted unless they confront terrorism rather than comply with it.

Information linking Saddam's regime to international terrorism was widely circulated before the war, which made Iraq look the second target, after Afghanistan, in the global war against terrorism (along with the rest of the "Axis of Evil"). September 11 triggered a policy change in the White House toward rogue states: now, terrorism, tyranny and weapons of mass destruction were all linked together as one evil network. Henceforth, the war against terrorism was no longer a purposeful "crusade" to defeat any particular enemy, but a combined, protracted and sustained worldwide effort to beat the intertwined evils of tyrannical regimes who utilize terrorism and who possess, or threaten to develop, weapons of mass destruction.

In Tony Blair's speech before the two Houses of Congress on 17 July 2003, where he renewed his loyalty to the US under George Bush and won 17 standing ovations, Blair embraced his host's view that terrorism was a "virus that had to be eradicated." This was a departure from Britain's pre-9/11 approach, expressed by Jack Straw, who, as Home Secretary in the late 1990s, turned England into a haven for Muslim terrorists. Pleas from Israel and Arab countries such as Egypt to extradite terrorists who had found shelter in his country went unheeded. This late awakening of the British[26] to the terrorist threat acknowledges that the war against Iraq was not only calculated to remove the tyrant and seize his arsenal of WMD, but

was also part and parcel of the war against world terrorism. The accumulated evidence against Saddam in this regard is fivefold: (1) his
encouragement and financing of terrorist movements such as Hamas; (2)
his ties to al-Qai'da which may lead to information of his support for 9/11;
(3) the existence in Iraq of terrorist training camps for Muslim radicals of
the Islamikaze type; (4) suspicions that Iraq was used by terrorist organizations for tests of chemical and biological weapons; and (5) suspicions that
Saddam maintained among his ex-patriots and other Arab and Muslim
groups in America, an infrastructure of covert agents that may one day rise
and act. We shall address some of these issues briefly.

Saddam and al-Qa'ida

The greatest and gravest indictment against Saddam in terms of his links
with terrorism are the documents linking him to al-Qa'ida. *Prima facie*, it
appears that nothing could link a hardened Ba'athist like Saddam, who
emerged as the leader of the most secular, nationalist and revolutionary
political organization in the Arab world, with a fanatic Islamist like Bin
Laden and his al-Qa'ida group. However, many Saddamists contend that
the dictator was playing the "Muslim card" whenever it was convenient, as
in the 1991 Gulf War, when he engaged the Islamic world to rally to him
and changed his flag to fit the occasion. There is little doubt that in the
process of practicing Islamic politics, he was influenced by it. Evidence of
this can be found in Saddam's direct support for Hamas and the families
of its martyrs and his embracing certain traits of Islamic behavior in his
public conduct. He latterly insisted on being shown in public during
Muslim worship; his speeches became sprinkled with Islamic symbols; and
he may have personally sought solace from two decades of war and misery
under the comforting wings of Allah.

In a letter to the Iraqi people published on 29 April just two weeks after
his regime was overthrown, Saddam uses many examples of Islamic
symbolism. The letter starts with the *basmalah* (the invocation of Allah, the
Compassionate, the Merciful) and a citation of a Qur'anic verse urging the
Believers to loyalty and resilience,[27] quite a feat for a fierce Ba'athist. The
letter then invokes the takeover of Baghdad by the Mongols in the thirteenth century, comparing it to the present-day American invasion. The
message was clear: just as the Islamic Empire of the Abbasids was threatened in medieval times by the Mongol barbarian Infidels, so the Muslim
world is today threatened by the Judeo-Christian barbarian Unbelievers.
Saddam repeatedly invoked Allah and implored him to give ultimate
victory to the Muslims.[28]

During the war journalists from two Western newspapers, the *Toronto
Star* and the British *Sunday Telegraph*, stumbled across hoards of docu-

ments that they claimed linked Saddam to al-Qa'ida, to the extent that in 1998 he sought to meet Bin Laden in person in order to establish a Baghdad–al-Qa'ida axis. It was reported in one document dated 19 February 2003, that another meeting was to take place in the Sudan, and that the French Foreign Ministry transmitted regularly to Saddam any deals it brokered with the US. One of those reports included details of a visit and talk between Jacques Chirac and Bush, when the French President was on a visit to Washington, ostensibly to offer his condolences for the 9/11 tragedy.[29]

Abu Iman al-Maliki, a veteran Iraqi Intelligence officer taken prisoner by the Kurds, attested to a meeting that had taken place in 1992 between Saddam and Ayman al-Zawahiri, Bin Laden's deputy. In an interview with ABC News, al-Maliki said:

> There is a relationship between al-Qa'ida and the Iraqi government. It began about the time of the Kuwait events [1990]. That is when the relationship developed and many delegations came to Baghdad. There are elements of al-Qa'ida training on suicide operations, assassinations, explosions, and the making of chemical substances, and they are supervised by a number of officers, experts from the Iraqi Intelligence's Explosives Division, the Assassinations Division, and other specialized departments . . . [30]

The *Guardian* previously reported in 1999 on the link between Iraq and al-Qa'ida, along with a warning from the Attorney-General of the Clinton Administration, Janet Reno, that a large-scale terrorist attack on the US was a "growing concern." The report followed a meeting between the Iraqi diplomat Faruq Hijazi and Osama bin Laden in 1998.[31] In the October 2002 issue of the *New Yorker*, Jeffrey Goldberg reported that the CIA had long downplayed the theory of an Iraq–al-Qa'ida connection, but cited a memo from CIA Director George Tenet to Senator Bob Graham, the Chairman of the Senate Intelligence Committee, where he warned that Iraq had provided training to al-Qai'da members in the areas of poisons and gases and making conventional bombs, and that there were indications that Iraq and al-Qa'ida had discussed safe havens and reciprocal non-aggression.[32]

Musab al-Zarqawi's group, who facilitated the murder of American diplomat Lawrence Foley in Amman, Jordan, in October 2002 and was himself linked to al-Qa'ida, having trained in its bases in Afghanistan, also had close relations with the Iraqi regime. In the autumn of 2001, al-Zarqawi received extensive medical treatment in Baghdad after he was wounded in Afghanistan. All experts concede that such hospitality could not have been offered to such a high-level terrorist without Saddam's personal agreement.[33]

Saddam's support for Palestinian terrorist groups enhanced his stature among the Palestinians in general, where he was popularly viewed as the new Saladin who would inflict defeat and humiliation upon the Americans. Indeed, official Iraqi support for terrorist attacks against Israeli civilians, a commitment to the destruction of Israel, financial support to the families of Islamikaze terrorists and generous free medical treatment, were offered to the Palestinian terrorist groups on an ongoing basis. The Abu Nidal terrorist group, founded in 1974 and headquartered in Baghdad between 1974 and 1983, had its chief Sabri al-Banna expelled from Baghdad in 1983 in return for America backing for Iraq in the Iran–Iraq War. Only after the war ended in 1988 did the Iraqis revert to sheltering al-Banna. The Palestine Liberation Front was also sponsored by Iraq. The PLF were responsible for the *Achille Lauro* highjacking in 1985; its leader, Mahmoud Abbas (*not* Abu Mazen), was exiled in Egypt. But in 1998 Abbas was given asylum in Baghdad. American troops arrested him in late April 2003, in Baghdad. Iraq, it was claimed, recruited and trained some of the PLF activists, equipped them with weapons and then dispatched them for terrorist attacks in Israel. Saddam also sponsored the Arab Liberation Front, headed by Rateb al-Amleh. Al-Amleh has been active in terrorist attacks against Israel, and the recipient of generous grants amounting to millions of dollars from Iraq since the outbreak of the al-Aqsa *Intifada*, both to finance operations and to compensate the families of martyrs.

A long trail of evidence exists linking the Iraqi regime to other terrorist organizations as well: the Mujahidin al-Khalk who operate within Iran, previously deployed against the Iraqi Kurds;[34] or the Abu Sayyaf Group in the southern Philippines, which, since 1995, has perpetrated many kidnappings for ransom. According to the American Department of State,[35] Iraq has been the main sponsor of Abu Sayyaf, information that was corroborated by Filipino sources.[36] But perhaps the most incriminating evidence has been the Ansar al-Islam base set up in a remote corner of Iraq, by Bin Laden's survivors from Afghanistan, on the triangular border between Iran, Iraq and the Kurdish autonomous area in north. They committed themselves to the establishment of a Qur'anic state to replace the present semi-autonomous Kurdish enclave. Ansar al-Islam operated under the supervision of Iraqi Intelligence, the redoubtable Mukhabarat, and are said to have developed an al-Qa'ida biological and chemical weapons laboratory for the production and distribution of poison gases. The base was heavily bombed before American Special Forces and Kurdish troops moved in to ensure its total destruction.

According to Mansoor I'jaz, Chairman of the Crescent Management Office in New York, who privately negotiated the Sudan's offer to share intelligence data on al-Qa'ida with the Clinton administration in 1997, an al-Qa'ida operative visited Baghdad for two weeks in March 1998. This set the stage for Faruq Hijazi, the Head of Iraqi Intelligence, to travel to Afghanistan to see Bin Laden for further negotiations. It is evident to Mansoor, in any case, that it was Iraq that provided the expertise, financial, logistical and intelligence support to al-Qa'ida for the American Embassy bombings in 1998. So emboldened were the terrorists by the state sponsorship of Iraq that it was natural that they would plan and execute larger and more lethal operations as the 9/11 attack.[37] Former CIA Director James Woolsey, who had served under President Clinton from 1993 to 1995, is also convinced of the link between Saddam and al-Qa'ida. He urged President Bush to promote the evidence that Saddam's regime had been involved in both 9/11 as well as the previous attempt to destroy the World Trade Center in 1993. He said in an interview:

> The Bush administration has not really pushed hard, I think, to uncover these various bits of evidence that may point to some types of links on some issues between al-Qa'ida and Iraq . . . It seems to me that it is important that the Iraqis were training not only their own thugs but also Islamists from other countries quite secretly at Salman Pak for years in the art of aircraft hijacking . . . Evidence tying the September 11 hijackers to the south Baghdad terrorist training camp has yet to surface, but that does not mean it is not relevant. Conceivably, people who trained them were themselves trained there. Other tactics were developed there which were passed on . . .
>
> [As to the 1993 bombing] the two lead bombers, the two smart guys who were supposed to escape and did, one was an Iraqi who had American citizenship. His name is Abdul Rahman Yasin and he fled back to Iraq and was under the protection of the Iraqi government there for years . . . Yasin's partner in the bombing, Ramzi Yussef, entered the US with an Iraqi passport. When Yussef's Manila apartment was raided by Filipino police in 1995, investigators discovered plans on his laptop computer to plant bombs on 12 US airliners and blow them up over the Pacific. An alternative plan called for Yussef to hijack the planes and crash them into US landmarks like the Twin Towers and the Pentagon . . . [38]

Former US Attorney for New York's southern district, Mary Jo White, who prosecuted Ramzi Yussef's case, revealed that Yussef warned US investigators that his compatriots would continue his work. Yussef, now serving a life sentence in a maximum security prison in Florence, Colorado, gave a statement to the FBI and the Secret Service, claiming that brothers of his would perform the planned bombing that he could not do. Apparently, the Bush administration prior to 9/11 had not pressed Yussef for more information on Iraq's role in his plot to destroy the Twin Towers. To Woolsey's mind, "there were enough connections between Iraq and al-Qa'ida that we ought to be looking at this very hard, as we capture files and people and hard disk drives and so on, and see what we can turn up."[39]

Members of the bi-partisan National Commission on Terrorist Attacks Upon the US received testimony from terrorist experts and academics that linked Iraq to 9/11. One member, former Secretary of the Navy John Lehman, indicated that the panel has already seen documents that point to a relationship between Iraq and al-Qa'ida. For Lehman, there was no doubt that Iraq trained terrorists in cultivating and using anthrax and in hijacking techniques at Salman Pak. Iraq's involvement in the Twin Towers attack has been argued for years by Laurie Mylroie, a fellow of the American Enterprise Institute in Washington and one of America's foremost experts on Iraqi affairs. She believes that Saddam's involvement in the 1993 attempt against the Twin Towers was the direct result of his defeat in 1991 and his burning desire to take revenge upon the US, by backing large-scale Islamist terrorist attacks.[40]

The Bush administration had previously asserted that there were ties between Iraq and al-Qa'ida, but many terrorism specialists and intelligence officials had publicly questioned whether radical Islamic cadres could have cooperated with Saddam's regime, and discounted the reports that Muhammad Atta, the chief operative of 9/11, had met with an Iraqi official in spring 2001. Examples, however, abound elsewhere in the Islamic world of Muslim fanatics, like Hamas, the Wahhabis or Hizbullah, cooperating with Marxist or secular groups like the Democratic Front. The fact is that the Iraqi official who met Atta, Ahmed Khalil al-Ani, is in US custody, and Iraq's role in helping al-Qa'ida in its sickest and most daring exploit will receive fresh scrutiny. Also under US custody now is Khalid Sheikh Muhammad, the Chief Operations Officer of al-Qa'ida, as well as other operatives, who may have acquired false Kuwaiti identities during the short-lived Iraqi occupation in 1990–1. Similarly, the Palestinian Muhammad Salameh, who was arrested in 1993 for his role in the World Trade Center bombing, made dozens of phone calls to Iraq over a period of a month in 1992.[41]

Another set of post-war indictments linking Saddam with al-Qa'ida came from Federal Judge Gilbert Merritt of Nashville, Tennessee, who was sent to Iraq as an expert to help rebuild the Iraqi judicial system. He filed a dispatch to his hometown paper, reporting:

Through an unusual set of circumstances, I have been given documentary evidence of the names and positions of the 600 closest people in Iraq to Saddam Hussein, as well as his ongoing relationship with Osama Bin Laden . . . I am looking at the document as I write this story from my hotel room overlooking the Tigris River in Baghdad . . .

One of the five lawyers with whom I have been working for the past five weeks had come to me and asked me whether a list of the 600 people closest to Saddam Hussein would be of any value now to the Americans. I said, yes, of course. He said that the list contains not only the names of the 55 "deck of cards" players who have been revealed so far, but also 550 others. When I began questioning him about the list, how he obtained it and what else it showed, he asked would it be of interest to the Americans to know that Saddam had an ongoing relationship with Bin Laden. I said yes, the Americans have, so far that I am aware, never been able to prove that relationship, but the President and others have said that they believe it exists. He said: "Well, Judge, there is no doubt it exists, and I will bring you the proof tomorrow."

So, today he brought me the proof, and there is no doubt in my mind that he is right. The document shows that an Iraqi Intelligence officer, Abd al-Karim Muhammad Aswad, assigned to the Iraqi Embassy in Pakistan, is "responsible for the coordination of activities with the Osama Bin Laden group." The document shows that it was written over the signature of Uday, the son of Saddam Hussein. The story of how the document came about is as follows . . .

Saddam gave Uday authority to control all the press and media outlets in Iraq. Uday was the publisher of the *Babylon Daily* political newspaper. On the front-page of the paper's four-page edition of November 14, 2002, there was a picture of Osama Bin Laden speaking, next to which was a picture of Saddam and his Revolutionary Council, together with stories of Israeli tanks attacking a group of Palestinians. On the back page was a story headlined "List of Honor." In a box below the headline was "A List of Men we Publish for the Public," with the lead sentence referring to a list of the "regime persons" with their names and positions. This list has 600 names and titles in three columns. It contains, for example, the names of the important officials who are members of Saddam's family, such as Uday himself, and then other high officials, including the 55 American "deck of cards" officials, some of whom have been apprehended. Half way down the middle column is written "Abd al-Karim Muhammad Aswad, Intelligence officer responsible for the coordination of activities with the Osama Bin Laden group at the Iraqi Embassy in Pakistan . . . "

Samir, the lawyer who brought this newspaper to me, and Zuhair, another lawyer with whom I have been working, translated the Arabic words and described what had happened in Baghdad the day it was published. Samir bought his paper from a newsstand at around 8:00 am, and within two hours, Iraqi Intelligence officers were going to each newsstand in Baghdad and confiscating the papers. They also went to the home of every person who they were told received a newspaper that day and confiscated it. Zuhair, who was the Counsel for the Arab League in Baghdad, did not receive delivery of his paper that day. He called his vendor who told him that there would be no newspaper that day. Samir's paper was never confiscated.

The only explanation for this strange set of events, according to the Iraqi lawyers, is that Uday, a somewhat impulsive and unbalanced individual, decided to publish this honor list at a time when the regime was under worldwide verbal attack in the press, especially by the US. It would, he thought make them more loyal and supportive of the regime. His father was furious, knowing that it revealed information about his supporters that should remain secret . . . At the time it was published, Saddam was denying that he had any relationship with Bin Laden, therefore he had all the newspapers confiscated, and he ordered that publication of the paper be stopped for 10 days.

This is the story of the Honor Roll of 600, and why I believe that President Bush was right when he alleged that Saddam was in cahoots with Osama and was coordinating activities with him. It does not prove that they engaged together in any particular act against the United States, but it seems to me strong proof that the two were in contact and conspiring to perform terrorist acts. Up until this time I have been skeptical about these claims. Now I have changed my mind. There is, however, one big problem remaining: they are both still at large and the combined forces of the free world have been unable to find them. Until we find and capture them, they will remain a threat – Saddam with the remnants of his army and supporters, in combination with the worldwide terrorist organiza-tion of Osama Bin Laden . . . [42]

This article carries intrinsic value, because its author cannot be suspected of political manipulation, and due to the sober and prudent language borrowed from the legal profession. Secretary Powell, in his memorable speech to the UN Security Council on 5 February 2003, stated that the Iraqi Embassy in Pakistan played the role of liaison between Baghdad and the al-Qa'ida. Despite his impeccable personal record, intellectual opponents of the administration refused to give credence to Powell's or the judge's claims. To this can be added the evidence linking Saddam to other inter-national Muslim terrorist organizations. Hamsiraji Sali, for example, the local commander of the Abu Sayyaf group in Cebu, southern Philippines, claimed that he received $20,000 annually from Iraq to spend on chemicals for bomb-making. Since Abu Sayyaf's affiliation to al-Qa'ida is beyond doubt, that partnership provides yet another piece of indirect evidence to Saddam's doings. Sali's claim came one week after an Iraqi diplomat, Husham Hussein, was expelled from Manila, amidst charges that he was in contact with Abu Sayyaf by telephone. Hussein may also have been a member of the Hussein family, though not of the caliber of liaison officer with al-Qa'ida in Pakistan; he was expelled after he received a call from an Abu Sayyaf member linked to the 2 October 2002 bombing in the city of Zamboanga, where one American serviceman was killed and another wounded. Several members of the Abu Sayyaf group had received explo-sives from Ramzi Yussef, who masterminded the 1993 Twin Towers attack.[43]

The American Security Agenda – Domestic and International

American troops made the search for al-Qa'ida and general terrorist links in Iraq one of the most pressing missions of the war. And the very fact that several terrorist targets were attacked and destroyed was evidence of terrorist links. In Sarget, near the Iranian border, US and Kurdish fighters eliminated what was believed to be a poison factory run by Arab al-Qa'ida refugees from Afghanistan. Nine precision-guided weapons hit that compound of the Ansar al-Islam (the Supporters of Islam) leaving only yawning craters. The air attack against the compound, described in detail by Secretary Powell at the Security Council, lasted one week, followed by a ground attack of American Special Forces aided by the Kurds. Some 250 Muslim fighters were believed to have been killed in all, with the survivors running away to hide in Iran. Stacks of raw intelligence were collected. According to the Chairman of the Joint Chiefs of Staff General Richard

Myers, laptop computers and documents were found, along with ricin samples, a poison made from castor beans. Myers said that the ricin that was discovered in London in late March 2003, came from the Sarget camp. Jalal Talabani, the Head of the Kurdish forces who fought alongside the Americans in that battle, said that many telephone books were found with numbers linking the Ansar to various quarters in the vast Islamic world, such as Saudi Arabia, Britain, the Palestinian territories, Jordan and Syria. As evidence, he held up a passport of a Moroccan man from Casablanca who was a member of the group killed during the fighting.[44] The Ansar compound structure was very reminiscent of the Alamut fortress where the medieval aassassins had enclosed themselves in an enclave from where they killed leaders handpicked by their spiritual head, known in Crusader literature as the "Old man from the Mountain."[45]

The reports reaching America about the destruction of the al-Qa'ida base in Iraq, which was presented as part of the global war on terrorism, were reinforced by both the inquiry of the National Commission on Terrorist Attacks Upon the United States, which was mandated to investigate American failures, intelligence or otherwise, to prevent the 9/11 horrors, and to recommend future measures; and at the same time, by the tough strictures imposed on Arab-Americans, some of them of Iraqi origin, by the Attorney-General's Office and the Home Front Secretary, which brought about the arrest and detaining of many Arabs. The triangular link was established in the minds of many Americans between the 9/11 attacks, with their acknowledged perpetrator, al-Qa'ida; the war in Iraq where the bases of al-Qa'ida were supposed to be searched and destroyed; and a minority of Arab-Americans who took advantage of America's generosity and hospitality to collaborate with outside Muslim fundamentalists. The result was the biggest domestic security threat since Pearl Harbor. Americans could not accept that breach of confidence, therefore they reconciled to the war in Iraq and to selective violations of civil liberties at home, all for the purpose of safeguarding their security.

The Chairman of the Panel of the National Commission, which is split evenly between Democrats and Republicans, is Thomas Kean, a Republican and former New Jersey governor; his Deputy is Lee Hamilton, a Democrat and a former House member from Indiana. Though the Commission was supposed to draft its report some time in May 2004, its hearings were considered relevant to the American public. The testimonies, especially of the families of the victims, were heartbreaking and kept hammering in the questions of how suspect immigrants could be let into the US while they constituted such a security threat to US citizens.[46]

On the Arab-American front, things were less clear-cut. Since the terrorist attacks President Bush has dubbed Islam as a "religion of peace," and he warned against anti-Muslim prejudice. Bush had reached out to

Muslims in the 2000 presidential elections, but he has also courted evangelical Christians who regard Islam as an evil religion and as the gravest danger to American national security. The matter was complicated further by anti-American statements made by various Shi'ite clerics in Iraq as well as other Muslim clerics in Saudi Arabia, Egypt and Jordan, which are generally considered pro-American. The arrest of some prominent Muslims in Florida and elsewhere in America, who were accused of representing Muslim terrorist groups, did not improve the suspicions that Muslims entertain toward the US, and vice versa. At home, the requirement for immigrants to register with the authorities that began concurrently with the opening of the War in Iraq and the consequent elevation of the national alert against terrorism, has provoked concerns about civil liberties and racial profiling from Muslims and Arabs. Despite protests from Muslim groups, the Pentagon invited the Reverend Franklin Graham, who called Islam "wicked and evil" following 9/11, to officiate on the Good Friday service while the war was still far from over.[47]

When American predictions of domestic terrorist acts during the War in Iraq failed to materialize, attention was shifted by intelligence analysts to the likelihood that a protracted American presence in Iraq after the war might cause a new wave of terrorism both in the US and against American interests abroad. President Mubarak had predicted that the War in Iraq would create "one hundred new Osama Bin Ladens." Some of the predictions regarding lone Islamikaze bombers have already been largely fulfilled, and they have been complemented by grenade attacks and sniper shootings against American patrols, camps in the heart of Iraq or lonely guards at American or Iraqi public institutions. Still, neither al-Qa'ida nor Arab countries who have been urged by Saddam to rebel against the US have responded.[48]

The continual harassment of US troops in Iraq cannot be considered terrorism as long as the targets are US troops and not civilians. This means that the contours of the war between the US and the world terrorist organizations may be changing, and that the battered international terrorists no longer have the means or the will to launch new operations on US soil, something that, in the long-run, if kept unchanged, will cut the Gordian knot between Iraq, international terrorism and the plight of Muslim Americans, at least in the eyes of American public opinion, if not the administration. The administration revived a 1996 law which makes it a crime to offer material support to any group designated by the US government as a terrorist organization. This means that even organizations such as Hamas, which collected funds in the US but operated exclusively against Israel, will no longer be able to maintain their front charities in the US.

Several groups and individuals were prosecuted under that statute, including a Florida Professor of Arab extraction who provided logistical and financial support to Palestinian Islamikaze and a Yemenite cleric who used a Brooklyn mosque to raise money and funnel it to al-Qa'ida. Even a prominent defense lawyer, Lynne Stewart, was charged of helping an imprisoned Sheikh to transmit messages to his terrorist followers in Egypt. Worse, from the point of view of some civil libertarians, is the atmosphere created when clerics in mosques are urged by the FBI to report on any suspicious visitor to their congregation, and to become informers for the counter-terrorism authorities, something that does not necessarily hold them in high esteem in the eyes of their congregations. The War in Iraq has put many mosque officials on high alert, but it has also turned away worshippers who feel they are spied on and that they have lost their freedom of speech.[49] A mosque in Santa Clara, California, that raised funds for food and medical supplies to be sent to Iraq, and was backed strongly by the local Muslim community, was shunned by several private donors who either contributed smaller sums than normal or refused to donate anything at all. Four Muslim charities were shut down by the government, accused of ties with terrorist groups, and several prominent Muslim donors were indicted or detained.

Usually so critical of civil rights and due process of law in other countries, America now finds itself guilty of having compromised these universal laws for the security of the nation. The US, which argues that these rights are impermeable, quickly sheds them whenever it is necessary to do so. A Muslim-Palestinian-American from Portland, Oregon, Maher Hawash, was detained for weeks on end, without charge, for an unspecified terrorist plot that the government refuses to describe, but is linked to some Taliban sympathizers who were planning to join the war against the US in Afghanistan. The secrecy of his case has outraged the Muslim community, despite the government's confirmation that his detention, like that of many others, was necessary to deter attacks. Other fellow Muslims are even afraid to contribute to his defense fund, lest they be accused as accomplices. The judge has banned the public from the court hearing and prohibited Hawash's lawyers from discussing the case in public. He had contributed to the Global Relief Foundation, prayed in the same Bilal Mosque as two apprehended suspects in terrorism, and gone to Hong Kong on his way to the Middle East, a route often taken by terrorists on their way to Afghanistan. When there was no end in sight to this process, his friends and supporters rallied on the steps of the Federal court house and demonstrated. Previous cases of Muslims who were similarly detained ended in indictments of terrorist conspiracies. Civil libertarians have accused the government of using those detentions as a preventive measure to buy time while searching for evidence. The Justice Department counters that only detention makes sure that a suspect does not tamper with witnesses or conspire to commit other crimes, and that each detention had been approved by a judge.[50]

Weapons of Mass Destruction (WMD)

Ever since Tony Blair's speech before the two Houses of Congress on 17 July 2003, where he conceded that history would forgive him and President Bush even if no weapons of mass destruction are found in Iraq, opponents of the war, in the US and Britain in particular, and elsewhere in general, have been "celebrating," as if the war had been in vain or as if there were no tyranny that was removed or terrorism that was battled. But that celebration seems premature, to say the least, not only because the search continues for WMD and vast possibilities still exist to find them, but also because there is such a weighty evidence of their existence, in the past if not in the present, that there should be no doubt about the validity of the Allied claims or the veracity of that "smoking gun." Evidence is indeed overwhelming and it is to be gleaned in the following domains:

1   Saddam Hussein had boasted in public since the 1980s of the development by his scientists of "binary" weapons of mass destruction, which presumably contain both chemical and biological weapons, and he threatened to use them to "burn half Israel"; others, like the Egyptians in the 1960s, used WMD in their wars (Egypt in Yemen, for example), but denied the fact or at least tried to hide it. Saddam is one of the few tyrants in history who threatened to use them, and backed his menace by actual manufacturing of the deadly substances.

2   Saddam used WMD both against the Iranians in the First Gulf War (1980–8) and the Kurds in Halabja in 1988; that means that even if Saddam had no weapons on the eve of the Third War, there is no denying that he had them in the past, and that he had used them.

3   Saddam himself had reported to the UN Chief Inspector Hans Blix, during the months leading up to the war, that he had certain quantities of biological and chemical weapons that he destroyed, but he provided no evidence of their destruction. In other words, while there is an Iraqi admission of past existence of those weapons, there is no proof that they were discarded.

4   Various foreign companies, especially some based in Germany, were caught trading in chemical substances with Iraq, which could provide the basis for the manufacture of WMD.

5   In the 1980s Saddam made tremendous efforts to develop missiles and a long-range "giant cannon," with the help of a Belgian scientist, which would be worthwhile developing only if it had WMD payloads to deliver.

6   When, in June 1981 Israel destroyed Saddam's nuclear program at the French Osirak, it was widely believed that the site was designed to produce nuclear weapons. Further evidence to that effect transpired over the years when Saddam's agents had attempted to smuggle out of

the US and Western European countries parts that are essential for the production of nuclear arms.

7   Prior to the Third Gulf War, an impressive body of evidence had been gleaned by British, American and Israeli intelligence, and most of it was presented by Secretary Powell to the Security Council.

8   During the war, widespread reporting was done in the American press, by independent investigative reporters, who accumulated a massive amount of evidence, circumstantial or otherwise, regarding the manufacturing of WMD. It is inconceivable that so many hiding places and secret sites, so many Iraqis who were banned from certain areas and so many restrictions around certain military camps, could all be fabrications with no grounding in reality.

9   UN inspectors, notably Mr Butler, the Australian Chief Inspector, who visited sites throughout Iraq, urged the public to learn from what the Iraqis tried to withhold from them, and from the obstacles they put before UN investigators, more than from the information they yielded under duress. The fact that the UN inspectors were on occasion prevented by or under threat of force, from accessing certain suspected sites, and only allowed on to them after delays, during which the Iraqis hid up the incriminating substances, also led the inspectors to believe that the Iraqi authorities were engaging in a systematic and organized campaign of concealment and denial.

10 Scientists claim that while nuclear weapons or facilities are difficult to hide, it is possible to conceal biological and chemical weapons, and that even if under duress the Iraqis destroyed the stocks they had of those deadly weapons, they certainly preserved their capacity to manufacture new ones at will.

11 The US special teams searching for WMD throughout Iraq have found many barrels of chemical substances, suspiciously hidden or buried under ground. The teams also found what appear to be mobile laboratories which could have manufactured WMD.

12 The clear possibility exists that during the months leading up to the war, Saddam had ample opportunity to conclude cooperation deals with other Arab and Islamic countries such as Syria, Iran, Pakistan or Libya, whereby weapons could be sheltered elsewhere in return for oil or money. One has to remember that since the end of the 1990 Iraq and Syria aided each other via the smuggling of vast amounts of Iraqi oil abroad, even as Syria was made a member of the Security Council of the UN.

Based on Secretary Powell's highly credible appearance at the UN Security Council, evidence does exist of Iraq's association with unconventional weapons, though much of that evidence is circumstantial. UN institutions are not a court of law: the fact that the majority of nations did not favor an incriminating American resolution spoke more about the self-interest of those countries than about the truth behind Iraq's WMD program. It is not the case that since the UN did not vote for something that meant that it did not exist or was the right decision. The UN record is replete with travesties of justice. In any case, once the US made the tragic mistake of apprising the Security Council of the Iraqi threat, it became evident that things were going to be decided by political considerations, envies and rivalries. But Secretary Powell's speech to the Council, an assessment of the threat posed by Saddam based on US, British and other foreign Intelligence services, remains a comprehensive portrayal of Iraq and its WMD. A summary of Colin Powell's main speech points follows.[51]

In mid-December 2002, weapons experts in one facility inspected by the UN were replaced by Iraqi Intelligence agents who were to deceive inspectors about the work that was being done there. On orders from Saddam, the Iraqis issued a false death certificate for one scientist who was sent into hiding, so that he could not be interrogated by the inspectors; in mid-January 2003, experts at one facility related to WMD had been ordered to stay at home away from work to avoid the inspectors. Workers from other facilities not engaged in unconventional weapons were to replace the absent workers; and a dozen Iraqi experts were placed under home arrest – not in their homes, but as a group in one of Saddam's guest houses. This is not the expected behavior of someone who has nothing to hide. Had the Iraqis been invited to the Security Council and allowed themselves to be interrogated under oath, it is doubtful that any one of them could stand the interrogation unscathed.

The examples cited by Secretary Powell gave ample indication of the systematic effort made by the Iraqis to keep key materials and people from the inspectors. This was not merely lack of cooperation, but a patent campaign to scuttle any meaningful inspection work. This should not be surprising since Saddam has specialized in such deceitful tactics since inspections began (1991–8), and it was precisely due to those tactics that the entire operation came to a halt (1998–2003) under the "arrangement" that the UN Secretary-General Kofi Annan had reached with Saddam Hussein. Little wonder then that the Secretary-General was not the most vocal voice in favor of resuming the inspections until they were demanded by the US, nor was he in favor of exposing Iraqi lies, which would have also incriminated Annan and his "understanding" with Saddam.

In the field of biological weapons, it had taken four years for the UN inspectors to get Iraq to admit that it was involved in biological manufacture. This admission, made in 1995, revealed vast quantities of these weapons. That meant that, while denying their existence, the Iraqis were hard at work producing and storing them. Iraq declared 8,500 liters of anthrax, while UNSCOM (United Nations Special Commission to Iraq) estimated that three times that quantity may have been manufactured. Moreover, the Iraqis have never accounted for all the biological weapons they admitted to producing, nor for the 400 weapons they had filled with those substances, which UN inspectors failed to locate. American Intelligence had amassed information about the continued manufacture of those weapons in the years since the inspectors were expelled by Saddam in 1998.

One of the most worrisome aspects of biological weapons was the existence of mobile production facilities. These trucks and train cars are specifically designed to evade detection. In any case, those mobile facilities could have manufactured enough biological agents to surpass anything the Iraqis had prior to 1990. A defecting Iraqi chemical engineer who supervised one of those facilities gave evidence in 2000 of the production of biological weapons and of an accident which killed 12 technicians on the site. He testified that production of those agents always started Thursdays at midnight, because the Iraqis thought the inspectors would not work on the Muslim holy day of Friday. Production continued until Friday evening, when the inspectors were likely to show up again. This testimony was corroborated by other independent Iraqi sources. The trucks, cars or trailers can easily be concealed because they are exactly the same, on the outside, as ordinary models of that particular vehicle. Indeed, during the Iraq War, even though many suspected vehicles of that sort were detected by special teams, they were hard to tell from others. In all, 18 mobile production units were available for the Iraqi manufacturing of WMD, which could churn out enough biological agents in one month (anthrax, ricin, aflatoxin and botulinum toxin) to kill many thousands of people. By 1998, the UN inspectors had concluded that the Iraqis had so perfected the dry version of these agents, which is the most lethal, that it was incorporated into the mobile units.

Other explored biological agents used in weapons can cause diseases such as gas gangrene, the plague, typhus, tetanus, cholera, camel pox, hemorrhagic fever and small pox. Lethal agents can be transmitted by infecting water sources and through the air. Iraq has even developed aerial fuel tanks for Mirage fighter jets to facilitate dispersion. Iraq has also developed four spray tanks mounted on unmanned MiG-21s, and no evidence exists that they were disposed of.

As to chemical weapons, UNSCOM had widely documented their development and manufacture, and one needs no better proof of their existence and of Saddam's readiness to use them than the fact that he used them in the war against Iran and against his own people in Halabja in 1988. Saddam has also never accounted for the thousands of shells and bombs filled with mustard gas and other chemical agents that were known to exist in Iraq. Only after the defection of Hussein Kamel, the late son-in-law of Saddam, did Iraq acknowledge possession of four tons of VX nerve gas, one drop of which is fatal. UNSCOM collected forensic evidence that demonstrates Iraq has not only produced this substance but has also developed weapons armed with the gas. Iraq has embedded much of its illicit weapons industry into civilian chemical plants; this dual-use production can be turned back and forth from civilian to military use in order to deceive prying eyes. These plants were built to willfully mislead inspection teams as to their function. Satellite photos shot as late as May 2002, for instance, showed unusual activity at the al-Musayyib complex, where Iraq transformed its chemical products into various weapons, including medium-range missiles and grenades, before dispatching them to designated secret locations. Another photo of the same site taken two months later revealed that the ground had been bulldozed and graded, indicating that the Iraqis had removed the crust of the earth in order to conceal evidence of years of ongoing chemical weapons activity.

Iraq ran an international network of clandestine procurement to purchase vital parts and substances for its WMD program: filters which separate micro-organisms; toxins used in biological weapons; equipment to concentrate the lethal agent; growth media for anthrax and botulinum toxin; sterilization equipment for laboratories; glass-lined reactors and pumps that can handle corrosive chemical agents; large amounts of thionyl chloride, a precursor for nerve and blister agents; and other substances. Even if Iraq were to explain that it needed all those substances for its legitimate chemical production, it would have to explain why it hid them from the inspectors, and why it took a tremendous intelligence effort, including eavesdropping on senior Iraqi commanders, to dig them up. By American estimates, the Iraqis had hundreds of tons of chemical agents, enough to fill thousands of weapons to cause widespread death. Saddam had given his field commanders the authorization to use those weapons under certain circumstances, itself evidence of their existence and of his intention to use them. Since the 1980s Saddam's regime had also been experimenting on humans to perfect his biological and chemical weapons. In 1995, 1,600 death-row prisoners were transferred to a special unit for such experiments. Eye-witnesses said the prisoners were tied to beds while tests were performed on them, and then autopsies were carried out to evaluate the efficacy of the products.

Regarding Iraq's nuclear capacity, which Saddam not only had never abandoned but remained determined to attain, the US provided substantial proof. Inspectors had been looking ever since 1991 for elements of a nuclear program but claimed to find nothing. However, Saddam did have a massive clandestine nuclear program: the fact that it was not discovered by UN teams only goes to show his ability to conceal it. Iraq's nuclear program covered various techniques to enrich uranium (electromagnetic isotope separation, gas centrifuge and gas diffusion), which cost billions of dollars. Iraq already possessed two out of the three elements needed for nuclear weapons: a cadre of expert scientists, and a bomb design. Since 1998 Saddam focused on acquiring the third element, fissile material, or the ability to enrich uranium. He made different tubes, which can be used as centrifuges. While American experts have identified those tubes as rotors for the centrifuges, the Iraqis claimed that they were to be used for the bodies of rockets in multiple rocket-launchers. This makes little sense, as their tolerance far exceeds what is the accepted standard in the American weapon industry. The Iraqis were also making efforts to acquire other parts of equipment that could be used to build gas centrifuges. Such efforts by the Saddam regime underline its ambition of manufacturing fissile material. The nuclear scientists' cadre, whom the press openly called the "nuclear mujahideen," were regularly praised and exhorted for their efforts.

In addition to weapons of mass destruction, Iraq also developed the means to deliver them, especially ballistic missiles and unmanned aerial vehicles UAVs. The means of delivery, which are too expensive just to deliver conventional payloads, are in themselves conclusive proof that the Iraqis were developing unconventional weapons. Before 1990 Iraq had developed many such missiles, and used them in attacks on its neighbors – Iran, Saudi Arabia, Kuwait and Israel – and longer range missiles were being developed. Despite the fact that the UN inspectors destroyed most of Saddam's missile capacity, he retained a few dozen of them with a range of up to 1,000 km. The two types of missiles Iraq had developed – al-Sumud and al-Fatah – violated the 150 km limit established by the Security Council. Moreover, the Iraqis had illegally imported 380 SA-2 rocket engines for the development of banned advanced rockets. Secretary Powell produced significant evidence to prove that the Iraqis were developing 1,200 km-range missiles that are forbidden by the UN resolutions and patently put in jeopardy Iraq's neighbors, because of their capacity to deliver unconventional weapons to each one of their major cities.

The UAVs (Unmanned Aerial Vehicles) have no other purpose than to carry and deliver unconventional payloads. Spray devices have been developed to attain greater efficiency in distributing the lethal substances over large areas. The UAVs have been fitted on MiG-21 Soviet aircraft, but Iraq has also been developing smaller vehicles for that specific purpose, called L-29s. While Iraq has declared this vehicle to have a range of 80 km, US Intelligence has discovered that in its test flights it covered a range of 500 km, without refuelling and on autopilot, which renders it lethal to Iraq's neighbors.[52]

Equipped with the knowledge that was laid out before the Security Council, which fully represented the working assumptions of Tommy Franks' troops, as soon as the American forces crossed into Iraqi territory they were on WMD alert, with specialized units of detection, protection and de-contamination accompanying every fighting unit. There were places and times where every soldier was on high alert, and despite the suffocating anti-WMD suits and masks, the troops wore them. That was particularly the case during the approach to Baghdad, when the Americans were convinced that Saddam would deploy all weapons at his disposal at his last confrontation with the Americans.[53] But that did not happen.

Various explanations are possible for their non-use. The most common explanation is that the American moves were so swift and overwhelming and they were always several steps ahead of the Iraqi field commanders, who never had the chance to evaluate the right time and place to use them. Add to that the disarray and collapsing systems of command and control under the American bombings, and you have a plausible reason why the Iraqis could not mobilize their WMD. But this explanation omits the fact that the Iraqis knew the Americans were coming for months and so had plenty of time to prepare for the assault. Another reason could be that Saddam's decision not to use WMD was politically motivated. That is Saddam did not want to confirm US suspicions by using WMD when he argued, and most of the world believed, he had none. This argument, however, overlooks the fact that the whole rationale for the stockpiling of such weapons is to use them to safeguard the regime. Furthermore, the self-defense line of reasoning, that Saddam never considered them an offensive tactic, makes no sense. No one was threatening Saddam with such weapons. Except for Egypt's use of chemical weapons in the Yemen in the 1960s, there is no record of the use of chemical warfare since World War I, except by Saddam. Besides, if he needed those weapons only in self-defense, why did he use them against the Kurds in 1988?

The only plausible explanation that remains is this: Saddam had plenty of WMD, which he built to use to promote his ambitions, both against factions of his own people and his neighbors. Very few of the latter also have them, even less would dare use them. He nevertheless came to the conclusion in the months building up to the war, that rather than vindicate the US and the inspectors who would ultimately find damaging proof of their existence, he would systematically eliminate any signs of their presence on his soil. An elaborate program of concealment was undertaken, matched only by the ongoing underground manufacturing of those substances. Whatever could be buried in the vast Iraqi desert, together with the large manufacturing facilities that existed there since the inspections started, "disappeared" in that fashion; whatever could be dissimulated as civilian-use substances, was transformed; what could be stored in neighboring friendly countries, such as Syria and Jordan, and (for a price) even Iran and Saudi Arabia, was hauled there; and what was left may have been shipped overseas to places like Sudan, Libya, or any country willing to take money for its storage; and the rest was simply destroyed. The destruction of missiles to satisfy UN inspectors in the weeks prior to the war were an example of that; another was the new top soil shown by Powell to the members of the Security Council.

On 26 March at the end of the first week of fighting, the Americans entered the three-square-mile compound near Najaf, some 100 miles south of the capital. Of particular interest was the information provided by an Iraqi general and other 30 officers, and another 300 POWs. The general claimed that he had nothing to do with unconventional weapons, but admitted that there were special bunkers and underground tunnels in the compound that neither he nor other senior officers could enter. When a team of the 75th Exploitation Task Force (XTF), formed of technicians of various disciplines and Special Forces, arrived at that site, they found a biological hazard sign on a wooden pallet with a crate in bunker No. 36, and markings on other crates in bunker No. 37 indicating CN-1, which is sometimes used for riot control agents.

The team also found artillery shells coated with a wax that is sometimes used on shells and bombs containing unconventional weapons. They also stumbled into 40 advanced Soviet-style masks with extra filters, indicating that WMD experiments were carried out there. Hydraulic triple-locked doors barred the entrance to some of the more-than 100 bunkers on the site, protected by electric fences and trenches. Another team, the Mobile Exploitation Team Bravo (MET-Bravo) visited a vast abandoned Iraqi air base at Talil in the south, its runways littered with war debris, plane wrecks and vehicles. Large quantities of weapons and ammunition, some from World War II, had been amassed haphazardly and left behind at the air base. The base had been heavily bombed by the Americans during the 1991 Gulf War, and was on the list of suspected sites, but according to the captain, "there was not any apparent rhyme or reason to the storage. Shells were mixed in with casings, fuses and mortar, piled high from floor to ceiling. It was all a jumble."[54]

Saddam had adopted a novel tactic of preserving what he could of his army and unconventional arsenals, avoiding initial combat and harassing the occupying troops only after the war was declared over and no WMD were found. The Americans had wrongly predicted that the Iraqis, withdrawing into Baghdad, would use chemical agents to contaminate the land between themselves and the advancing US troops. The assumption was based on the experiences of the First Gulf War (1980–8), where the Iraqis laid down mustard gas behind the Iranian forces, then bombarded the front lines with sarin nerve gas. The goal was to drive the retreating sarin-exposed Iranians into the mustard trap, and the Americans were afraid that the same tactic might be repeated against them to create killing zones around them as they approached Baghdad. The fact that Iraq is not a signatory to the Chemical Weapons Convention (1993) increased suspicions among the Americans.[55]

Two weeks into the war, the Americans had explored a dozen of the several hundred suspected sites, but still no smoking gun had been found. The official explanation was that most of the suspected locations were still under Iraqi control, in the Baghdad and Tikrit areas, and that after

America took over the entire territory the search would be conducted in earnest. Meanwhile, at an industrial plant in Latifiya, south of Baghdad, troops found thousands of boxes of white powder, a suspected chemical agent, but it was later identified as regular explosives. The 75th XTF, much to its frustration, found itself training in northern Iraq rather than making headway in the investigations process, while the American administration were now talking about restoring civil rights to Iraq, building a democracy and destroying the infrastructure of terrorism in the country. They still expressed their faith, at least in public, that WMD would be located sooner or later. The media, rather than producing investigative journalism, simply resorted to anti-government reports, accusing the American and British leaders of deception.

In one incident, the Americans authorized the use of tear gas against rioters in Iraq in order to avert the use of live fire to quell disturbances. Experts and intellectuals claimed that America, who is a signatory to the Chemical Weapons Convention, would be violating its signature – tear gas being one of the prohibited substances. However, there exists in the American legal system an executive order from 1975, which has since become American national policy, allowing tear gas to be used for certain defensive purposes, such as when civilians were being used to screen an attack, as was the case in Iraq. The Chemical Weapons Convention had banned tear gas against armed forces for fear that it might escalate to the use of other chemical agents, but that was clearly not the case here. Opponents of the war found here an opportunity to claim that the use of tear gas in the war entitled the Iraqis to retaliate with chemical weapons of their own, in self-defense.[56] Absurdity had come full circle.

In the Karbalah area, while the Americans were searching an empty military camp where Palestinians and other foreign volunteers were supposedly trained, troops found several drums which they thought may contain deadly nerve agents and mustard gas, but decided to reserve their final judgment until the 75th XTF could test the findings. American troops also discovered an unusually large selection of chemical protection gear. Some soldiers became ill, probably auto-suggestion, and they put on their chemical protection suits. The chemical unit identified the substance as CN, a riot-control gas that causes vomiting and blisters. A second 20-gallon drum was identified as containing sarin and tabun, two nerve agents. Another 55-gallon drum was said to have tested positive for mustard gas. The suspected materials were not packaged into warheads or artillery shells, something which should have raised suspicions as to their lethal effect.[57] Reporters were extremely prudent regarding the find, qualifying their writing with "possibles" and "maybes." One reporter even warned that tests in the field can be inconclusive, because the kits for preliminary testing were designed to err on the side of caution, while the large and precise instruments – the gas chromatograph and the mass spectometer – which break up the chemicals into their components and then compare them to libraries of known substances, are too large and too complex to be placed in the field. The Iraqis were known to have developed, in the 1980s, large quantities of mustard, tabun and sarin chemicals. The first tests showed that residues of these agents might still have lingered in the camp.[58] This ambiguous discovery demonstrates the deception the Iraqi program was based upon: Any lethal material can be depicted as innocent, and any residue of chemical substances can be dismissed as fertilizer.

When questions relating to circumstantial evidence are not asked, and testing in military units is limited to matter-of-fact, mechanical gauging, then one understands why the testing units would repeat their refrain of "no-conclusive evidence," and of "frustration" at their inability to dig up the findings that were their very *raison d'être*. By their repeated expression of "disappointment" that they did not find the incriminating material, while it was laying right there all around them, the testers ignored the underlying truth. When a "smoking gun" is not found in a homicide case, the spent cartridges, the body, the blood stains, the hair and fingerprints of the assassin are sufficient incriminating proof. Yet when sensors invariably detected chemical materials in every suspected Iraqi camp, the chemical liquid found was described as "probably part of organo-phosphates used in pesticides." When such a finding was announced by the Mobile Exploitation Team Alpha in Muhawish, a town in the valley of the Euphrates eminently suited to agriculture, one could understand the inconclusiveness of the findings. But in most other cases, where there was no agricultural activity, the testing teams failed to provide reasoned, logical hypotheses for the existence of substantial volumes of chemical agents. In Muhawish, American soldiers reported nausea and welts and a sophisticated detector showed the presence of a gas agent, but the verdict reached was organophosphates. No questions were asked why the Iraqis went to great lengths to hide eleven 20-gallon and three 55-gallon drums of apparently harmless thin clear liquid. No investigative reporting was done on the question of why the soldier who yielded this information asked not to be identified.[59] The day before Baghdad fell, Mobile Exploitation Team Alpha, of the 75th XTF, was dispatched for a "three hour mission" to explore the Tabook State Company in a small town near Karbalah, to check on some "underground barrels of mysterious origin." Two days later the team was still there, opening large buried storage containers. They also found foreign equipment recently imported, but "it was not clear that it was used in any weapons program."[60]

In Kirkuk American paratroopers discovered "suspicious warheads and rocket components" just outside the Iraqi government offices in town, again characterized as a "tantalizing but inconclusive find," because the officers could not determine whether they were of a design prohibited by UN resolutions, or they were built to hold chemical or biological munitions. Back in Washington, it was revealed that the Americans were now setting their sights on three dozen sites in the search for illegal weapons, selected from among the list of 1,000 laboratories, plants, military installations or storage facilities that were initially suspected of manufacturing WMD or storing parts of them. In the preceding week the Americans had retrieved file cabinets of laboratory manuals and technical papers at some of the sites where they had looked for banned weapons. The Pentagon was in the process of collecting documentation about the prohibited weapons and war crimes committed by the regime but the best hopes of the administration were now pinned on human intelligence to be extracted from senior Iraqi officers who would know where the materials had been hidden, or what happened to them. Progress in the investigation of Iraq's al-Qa'ida ties, which had so far also been "inconclusive," might throw some light on the manufacturing of ricin and other dangerous gases and chemicals by the defeated Ansar al-Islam in northern Iraq. General Myers said that he believed the ricin gas found in an apartment in London in January 2003 had originated from the Ansar camp in northern Iraq.[61]

At Karbalah a search team found radioactive materials in a maintenance building, and "dual use" biological equipment that could be switched to either civilian or military use. A nuclear detection team removed seven canisters containing a radioactive isotope, cesium, which was used to calibrate machinery in the many buildings and production facilities under construction on the site. After a week-long survey, experts concluded that the specific purpose of parts of that giant installation "remained a mystery," something that could hardly be used to clear the Iraqi regime of the WMD accusations. The plant was one of Iraq's leading ammunition manufacturing locations and it was under a large-scale expansion project when the war broke out. The plant had been visited by the UN inspection teams in February 2003, but the delay in letting them into the plant suggests Saddam had things to hide, which explains why the inspectors found only "suspicious" materials. It was not until American troops revisited the site for a second time that they came across the biggest find of all – 11 sealed and buried containers. Some of them were opened and a small chemical platoon was left behind to secure them, but the massive looting of the site by thousands of impoverished Iraqis from the surrounding villages, left the containers clean of any findings when finally a specialized team arrived to take stock of what was there.[62]

About 50 experts, American and foreign, some of whom had worked for the UN inspection teams previously, criticized American military search efforts as "superficial" and "misguided," probably based on their inability to piece together the evidence they found into an incriminating whole. The administration, which finally awoke to the ineptitude of the troops on the ground, and even the XTF units which followed them, to locate WMD, was now considering dispatching civilian teams to Iraq, even though Paul

Wolfowitz, the Deputy Secretary of Defense visiting Iraq in mid-July admitted that the search for WMD had been overtaken by the more urgent task of bringing order back to the country. The civilians' task would be, as a military official termed it: "To tell the difference between Saddam's strategic talcum-reserves and anthrax."[63] At long last, someone understood that the purely technical, factual method would not work any more.

There was, however, infighting and competition between the two Pentagon agencies – the Defense Intelligence Agency, which was supposed to coordinate the civilian effort, and the Defense Threat Reduction Agency, in charge of destroying unconventional weapons. The Iraq Survey Group was assigned to recruit the civilian experts from among a pool of 300 UN inspectors from various UN agencies who had previous field experience in Iraq. According to the Pentagon, the idea of recruiting the specialized civilians had originated from the early stages of the war planning, and was not the result of the incompetence of the built-in military teams. The failure of the detection teams to come up with anything beyond the "no conclusive" formula certainly accelerated the recruiting process. They received refresher training in Fort Benning, and were to join the 1,000-man effort to search for WMD, of which they would be the core of experts.[64] In the meantime, however, the skeptics' hands were strengthened by the fact that no weapons had been found, months into the post-war period. The skeptics offered no explanation, however, for all the mysteries, quandaries, questions and hide-and-seek games that Saddam played for years with the UN inspection teams.

After the war, a picture began to emerge of what had happened to the WMD programs in Iraq. An Iraqi scientist who claimed to have worked in Iraq's chemical weapons industry for more than a decade told an American military team that Iraq had destroyed chemical and biological weapons and equipment only days before the war began. He led the Americans to a supply of materials used to build illegal weapons which he claimed to have buried, as evidence of his country's illicit weapons program. He also said that his country had sent in secret unconventional weapons and technology to Syria, starting in the mid-1990s, and that more recently his authorities were cooperating with al-Qa'ida. He reiterated that Saddam had destroyed, as early as the 1990s, some stockpiles of deadly agents, shipped others to Syria and focused research instead on programs impervious to detection by outside inspectors. Mobile Exploitation Team Alpha considered the scientist credible, especially after they verified on the ground some of the details he gave them, but for his own safety they could not disclose his identity. These findings also lend credence to the assurances of the administration on the eve of the war that it was out to destroy those weapons, and its later contention that it would take human intelligence provided by Iraqi defectors to locate evidence of the hidden chemical and biological programs. Significantly, the captured scientist revealed that four days before Bush gave Saddam the final ultimatum, Iraqi officials set fire to a warehouse where biological weapons research and development were conducted, and that months before the war he had watched Iraqi officials bury chemical precursors and other sensitive material, to conceal and preserve the weapons and material for future use. He showed the Americans documents, samples and other evidence of the program that he claimed to have stolen to prove that it existed, if proof was needed.[65]

This evidence and testimony was not acceptable to the war's critics. In the post-war period, attacks centered by both European pundits and the opposition press in the US and Britain upon the "cooked evidence" that Bush and Blair were accused of having staged to lure their countries into war. The *Daily Telegraph* argued that "Tony Blair stands charged in effect of committing British troops on the basis of a lie,"[66] and *Le Monde* claimed that "what we are witnessing is probably one of the biggest state lies in years. The US was in fact bluffing when its published its documentary proof . . . The weapons of mass destruction were just a pretext . . . "[67]

This heated public debate further escalated with the eruption of the David Kelly–BBC scandal (and later Hutton Inquiry) in Britain and the admission in the US by George Tenet that he was the origin of the erroneous note introduced into Bush's State of the Union speech in January 2003 accusing Iraq of having purchased uranium from Niger. For the Bush administration, however, as voiced by Condoleezza Rice, the National Security Adviser, it was essential for the disarming nation, in this case Iraq, to show its goodwill and intention by giving the international community unrestricted access to its installations, exactly as South Africa and the Ukraine had done with regard to their nuclear programs. Otherwise, Saddam's regime carried no credibility in terms of its WMD threat, even if it had begun the process of eliminating its weapons stockpiles.[68] Other observers who have also concluded that Saddam did have stockpiles of prohibited weapons, founded their claims on Saddam's silence regarding what he had done with the thousands of liters of anthrax and the thousands of tons of VX that he had admitted to owning in the 1990s. Therefore, the only remaining logical question was how far he progressed since 1998, when the inspectors were expelled. And when they resumed their searches in the fall of 2002, following the Security Council Resolution, the thousands of pages his experts wrote in response to the demands of the UN failed to provide post-1998 answers. Moreover, in a February 1998 speech, the then President Bill Clinton described the frightening proportions of the chemical and biological arsenal of Saddam, and urged the world to address that threat. No voluntary disarmament is known to have been done by Saddam since; hence the hesitation of many to believe that, on the eve of the Iraq War, all those agents had suddenly evaporated.[69]

In an interview on Polish television, President Bush was remarkably keen to assure his audience that some banned weapons had been found by the search teams in Iraq, and not only the mobile laboratories which had received wide coverage by the media. General Keith Dayton, who heads the search team effort in Iraq, has said that his team would shift the focus from suspicious sites to areas where documents, interviews with Iraqis and other clues suggesting where biological or chemical weapons may be hidden.[70] One would think that both speakers were referring to the considerable progress made after they interrogated some of the defectors and renegades who fell into their hands. The critics, however, were not interested in manufacturing machines or labs; they wanted to see the weaponized substances themselves. In Britain, the criticism of Tony Blair was so feverish that no amount of proofs of the cruelty of the defunct regime of Saddam was enough to silence the critics: The mass grave of 200 children who had been burned alive that was discovered near Kirkuk, was, for many, deemed an unsatisfactory justification for the removal of Saddam. A reporter who visited western Iraq was startled by the vast amount of closed military compounds in the heart of the uninhabited desert, with hundreds of buildings, laboratories, hangars, bunkers and silos stretching to the horizon, and for which Iraqi officials never provided a plausible explanation of their use. For that reporter, it was not a question of whether or not Iraq *had* those weapons, but its *capacity* to manufacture them.[71]

The reports about the discovery of Saddam's plans to revive his nuclear program served as ammunition to the pro-war lobby. After all, the revelations of mass graves, torture, oppression, arrests and executions, corruption and the siphoning of public funds to Saddam's cronies, all indicated a regime worse than Stalin's and not far behind Hitler's. During the previous Gulf War, Iraq had stored biological arms in pits dug in the desert or in abandoned railroad tunnels. The Iraqi scientist who led the Americans to the site where uranium enrichment equipment was buried, was, like most WMD personnel, part of the Special Security Organization under Qusay's control. People should realize, the pro-war advocats contested, how difficult it is to extract the information from a country dominated by the dual instruments of fear and repression. In this framework, critics should be satisfied with discovering the implements that make nuclear weapons, even if the bomb itself has not been found or was not yet manufactured.[72]

On 21 June, US forces broke into an abandoned community hall in Baghdad and seized piles of intelligence equipment and top secret documents. Some documents referred to Iraq's nuclear programs. They were seized on the sixth day of a nationwide operation called "Desert Scorpion." Ninety raids were conducted in all, yielding 540 suspects, 22 of them by troops of the 1st Armored Division who had relieved parts of the Marines and the 3rd Infantry after they had fought the battle of Baghdad. Another three raids were made by the 4th Infantry in the area of Kirkuk in the north. In some of the seized documents, there were manifests for the delivery of communications equipment to the Iraqi nuclear agency. One letter, dated February 7, 1998, from the National Security Council of Iraq, was addressed to the Iraqi Nuclear Agency, with a carbon copy to the Mukhabarat (the Secret Police), confirming that not only was there a nuclear program but that it was secret.[73] The US has been sitting on much more information, discovered after the reform and reinforcement of the search teams; it is not yet ready to make any significant early disclosures, as this might jeopardize the effort's continuation. According to leaked information, many countries, including France and Germany, would find themselves in an embarrassing situation: Many of the Iraqi WMD scientists, for example, traveled to Syria with French passports.[74] Pending the scandals that are bound to rise when more information becomes available, it is worth concluding with comments from Rolf Ekeus, the first Chief of the UN Inspectors in Iraq, who had accumulated more Iraq-hours following the 1991 Gulf War than anyone else:

> It is difficult to understand the extent to which the terror of the Saddam years has penetrated his unhappy nation . . . As long as Hussein and his sons are not apprehended or proven dead, few of any of those involved in the weapons programs will provide information of their activities . . . The chemical and biological structures in Iraq constitute formidable international threats through potential links with terrorism . . . These were major threats against Iran, the Kurdish and Sh'ite populations of Iraq, and Israel . . . The Iraqi nuclear programs lacked access to fissile material but were advanced with regard to weapon design, with competition with Iran as a major driving factor . . . The fall of Saddam should give it an opportunity to rethink its own nuclear weapons program . . .
>
> This is enough to justify the international military intervention undertaken by the US and Britain. To accept the alternative – letting Hussein remain in power with his chemical and biological weapons capacity – would have been to continue to tolerate a destabilizing arms race in the Gulf, including future nuclearization of the area . . . and the continued terrorization of the Iraqi people . . . [75]

7

Ruling from Horseback

Chinese history tells us that when China was overrun by the Mongols who established the Yuan Dynasty (1279–1368) under Kubilai Khan, Chinese scholars, who were much better at Confucian philosophy and ethics than warfare, told the occupiers, referring to their swift horsemanship: "You can conquer China from horseback, but you cannot rule it from horseback." The Mongols, who tried to overturn the traditional Chinese order and put themselves, instead of the Chinese elite of literati, at the apex of society, found their reign short-lived. The Mongols passed into history, but their lesson was not lost on the Manchus, who conquered China in 1644 but ruled it for a full dynastic cycle of 300 years until 1911, as the Qing, the last Imperial Dynasty of China, when the Empire collapsed. The Manchus' secret was that they learned China before they conquered it; they were not arrogant conquerors.

When the swift conquest of Iraq from tank-back is reflected upon, along with the seeming propensity among Americans to rule the proud and rebellious Iraqis from tank-back, one cannot escape the analogy. As Tom Friedman has aptly put it: "The Americans had better understand that 'shock and awe' is not just for war making, it is an everyday tool for running this place."[1] The Americans have made it clear that they wish to institute their form of democracy, their idea of institutions, and to retain their veto power even as an Iraqi Council (of their choice) deliberates the needs of the population.

War does not determine who is right, but rather who is left. The success or failure of a war can be gauged against the declared war aims. The main aims of the Third Gulf War, aside from the hidden agenda, seem to have been fulfilled with skill and rapidity, thanks to the meticulous planning, the daring execution of the battle plan, solid American leadership, and the good sense of proportion and of judgment that was maintained throughout the hostilities. Saddam Hussein was effectively removed from power; his two sons have been killed; most of his cronies on the deck of cards have been eliminated or are in custody; Iraq is disarmed and its armies disbanded and no longer poses a threat to its neighbors; the tyrannical system of terror has been dismantled; the minorities have been disengaged from oppression; and the waste and corruption of the Ba'ath regime ended. All that at a remarkably low price, human and economic, both for the US and its allies, and for the Iraqi people. Wars that Saddam waged in the past had cost far more and lasted much longer. Even the hidden agenda seems to have accomplished stunning achievements: The oil industry has been put reasonably back on track and is undergoing renovation, expansion and modernization; the bases of international terror in Iraq were destroyed and the links of the regime with outside terrorist organizations has been severed; and the much-feared weapons of mass destruction, or what remained of them, have been sought, destroyed or otherwise monitored.

There are four issues, however, that will determine the ultimate fate of the Anglo-American venture in Iraq: (1) to what extent their achievements in the war are permanent; (2) what sort of legacy they will leave behind when they transfer back to the Iraqis the reins of their government; (3) what kind of interim regime they will be able to establish until the Iraqis are able to make their own choices; and (4) how heavy-handed or sensitive they will be in the transitional period of ruling from horse-back. We shall discuss these issues against the backdrop of Iraqi domestic divisions and conflicting interests, the American attempts to pacify post-war Iraq, the competing leaderships emerging in Iraq, Iraq's relationships with other countries, and the long-term American interests in the country after order and self-government are achieved.

Let us begin with the main arguments of a general assessment of the war that was done at the GLORIA (Global Research in International Affairs) Center in Tel Aviv in a joint conference of scholars and officials from the Department of State. There was consensus that, on the military level, the victory in the war was not only the result of Anglo-American success, but also of Iraqi incompetence. Opinions differed, however, on what may happen after the war. Some thought that the long-term American position in Iraq might become untenable once they realize that it is impossible to impose a Western democracy. Others argued that the resilience of Iraqi nationalism and pride, over and beyond communal and religious differences, was what prevented Saddam from implementing his scorched earth policy in the face of the American invasion, and will contribute to holding Iraq together through the upcoming tribulations of rebuilding the country. Participants on the panel said that the US would have to plan for a long stay to ensure stability and state-building in Iraq, because the army, which was the main pillar of the regime, had disintegrated and it would take a long time to rebuild a new one, from the bottom up, divorced from politics. Others thought that the spread of half a million skilled soldiers among the population May on the contrary, not only increase unemployment and dissatisfaction, but also foment unrest and political opposition. A disciplined national force was better for stability than a scattered and uncontrolled mob, which, if it retains its weapons and affiliation with its religious and communal origins, may increase instability and separatism.[2]

One panelist thought that leaving Iraq without a strong national army would alter the strategic balance in the entire Gulf area, inasmuch as Iran would emerge as the unequalled, preponderant power. Others remarked, that unlike the previous Gulf War which sanctified the status quo and the regimes in place across the Middle East (even Syria had no qualms about taking part in the alliance which fought Saddam), this time the war was all about change – political, economic and social: therefore the existing Arab regimes were reluctant to participate in the war and are afraid after it of what might unfold in its wake, as America has been signaling that it wants to use the changes in Iraq as leverage for changes elsewhere in the region. Therefore, one panelist argued, the success or failure of the war will be gauged by what the Americans will achieve in Iraq and to what extent that will serve as a model elsewhere. The Arab street, it was agreed, will judge the Iraqi model by the extent to which normal life, security, public order and alleviation of fear and oppression are established on the streets of Baghdad. On the other hand, the Iraqi people will not tolerate too long an American stay, which it would regard as a neo-colonialist occupation, nor will the American public countenance too long an occupation particularly if it becomes too costly in human and economic terms. It was suggested that the Arab countries should be differentiated into the non-Gulf states, like Egypt, Syria and Lebanon, which will not benefit from the war, and the Gulf states (such as Kuwait), for whom the removal of Saddam ends their main security threat.[3]

Unless the US succeeds in returning Iraq to normal soon and visibly betters the life of the common citizenry, the war would not have been worthwhile. Moreover, unless America makes salient progress in demonstrating that the options of government it is suggesting are better and work better, involving some kind of workable harmony between the various groups, it will not succeed in persuading the Iraqi street that the situation has markedly improved compared to Saddam's times and, worse, it will not be able to hold on to the bases, the oil and the regional hegemony it has achieved thus far. As long as America's efforts in Iraq do not bear fruit, no regional changes, no reforms, no democratization and no re-deployment of forces and alliances can be accomplished. The task at hand, therefore, is threefold: (1) to achieve peace and security, law and order; then (2) rebuild Iraq economically, institutionally and politically; then (3) reach an understanding with the new Iraqi government about the American presence, influence and interests in Iraq after the end of the occupation. Only then will the US have ample leverage with which to significantly alter the political and social make-up of the rest of the Middle East.

Normalization, Security and Public Order

To no small extent, the American ability to secure peace and normalization will be determined by, and measured against, their success in their fight against the guerilla war that has been developing against them. Failure to win the guerilla war would mean the continuing threat to security in the country, and would create, in the minds of Iraqis, an image of a weak America, with a tenuous grip on the country. It is the frequency and brazenness of the attacks against US forces which has brought the specter of a protracted war in Iraq. The attacks have meant a delay in the withdrawal of American forces, which is essential to the lowering of the coercive military profile of the American presence in the short run and emphasizing the cooperational civilian partnership between the US and Iraq in the long term. As long as Americans in uniform are targeted and need to remain vigilant, they cannot consider the war over. What is worrying about the American death toll under enemy fire since the formal end of the war, is the gradual but continuing rise in the number of deaths: six were killed in May 16 in June, with similar figures for July, August and September. By October, more than 100 US soldiers had been killed since the Pentagon declared the end of combat operations. There was an assumption in the American Command that it was the uncertainty about the final and irreversible removal of Saddam's regime which encouraged his remaining supporters to pursue their guerilla tactics against the American forces. The death of Saddam could not come too quickly for the Americans. The elimination of Saddam's sons in Mosul in mid-July was also calculated by the Americans to demonstrate to the Iraqi public that the regime, with its heirs eliminated, was dead. Their decision to present photographic evidence of Uday and Qussay's deaths, contrary to American wont, was in sync with attempts to calm the security situation. Whether that controversial move will achieve its goal is hard to tell. In any case, the American Command believes that previous assessments that they were fighting the last remnants of pro-Saddam opposition were too optimistic, and that the plurality of opposition groups, some of whom are supported from the outside, prompts them to evaluate the prospects for peace much more realistically.[4] That pictured has not drastically changed since the capture of Saddam in December 2003.

What makes the Americans' task difficult are not the occasional frustrated or angry Iraqis who pelt a few rocks on a passing American patrol which searched their homes, but the sophistication with which seemingly innocent civilians approach a roadblock and then toss grenades at the unsuspecting soldiers, or American soldiers on guard in small numbers, who are snatched with their equipment and then found murdered. The continued attacks mean that troops tend to act more aggressively when questioning potentially dangerous suspects and keep Iraqis generally at a greater distance which in turn estranges them from the Iraqis who become more and more convinced that Americans are occupiers and not liberators. That in turn has emboldened the opposition to the American presence in Iraq to hasten their departure by committing acts of sabotage against the occupying troops. Only when the guerilla operations were launched against American troops did the US begin to understand the negative result of allowing the Iraqi soldiers in Baghdad, Kirkuk, Najaf etc. to escape: these soldiers had kept their forces intact, and could now attack the US on their own terms. Moreover, the Sunni part of the population, concentrated in the Sunni Triangle in the northwest, which stands to lose most from a continued American presence, is also the most financially able to encourage the resistance groups. There were also ambushes against both the British and the Americans in the Shi'ite areas in the south, which inflicted several casualties.[5] The Americans responded violently with the Peninsula Strike in mid-June which brought about the killing of 113 Iraqis and foreigners and the arrest of 400 more, followed by the Desert Scorpion operation, in order to eradicate the opposition, which circulates tracts under such ominous names as "The Army of Muhammad," and the "Iraq Liberation Army."[6]

The unexpected scope of those "seek and destroy" operations which evoked among the Americans memories of Vietnam, turned the Sunnite Triangle into so battle-ridden and hazardous a terrain that some European reporters, gleefully documented the troubles confronting the US in Iraq and characterized these hostilities as the "resumption of combat." The Americans first closed off a peninsula delineated by the path of the Tigris river (hence the codename Peninsula Strike) where some of the guerillas found refuge, and then used attack helicopters and drones to mop up the encircled area. Among the 400 suspects captured were 30 members of the Ba'ath Party. A dozen more who attempted to flee in a boat were caught up in a river patrol. A few caches of weapons were discovered and seized, probably hidden by the withdrawing forces who did not fight in the cities and elected to face the Americans in guerilla warfare. During the operation, the American Air Force bombed a "terrorist training camp north of Baghdad," and lost an Apache in the process. The arrival of more foreign troops to reinforce the Americans – Danes and Dutch to the British zone in the south, Poles, Italians, Spaniards, Central Americans and others to the north – was likely to render peace-keeping operations an international affair and reduce the stigma of "occupation" attached to the Americans.[7]

It will take months for the Iraqis to outgrow the trauma they experienced in the wake of the collapse of the Ba'ath regime. No one can forget the chaotic scenes that followed liberation, to the extent that there were even calls for Saddam's return (in Arab tradition "sixty years of tyranny 'are always thought better than' one day of lawlessness and chaos"). Nor can anyone forget the total collapse of basic services: electricity and water, gas and telephone communications, all suddenly unavailable, causing untold misery. Places of work and sources of livelihood that the predominant public sector afforded the populace were no more: soldiers and policemen, workers and day laborers, government officials and teachers, were all payless, aimlessly roaming the streets and worried about what the next day may bring. Iraqis protested loudly for the restoration of civilian life: "Restore Order!" "Provide Security," "Stop the Looting!" even as American troops, under the brief term of Jay Garner, were desperately attempting to resume electricity supply first, because everything else – water pumps, oil pumps, food conservation, refrigeration – depended upon electricity.

To begin the long process of restoring order, the US military set a deadline to Iraqis to hand in automatic and heavy weapons. Some weapons were turned in, though their quantity could be described as a "drop in the ocean,"[8] given that many Iraqis freely walked around with guns. Stolen weapons, from pistols and assault rifles to anti-tank grenades, were also on sale in the streets, much like the open arms markets of Peshawar during the first Afghanistan War (1979–89). Anarchy and an abundance of weapons, combined with high unemployment and poverty, produced a crime rate which reached unprecedented levels. Security was at its worst in modern Iraqi history. Even electricity workers, who were valiantly trying to repair the damaged grids from the war, were often ambushed by looters and robbers, who stole cables and equipment. Gradually, as the Civilian Administration started to pay salaries, many former policemen and other officials reported to their jobs, and others were recruited anew and sent to retrain in police academies. The problem was that, like in any state machinery under occupation, anyone who was hired by the occupying administration could be accused as "collaborator," and made a target for murder or intimidation.[9] Saddam's supporters still lingered, perhaps as part of the strategy of withdrawal from the big cities, in order to preserve the skilled fighting personnel and their weapons for the guerilla war being waged on a daily basis on American forces. Re-establishing security and peace did not only mean crime-stopping. There were also the wider issues of redressing justice to the many thousands of families who lost loved ones during Saddam's rule. Their families now demanded justice, or at least the identification of their remains among Iraq's mass graves.[10] Returning to normalcy meant reopening schools and ensuring that 25 percent of the population enjoyed some kind of routine. On the welcoming blackboards in classes some American officials had scribbled, "Iraq is Free," a message that did not yet carry any real meaning to the citizenry.[11]

Marsh Arabs after Saddam

In the aftermath of war, basic communal and individual freedoms were restored. Shi'ites who under Saddam had to endure restrictions on their movements (such as pilgrimages) now exercised their right to do so. Marsh Arabs, who had lived for thousands of years in the area around Amara, in the marshland that had been formed by the flow of the Tigris just before it converged with the Euphrates into Shatt al-Arab, suffered terribly under Saddam. Saddam sought to eliminate the marsh culture: he drained the wetlands, set the reeds on fire, and executed thousands of residents, until their population dwindled to fewer than 20,000 (compared to half a million in the 1950s). When the war broke out, lawlessness ruled across the area, which was infested with bandits and criminals. In the 1980s during the war with Iran, many people who ran away from the regime arrived to hide in the marsh jungle. Chemical weapons were used by the Iraqis on Iranian infiltrators. In the late 1980s, a local hero rose against Saddam's regime and inflicted considerable damage on the Iraqi troops sent to quell them. That local hero, Karim Mahood, fought Saddam until 1997 and then fled to the US, but has now returned to Iraq with the forces of Ahmed Chalabi.

In 1991 Saddam ordered the drainage of 8,000 sq. m of land, from Nasiriya in the west, Kut in the north and Basra in the south, an area roughly the size of New Jersey or Israel. He built up dams on the water beds that branched off the Tigris and the Euphrates and used to feed the marshes, then in 1993 completed the digging of a channel that drained the rest of the water, and in every dried up area the army burned the reeds. About 50 percent of the marshes were destroyed, eliminating not only human habitats but also wildlife: According to environmental agencies, 11 bird species and three mammal species are believed to have been made extinct as a result of Saddam's actions. The Marsh Arabs who were not killed either moved to Iran or to larger towns. Now that Saddam is gone, former residents of the marshes are hoping to reclaim the marshes for themselves. Some waters have already begun to be released from the dams. Villages that had been cut off from water supplies suddenly began to revive.

The Dinar

One of the chief concerns of the populace was the value of the money they held. After Baghdad fell, thousands of Iraqis gathered outside the doors of the Iraqi Central Bank, seeking to exchange their 10,000 dinar bills (valued at less than $10 due to the huge inflation, compared to $3.5 for one dinar in 1990), for small denominations. Since the war ended, traders and shopkeepers were charging a 25 percent fee on the 10,000 dinar bills, the largest in circulation, after word spread that some of them were counterfeit. With most of the banks closed the entire monetary system was crippled and no official exchange rate could be enforced. This had a knock-on effect for civilians receiving their first salaries. When they received them, the employees who were paid in 10,000 dinar bills saw their value diminish by 25 percent when they exchanged them at markets. The large dinar bills have become a liability and employees now saw their income sharply reduced and their savings jeopardized. The new government will have to decide on what drastic measures to take in order to stabilize the dinar, or replace it with a new currency. American Treasury Department officials have been hard at work trying to stabilize the situation by declaring the 10,000 dinar bills valid at their face value, and the Central Bank has started again to print new money bills, especially the 250 dinars, the most common in use. Furthermore, state and private lenders were ordered to open their gates so as to help restore confidence in the currency. To provide for emergency payments of salaries and other needs, funds were levied from the $1.7 billion of frozen Iraqi assets in the US, but the salaries for April and May were being paid with Iraqi money. Since the dinar does not have any backing in foreign reserves, the self-contained Iraqi economy does not ply to economic theory, and its administrators are free to do what they like, including printing money without worrying about inflation.[12]

The New Press

The press in Iraq, especially in Baghdad, was a success story of post-war liberation. It was as if all the intellectual fervor and curiosity that had been oppressed by the Ba'ath system was released like a wound spring. In one single day in June, barely two months after the war, three new publications appeared in the newsstands: a broadsheet called *al-Hawadith* (News, Events); *al-Huriyya* (Liberty), published by the Arab Democratic National Movement; and *al-Qabas* (The Light), which highlighted disputes between the fledgling American civil administration and local Iraqi leaders. These were only part of a panoply of new dailies and journals, Arab and Kurdish, Islamic and secular, which filled the streets and sold large numbers despite the impoverished state of the Iraqi economy. It was a contrast, and a break from the official Ba'ath organs (*al-Jumhuriyya* and *al-Qadisiyya*) which were mere mouthpieces for the regime. *Az-Zaman* (Time), a pro-democracy paper formerly based in London, moved in April 2003 to Baghdad along with a Communist Party daily. The more than 70 new publications, most of them pro-reform and supportive of freedom of the press, both condemned in various degrees the American presence in Iraq, but also exposed the crimes of Saddam. Suddenly political cartoon and color photos, gossip and small talk filled the pages of the dailies. The new press succeeded partly due to the availability of only one American-sponsored television news program, which could not satisfy the public's hunger for knowledge.[13]

Radio and Television

While the new administration was yet to announce its plans regarding the state media in the new Iraq, the former director of the Voice of America, Robert Reilly, was already at work with Iraqis on future radio and TV programs. Rumors were rife that former CIA Director James Woolsey was being considered as an adviser to the new Minister of Information.[14] If that rumor materialized, the Americans would be plying to one of the autocratic characteristics of Iraq and the Arab world in general, where Ministers of Information (or National Guidance in some places) censor the press and make sure that news items are standardized. Ministries of Information are essentially propaganda apparatuses, designed to shape public opinion via the state media tools. Leaving the structure of the ministry intact and nominating a former head of the CIA to counsel it would signal to liberal Iraqis that nothing had changed in the area of media control.

Since Iraqi radio and television facilities had been bombed during the war, an American C-130 transport plane, equipped as a broadcasting station and nicknamed Commander Solo, had been overflying Iraq and transmitting programs developed by the Broadcast Board of Governors, a US agency that oversees the Voice of America and other government-sponsored media projects. Their one-hour daily program, called "Iraq and the World," was anchored by Iraqi exiles and was dubbed as "primitive" by Iraqi TV. The show consisted mainly of excerpts from the three major American networks, except for CNN, which refused to participate. The program was criticized by many intellectuals and Iraqi television workers, who expressed their "disgust" at the broadcasts across Iraq, which, they claimed, "show us what they want to show us." Some workers were adamant that they would not work under American tutelage, insisting that America should provide security, not jobs. Given the views of veteran Iraqi television and radio workers, the new administration may find its broadcasts falling on deaf ears.[15]

Women and Children

The weaker elements of society, especially in traditional, patriarchal Islamic countries, have been women and children. Saddam's secular, anticleric regime, however, meant that women enjoyed greater freedom in Iraq than elsewhere. Post-Saddam, Iraqi women are wary that the democratization of society might prompt its clericalization, which in turn could mean a curtailment of their rights. They are most afraid of the notion that should a cleric be elected head of state, they could lose their relatively emancipated status. The newfound religious freedom as enjoyed by the Shi'ites is a mostly male celebration, reflecting male desires to establish an Islamic state, the symbol of male freedom and, conversely, female oppression. The rising religious fervor (including clerics urging all women to wear the hijab), after decades of religious oppression, has struck a chord in many men, who, having previously taken orders from the Ba'ath, now follow the advice of clerics. Particularly worrisome for women has been the gradual Islamization of Iraqi society. If, one decade ago, only two or three women in college covered their heads, now the reverse is true.[16] Young women have seen their rights restricted recently, especially toward the end of Saddam's regime, when he was more easily influenced by Sunnite clerics. One law he introduced was that women younger than 45 had to be accompanied on their travels by a male chaperon from their nuclear family. This constituted a blow to the women who witnessed a growing general public mood of conservatism which still upheld arranged marriages and head scarves. This is a far cry from the 1950s when young Iraqi women, free from the veil and the scarf, could travel abroad to get an advanced education or as non-married diplomats. The opinion of middle-class and upper-middle class Iraqi women, however, may not be shared by poor female Shi'ites or uneducated Kurdish women.

The Iraq war has also had a significant effect on the children in the country. In Baghdad and Basra, children have been seen riding US tanks, or asking American troops for sweets and other items. For the children, military and Fedayeen bases that had been out-of-bounds were suddenly left abandoned for them to play in, with often tragic consequences. The problems facing the civil administration in trying to restore children's lives to normal has been, first, keeping them away from dangerous areas, and second, getting them back to school. This has proved difficult, as many children, especially from the poor neighborhoods, returned to their schools only to find them stripped from all their equipment that had been looted. In the cities generally, the Iraqis had often turned schools into theaters of operation and stocked them with ammunition, at the detriment of children's safety.[17] In one incident at the end of April five boys aged between six and twelve found an abandoned artillery shell outside Kirkuk, which blew up in their faces, leaving them with permanent scars. Similar incidents unfolded throughout Iraq, with the consequence that more children (and civilians in general) were killed or maimed after the war than during it. Hundreds of children remained limbless in the aftermath of the war, and the new Civil Administration will have to care for their rehabilitation if they are to be included in the process of normalization.[18]

When some schools reopened in the beginning of May more teachers and students stayed at home than arrived for classes, fearing for their safety, since only a fraction of the schools were checked and cleared of weapons and unexploded ordnance by overstretched American troops. Still, it was essential for US soldiers to be vigilant at the entrance of every school to help the population regain confidence in the upcoming normalization efforts. In places where that was successful, it was a pleasure to see children dressed in uniforms and resuming classes. Some of the kids who had been deprived by the long years of embargoes and wars, were now hoping that the Americans would "bring them the bananas, oranges and apples" they had longed for. However, the school turnout, generally, was low. Having spent a week clearing up one elementary school in Baghdad of the waste that the military and Fedayeen had left behind them in preparation for the return of 800 students, only 30 showed up on the first day of school. The children were greeted with hugs and kisses, and for the first time they did not have to begin their day by pledging their love and devotion to Saddam. Teachers were now free to denounce Saddam's version of history which had contaminated children's textbooks, and were elated to recount to the children the pleasure they felt at finally being able to watch more than the one state-sponsored Iraqi television channel.[19]

Nuclear and Chemical Waste

Another daunting task that fell to the Civil Administration was clearing Iraq of the sediments of nuclear and chemical waste that had accumulated over the years. In an abandoned range near Amariya, just west of Baghdad, an American team discovered a radioactive cobalt-60 site. There was, however, no location designated by the coalition where dangerous material could be separated and stored. Some of the material uncovered at weapons sites in Iraq could be used to make "dirty bombs," and other less lethal material could also cause damage to the population in the long run. One of the pits in the Amariya range was reportedly registering a level of radiation 1,000 times the normal, though a later verification found it lower than the initial level. The test range was not on the list of the more-than 900 sites that had been designated dangerous sites where weapons of mass destruction were made or tested or stored – an indication, perhaps, of its secrecy. According to the experts, the range had been used in the past to test the exposure of troops and equipment to the effects of radiation in a simulated battlefield. They recommended that efforts be made to secure the underground sources and neutralize them. Nuclear and chemical disposal was not something the American administration and the military had banked on encountering.[20]

Historical Artifacts

On 3 July, US Marines reserve Colonel Matthew Bogdanos, the former head of the team engaged in the recovery of stolen artifacts, arranged for a special exhibit of the National Museum treasures, which had not been shown to the public since 1991, when, out of fear for the safety of the items, they were deposited in the vaults of the Central Bank. Among the articles featured was the gold jewelery of an ancient monarch, known as the Treasure of Nimrod. During the American attack on Baghdad, the vaults of the bank were flooded and it was impossible to recover the hoard until the water was pumped up. In the eight days of looting prior to the Americans' arrival, some 6,000 items were stolen. One of the most valuable pieces, the Warka vase, was returned, but another 32 major exhibits remain missing. Initially, reports about the extent of the looting were found to have been exaggerated and the Americans accused the museum staff of having deliberately inflated the volume of the thefts and misled world opinion. Apparently concerned that the looters might return, the staff did not reveal to journalists that many artifacts had been moved to store rooms or sent to bunkers elsewhere. Only when the military team arrived on 22 April was the proper assessment made, but it took several weeks, first because of essential repairs to the generator, and second because many women who worked in sorting out the stocks, refused to work for more than a few hours a day out of concern for their safety. It turned out that while most of the staff was concerned about the exhibits and began emptying the show cases three weeks prior to the war for safe-keeping, some of them informed professional thieves of the locations of certain items.[21] In addition, new reports emerged at a special conference convened by UNESCO in Paris which confirmed that the Iraqi National Library and Archives in Baghdad had also been looted and burned, as well as the Library of Manuscripts attached to the Ministry of Awqaf (Religious Endowments), and the Saddam Centre for Manuscripts in Baghdad, all of which suffered irreparable damage. The Gulbenkian Museum of Modern Art in the Iraqi capital and its collection of paintings had been burned. And the blame for all this was laid by the Arab world and others at America's door. In their defense the Americans could point to a long "tradition" of the looting of archaeological sites, where armed gangs, sometimes numbering hundreds, "descended on sites and stripped them bare."[22]

Fedayeen Saddam

Among the elements of instability one should also count the Fedayeen Saddam recruited by the regime to keep Iraqi citizens in check. Opposition groups in Iraq put their number at 50,000, organized in brigades of 3,000 each, one for each of the 18 provinces. They were created by Uday in 1991, mainly for the purpose of quelling the Shi'ite rebels in the south, but were soon handed over to Qusay. The organization largely recruited teenagers from impoverished families. The Fedayeen Saddam were trained in the infamous camps of Salman Pak, where they were brainwashed into believing that the continuation of the Ba'ath regime was of paramount importance. The units had pre-prepared stashes of weapons; they traveled as inconspicuous civilians, utilizing the element of surprise against their enemies. This covert nature of their operations instilled fear among the general populace, and paranoia. Their ability to melt into the population means that the Americans are having a hard time finding them and eliminating their presence virtually everywhere in Iraq.[23]

Foreign Fighters

Peace and security can only be achieved by defeating the elements of instability and opposition in Iraq, and these include foreign elements that had been permitted, even encouraged, by the Saddam regime. Western peaceniks were invited or volunteered to protect Iraq from the war, offering to act as human shields. They scattered to the winds as soon as American bombing began. Much more worrying are the thousands of foreigners, mainly Palestinian, Jordanian, Syrian and other Arabs, but also Chechnyan and possibly Bosnian and other Muslims, who regarded Saddam as the defender of Islam, a latter-day Saladin. Many of these fighters, like Ansar al-Islam, were refugees of the survivors of the first and second Afghanistan wars (1979–89 and 2001, respectively), known as "Afghans," who sought new bases in parts of the Islamic world difficult to access for the West, such as the Yemen, northwestern Pakistan and the Iraq–Iran border, to pursue their fanatic *Jihad*, by means of terrorism and development of WMD. Many of the terrorists responsible for the attacks against American soldiers in the past six months, have done so as part of their anti-American struggle.

The most troubling threat has been the Mujahideen Khalq, an Iranian opposition group that Saddam allowed to operate from Iraq against the Iranian clerical regime. Acting upon a decision by President Bush, the American commanders in Iraq have entered into discussions with the Mujahideen about surrendering their weapons and ensuring they can no longer operate as an armed force in Iraqi territory. The Mujahideen had been listed as a terrorist organization by the Americans since 1997, and under the terms of their initial understanding with American commanders, signed on 15 April they were allowed to keep their arms and their camps near the Iranian borders,[24] but since they had supported the taking of American hostages in Teheran in 1979 and they operated bombs against

Iranian civilians, which had caused them to be listed on a par with the Hamas and the Hizbullah, the Bush administration decided to intervene to disarm them in order to lessen its already heavy burden of keeping the peace in Iraq. The Mujahideen number some 10,000 members, 3,000 of them combatants under the Badr Brigade, divided between five camps; they kept strictly to their ceasefire agreement with the Americans after Saddam was deposed. Under the new arrangement devised in Washington, however, the Mujahideen will have to surrender their weapons and move to designated "safe areas," with the Americans taking responsibility for their security, so that guns in all Iraq can only be held by a central government force under American supervision.[25]

Rebuilding Iraq

Rebuilding Iraq economically, institutionally and politically means the transition from the rule by dictatorship into a country that has elected accountable leaders who are subject to the law. Economically, the major issue is not only one of proper conduct and ethics in the handling of public money but also of building a national Treasury that belongs to all the people, with its monies dispensed according to the budgetary laws. Reviving the oil industry, lifting the UN sanctions so that Iraq could compete with its oil and other products in the world market, directing funds to social services, investment, industry, agriculture, irrigation systems and public transportation, were all targets for the Civil Administration to aim for. Other key matters included: (1) modernizing and expanding the oil industry to maximize the income from it and increase spending on education and on pulling Iraq out of poverty; (2) bringing in private investors to develop new technologies and employ the highly-skilled Iraqi professionals in constructive and money-making enterprises; and (3) affording every Iraqi child an education, medical care, freedom from want and a peaceful future. A daunting and ambitious program, this necessitated the healing of relations between the sectarian, communal and religious divisions and the drawing-up of an harmonious consensus on how to distribute fairly the wealth of the country to all its citizens.

Stolen Funds

To start with, the Americans made an effort to retrieve some of the monies stolen by Saddam and his sons in order to begin to finance the rebuilding of Iraq, until the oil exports, which are at the center of this program, can carry the brunt of the envisaged financial outlays. American officials in Washington announced in mid-May that they located the $1 billion taken from the Iraqi Treasury prior to the US invasion by Qusay Hussein. The money was packed in 191 numbered boxes, which appear to be part of the 236 boxes taken on late night of 18 March by Qusay, just one day before the American air-attacks were launched. The fact that the money was found in Baghdad suggested to some observers that either Saddam was unable to move the funds out of Iraq due to the American attack, or he believed he could retrieve them later. Storing his money and waiting to retrieve it ties in with the notion that Saddam decided to keep his forces intact by ordering their withdrawal: the money that was to be kept in safe places in Baghdad would surely have financed the continued guerilla war against the Americans. Saddam must have counted on the continued harassment of the Americans by the remnants of his defeated army, with the backing of that money, until the rate of American casualties forced an administration faced with long-term attrition to withdraw, paving the way for his triumphant return. Lebanon has also announced it found another half-billion dollars placed in its banks. In all, the US has said that it found more than $2 billion, though it still had trouble accounting for one-half of the $2 billion frozen by various countries during the 1991 Gulf War. But once they were on the tracks of Saddam's stolen money, the Americans did not let up in pursuit of their investigations.[26]

An American Army Reserve Unit discovered $4 million in cash in a compound that had been home to Special Republican Guard officers. The L-shaped bunker where the money was hidden may have more sealed compartments. This was evidence that the tampering with the public treasury was not the exclusive domain of Saddam and the leadership. The money was hidden on 16 March just three days before the eruption of the war, according to a statement in Arabic signed by five people. Corruption in Ba'athist Iraq had spread to all levels of authority. The box, elaborately sealed and locked, contained 40,000 $100 bills. Days later, another military unit stumbled upon a sealed cottage that contained $650 million in cash. Newly-poured concrete, bricked-over rooms, and hollow floors in some guard houses were clues to the sophisticated campaign of concealment that had taken place. These precautions illustrate the priority lent by Saddam to caches of weapons and cash over the needs of his starving people.[27]

Oil Exports

A measure of the urgency with which the Americans and the emerging new Iraqi authorities view the resumption of the oil exports as the key to reconstruction, is the speed with which the oil industry has been recovering and rapidly approaching its pre-sanctions capacity, with the goal to double it within the next few coming years if and when security is established. Thamir Ghadhban, the Director-General of the Oil Ministry, who was appointed by Jay Garner as Acting Minister, has already announced that Iraq will reach its 1.5 million b/d pre-war capacity by mid-June 2003, with further dramatic increases promised in the years to come. Ghadhban's workers received their first salaries from the American Civil Administration in late May at the same time as the United Nations Security Council approved a US-drafted resolution giving the US and Britain broad powers to run Iraq and its oil industry, ending 23 years of sanctions that had crippled Iraq's economy. The Administration also paid the salaries of the 40,000 workers of the Electricity Company, without which no production, including the oil industry, could be resumed.[28] Even though the Americans have thus far financed the rebuilding of Iraq's faltering national economy, the wealthy elite of the country also want some of the potential profits. They emerged unscathed from the Saddam regime because they knew how to please it by paying bribes and giving expensive gifts. Now, depending on the Americans' ability to successfully collaborate with them, they are rich and powerful enough to help pull their country out of economic slump, reorganize its industrial and commercial base, revive tourism and agriculture and resume dormant international trade ties. Elite families such as the Duleimi, Khudairy, Bunnia, al-Janabi and Kubba had been well known in Iraq before Saddam and they have outlived him, a measure of their adaptability to changing circumstances and of their business acumen. Members of their families are Western-educated and they have substantial economic interests in Britain, Syria, Jordan, Saudi Arabia and Dubai. Some of these families lived in exile during Saddam's rule, but they are now primed to face the new challenge, and are already exploring new opportunities in cellphone communications, commercial television, airlines, car dealerships and post-war reconstruction. Many of these families are sworn enemies of returning exiles vying for the leadership of the country, like Ahmed Chalabi, the returning Head of the Washington-based Iraqi National Congress. Some have decided to struggle for political power against Chalabi and the other exiles, and built a political party, the Iraqi Republican Group, to contend in the political arena.[29]

Agriculture

Apart from oil and business, one of the basic economic infrastructures of the country is its prosperous agriculture. With an abundance of water, the fertile valleys of the great rivers, plenty of experience in land cultivation and the warm climate, Iraqi soil is capable of providing the food for all its people, and beyond. Iraq is one of the major world exporters of dates. It was the productivity of dates that Saddam was counting on when he defied the UN embargo and counseled his people to eat dates and drink water, both of which there was plenty. After the war, landowners met in the Mosul area to discuss the problems of the upcoming barley harvest. As there was no government in Baghdad, the Central Bank was looted and fuel was in short supply the crops might rot in the fields, with disastrous losses for the growers and the programs for feeding the population. The Mosul region produces half the country's crop of wheat and barley. In the past, the government would set the price and pay the farmers their dues, but now without a government or a central bank to pay the cost, they were lost. An American general with the 101st airborne, which had taken over the area following the conquest of Baghdad, had to deal with this novel problem. For the new government the farmers' dependence on government and the government's role in price setting would have to be eliminated, and the Iraqi farmers guided toward a market economy. During the nationalization policy of the Ba'ath in 1971, large farms were broken up so that no farmer could have more than 250 hectares.

Another aspect of the land economy is the ethnic dispute between the Arabs and Kurds. The Kurds wish to reclaim lands from which they were ejected by Saddam and were subsequently settled by Arabs. With about 10 percent of the land contested in northern Iraq, the Americans are attempting to find interim solutions by dividing the crops between the owners and the farmers who till the land. This is another sensitive issue that a new government will have to tackle in order to revive and modernize the most promising sector of the economy – agriculture – after oil.[30]

Social and Political Reorganization

The American war aims and their vow to bring democracy to Iraq are a repetition of what Britain had undertaken 80 years earlier when the Iraqi state was established. In August 1922, the Interior Ministry of Mesopotamia announced that Prince Faysal, who had been brought from Hijaz in Arabia, had won the referendum by a comfortable majority, to be installed as a constitutional monarch, and a few days later he was sworn in as the King of Iraq. The British Colonial Secretary, Winston Churchill, had succeeded in his mission. When Churchill deliberated a year earlier at the Semiramis Hotel in Cairo in March 1921, over the future of the Middle East, he made it clear that Faysal's crowning must be seen "as if the proposal derives from the will of the local population and not from Britain."[31] What else is new? In 1922, the referendum was a fraud, as the British arrested and exiled anyone who might have endangered the proceedings, and the local population was engaged in murder and violence against the rulers. When Churchill grew weary and suggested a withdrawal, his prime minister retorted that Britain was staying in Iraq only because of Mosul and its oil deposits.

Immediately after the American victory was declared, a conference was held in Nasiriya, attended by Iraqi tribal and religious leaders to discuss the future of their country. At the end of April a ten-hour political conference between 300 Iraqi leaders convened under joint American and British sponsorship. President Bush's Special Envoy, Zalmay Khalilzad, called for another national conference in May to decide upon a leadership council or a single agreed head of state, but none of the candidates to lead the transitional government, including Ahmed Chalabi, attended that meeting. Their absence was an attempt by the organizers to prevent "grandstanding," but instead the Shi'ites clerics attended. The Iranian-sponsored Supreme Council for the Islamic Revolution in Iraq, which had boycotted the Nasiriya preliminary assembly, were invited and their representatives attended, but not far from the conference hall, several thousand protesters affiliated with a Shi'ite theological college in Najaf denounced the meeting as unrepresentative of religious Shi'ism. According to Khalilzad, rather than talking about a "new governing body," the conference decided that the next meeting, to be held in Baghdad, would select a "transitional government," which meant a self-designated body, and not an American-appointed set of Iraqi "representatives" following Civil Administration policy.[32]

The American strategy for reviving the political leadership and local government is to approach civic leaders, urging them to take on the task of administering their localities, and providing the necessary protection and support to them. This approach has sometimes backfired. In Baghdad the Americans found it difficult to locate leaders willing to take on responsibility. They had sporadic successes in working with groups of leaders, businessmen and clerics in some neighborhoods, but the administration of the city through an integrated local government remained problematic. The one provisional governor who stepped forward to take up the job, Muhammad Zubeidi, was arrested by the Americans. Chalabi, their hand-picked choice for the national leadership, was also stifled by the infightings within each community, the disagreements between various interest groups, the enmities between various ethnic and religious denominations, and Syrian and Iranian agents who have been operating on the ground.[33] This power vacuum was in part created by the military influence in Saddam's government. With so many of his ministers also generals or former generals, and therefore US military targets, there was a lack of civilian leaders.

Basra is a good example of the dependence of the occupiers on local leadership on the one hand, and the vital role that tribal chiefs can fill in returning the country to normalcy on the other. British forces called on the help of a senior tribal leader to restore civilian rule in Basra, as they faced criticism for not preventing looting among the civilian population. The unnamed Sheikh pledged to draw up an interim committee to run the city following the collapse of the Iraqi government, and to form a leadership of the Basra representatives of the local people. The remarkable latitude given to the traditional tribal chief was either an admission that the British did not want to rule the Iraqis, or a demonstration of the vitality of the traditional tribal organization of society in spite of the long repression under Saddam.[34]

The role of the tribes and their chiefs in Iraq, one of the pillars of Saddam's rule, will exert a great impact on the Americans' ability to control the situation in Iraq. The Iraqis are not only divided into ethnic groups and religions; they are also members of tribes. Some 150 large tribes and 2,000 smaller clans exist in Iraqi society, and many have relatives in Turkey, Saudi Arabia, Syria and Jordan. For years they allied themselves with the rulers of those countries. Their status diminished in modern Iraq with the rise of urban elites who took over the leadership of the country. But Saddam's rise to power, coupled with his strong identification as a member of the powerful Tikrit clan, brought the tribal chieftains back into the picture as his allies in power. During the first Gulf War, the Iran–Iraq War, it was the tribal chiefs who recruited most of the soldiers; in return they received grants and gifts and retained their previous political authority. For example, the sheikh of the powerful al-Jabouri tribe provided 50,000 men to the military after Saddam helped him against another tribe and gave him cash and other gifts. Following the war, the tribe was enriched through the reconstruction contracts that Saddam gave members of the tribe. But Saddam also knew how to punish tribes that were perceived as threatening his monopoly on power. In 1989 he distanced himself from the same Jabouri tribe which, for Saddam, had grown too strong. The canceling of gifts and contracts to the tribe generated animosity, which ended in attempts to assassinate Saddam and large-scale retaliations that left many tribesmen dead. The chief of the tribe, who was abroad during the retaliatory raids, remained in Damascus to handle the affairs of his tribe, concluding alliances with Shi'ite and Kurdish tribes within Iraq. In 1993 the Jaburis failed in another attempt to assassinate Saddam.[35]

Saddam's relations with the tribal chieftains were dominated by suspicions and paranoia. The Iraqi tribes are prepared to be loyal to anyone who maintains their status and continues to finance their activities. In 2000 there were reports of clashes between the Iraqi army and the Bani Hassan tribe in southern Iraq over the government's decision to redistribute lands at the expense of some tribe members. Three dozen men were killed on both sides before the plans for land allocation were shelved. On the highway leading to Mosul a sign reads, "Territory of al-Duleimi Tribe – Sword in the Hand of the Leader." This tribe had also rebelled in 1999 and was crushed by the army, but later cash bribes, along with the complicit agreement between the government and the tribe that its smuggling activities could be pursued, meant the tribal allegiance was switched. Prior to the 2003 war, and knowing that command and control might be cut off due to Allied bombings, Saddam gave the tribal Sheikhs the operational responsibility to delay Allied forces and harass them, to keep control of the roads and launch guerilla attacks. By giving them cash and weapons in preparation for the war, Saddam made them indebted to him. This gave the tribal heads a role in local government, in the distribution of food and medicine and protection against plunder – roles that will be important when local government is re-installed in post-war Iraq. It was this realization that prompted the Civil Administration to involve the tribes in the leadership gatherings on the future of Iraq.[36] Since tribal loyalties cut across religious and ethnic divisions, this complicates the demographic situation even further, to the point where it is hard to see how a united Iraq can emerge by consensus from this chaotic state of divisions.

The key issue, then, is leadership. The Civil Administration, headed by diplomat Paul Bremer, has appointed 25 members from all factions and groups, into a Ruling Council, lending proper weight to the country's Shi'ite majority by allocating them a majority of the seats, giving the Kurds and Sunnites an equal number, with the rest belonging to Turkomans and Assyrians. But the Council has already come under fire over the veto powers that Bremer maintains; he is able to overturn any decision of the council. Consequently, members of the Council threatened to quit, which does not bode well for the future unity of the council. In mid-June 600 Sheikhs from around Iraq met in a huge tent pitched near Baghdad International Airport, at the call of the Association of the Sheikhs (established after the removal of Saddam), with Colonel Drenner, a representative of the Civil Administration, present as an observer.

Sheikh al-Jawari, who initiated the meeting, read the prepared text of a concluding resolution which called for the formation of a new Iraqi government as soon as possible, releasing frozen Iraqi funds from abroad, settling the problem of Iraqi foreign debt, retrieving the stolen Iraqi antiquities, providing food for all Iraqis, guaranteeing salaries and pensions and granting amnesty to members of the Ba'ath Party and of Saddam's regime. Thamer al-Duleimi was challenged on the last point of pardon to the servants of the *ancien regime*, and accused of being a "traitor and an agent of Saddam." The speaker defended himself, pleading that he was never a member of the Ba'ath and that his five brothers had been killed by the dictator, going on to explain that not all former Ba'athists were criminals and only those guilty of crimes should be prosecuted in a court of law. The chiefs of the Shi'ites, who had suffered the most under the regime, and now the council majority, made the most vocal calls for Ba'athists to be punished; while the Sunnis, the most privileged group under Saddam, now stood to lose the most in the new Iraq, and preached a more conciliatory tone to try and maintain the status quo. This was a measure of the extent to which the new freedom of speech which emerged after the Saddam era of *divide et impera*, could erupt into disagreements and conflicts.[37]

Within two months of Saddam's fall, some 70 political parties and groupings had emerged. While the 600 Sheikhs, out of the 800 members of the new Association representing 1,000 tribes and clans (with a total of three million clan members), were arguing, the Americans maintained a low profile. The aggregate power of these clans could be the most pronounced in the country. Ethnic and religious loyalties, internal dissent and hostility mean that such a union is, at best, highly unlikely. The clan heads are demanding two representatives in any future government, short of which they threaten to become another movement for national liberation – thereby rejecting the possibility of a national consensus. For that reason, the heads of the clans are skeptical of American efforts to organize a democratically-elected government.[38] What the Americans have done so far, in establishing the Ruling Council, can only lead to disaster. A regime of strictly designated ethno-homogenous positions, as seen in Lebanon, where the head of state will always be a Shi'ite, to satisfy the numerical majority, and certain ministries are allocated to the Kurds, the Sunnites etc., will not only *not* contribute to a government of national unity, but threatens to perpetuate the divisions by permitting every minister to regard his ministerial duty, not as a national responsibility but as a private domain of interest. An efficient Iraqi government will not be generated by that system.

Ahmed Chalabi

Ahmed Chalabi is a Western-educated Shi'ite, extremely talented and patriotic by all accounts, but highly controversial in Iraq and elsewhere, and favored by the Pentagon for the leadership of his country. The Pentagon swears by Chalabi's commitment to democracy, to the West and to the Middle Eastern peace process, citing his leadership of the Iraqi National Congress. Other officials, however, are skeptical that a man who has spent most of his adult life in exile can succeed in the chaotic and diverse Iraqi political landscape. Chalabi's entourage, which includes about 700 fighters, was flown by the US to Iraq and based at the Talil air base in the south at the behest of the Pentagon. After Baghdad fell, some of Chalabi's men (called the Free Iraqi Freedom Fighters) helped capture one of Saddam's aides who was on the most wanted list. A US C-130 plane landed in Shatrah on 11 April carrying 300 members of the Free Iraqi Forces, under the supervision of the US Special Operations Forces. The troops, who were at first mistaken by the locals as Marines, were acclaimed when they identified themselves as returning Iraqis. US forces had been reluctant to take the exiled fighters to Baghdad for fear of violent encounters. The fighters were enjoying favors from the Pentagon in terms of transportation, training, uniforms and arms. The previous week, the US Air Force flew another 600 Free Iraqis to Nasiriya from northern Iraq. More potential recruits showed up on a daily basis – the nucleus of the new Iraqi Army. Most of the men entered northern Iraq independently from Syria and Iran, and the Americans feared they had brought those nations' indoctrinations and beliefs with them. Many of the recruits were as young as 16, and they were split into companies by cities and regions of origin, hoping that they would eventually be deployed to those areas. They were armed with Iraqi weapons from the 1991 Gulf War and wore American uniforms. In Shatrah they carried out assigned operations such as manning check posts, arresting suspects, searching, collecting and destroying weapons and ammunition, all under supervision of the Special Forces.[39]

The Americans remained concerned about the role and future of Chalabi's men, fearing that they might become a sinister security force not dissimilar to Saddam's. Only a few weeks after establishing the Free Iraqi Force, American commanders were deliberating whether to dissolve it or integrate it wholly within the American military. They also were angered by reports that Chalabi was already crediting himself with the restoration of the Basra railway that the British had been toiling on, in order to resume the transport of goods and oil northward. Chalabi needed to be seen as decisive in order to build his political base, but the Americans clearly wanted to be the only power in the land able to make appointments and delegate authority.[40] Chalabi has nevertheless succeeded in mobilizing some political support, including the Kubba family, wealthy merchants from Baghdad. In monarchical Iraq both the Kubba and Chalabi families belonged to the capital's elite. Both were secular Shi'ites, made great fortunes and enjoyed the privileges of belonging to the upper class. The Chalabis had fled after the 1958 Revolution, leaving behind their mansions and other belongings, but the Kubbas stayed on, clinging to their trade and property. The Kubba clan is, however, divided in its support for Chalabi.[41] Chalabi, who had stayed abroad for decades, and whose National Congress was permanently excluded from the Iraqi news and politics, is not a familiar face to many Iraqis, especially the younger generation. Many older Iraqis remember Chalabi's father as an honorable person, but doubt whether the son, who has been absent from Iraq since the age of 13, has any legitimate claim to rule the country. Even his supporters in the Kubba clan have backed him because of his lineage, not because of his political ideas or his plans for leading post-war Iraq.

Other Leadership Contenders

But Chalabi, who has been establishing himself as a serious candidate for the leadership, and the prominent Sh'ite clerics, such as Hakim and Sadr, are not the only choices for voters. There are prominent individuals such as the veterans Adnan Pachachi, and Sa'ad al-Janabi, and various groups including the Iraqi National Accord Group (another organization of exiles with CIA connections). Al-Janabi has seen his support increase and is often mentioned as a serious contender for the leadership. He formed his own organization, the Iraqi Republican Group, and generated dialogue between his staff and the Civil Administration both under Garner and latterly Bremer. He is advised by a former CIA operative, Whitley Bruner, who is an old hand at Middle East politics and has been involved for years in cultivating Iraqi opposition groups. Al-Janabi lived in exile for many years, and faces accusations that he was involved in corrupt business dealings with the Saddam regime and worked for the Iraqi *Mukhabarat* and for Saddam's sons-in-law. He made a fortune by monopolizing distribution of a brand of cigarettes imported by Saddam's family. In the 1990s he moved to the US, but according to reports, in 1998 he was talked into collaborating with the *Mukhabarat* service from his base in New York.[42]

Another serious figure who may impact on Iraqi politics is Kanan Makiya, a leading Iraqi intellectual and freedom fighter, who is close to President Bush. He visited Iraq after the war and reported that, in the ensuing power vacuum, especially in the south, "anti-democratic" Shi'ite clerics were filling the void. He supports the enlargement of the National Congress' militia, and laments the fact that the American command seems to obstruct their path. He has complained that the CIA, who he claims are opposed to a democratic Iraq, is undermining politics by shuttling former General Nizar al-Khazraji out of Denmark; al-Khazraji had been charged for his role in war crimes against the Kurds. Above all, Makiya worries about Washington infighting over the future of Iraq, with the Department of State undermining Bush's vision of a democratic Iraq and the Pentagon supporting Chalabi. He has called upon America to openly align with the democrats in Iraq, and asked Bush not to leave the future of Iraq in the hands of those who "will erect new statues instead of those of the tyrant that were destroyed."[43] Makiya, who is thoroughly Westernized and opposed to the clerics as political figures, favors democrats like Chalabi. But then, what kind of democracy would that be if the majority Shi'ites who may prefer their clerics as political leaders are banned from the process just because they do not believe in the Western style of democracy? Even if they did compete in democratic elections, questions are raised as to whether the Americans would allow the election of a radical Islamic cleric to stand.

Land Claims

Apart from the tribal, religious, factional and ethnic conflicts which afflict Iraqi society, there is also the problematic issue of contradictory claims between Arabs and Kurds over titles to the land. In mid-May a crowd of angry Kurds, who had aided the conquest of northern Iraq, now confronted a small garrison of American troops near Domees in the northern Kurdish autonomous region, claiming that Kurdistan had been their homeland from time immemorial and the Arabs had no right to settle in it. Later, an Arab crowd approached the same American garrison, demanding their return to the houses and lands they had been expelled from during the Iraq War. In the cities of Domees, Kirkuk and Dohuk, Kurds who had been kicked off their land by Saddam returned during the war and evicted the Arabs who had replaced them. Now both groups are claiming competing titles to the land, and the Americans must settle the issue. Even in Domees, for example, where the Americans had worked out a settlement under which the Kurds were to leave, returning convoys of Arabs were still held at roadblocks, signifying that under such shaky circumstances, any agreement would be flimsy at best.

The lands were originally Kurdish: Saddam expropriated the lands and executed many of their Kurdish inhabitants after their failed rebellion in 1991. However, new deeds were given by the Government to the new settlers, some of the claims were paid for and since resold, and Saddam razed many existing Kurdish villages and built new housing blocks to accommodate the Arabs, mainly senior officers and Ba'ath officials' families. When the war began in March many Arabs fled to avoid American air-strikes and Kurdish assaults, at which juncture the Kurdish Democratic Party, which ruled the northern Kurdish autonomous enclave, distributed the vacated houses to the Kurds.[44] When the Arab residents returned to their lands they demanded their homes back, and since then they have been holding demonstrations opposite the American base in Mosul to press their demand. The Americans decided against Kurdish claims and backed the Arabs over the settlement issue. The Arabs have since retaken possession of their properties, but relations between the two groups are dangerously unstable.

Independent of their land claims, the Kurds also demanded a stake in the huge Kirkuk oil industry but this demand was quickly denied by the Americans, who could ill-afford to start a new bout of claims and counterclaims. This is in spite of the state of affairs where former senior Ba'ath officials still occupy senior positions in North Oil. The Kurds have been frustrated by the fact that the high hopes they had entertained for the arrival of their American allies did not translate into the removal of Saddam's cronies from control of the oil industry; in essence, the Ba'ath was still in control of northern Iraq's biggest asset, and the Kurds were still landless. The Americans were probably concerned at that point about the need for a quick and effective resumption of oil exports even if it was with politically incorrect figures. While in the city council of Kirkuk the Kurds and other minorities got their worth in political representation, they remained frustrated that in the oil industry they did not reap any benefits – another potentially explosive issue in the future.[45]

Shi'ite Politics in Post-War Iraq

In the Shi'ite majority, which is the most likely to benefit from the changes, there is a deep-seated frustration over the pace of political change, not only because the Shi'ites are themselves divided between those who vie for an Iraqi Muslim state, advocates of an Iranian-sponsored Muslim state and those who dream of an all-Iraqi secular state, but they are all afraid that long election postponements might damage their leadership credentials, as their initial support fades. Shi'ite demonstrations have repeatedly warned the Americans that they should end their occupation and let the Iraqis rule themselves, even though they know that a sudden withdrawal would leave the country in total anarchy and pave the way for the return of Saddam or some other dictator. Other Shi'ite groups, supported by various clerics, are clamoring for an Islamic Republic, knowing full well that no consensus can be formed around this proposition by many other Iraqi groups, least of all by the Americans, who risk seeing their achievements in Iraq evaporate should they allow such an event to pass. Meanwhile 10,000 Shi'ites demonstrated in the center of Basra demanding the right of self-government. Led by their local clerics, they rallied outside the offices of the British Governor to protest the dissolution on 24 May of the Basra Council installed by the British when they took over the city, which had been replaced by a commission headed by a British officer (a replica of the Governing Council in Baghdad appointed by the Americans and headed by the Overseer of the Civil Administration, who retained veto powers).[46]

The big question with the Shi'ites has been whether they would keep to their traditional view that clerics should stay out of politics or if they would follow in the footsteps of Ayatullah Khomeini. In Iraq, two firebrand Shi'ite clerics, young Muftadah al-Sadr, who comes from a great clerical family, and the venerated Muhammad Bakr al-Hakim, Iran's favorite Iraqi cleric, have been capitalizing on the removal of Saddam and, through a mixture of intimidation and political demonstrations, are trying to humiliate and silence their peers, like Grand Ayatullah Ali Sistani from Najaf, who was declared in favor of a multi-faith, secular and democratic Iraq. Unlike the Iranian Shah in the pre-Islamic Revolution, who was wary of acting harshly against senior clerics, Saddam had no compunctions about killing, jailing or putting them under house arrest for disobedience. What is more, while Khomeini had cultivated, during his years of exile, a base of support among younger clerics, the Iranian-sponsored Iraqi clerics do not have that domestic base of loyalists.

Most of the Iraqi clergy, due to the state controlled media apparatus under Saddam, was not aware that the Islamic Revolution in Teheran had turned sour and that reformists and students were protesting against Khomeini's rule. In the new Iraq such information is freely available, and when they realize what is happening in Iran, many Shi'ites might slightly dilute their revolutionary zeal, in which case Sadr and Hakim might lose some of their constituencies. The Americans are, in any case, virulently opposed to the Iranian model, and their swift arrest of a self-proclaimed mayor of Baghdad who supported an Islamic Republic in Iraq sent a strong message to the Shi'ites. Hakim and Sadr, however, continue to exploit the power vacuum in the country, extending their services to their neighborhood mosques, something that will strengthen their hand in future elections. And the murder of Abd-al-Majid al-Khui, the American-supported son of the great Shi'ite luminary and anti-Khomeini and anti-Saddam, alerted both the Shi'ite hierarchy and the Civil Administration in Iraq to the strong resolve of some Muslims for Iraq to become an Islamic state.[47]

The debate over the soul of Iraq has resulted in exiles in Iran returning to Iraq, and vice versa. Dozens of Iraqi clerics who had spent several decades in exile in Qum, the Iranian Holy City, were now on their way back home. One of them was Muhammad Hassani, who headed a religious school in Qum, one of 15 designed for the Iraqis. His and others' return to the shrines of traditional Shi'a was seen as competition to Qum, the home and spiritual center of the hardline Ayatollahs of Iran and disciples of the Khomeini school which professes the rule of the clerics. Now that the centers of Shi'a in Iraq became accessible, the clerics feared that Najaf would once again take its primacy when the seminaries recommenced and the traditional Shi'ite teachings – that the Government and Islam should be separate – might prevail once again. Other moderate Shi'ites in Iran who also believe in freer religious studies divorced from politics, like Ayatullah Javad Tabrizi, have also said that they would return to Najaf as soon as the situation stabilizes.

Najaf was for centuries the center of the Shi'a, because its titular founder, Ali, is buried there. The most prestigious theology schools were always based in Najaf. But when the Ba'ath, and then Saddam, circumscribed the freedom of worship, persecuted the Shi'ite clerics and killed or arrested many of them, many fled Najaf, and the city subsequently lost its vigor and primacy. The eclipse of Najaf was concurrent with the rise of the Islamic Revolution in Iran, which made Qum a competitive center of learning, with some 30,000 clerics seeking knowledge and interpretations of the great Ayatollahs. Qum, although important, can never historically or spiritually compete with Najaf since it "only" houses the tomb of the sister of Imam Reza, the eighth Imam. The return of Najaf to the Shi'a also coincides (the Shi'ites would say that it was so determined by Allah) with the struggle in Iran between the reformists of President Khatami and the student movement, who favor a more open society and regime, and the Khamenei obscurantist clique which rules the country and adopts a strict Islamic approach to government. Iran has also provided, for the past 20 years, financial support to the Iraqi Supreme Council of the Islamic Revolution, which advocates an Iranian-style Shi'ism in Iraq, led by Ayatullah Bakr Hakim. That faction is close to the Iranian conservatives, and its troops, the Badr Brigade, were trained by the Revolutionary Guards of Iran. The faction has the potential to be a significant voice in Iraqi politics as the arena opens up for competition. The decree issued by the Qum-based Iraqi theologian Khadem al-Haeri denouncing the American invasion of Iraq and calling upon exiled Shi'ites to return to Iraq and battle the Great Satan there, is indicative of Hakim's politics. But though the Supreme Council, via its Darol-Hakameh Institute in Qum, helps the returning clerics to Iraq, there is no telling what their political tendencies or loyalties will be once they are absorbed back into the social tissue of their country. At any rate, even the clerics who oppose the Iranian Islamic state model advocate some sort of Islamic state to reflect their majority of the population.[48]

Ayatullah Muhammad Bakr al-Hakim, who lived in Iran for 32 years, has returned to Najaf with a large retinue and generated speculation as to his intentions. He stopped along the way to Najaf at various Shi'ite centers and, like an experienced campaigner, addressed large crowds. It is believed that his staunch opposition to Saddam gives him the legitimacy to nego- tiate on behalf of the Shi'ite majority in the constitution of any future government. Under the terms of the agreement with Washington which allowed him to return, the Badr Brigade must play only a very limited role as Hakim's personal guard. After Basra, he traveled to Nasiriya and wept publicly when recalling the torture of the Shi'ites by Saddam during the uprising. He was accompanied from Basra by busloads of supporters, while thousands of sympathetic Shi'ites decorated his trek to Najaf. But beyond their immediate circles of zealots, there seems to be little mainstream enthu- siasm for Hakim or the other returning exiles. Those who opposed Hakim openly, did so on the basis of his estrangement from the Iraqi scene for years and thus translated his lack of experience in the daily workings of Saddam's rule into a question mark over his leadership credentials.[49] His murder later in 2003 was an indicative comment of this mood.

The fanatical crowds who deliriously greeted Hakim, shouting: "With our soul and blood we shall sacrifice for you Hakim!" belied Hakim's inability to secure the support of the highest priests in the land. He knew that his political success hinged on the support of Ali Sistani, the supreme leader of the Hawza Shi'ite Council, who was still considered the absolute authority of Shi'ite law in Iraq. Sistani had never considered Hakim a member of the Hawza, which is supported by a majority of the Shi'ites of Iraq. Neither he nor his son and possible heir attended the reception held by the Shi'ite crowds for Hakim when he reached Najaf. While the Secretary-General of the Supreme Council, Ali Najafi, did attend, the three other leaders of the Shi'a, all based in Najaf, also declined the invitation. One of them, the young upstart Muftadah al-Sadr, the son of the hugely- popular Muhammad Sadiq al-Sadr who had been murdered by Saddam, has been one of Hakim's most virulent critics: Sadr's assistant accused Hakim of masquerading as a *marja'*, that is, a supreme spiritual leader, which he clearly was not. Much of the income of Sistani and Sadr comes from the annual tithe Shi'ites pay to their religious leaders, about one-fifth of their total income; the leaders then distribute funds among the Believers the way they see fit. But their levies are insignificant compared to the efficient machine of the Supreme Council, accompanied by the Badr Brigades, which stopped in all towns and villages along the 500 km route from Basra to Najaf, distributing pictures of Hakim and calling upon the people to welcome the returning leader. Suspicions, of course, were raised that Hakim's campaign was funded using foreign (Iranian) money, propaganda and organization to try and pave Hakim's way into the recognized leadership of Iraqi Shi'ites in the new Iraq.[50] His death, which leaves his organization unscathed, might provide new leadership.

The leadership of the Shi'a will be decided between clerical scholarship with its built-in veneration by the populace, and a new brand of leadership, modeled on Iran, where the leader, and his qualities to mobilize the country, take the primacy. The former do not wish to deviate from the traditional Iraqi and Shi'ite political model, while the latter, personified by Hakim until his death, and following the charismatic leadership provided by Khomeini, strive to apply the principle of *wilayat-al-faqih.* When Hakim gave his speech/sermon in Najaf he was careful not to speak against anyone, thus positing himself as the leader of all Shi'ites, while Sadr's people boycotted him and demonstrated against him. Nonetheless, Hakim and Sadr agreed on one principle – namely the need for *Jihad.* Hakim's supporters claim that Iraqis have already sacrificed millions of lives to rid themselves of Saddam, and unlike the Saudis, they were ready to sacrifice many more and set aside their differences to expel the "colonialists." This is a powerful appeal which concords with the many *fatwas* being issued throughout Iraq, and not only by supporters of Hakim, declaring that, should the Americans outstay their welcome, they would be forced out through a *Jihad.* The *Jihad* as a mobilizing factor is a clear and present danger, given the tradition of suffering and sacrifice in Shi'a Islam and the self-flagellation witnessed on Ashura day after the fall of Saddam. However, although a *Jihad* declared by Hakim or anyone else against the Americans would be difficult to extinguish, many Iraqi professionals and educated citizens prefer secular candidates like Chalabi, for their moderate views and their ties with America, which are considered vital for the rebuilding of the country.[51]

On 21 June 2003, 3,000 supporters of several senior Shi'ite clerics in Iraq held a demonstration in front of the Civil Administration compound in Baghdad and demanded an end to the occupation. The peaceful nature of the protests reflected Sistani's view that, although the American occupation is wrong, it is a necessary transitory measure to prevent anarchy, as opposed to al-Hakim, who explicitly called for a strict Islamic Republic modeled after Iran. Even those who openly oppose the American presence in Iraq have so far refrained from issuing any *fatwa* ordering their followers to rise against the occupiers. It is generally recognized that Iraq will need massive amounts of American aid in order to rehabilitate the country, and if the Americans should be forced to leave before their task is accomplished, the country may slide into anarchy. An early withdrawal of the Americans might also provoke internecine battles between the various Shi'ite factions for regional hegemony.[52]

The Sunnites after the War

Apart from the majority Shi'ites and their factional rifts, and the Kurds vying for a state of their own in the north, there are the Sunnites, the ruling elite of the modern Iraqi state since its inception. Feeling that their position at the summit of Iraqi society may be under threat, they have been demonstrating in Baghdad on an almost daily basis. Many of them are Ba'ath loyalists, Republican Guard or government officials demanding salaries or pensions. They are seconded by Sunni fundamentalist or nationalist factions, and the combined power of these groups, coupled with the guerilla recruits who are mainly recruited by the Sunnites, constitutes a growing nuisance to the Americans. The Iraq Islamic Party (IIP), led by Iyad al-Samarai, and the pan-Islamic *Hizb al-Tahrir* (the Liberation Party), led by Usama al-Tikriti, are extant from the Saddam regime which co-opted them side-by-side with the predominant Ba'ath Party. These opposition groups against US occupation, may even achieve Shi'ite and Kurdish support, ostensibly to protest the decision to delay elections by Paul Bremer. The insulting remark that the "the Iraqis are not yet ripe for such elections" may mobilize anti-American groups. Evidently, the Americans are loathe to surrender power to a self-appointed tribal and factional Iraqi government, or a Shi'ite-dominated one which, upon attaining power, would likely challenge American political and economic hegemony in an attempt to oust the US from the Arab world.

The Sunni population in Iraq, although angry at the American conquest, in keeping with the Sunnite tradition of preferring rule over chaos, has decided to take the moderate path in order to appease the Americans. But despite their declarations of tolerance they did not hide their belief that Islam will again prevail as in the past. One of the Sunni Imams, Sheikh Jamal al-Nazzal, gave a speech in a mosque in Faluja, a rebellious city in the Sunnite Triangle, one week after clashes between American troops and demonstrators resulted in many civilian casualties:[53]

We appeal to the Christians, the People of the Book, in the East and the West to look at Islam and compare it with their New Testament. All are books from Allah . . . You Americans are Christians? Then read the New Testament which says that you must act justly. We appeal to the Americans who entered Faluja and quote the words of Jesus to them: "If someone strikes you on the right cheek, turn the left cheek." But America struck us first, with uncalled for and unacceptable force, in Baghdad and other places. In our city they struck us on the right cheek and on the left cheek and from above, from the front and from behind, and their planes hover over our city, verily above the houses. Their tanks and armored vehicles drive through the streets and aim their weapons at people. They say that America does not act with terror. By Allah, this is the gravest terror . . .

In our city there are no weapons, no weapons of mass destruction, only weapons of mass construction and good deeds, the Qur'an, prayers. This is our weapon . . . We are people of comprehensive justice, for Islam and other religions . . . Why does America violate the sanctity of Islam in these lands? They make a fuss when the Taliban destroyed idols of Buddha, but aren't emotions raging in the Muslim world when Americans and Europeans destroy the sanctity of human life in Iraq? Did you find missiles or bombs in Faluja? Is that why you are killing our children? We must act with rationality and faith and according to the way of the Qur'an, the way of Muhammad. We call on the American forces to leave our city. We will protect our own city, children . . . [54]

Whatever the American reforms in the political system of Iraq, it is evident that the Ba'ath, the symbol of Saddam's terrifying monopoly of power, has seen its influence wane; at best, it can hope to exist as one of the dozens of political parties that have emerged after the war. But the Ba'ath's influence is deeply rooted in Arab politics and its Muslim supporters need re-education the way defeated Germany in the aftermath of the war needed a de-Nazification program. Hence the de-Ba'athification that both Chalabi and the Americans are looking at: the former, because without dismantling the mono-party-oriented Ba'ath structure Chalabi cannot compete in a new multi-party system; the latter because, as Donald Rumsfeld has declared, "we will not allow the Iraqi people's democratic transition to be hijacked by those who wish to install another kind of dictatorship."[55] He means, of course, that "a vocal minority clamoring to transform Iraq in Iran's image will not be permitted to do so," but the same principle applies. The Arab nationalists who created the Ba'ath had been deeply impressed by National Socialism in Germany and they embraced its beliefs and values, directing their zeal against the same enemy in the Middle East: the British and Zionism. In 1941, the emergence of a pro-Nazi regime in Iraq was aborted only thanks to a British invasion. After 1945, it was the Soviet Union who sponsored Ba'athism and strengthened its totalitarian base. Since then, the suppression of any opposition by the secret police and massacres of rebellious populations, have been characteristic of the Ba'ath regimes in Iraq and Syria.[56]

The Future of the Iraqi Army

Iraq's notorious army, which supported the regime and served as the symbol of Iraqi nationalism, is planned to be reconstituted as a small (around 40,000 men) armed force and protector of the new democratic regime. There are real difficulties facing such a plan, however. All Arab regimes consider the size of their armies as a yardstick of their national pride and mark of independence; therefore, it is hard to imagine how a restriction on military capacity could be enforced in the long run, even if the new government is persuaded to accept these limitations in the first place.[57]

In the meantime, however, to prevent unrest, the Allies are paying the salaries of 250,000 unemployed soldiers, provided they renounce their Ba'ath affiliation. In doing so, they not only wish to guarantee that the dismissed soldiers would not add to the organized resistance against their presence in Iraq, but this also indicates that the Americans will be relying on their own firepower for the duration of their stay in Iraq. In any case, the urgency of rebuilding an Iraqi army is linked to the general sense of concern growing in the Civil Administration that, unless they hasten the pace of building the new institutions of power in new Iraq, and are seen to be fulfilling their promise to hand over power to the Iraqi authorities, the resistance against the occupation could increase and the rate of American and other allies' casualties might render their long-term presence untenable. That is why Paul Bremer had announced the creation of the Governing Council, which is primarily a consultant to the Allies. In July 2003, Bremer commissioned the drafting of a new Iraqi Constitution, while he promised that the next free elections could be held within a year thereafter, following which national sovereignty would be transferred from the Civil Administration to the Iraqi people. Various Iraqi political leaders have already expressed their disappointment at this postponement and they are pressing for early elections. Recruitment for the new army started in early July for the first "light infantry division" of 12,000 men, and their training was entrusted to General Paul Eaton, the former commandant of the US Army Infantry School at Fort Benning in Georgia, whose rank also enables him to command the force when it is ready to operate.[58]

However, when the new national army is established, the issue of the other surviving militias remains. Most problematic would be the Kurdish 70,000-man Pesh Merga. Were they to be dissolved? Who could realistically enforce such a dissolution should the Kurds reject the idea? Saddam had tried but failed to disband the Pesh Merga, and with more men than the Americans have at their disposal. Nor are the Kurds enemies of the United States. In May when all Iraqis were ordered by General David McKiernan, the top US Commander in Iraq, to turn in their heavy weapons, he exempted the Kurds, who were allowed to retain their tanks, artillery and heavy machine guns. Some of the leaders of the two rival

Kurdish factions – the Kurdistan Democratic Party (KDP) of Massoud Barazani, and the Patriotic Union of Kurdistan (PUK) of Jalal Talabani – have expressed their wish to become part of the new Iraqi Army. While their wish to integrate, rather than secede, was considered positive by those who maintain that Iraqi integrity must be preserved, the proposition of integrating a 70,000-man militia into an army not supposed to number more than 40,000 men in total means that their offer is likely to be rejected.

America's Future in Iraq

America came to Iraq to overthrow a tyrant and build a new state and a new society, in the process reaping some strategic and economic profit. But it did not come with a clean slate of demands either. Ever since Congress passed the Flatow Amendment[59] in 1996, Americans with terrorism-related claims against foreign countries have had the legal ability to sue nations on the Department of State list of countries sponsoring terrorism. Before then, Americans were prevented from making such claims because foreign nations were protected from legal and financial liability under the Foreign Sovereign Immunities Act. Despite the Amendment, the Department of State opposed efforts by American citizens to recover monetary damages from frozen foreign assets in the US, due to the potential risk the US faced in terms of damaging already sensitive relations with countries on the list. But as part of the Executive Order that President Bush issued on 20 March 2003, payments were being issued to American plaintiffs who had success-fully sued Iraq in American courts but who had been unable to collect from the frozen monies in the US. Until then, Americans who won their suits against Iraq on account of abuses dating from the previous Gulf War were unable to get the US government to enforce the judgments on their behalf. When the Executive Order was issued, some $300 million was released to make such payments, while the US government confiscated all the remaining frozen assets to help pay for the reconstruction of Iraq after the war. However, while those plaintiffs who received their judgments were compensated, others who were still pursuing the legal process were suddenly denied the funds to pay their claims should they prove successful. The latest judgment was delivered on 7 May when a federal judge in Manhattan awarded $104 million in damage to the families of two victims of 9/11, after the judge determined that there was sufficient evidence to establish that Iraq provided material support to Osama bin Laden prior to the attack on the Twin Towers.[60] Aside from the legal angle of convicting the Iraqi regime for its ties and cooperation with al-Qa'ida, while the issue is still debated in the US and the media, new legal problems have arisen for the future relations between the US and the New Iraq. Namely, can any future (or previous) Iraqi government be sued for payment by any of the ongoing US cases after the frozen monies have been confiscated by the US government? Certainly, there is a legal continuity between governments, and any new Iraqi regime can, theoretically, be held responsible for the damages of its predecessor. But will the US government risk its relationships with the New Iraq being soured by these claims, which may involve potentially many millions of dollars?

All the endeavors to put Iraq on a new domestic course will go to waste without a new legal base to underpin the entire system. Pending the drafting of a new constitution, there is an urgent need to reinvent Iraq's legal system. In the Arab and Islamic worlds, a constitution is not a permanent document, nor is it a guarantee against the infringement and abuse of human rights. Rather it is the deed of individual governments and dictators who tailor the constitutions to secure their own status and reinforce their own internal political primacy. Instead of a constitution protecting the public against tyranny, it is the tyrant who is the protector, often against the public will (in a mural in Baghdad, Saddam is depicted holding the scales of justice). To ensure that Iraq's free and democratic future is permanent, a new legal system based on the Western concept of law needs to be devised, one which recognizes contractual obligations and mutual recognition of interests without regarding the American presence as an occupation or as a coercive element.

Saddam's legal system was based on bribery and corruption. In each district there were matrimonial courts, civil courts and criminal courts. Judges in civil and criminal courts were selected from among the lawyers who had attended a two-year training course. Serious crimes were handled by three-judge panel courts; but political crimes were dealt with by the Revolutionary Courts that came under Saddam's direct supervision. American military and civilian teams of jurists, comprising experienced judges, attorneys and private practitioners of law, met with local Iraqi lawyers and former judges, in an attempt to rescue the country from the "legal" apparatus that had brutalized it for three decades. Colonel Marc Warren, the staff judge advocate for V Corps, which has been in charge of Iraq since the formal end of the war, has been diligently trying to establish a group of Iraqi individuals to initiate the new judicial system, and to get a new court system and a public record system operational. The US contribution to a new Iraqi legal system may be the most lasting influence that America leaves behind in Iraq.[61]

Without question, America has made radical changes to Iraq already: First, the Iraqi state was shaken to its foundation; second, a new mode of thinking was introduced to the Iraqi people that might be transmitted to other Arabs in general; and third, by practice and example, the groundwork for modern statecraft has been established. While America is prepared to accept almost any regime in Iraq that would respect the rights of its citizens and its neighboring countries, like Jordan or Egypt, President

Bush has made it clear that he will not tolerate an Islamic regime in Iraq. That is because the US is opposed in principle to theocratic states – which is precisely what some Iraqi Shi'ite factions want to establish. Contrary to the general Muslim conviction that the US sees Islam as the enemy, America does not, historically, wage war against democratic or liberal states, or against any religion *per se*, because religion belongs to the domain of the individual, something which is guaranteed by American culture, tradition and its Constitution.[62]

Iraqis will come to realize that the Sunnite center, which was the focus of their modern history, must surrender its power to the previously peripheral forces of the Shi'ite majority and the Kurds. That realization signifies that the centralized state system maintained by the Sunni elite through a regime of tyranny and oppression that yielded nothing to the periphery, will have to be decentralized and opened up. The main instruments of power – the Army, the Ba'ath and security apparatus – have collapsed, creating a vacuum that only the ethnic and religious communities can fill. The Americans, who are committed to the integrity and diversity of the Iraqi state, must carefully negotiate between the emerging de-centralization process and the imperative to maintain some sort of overarching central authority. Most prominent is the revolutionary role of the Kurds, the only Iraqi element to have fully participated in the war on the American side. For that purpose, and having been emboldened by their decade of autonomy and their alliance with the US in the war, their two rival factions have established their HQs in Baghdad, willing to participate in the new democratic system. The Shi'ites, too, have gained. Their factionalism, which is even more fractious than the Kurds', and which does not allow them any united front *vis-à-vis* their rivals notwithstanding, they can all express their views and worship freely; under US control, which believes in the rule of the majority, the Shi'ites will no longer be on the fringes of Iraqi political life. All Iraqis have learned that beyond their tribal tradition, they can cultivate a multi-party system sustained by a multifarious free press, as seen in both the tribal associations involved in the process of government-building, and the hundreds of political parties, papers and journals that have emerged from the post-war chaos.[63]

8

Arab and Muslim Fears: Images, Loyalties, Wishes, Delusions

One of the most fascinating aspects of the Third Gulf War was the world of fears, wishes and delusions that the Arab and Muslim worlds found themselves in before, during and after the war. This is not only due to the direct way those worlds related to the war, given that a "sister" Arab and Muslim state of great importance was involved, but also because the Muslim and Arab worlds had faced the same quandary twice before – and each time had responded differently. The various reactions of the states of the Middle East to the Iran–Iraq, Gulf, and Iraq wars, was counter to the principle of Arab solidarity – that no Arab leader can afford to be caught as violating, and which has been used to promote the idea of "Arab Nation" since the era of Nasser.

During the First Gulf War (1980–8), waged by Iraq against Iran, Arabism and Arab solidarity brought practically all the Arab world, especially in the *Mashriq* (the eastern part), not only to support Saddam but also to foot the bill of the war, especially by wealthy Kuwait, Saudi Arabia and other Gulf states. Other countries of more modest means, notably Egypt and Jordan, helped by either sending workers to operate the Iraqi economy while Iraqi men fought on the front lines, or facilitated trade through their territory to overcome the blocking of the Gulf by burning fires and bombardments.

The invasion of Kuwait by Iraq in 1990 caused immediate consternation and shock throughout the Arab world, not only because they thought it was wrong or unjust for one Arab member of the 23-nation Arab League to attack another, but because Arab leaders such as the Presidents of Egypt and the Yemen and the monarchs of Saudi Arabia and Kuwait felt "betrayed" by their ally who did not even consult with them, and frightened by a formidable, ruthless and aggressive neighbor, with no respect for law, borders, neighbors or stability in the Gulf area. Because America was also set to dislodge Saddam from his occupation of Kuwait, the other Gulf states could afford to join the American-led coalition. Even isolated Syria was happy to comply to the Arab consensus.

President Bush's determination to fight world terrorism post-9/11, even at the price of violating taboos, over-stepping conventional wisdom, killing holy cows, and going to war, if necessary, to eradicate the "Axis of Evil," has changed the perception of the US in the Arab street in the 13 years since the 1991 Gulf War. For the Arabs and Muslims, new dilemmas emerged that they had to deal with, primarily the issue of siding with a world power that was not very popular after the Afghan war, instead of supporting another Arab and Islamic country under attack, in this case Iraq. Since most of those countries had supported, openly or latently, Islamic terrorism, in one fashion or another, as long as it was not directed against their domestic regimes, their publics could not understand why their governments should collaborate with the US against fellow Arabs and Muslims. On the other hand, the Arab leaders were in a bind: if they did not support America's campaign against Saddam, they would not only lose its economic and strategic support, but if they were not explicitly "for" the War against Terror, they might be considered "against" it as Bush had warned, making them potential targets if they could not control the anti-American hatred that was brewing among their crowds, as expressed by their media since the horrors of 9/11.[1]

The question of Arab and Muslim attitudes toward the 2003 Iraq War, which was imposed on the region, from their point of view, at the wrong time, against the wrong targets and sometimes against their own best interests, sometimes forced them to make choices and then to renege on them, to make declarations and then retract them, to allow the populace to let off its anger, and then to quell it. Such policy was often seen as hesitant and zigzagging at best, cowardly and hypocritical at worse, especially by their own critics. We shall examine this problem through four different prisms: first, the evolution of the attitudes as expressed by the media and public statements of the politicians, and as they evolved before, during and after the war; then, the often negative, sometimes Satanic images of America that were crystallized in the state-controlled Arabic press and which did not differ in essence from the old stereotypes that have been cultivated in the Arab world for years; third, the amazing process of self-flagellation, especially by audacious Arab and Muslim intellectuals who dared to ask what was wrong with themselves; and finally, the realization that the War in Iraq had changed the political and social landscapes of the Middle East which will affect all regimes in the region, from the fear from democratization that will topple the existing regimes, to the permanent presence of the Americans in the area and the return of colonialism and imperialism.

Arab and Muslims Attitudes to the War

On the eve of the war, countries that were against it, like Syria, led the campaign of anti-Americanism while others, like Egypt and Saudi Arabia, were ambivalent. The Kuwaitis, who stood to gain the most from Saddam's defeat, were enthusiastic about the prospects of the approaching war. One Kuwaiti editorial warned Saddam that he should either resign or face being "dragged,"[2] a reference to when Abdul Karim Qassem toppled the monarchy in Iraq in July 1958, Nuri Sa'id was killed and his body dragged behind a car in the streets of Baghdad to the enthusiastic cheers of the mobs. Syria, seconded by Libya and against the background of the prepa-rations for war, saw President Jacques Chirac of France appear as the hero of the Arabs. Under the title "The Summit of the Bloodthirsty," the mouth-piece of the Syrian regime condemned the Summit in the Azores between Bush, Blair and Aznar, arguing that the choice of an isolated place for the conference indicated the "fear of international anger," which made it the "summit of the isolated and the rejected." According to the author, the anticipated aggressive war would only increase, not decrease terrorism across the world.[3] The volunteers called upon the entire Islamic Nation, which "numbers 1.4 billion Muslims, to flock to the training camps in Iraq." A Syrian volunteer warned:

> Listen Oh Bush, Listen Oh America! . . . We are not the aggressors, we did not cross oceans in order to slaughter your children, your women, and, most impor-tantly . . . your religion. We merely came as martyrdom seekers in order to champion the words: Allah is the Greatest, Allah is the Greatest, Allah is the Greatest![4]

While opposition media were unreservedly set against the war throughout the Arab and Muslim world, the mainstream papers, which are owned and guided by the establishment, were much more ambivalent. On the one hand, they were bound by their public to declare the illegitimacy of the war, but they also had to soften the attacks against America to respond to the policies of their governments, especially in countries that were supposed to act as "allies of the US." Those known to be in opposition had much less compunction about putting the blame on the Americans and expressing their sympathy to the Iraqi people. Establishment writers were also concerned about internal dissention, whereby the masses refused to follow their leadership, and mass demonstrations had to be quelled.

Friday sermons were appropriate forums for preachers to urge Muslims to join the war against America throughout the Muslim world. Even Qatar, the new US ally which hosted Centcom during the war, forgot to tell its clerics of its change of attitude toward America, judging by their virulent anti-American attacks. Dr Zahrani, whose sermon was broadcast live on national television, called upon all Muslims to join. He said:

> Oh our people! Why are you sitting cross-handed? The fighting is a duty, for the Crusaders have returned once again . . . Their war against Islam has its motives . . . Did Islam ever fight to gain other peoples' resources or to destroy them? Is

warfare permitted in Islam to to impose the faith on others? Did Islam ever fight to encompass others within its social and religious system? Never! War in Islam is only permitted to thwart aggression, to react to aggressive enemies. Peace is the basis for the relationship between Islam and other faiths . . . Is this the approach that prevails in other creeds? Of course not . . .

Islam forbids war to the Muslims against whoever conducts himself in peace and prohibits peace with whoever fights against them. This is the balance that exists in Islam. So let us examine the motivation of others to wage war. Are they humane motives? Let us examine the non-Muslim creeds – the Jewish and the Christian . . . What lay behind their wars? Is it justice or freedom as they claim?

President Bush and his administration are pushed by their Judaic-Christian-Zionist faith to fight and kill. The belief in the coming of the Messiah is common to all three religions . . . . But did Islam direct us, in the name of this belief, to kill any people or destroy his houses? Never! . . . [6]

A Palestinian preacher, Sheikh Ibrahim Mdeiras, repeated the same ideas, in similar words, on the same day, on Palestinian Authority Television, urging:

Oh Muslims! Wake up from your slumber! It is your faith that is under attack! Iraq is also attacked for economic and strategic reasons, and as a personal vendetta, but there are also historical and religious reasons . . . America has been suffering from an economic recession that has almost eliminated it, there-fore she needs a war that would bring in gains and boost the standard of living of the Americans . . . Iraq has been the only country in the Gulf whose oil is not under American domination . . . .

This is a religious war . . . Exactly as Palestine is sacred, so is Iraq, because the Prophet has said that in the hadith and Sunna . . . The Iraqis who defend justice are martyrs. Iraq is sacred because there is a golden mountain there, as the Prophet has said. The Crusaders know about that golden mountain, for which they came to Iraq, but that mountain will turn Iraq into a cemetery for the invaders and the Infidels. So said the Prophet . . .

America will be annihilated, Allah Willing, and Palestine, Iraq and the Middle East will become the cemetery of the oppressors . . . The Arab peoples should topple their regimes . . . Where are those who turned the world upside down when the Buddha statues were blown up in Afghanistan? Many Muslim clerics and rulers went there to plead, pretending that they were archaeological finds.

Even more vitriolic communiqués were published by the Arab Liberation Front, a pro-Iraqi organization, which called upon demonstrators in Gaza to "assemble around Iraq under the banner of *Jihad*, against aggression, and attack foreign bases." The Palestinian prisoners in Israeli jails also published a communiqué, a measure of their "oppression and torture" in Israeli custody, urging "all free Arabs and free people in the world, of all creeds and nations, to support the Iraqi people, not just by demonstrations but by pursuing *Jihad*, fighting and struggle, by all means, like attacking American and British occupied bases and uprooting their embassies."[6]

In the past few years, ceremonies were held throughout the Palestinian territories by pro-Iraqi organizations like the Arab Liberation Front and the Ba'ath for the families of Islamikaze bombers; thousands of dollars were distributed to them on behalf of Saddam. But since outbreak of the war, slogans in support of Iraq were orchestrated at those ceremonies, often in the presence of senior officials of the Palestinian Authority, comparing the occupation of Iraq with that of the territories. The leader of the Liberation Front, who distributed money to the families of 22 recent Islamikaze said: "As we honor the martyrs today, we are renewing our alliance with our brothers in Iraq. Our Palestinian people will never forget, despite its suffering, the plight of the Iraqi people." He praised Saddam Hussein and stated that he had donated so far $5 million for the families of the martyrs. In another gathering in Gaza, the speaker urged the Iraqis to rise against the Anglo-American aggression. Member of the Palestinian Parliament Dr Kamal al-Sharafi said: "the believing and resilient Iraqi people will win the war . . . and will enjoy peace and stability." He urged his audience to honor the blood of the martyrs "and to follow in their footsteps until we regain our rights and establish an independent state."[7] The Jenin refugee camp, which has become a source of Islamikaze terrorism against Israel, decided to name its central square after Ali Na'mani, the first Iraqi killed in the war, as an expression of "strengthening the blood relations between the Iraqis and the Palestinians who are glittering in the skies of the Arab nation."[8]

Palestinian children were also mobilized to the campaign of identification with the Iraqi people and its children. A project entitled "wipe off the tears of Baghdad," organized by the Islamic *Shura* of the Rafah Children, called upon Palestinian families to establish contacts with Iraqi families and to tell them that the Palestinians shared with them the siege and the suffering.[9] A Palestinian child who contacted an Iraqi family reported that he expressed to them the joy of the Palestinians at their resilience in the war, and at their success in seizing the two American pilots whose airplane had been downed. The Palestinian Muslim children also staged a mock trial of the Arab regimes, whom they urged to support Palestinian and Iraqi children and to "expel the ambassadors of the US, Britain and what is called 'Israel'," to oppose "aggression and greedy invaders, to stop the export of oil, and to use it for the purpose of putting an end to the aggression against Iraq." The Arab rulers were also required to "leave office, to declare *Jihad* for the sake of Allah, and to repent and ask Allah for pardon." The Young Palestinian Parliament, established by the dominant Fatah group in the PLO, ran another mock trial of President Bush, where he was accused of "murdering Palestinian children and perpetrating war crimes." During the "trial," a child wearing a Bush mask sat in a cage, surrounded by other children dressed as policemen, who "guarded" him. The list of indictments against him was lengthy and heavy : "bombing civilians in Afghanistan, killing Iraqi children, leading the world to war, attempting to take over oil and other resources throughout the world, and an unqualified support to the Sharon Government which leads a total war against the Palestinians." The verdict concluded that as Bush was found a "war criminal, his case would be transferred to the War Crime Tribunal in the Hague."[10]

Not to be outdone by its Fatah rivals, the Hamas weekly for children, *Al-Fateh* (the Conqueror), which often sports a child of that name, mounted on a horse and wielding a sword, addressed an open letter to the "Beloved Children of Iraq":

> We have been looking at you even before your images were broadcast on television . . . We are watching the martyrs among you who were torn to pieces by the missiles and bombs of the oppressive Americans and Britons, and their pure remains dispersed to all winds, with their heads one way, their hands another way, and their legs elsewhere. We see their fresh bodies burned by the fire of the invaders, and were blackened by the arson, the darkness, the hatred and the greed showered on them . . . The misery of their souls [the Anglo-Americans], that are dipped in the Jewish mud, and drawing inspiration from Jewish oppression, heresy and barbarism, causes them to incinerate Iraqi children with a cruelty that raises the envy of wolves, hyenas and all the predators of the forests and deserts . . .

As the war proceeded, the divisions in the Arab and Islamic world deepened, to the point that some of their leaders did not talk to each other, and insulting messages flew between capitals. The War in Iraq attained new epithets, such as the "war of aggression," "war of hatred," "invasion of Iraq" and so forth. The main axis of tension ran between Egypt, Syria and Kuwait. Egypt was accused of supporting the war, Kuwait for creating the conditions that led to the war, and the latter threatened to halt its financial aid to Syria and Lebanon, arguing that when missiles were fired on it, neither Syria or Lebanon condemned the attack even as they were recipients of Kuwaiti financial aid. Kuwait asked why should they continue the generous financing of projects in those countries while they opposed the war and calumniated their benefactor. In this war of words, the Syrians presented in their newspapers cartoons from Kuwaiti publications where the Iraqis were mocked for the defense of their country, and asked whether dollars were more important to the Kuwaitis than the blood and tears of children. They criticized the Kuwaitis, who based themselves on "American propaganda which justifies aggression," for ridiculing Iraqi defenses while "our Iraqi nation stands firm against the invaders in this war of aggression, and while it is incumbent on all of us to stand shoulder to shoulder against the enemy." In its extreme role of unreservedly standing up to America, official Syria found itself isolated, clashing with some Arab countries. Syrian demonstrators marched to the embassies of the US and Egypt in Damascus, demonstrators claiming, inter alia, that both had become "Zionist states" and "wanted to make the entire region Zionist." Mubarak, who had warned before the war that if triggered it would cause the rise of "a hundred Bin Ladens," reacted to the demonstrations by stating that Syria was a strategic ally of his country, and that sometimes there are disagreements between the two. Syria, which remained on the American list of states that support terrorism in spite of its cooperation with the US in providing intelligence on al-Qa'ida, genuinely believed that it was treated unfairly by the Americans, who "are enslaved by the Israeli position with its hands tied by the American-Jewish lobby."[11]

Egypt also was licking its wounds from the huge losses it suffered in tourism and the income of the thousands of Egyptians who worked in Iraq. Mubarak was insistent all along that though Saddam "must go," his departure should not be enforced by war (but he did not offer an alternative scenario on how to move the tyrant from his grip on power). Mubarak had every reason to worry due to the added threat of the Muslim fundamentalists, who in spite of their harsh oppression for years, were still much in evidence and ready to capitalize on the war and the deteriorating economy, both of which aroused much discontent. Popular demonstrations in Cairo gained in strength, and there were many points when it was feared that the security forces would be unable to control the restive masses. Susanne Mubarak, the President's wife, opened a bank account and tried to elicit donations for the people of Iraq, hoping thereby to allay public anger. But their anger was directed both against the war and Mubarak who "did nothing to prevent it." Even the bastion of the West in Cairo, the American University, was the area of threatening unrest, as the students took down the American flags and chanted : "Down, down USA! The CIA won't control us!" A poem by Amal Dankal, *The Stone Cake*, which had been read in 1972 at a massive gathering that demanded that President Sadat liberate Sinai from Israel, was read by students on this occasion too:

Show weapons
Death will fall and the heart will scatter
like a string of prayer beads . . .
Raise weapons and follow me
I am the repentance for tomorrow and yesterday
My banner – two bones and a skull
and my slogan: this morning![12]

Mubarak had tried to harness Sheikh Tantawi, the Sheikh of Al-Azhar University and the highest authority in established in Islam in the Arab world, to placate the opposition at home. Tantawi did part of the job assigned to him by the President who had appointed him to the job, but as in the case of the Islamikaze bombings, which he simultaneously sanctified and condemned, his position remained ambivalent. Prior to the war, he was on record as supporting an all-out *Jihad* against the Americans and

Islamikaze attacks against them, but he also was in favor of Saddam's abdication as an exit from the crisis. He then dismissed from office Sheikh Ali abu al-Hassan, the Head of the Fatwa Division of al-Azhar, for having voiced the principle of the duty of all Muslims to fight against invaders of Muslim land, which meant that the resistance to the Americans and British in Iraq was obligatory. Abu al-Hassan also prohibited Muslims to hold American citizenship, which signified the de-legitimation of the 6 million or so Muslim-Americans. He explained that his dismissal was due to the protest of the American and British Ambassadors in Cairo.[13] A few days later, Sheikh Tantawi himself approved the principle of Muslim duty to fight invaders, though he opposed the epithet of "Crusader War" that other Muslim clerics had attached to the Iraqi confrontation.[14] Tantawi's zigzagging views once again reverted to his tougher message when he condemned a Shi'ite cleric exiled in the US who had called the Iraqi military to surrender in order to save lives, and confirmed the duty of Muslims to defend their land, stressing that it was "a huge sin to abandon fellow Muslims and to refrain from fighting for them anywhere in the world."[15] In his later statements, Tantawi came out fully in favor of *Jihad* against "American aggression" and encouraged the Iraqis and volunteers who went to fight for them to pursue their holy war.[16]

The fall of Baghdad instigated a flow of emotions that is hard for non-Muslims to identify with, but in light of the centrality of Baghdad in the Muslim consciousness it becomes easier to comprehend. In spite of the general consternation in the Arab world, except for some "islands" of liberalism, some nuances emerged which represented the differences between the establishment and popular sentiment, and between those who supported America, though half-heartedly, and those who remained adamantly anti-American or pro-Iraq and pro-Saddam to the bitter end. The lone voices of dissent were voiced abroad and in the Arab world so stifled that they were not heard by the wide Arab audiences. Despair and a macabre humor characterized the content and tone of the reports of the downfall of Baghdad and Saddam in all the Arab and much of the Islamic press. In London, the pro-Saudi daily *al-Hayat* editorialized:

> They used to shower him with flowers and adulate his statues, which they bypassed with fear. No one ever dared to smile of tell a joke. What a change! Now they throw abuses at his pictures and hang ropes on his statues, in front of the invaders. Where are the Republican Guards? Where is Qusay and the Special Republican Guards? Where is Chemical Ali who can replicate thousands of Halabjas?
>
> Television has fallen silent and al-Sahhaf [the Information Minister] has disappeared . . . The "Infidel Flghters" [his term for the American troops], have been sweeping through the city. The battle of Baghdad never took place, and the invaders did not have to commit suicide at the walls, because tanks advanced and cut like knives through the veins. It is too late. There is no longer need to

convene the leadership of the Ba'ath, nor the Revolutionary Council. There is
no more need for [Revolutionary Council Members and Vice-Presidents] Izzat
Ibrahim and Taha Yassin Ramadan, and Tariq Aziz has nothing more to explain
or justify . . . [17]

The mainstream dailies in Egypt, who would not write anything contradicting the regime, were numb the day after the fall of Baghdad, and elected
to suspend their fiery writings and to escape to secondary issues. *Al-Ahram*
reported in its main headline the neutral news of "The Fall of Central
Power in Baghdad," with the editorial dealing with a "tragic health crisis"
in Iraq and the editor treating the paramount issue of the struggle in
Washington between various approaches with regard to the future of
Iraq.[18] The second most important daily, *al-Akhbar*, decided that the main
headline should be "A Surprising Collapse of Saddam's Regime," but did
not devote any of its editorials to the momentous events in Baghdad, except
than writing about the "Human Suffering of the Iraqi People" ; nothing
about the joy and exhilaration and the iconoclasm that reigned over
Baghdad. Its chief editor elected to write about the Arab journalist who
was killed in Baghdad.[19]

Everybody in the Arab world clamors for democracy in Iraq but they do
not tell us how democracy can grow from a tradition of tyranny, unless
aided from the outside, and it is to that aid that they are universally
opposed. It is either one of two things: they do not understand what democracy means and how people must be educated to it, and then by it; or they
are afraid lest it encroaches upon their own territory, which is not to the
liking of the existing regimes there. The same obtuseness one finds in the
Palestinian media that mourned, for the most part, the fall of Baghdad. The
daily *al-Ayyam*, which routinely appears in color, was printed on this occasion in black-and-white, as a symbol of mourning, while another, *al-Quds*,
elected to put on the front page the statue of Saddam in Liberation Square
in Baghdad standing defiantly erect, at variance with the pictures of
toppled Saddam that were seen all over the world. The editor of one daily
blamed the fall of Baghdad on the "lack of wise military plans which
prevented the application of the basic principles of urban warfare, such as
tunnels and obstacles, road mines and fortifications, and leaving Iraqi
tanks exposed to air attacks . . . " By contrast, he said, even the resistance
in the Jenin refugee camp was more efficient than Baghdad's. He also
laments missing the opportunity of "averting disaster" had an agreement
been reached prior to the war.[20]

The prevailing line of denial, which signals that the Palestinians would
not admit that they were wrong in their evaluation and support for
Saddam, continued. An official of the Palestinian Authority, Vice-Minister
Ali Sadeq, who doubles up as a columnist in a Palestinian daily, refuses to
let go of his adulation of Saddam, by claiming that he was a "thorn in the

eyes of the Imperialists," by keeping the "flame burning," a rather vague and uninformative appraisal. He declares in no uncertain terms, "We shall not change our minds, be the humiliation and the distortion deep as they may be." Even though he admitted that Saddam had made some mistakes, those are by necessity part of the deeds of great leaders who rule intricate societies, in dangerous geographical regions, in difficult times. He did not explain which are Saddam's "mistakes": the mass graves, the corruption, the reign of terror, or the war he waged against his neighbors, thereby making his region "dangerous," but that observation augurs ill for the future Palestinian state, if a senior official regards Saddam's disaster a "mistake of a great leader."

Most fascinating and revealing have been the testimonies about the fall of Baghdad recorded by the Arab media from Arab volunteers, who were on the spot and contributed their share to the quandary of that swifter-than-anticipated surrender. A Yemenite volunteer, who returned home to Sana'a via Damascus (evidence of Syria serving as a transit for fugitives from the war), told his story:

> Baghdad did not fall; it handed over to the invaders in a stunning move. While we [the foreign volunteers] were fighting in groups in the various neighborhoods of Baghdad, the Iraqis asked us to leave our trenches, to throw away our weapons and to return to our countries of origin. Our mission then became to survive, in the hope that we would be able to return to our homes, when we realized that our stay had become a liability to the collapsing Iraqis in the face of the invading armies . . .

This straightforward account, which was corroborated in many details by other accounts of this sort, the hypothesis discussed earlier regarding the mystery of the fall of Baghdad, Mosul, Kirkuk and other cities without battle in spite of the presence there of some of the choice Republican Guards divisions. This tends to confirm that some contingency plan existed in the Iraqi Command that, when it became clear that the American attacks were overwhelming, it was better to preserve some Iraqi troops and their weapons for the guerilla warfare after the war, and possibly for the recon-stitution of the armed forces in the future, rather than let all of them be decimated by the grinding bombings and precision shelling of the invaders. Some volunteers imputed the fall of Baghdad to the "unimaginable inten-sity and destruction of the American bombings," which by the fourth day before the fall of Baghdad had made the Iraqi guns, Katyusha rocket launchers, ground-to-air missiles and even the tanks that were dug in under trees at the entrance of every neighborhood on the Tigris river, completely inefficient. This was augmented by the fact that many civilians asked the volunteers not to shoot lest they attracted responses from Americans, which might hurt their houses.

Arab and Muslim Images of America

During the initial stages of the war, when Iraqi television was still broad-casting, the Americans were depicted as cruel and lawless predators, and President Bush, who had given an ultimatum to Saddam to leave power and prevent war, as the personification of evil. Every day, clerics and foreign volunteers, guided by the Iraqi propaganda machine, streamed to the television studios to give their version of how they conceived of America, who was in fact waging war against the Iraqi people, not Saddam, because "Iraq is Saddam and Saddam is Iraq," or "Saddam is Iraq, and the entire nation and the whole of humanity." Iraqi soldiers said that they were ready to sacrifice themselves for Iraq and Saddam. One of them described "little Bush" as having made up false accusations against Saddam and Iraq in order to launch their attack. They swore to teach America a lesson, and that the Americans would not succeed in harming "even one inch of Iraqi territory," and pledged that the "arrogant Americans" would be smashed against the "proud mountain called Iraq." Others, repeating Saddam's own images and wordings, promised that Iraq would become the "cemetery of the Americans." A woman said that her compatriots raised their children from young age to become martyrs and perform *fida'i* operations, that Iraq was the "land of the prophets, of heroism and of Saddam," therefore the Iraqis dismissed the accusation made by "criminal Bush" against the "hero of Iraq and the Arab nation – Saddam," and that he had better prepare coffins for his troops along Iraq's borders, because they will not have entered it.[21]

Even in Qatar, the country that hosted General Franks's HQ during the war, national television broadcast a sermon by a cleric calling upon Muslims to fight the Crusaders who "once again have brought corruption to the lands of Islam." He accused the medieval Crusaders of having entered the Aqsa Mosque and slaughtered 70,000 Muslims, and knew no pity for children and the old. Because of these Crusades, the cleric claimed, all the land is burning with terrorism, despite the huge demonstration across the world against what is happening in Iraq and Palestine. He said that in fact the War in Iraq and Palestine is being waged against humanity, in order to take Iraq's resources. Bush and his administration were singled out by this cleric, Dr Nasser al-Zahrani, as "believers in a Jewish-Christian-Zionism creed, which push them to fighting and killing." He said:

> the Jews and the Christian Right believe that the Messiah will not return until Greater Israel, from the Nile to the Euphrates is established . . . Therefore they think that there no escape from expelling all the population of Palestine and Iraq, and part of Egypt's . . .

Palestinian state television equally charitable toward Bush, who was dubbed the "Pharaoh" of our age; but exactly as Allah had drowned

Pharaoh in the ocean, and has been since drowning the Pharaohs of each generation, so will He drown America and with it "all tyrants." America was called the "Crusader-Zionist," who launched war against "our Iraq of Islam and Arabism, of culture and history." The Friday preacher, Sheikh Ibrahim Mdeiras, reminded his audience that he had warned that if America vanquished Afghanistan, it would turn against Iraq, and now that Iraq is under attack, Lebanon and Syria will follow. This Crusader-Zionist war, said he, was declared by the little Paharoh, Bush, as a revenge for the defeat of Pharaoh the father as a result of which he lost his power. To remove the family shame, the "little Pharaoh" came back to power and the only way to redeem the family was to remove Saddam. Bush, he insisted, also wished to take revenge for the defeat of his ancestors – the Persians and the Byzantines whose faltering culture was superseded by Islamic civilization in Iraq.[22]

Some mainstream Arab media, even of countries "friendly" to the US, did not hide their hostility to the Americans since the outset of the war and painted the world power as greedy, full of ill-will, scheming and barbarous:

> This is a historical paradox that the newest culture has been battling against the oldest under false pretense, while in fact eying its natural resources. The northern countries have always accused the southern states of backwardness and barbarism, but it turns out that the men of the vacuum bombs, missiles and modern technology is identical with the men of the stone age . . . The world has discovered that technological and cultural advance have engendered the distortion of the principles of human rights, the preservation of the environment, and peaceful co-existence. This is proven by the fact that the vanishing of the Soviet deterrence has given rise to the greedy ambition of the US in the world . . .

Iran soon joined the chorus of anti-Americanism, especially after Saddam's fall and there was a "danger" from the Iranian viewpoint, of a permanent American presence on Iran's doorstep. Former President Rafsanjani made it clear that "no one would agree for a retired American General to become the ruler of Iraqi people," if one takes into account that all the Americans are interested in is control of Iraq's oil resources and serve the interests of Israel. He accused the Americans of pursuing their "crimes under the cover of liberty and democracy."[23] President Khatami was more sober and he condemned the American disregard for the UN and the damage caused thereby, and urged the US to leave the Iraqi future in the hands of the Iraqi people, but did not explain how that could be done if the Americans heeded the UN and Saddam remained in place.[24] Other senior Iranian officials were subdued enough to clamor only for a UN role in Iraq, fearing that continued American control of the country would endanger Iran. One of them argued, that despite Saddam's tyrannical nature, it would be a "great insult" to the Iraqi people to be ruled by an "American military ruler," because it should be ruled by "democracy," with ethnic and tribal groups participating. Like the Arabs who suddenly discovered that democracy was "good" for Iraq, so did official Iran.[25] The Iranian press was much more critical and specific. The reformist paper *Iran Daily*, who accused the Americans of installing a new "world disorder," said that the Anglo-American invasion had proved that those who have the military might also hold the power of decision, thus making the UN irrelevant, and expanding the American agenda beyond the control of oil or the removal of Saddam. The paper lamented the break of "Arab solidarity following the bombardments which set out from Kuwait," but emphasized the need for an overhaul of inter-Arab relations, for a "true" democratization of the Arab and Islamic worlds, that would prevent dictators like Saddam rising to power; and for a re-examination of the relations between the Arab and Islamic worlds with Europe, taking into account the support of some European nations for the attack. The author concluded by determining that "the American attack has removed the moral basis of the US and Europe to preach to others about rights, democracy and the rule of law.[26]

Arab and Muslim Self-Flagellation

While war loomed in Iraq, great debates were raging in the press of the Arab world regarding its probablity and usefulness. The most unusual of those write-ups, far from putting the blame on others, notably the West, Zionism,and especially the US, sought fault in the Arabs themselves, their tyrannical regimes, the hypocrisy of their rulers and their failure to come to Iraq's aid in spite of their bombastic statements. Those criticisms are worth studying and reporting because they are the only glimmer of hope that, if pursued and internalized, they might one day help create the foundations of a new society and culture. Most daring in their criticism of Saddam's policy which led to the war were the Arabic newspapers in London which once again epitomized the widely-accepted notion that the further one is from an Arab capital the higher the degree of freedom of expression. *Al-Hayat*, for example, harshly bashed Saddam's "mentality" and narcissism. But Saddam was, in addition, prone to shifting political positions, from a secularist to an Islamist, according to his needs, and with his speeches he served the "worst of American propaganda." The paper mocked Saddam's call for *Jihad* and his war-cries "*Allah Akbar!*" with his mobilizing pledge to "revive Palestine" and his cursing of Zionism, thus championing the cause of Arab nationalism. The author of the editorial said that Bush's evangelism which is committed to "liberate Iraq," turns Saddam's warlike speeches into a cause for pity rather than for anger.[27]

Articles of this sort could not have been published in Syria or Saudi Arabia or Libya; it is significant that only the more westernized societies of Lebanon or Jordan, or Arabs who live and write from London, were sensitive to the horrors of Saddam's reign of terror. Another writer declared that only those who denounced the mass graves should have a say in demanding the ousting of American troops from Iraq. Those who wanted to begin a new era in Iraqi history and erase the memory of Saddam were dangerous, because that would leave the door wide open to a return of the Saddam phenomenon, and of new mass graves. He cited the model of Poland, where 4,000 Polish officers were eliminated by Stalin at the Katin Forest; the site has become a national memorial both in Poland's national culture and in the relations between Poland and the Soviet Union. In the case of Saddam, the number of his victims amounted to over a million people, forcing the Arabs to face their schismatic personality: those who want to turn the page are those who oppose the US; but should everyone forget and everyone oppose the US, their road would necessarily give rise to a new Saddam. He emphasized that only those who condemned the mass graves should be allowed to oppose the US, because otherwise it is hard to comprehend how one can take so much interest in Iraq's liberation, and at the same time be disinterested in the collective death of the Iraqis. Only those who turn the graves into memorials, as a lesson for the future, will be credible when they urge the end of American occupation. The prerequisite to ensure that the phenomenon of the mass graves will not recur is an open discussion of what has caused them, how tyrants dominate people's lives by using bombastic slogans and dogmatic formulae.[28]

When Baghdad fell, and as the shock was slowly digested, in an Arabic newspaper appearing in London columnist abd al-Rahman al-Rashid, a liberal who had lashed out against Saddam's regime throughout the war and against the pro-Iraqi coverage of the war in the Arabic media, now celebrated the fact that "Saddam was not the only one to fall." He said that more important of Saddam's fall was the collapse of "the great lies which accompanied him and praised him" and of the minds which "insisted on distorting fact and history." He rejoiced that the Arab media, which had tried for 30 years to convince their audiences that they were watching an Iraq of the people and its leader of the people, could now see for themselves the masses which toppled Saddam's statues, tore up his pictures and urinated on them. To his mind, the real story was not the fall of Saddam, who would have succumbed in any case, but the challenge to the social and political conventions which dissolved in real time as people watched. The Arab regimes which have claimed over the past half century that they represented and shaped the culture, politics and media of the Arab public, were transformed into a mockery. He took the Arab media to task for presenting the accidental death of an Arab journalist (together with many non-Arab others) in the war as "proof" that the Americans wished to silence the unfavorable Arab reporting, and concluded that in the war, two groups of Arabs came to the fore: the majority that supported Saddam in his "war of honor and survival" against foreign plots; and a reticent group that was mainly in Iraq and could not express itself, who knew that it was a war of liberation, at the very least, from a murderous and corrupt regime. While all previous wars had been against Israel or between regimes, this time it was waged against the "miserable state of the Arabs."[29]

Arab and Muslim Lessons from the War

The one lesson that was articulated by all those who wrote about the war in the Arab and Muslim media, is the total Arab failure at modernization and at learning the secrets of modern warfare. Not since the disaster of 1967, when the Arabs were swiftly defeated in six days of war by small Israel, had the Arab world experienced such a humiliation, which could not be explained away only by overwhelming American technology or by the souring relationship between the people and the regime in Iraq. Twelve years earlier, the people of Kuwait and Kuwait City had been conquered with the same ease as Baghdad by the Marines, despite the fact the the Kuwaitis supposedly supported their sheikh, who run away rather than stood up to defend his country, after all the untold billions that he, and the other Gulf states, had spent on technology and modernizing their armies. Saudi Arabia itself, with its population more than double that of Israel, and with virtually unlimited resources and access to American arsenals, could have developed over the past decades an army which could have easily defeated Iraq. The explanation lies elsewhere and it is beyond the purview of this study to try to unravel it. Suffice to say, that after Baghdad, the Arabs will have to go, as after 1967, through a painful and humiliating soul-searching process, that might bring them to the conclusion that modern warfare is not for them and abandon it in their international relations, instead adopting more peaceful means (unlikely); or that building modern and victorious armies requires building from the foundation modern nations, with democratic and open institutions, where more identification between the people and the regime can be cultivated and the conviction is implanted that the army is to be used to defend the country when it is attacked (slightly less unlikely).

A courageous Arab journalist writes that, while half a century after Hitler, the Germans have not yet been cleansed by the crimes done by the Third Reich, the Arab world has not yet awoken to the abominable crimes of Saddam. His horrors, gradually being revealed will leave a lashing scar on Iraq, but also on every Arab. For Arabism today also "carries huge doses of barbarism and hatred," says he. He admits that when opponents of the regime were seen blown up to pieces on television screens, while their executioners were applauding, he felt that "something dear to our human honor was also blown up." He emphasizes that it was precisely those murderers, who voiced slogans of progress and nationalism, who also committed those unprecedented acts of barbarism and sent the skulls of their victims in boxes to Saddam's sons. In the mass graves skulls of people were found perforated with bullets, and mothers still attached to their children, who were murdered with them. And in the face of all this, no word of regret, remorse or apology came from anyone who knew and witnessed, to help wipe the shame from the faces of all Arabs, who demonstrated against the war with pictures of Saddam, the perpetrator of those horrors. The Arab journalist was at a loss as to what should be done post-Saddam: to rebuild the Arab League, which has become morally bankrupt, or to build anew the shameful image of Arabism? He said that all Arabs ought to apologize for Saddam's crimes against all the people who were murdered, especially those Arabs who supported Saddam "in defense of the Iraqi people."[30]

A Jordanian writer argued that, the mass graves of Saddam made the horrendous Halabja murder by gas of 5,000 Kurds (1988) looked like a "minor episode" in the bloody recent history of Iraq. Saddam acted impartially to all regions and groups in Iraq inasmuch as his acts of terror were spread evenly throughout the country. The lessons to be learned from Saddam's regime, according to this writer, are:

a. Saddam's regime had reached the "heights" of Pol Pot's Khmer Rouge, and compared to him, all "Arab capitals would look like oases of democracy and human rights."
b. It was wrong to believe that a change could be operated from within Iraq, in view of the horrors that the Iraqis were exposed to for three decades.
c. No need to look for the reasons to Saddam's collapse. It was the mass graves, and not the plots and the acts of treason the Arabs were looking for.
d. All those who condemned democracy as a Western innovation [bid'a – prohibited by Shari'a Law] and dismissed it as inadequate for the Arabs, have grown up either in totalitarian Marxism or fundamentalist Islam, therefore they had better learn that self-criticism is a good quality, while reticence in the face of war crimes is tantamount to cooperation with the criminals.[31]

Thomas Friedman of the *New York Times* quoted Amr Mussa, the former militant Egyptian Foreign Minister, and now the Secretary of the 23-nation Arab League as saying that had the appointed Governing Council of Iraq been elected instead of appointed, it would have had genuine power and credibility. Friedman takes the Secretary to task for his hypocrisy and shamelessness, because in his organization not one government was elected and without the American intervention that he vehemently opposed, the Iraqi people would not have been given the chance to democratize. Friedman rightly detects the state of fear and denial throughout the Arab world, but wrongly observes, nevertheless, that no debate has been taking place about the Iraq regime and its sequels.[32] Some courageous and pioneering Arab writers did open such a debate, though not on the universal scale that we are accustomed to in the West, and without certitude about whether it would fall flat on its face, like the 1967 and 1991 debates, or if something constructive may develop out of it. It is significant that even the most supportive press for Saddam in the Arab world, the Palestinian, there is some recognition of the disaster that Saddam had created and hope for a better future if the right lessons are drawn. It is instructive to see one of those Palestinians plea for change in the Arab world:

> Maybe this catastrophe, which has joined the long series of other disasters and defeats incurred by the Arabs over the past century, will create a new consciousness and clarity of thinking in the Arab and Islamic worlds, which everyone knows are in a state of retreat, cultural backwardness, and disintegration, and which cannot even cooperate among themselves on the one hand, and with others on the other . . .
>
> What happened in Baghdad yesterday was not the last page in the history of that venerable city. Amidst the ruins of the bombings and the parts of the bodies of the victims: children, women and the elderly, who defended the glory of our nation, lay the seeds that will prove to the world one day, we hope soon, that Baghdad will know a new revival . . . [33]

Al-Qa'ida's lessons from the war, like those of Hamas, were that guerilla warfare, including by Islamikaze, should be pursued against the Americans. On their Web site, which changes IP address every second day, and under the heading of "The Crusader War against Iraq," al-Qa'ida publishes its summary of the war and its lessons, in a series of 35 articles, based on so many questions that were raised in the first article and answered one by one in each daily article. In the seventh article, written after the fall of Baghdad, al-Qa'ida promulgated its recipe for the continuation of the struggle. The article is strikingly realistic, cruelly factual and analytical and aware of the facts and developments, in contrast with the denials and fantasies of most Arabs and Muslims:

> What happened today in Baghdad, with the entrance of the Crusader forces there without battle, was not surprising for those who scrutinize things from a military point of view, because their entrance to the Capital had been expected sooner or later, and the terrain did not allow the Iraqi defense to stand fast, as long as it operated as a regular army . . .
>
> Yes, we have to admit our surprise at the ease with which they entered the city, and at the lack of any resistance to their advance. We simply cannot understand where did all those thousands of regular Iraqi soldiers disappear. We had expected some resistance, at least of the sort that was evident at Umm Qasr [the southern port taken by the British]. Despite our lack of knowledge as to the reasons for that, we are nevertheless convinced that even had the resistance in Baghdad taken place with regular forces, it would have ultimately collapsed

after a while. It seems that the Iraqi commanders too understood that using regular forces could have constituted a defense for a few weeks, and then it would have collapsed because the elements for a resilient resistance were not there. The Iraqi Minister of Defense, Sultan Hashem, said on the sixth day of the war that though a siege would be laid around Baghdad it would not fall. But the fact that they were convinced that there would be a siege was enough for them to draw the conclusion that they could not hold indefinitely through the use of regular forces . . .

Al-Qa'ida is not only talking, it is also doing. With its head, Osama bin Laden, still at large, he has been free to conclude that the soft belly of America today is in Iraq, like Russia's in Chechnya, and therefore it is time to strike. A preview of that was evident in May 2003, when a series of bombings masterminded by al-Qa'ida in Chechnya, Morocco, Saudi Arabia and Pakistan, left 100 people dead. More bombings have occurred in Iraq since then, on an almost daily basis, though they have dwindled since the capture of Saddam. But the great fear is that Bin Laden may plan a mega-terrorist act against a Western city using non-conventional weapons, and his bases in the Middle East, the Horn of Africa, and South-east Asia that have remained intact, as the 7 August explosion of the hotel in Jakarta has shown.[34] Exploiting the lawlessness in Lebanon, al-Qa'ida has set up a new base at the Ain al-Hilweh refugee camp near the port of Saida (Sidon) in the south.[35] Perhaps most interesting, wide-ranging and likely to be listened to by the entire Islamic world, are the lessons drawn by Sheikh al-Qaradawi, the popular and authoritative luminary among the Sunni fundamentalists, an Egyptian who lives in exile in Doha, Qatar (ironically the seat of Centcom during the war). Because he had undergone surgery, he was not heard of during the war, but as soon as he was released from hospital, he gave his much awaited, heeded and listened to Friday sermon at the mosque in the Qatari capital. His observations, mostly tinged with the aftermath of the War in Iraq, can be summarized in several important points:

1   Military power rules the world, not the law, because might can impose its will, and America invaded and coccupied Iraq in spite of the whole world's opposition. There was nothing one could do.
2   America is accountable to no one, though it demands accountability from all the rest; America did not go into Iraq to dismantle unconventional weapons or to rescue the Iraqis from Saddam, but to destroy Iraq's military power in order to pave the way for Israel to monopolize the arsenal it has and not to allow it to fall in others' hands.
3   Oppression comes to an end; Saddam's regime was of the most oppressive on earth, and in the Arab and Islamic land. It was oppression and tyranny which paved the way to the coming of the Americans and the

British to the area, to the war in Kuwait and to the First Gulf War before it.

4   It is recommended to the Iraqi people and all its ethnic and religious components to stand together in the face of the disaster, because they all have a common target, a common enemy and a common campaign; they should forget marginal debates and not exaggerate retribution against the Ba'ath Party members. The true membership is only a few thousands, while the Iraqi people is not Ba'athist by default. It was oppressed by the tyranny of Saddam.

5   The lessons of Baghdad should be applied to the Land of the Prophets [Palestine] where many have "sold their souls to Allah." The *Intifada* has reflected a proud and heroic nation that is not afraid of death, and wishes liberty, to live honorably or become martyrs. It is inconceivable that such a nation should die, despite the efforts of the Zionist state and its strategic partner, the US. Summits in Sharm al-Sheikh and Aqaba saw Bush honored by Arab rulers because he defeated Arab people, and they wished to crown him as the king of the world. That was to give legitimacy to the new measure concocted by the US and Israel, to provoke the Palestinian Authority to fight its brothers, for the Road Map opens that door and demands the end of the *Intifada*, silencing opposition, eliminating resistance and collecting weapons, so that Israel can monopolize their use.

6   He categorically condemned the killings in the Islamikaze acts in Morocco and Saudi Arabia. He said that such acts were done in the past in Islamic countries but they produced no results, no regime changes and no toppling of governments, except that thousands of Islamists were incarcerated.[36]

The most important elements in this remarkable document are:

First, that the US in general and President Bush in particular, will be engraved in the minds of Muslims for years to come as the parallels of the Mongols and Hulagu, respectively, regardless of the facts. The incalculable humiliation caused to all Arabs and Muslims by the fall of Baghdad to the Mongols has been repeated and instilled in the minds of Arab and Muslim children for 800 years. Only the accusation of the enemy as a barbarian, a destroyer of civilization, who knows no rules of combat and indiscriminately slaughters Muslims, can somehow mitigate the sense of loss, humiliation, helplessness and disgust that they felt, and are cultivating now with regard to the Americans. Those historical parallels, of which Arabs are fond of, have already been picked up by other Arab and Muslim media, and are sure to remain ingrained in Muslims minds for generations to come, instigating countless acts of retribution and terror against the Americans. Qaradawi is not just another cleric; his language is emulated and his reasoning repeated in many circles, and this ensures its longevity. The only consolation Muslims may feel is that the Mongols had eventually converted to Islam after they wreaked their havoc, and Osama bin Laden's pleas, seconded by other Muslim fundamentalists, to the Americans to convert to Islam and thus resolve the problems of the world, can be seen in this light.

Secondly, the extraordinary appeal of the Sheikh, one of the most vehement supporters of the *Intifada*, on the Palestinians, including the Islamists among them who swear by his name, to give up the territories of Israel Proper (1948) and concentrate on the demand from Israel to evacuate the territories of the West Bank and Gaza, is a novelty. The Hamas and Islamic Jihad have been adamant on their claim to the entire Palestine territory, and there is no telling how they might refer to this conciliatory démarche of their venerated spiritual mentor, who had in the past supported even their Islamikaze acts. Even the Islamists groups, like the Palestinian Authority, have never given up the Palestine of 1948, by their very demand for their right of return, which in effect means a return to the very places the Sheikh has spelled out as non-retrievable. Perhaps the Sheikh has realized, under the strong impression of the American victory in Iraq, that the US would not let the Arabs dismantle Israel by claiming its territory, and therefore he counseled to accept what is retrievable, though in effect he rejected the Road Map and the current policy of negotiation between the parties. Only future declarations of the Sheikh can resolve those contradictions.

Iraq, America and the New Middle East

9

Once the current issues of security which predominate American policy in Iraq are resolved (and given the current rate of attacks on American troops, there are no certainties that the security situation will improve), the US agenda will be dominated by the questions of restructuring the entire social and political order in Iraq, together with issues of economic reconstruction. The problems look almost insurmountable; it is too early to say if, when and how, the US will succeed, but under the firm leadership of Paul Bremer, the first tentative steps toward a free Iraq are being made.

The Future of Iraq

Paul Bremer nominated the 25 members of the Iraqi Governing Council (IGC), which possesses deliberating powers and the capacity to make practical policy recommendations – though its actual decision-making and execution powers are still uncertain – but are subject to the vetoing by the American Civil Administration. This is the most representative body the Iraqis have had, at least since the rise of the Ba'ath in the 1960s. It is not representative in the sense that it was elected, because it was not, but it presents, perhaps for the first time in modern Iraqi history, a proportionate representation of the ethnic and religious groups and accords extra political weight to the demographically dominant Shi'ite population (60% of Iraqis) who had never occupied a government role in Iraqi politics.

After 80 years of turbulent and violent independence that culminated in Saddam's dictatorship, which did little to justify the concept of "territorial integrity" in Iraq, the US now has a unique opportunity to try the two-states solution, experimented with (successfully) in Kosovo/Serbia and Montenegro, and (unsuccessfully) in Israel and the West Bank and Gaza. Tearing the existing polity apart would disrupt the fragile bonds Iraqi society is built on; but re-creating Iraq into separate, ethnically homogeneous states – Kurdistan, a Shi'ite state in the south, a Sunni republic in the center – may provide an answer to the country's problems. Under

Saddam things were getting worse, with the proportion of the Shi'ites increasing, and their suppression therefore becoming more difficult, and the Kurds demanding independence; but it was not in Saddam's personal interest to end the hegemony of the Sunnite elite which sustained him through the military and the machinery of the Ba'ath. The postwar condition arguably presents the Civil Administration with the best moment to seize the opportunity and stabilize the country's borders and demography in order to create long-term peace and prosperity.

Certainly, the Governing Council is temporary and should pave the way to national elections within a year. What then? What if the Kurds vote for their two rival parties, the Shi'ites remain clustered around their religious leaders, and the tribes campaign for their tribal interests? Within such a fragmented society, which has never had a democratic system, what hope is there to establish a democratic system based on political parties, the way Chalabi and others have been hard at work to achieve? Can all Iraqis accept majority rule? Is it at all feasible to continue to constrain all Iraqis to live together if there is nothing in common between Kurd and Shi'ite, Sunnite and Assyrian? The Kurds, for one, feeding on the experience of virtual autonomy they enjoyed between the Second and Third Gulf Wars, would certainly opt to preserve the status quo, and if given independence with the oil fields of Kirkuk and Mosul, they would certainly be able to establish a long overdue independent state with a Kurdish majority, while preserving the rights of the Sunni, Assyrian and Turkoman minorities. The Turks, the Iranians, and the Syrians, however, would reject the proposition. So what? Since when have those oppressive regimes had any meaningful say in Kurdish affairs? They can protest, but they are powerless against such a proposal. Quite the contrary, a Kurdish state might inspire the other Kurds to rise and demand their right of self-determination supported by the entire international community. With an American presence in Iraq, none of those countries would dare to suppress such a process. Ultimately, the 35 million Kurds (three times the population of the Palestinians), could enjoy the liberty that has been denied them for a century, while Palestinian autonomy demands have been internationally heeded and actively supported.

If the Shi'ites are able to unite their various factions and agree on a model of government, they will quickly realize that this model could not realistically include the Kurdish northern Iraq. In that event, they will probably seek to consolidate their own regions of Iraq (where they constitute the 80 percent majority), including the Sunnites in a new role as a minority group whose citizenship and human rights would be enshrined in any future government constitution. This model, based on the riches of the southern oil fields of Rumeila, if it can establish all-Arab political parties where Shi'ites, Sunnites, and other minorities can participate, with its capital Baghdad intact and mixing together Shi'ites, Sunnites, Kurds, and others, will have a very strong opportunity to develop into a free and prosperous state, living in peace with its neighbors. It is expected that the proposed partition of Iraq will raise opposition from the slogan-wielding parties who advocate the "territorial integrity" of Iraq. But one has to recall that modern Iraq was created when three separate provinces of the Ottoman Empire (Mosul, Baghdad, and Basra) were artificially merged together after World War I, but never truly developed into an integrated society. What is wrong with giving a new opportunity to those Iraqi Arabs – Sunnis and Shi'ites – to build a new state together, and rescue from their yoke the restive Kurds? After all, the latter are as numerous as the Sunnites, and in aggregate with other Kurds, who might subscribe to independence, they even surpass the combined numbers of all Arabs in Iraq.

In the long run, after the disastrous experience of the past 80 years, especially the rule of Saddam, which did nothing to justify or uphold the concept or "territorial integrity" in Iraq, there is now a unique opportunity to enact the suggested concept of two states, just like the Israeli rule of the West Bank and Gaza for 35 years has given rise to the widely accepted and anticipated two-state solution. Although tearing an existing polity apart will cause many pains and tribulations, it is better to resolve the problem once and for all, in a long and uneasy process of healing, than continuing the existing situation which has proven patently untenable, and promises to grip all components of today's Iraq in misery and conflict for generations to come. Great statesmanship does not reside in the choice between the good and bad, the easy and the uneasy, the soft and the harsh option; that would be too simple. It resides in seizing the bad, which is the situation today, before it becomes worse. Under Saddam things were getting worse, with the proportion of the Shi'ites increasing, and their suppression concomitantly, and the Kurds becoming impatient; but he was not the man destined to take a decision which would have been to the detriment of his power and the hegemony of the Sunnite elite which sustained him through the military and the machinery of the Ba'ath. The post-war condition, where that regime has been irreversibly removed, is arguably the best moment to seize this new opportunity.

Paul Bremer has pledged that a commission to draft the new Constitution "by Iraqis for Iraqis," which promises to be a long process, would decide the new contours of the Iraqi state. No other culture has written as many constitutions as the Arabs. In the West, a constitution is permanent and outlasts transient governments; it is conceived as a bulwark to protect the citizens from the vagaries of governments or the abuses of whimsical rulers. It is also a yardstick to gauge the legality of new laws, and provisions are made that the court system protects the constitution from violation. In the Arab world it is a quite different story, with the incumbent dictator dispensing constitutions one after the other, as a measure of his good intentions, generosity, and plans to benefit the people, which usually remain unfulfilled. They are written in rosy and pompous language, invoking lofty principles (the pinnacle of liberalism and democracy), but after they are promulgated, the ruler does what he wishes, his diktat is the law, and whoever protests the violation of the constitution is suppressed. Like Samuel Johnson, who was once told of his friend who had been unhappily married for many years, but upon the death of his wife had married again, to which the philosopher retorted "that is the triumph of hope over experience," one has to accompany Bremer's optimistic hopes with the rather dismal historical experience in this regard. Leaving it to the Iraqis to agree, let alone to decide, upon the terms of the constitution, and then on the new system of government, could be a frustratingly protracted process that may never come to fruition, and if there is one it may be never implemented if the terms of reference, the deadlines, the timetables and so on are not defined for them by the Americans.

When a constitution, acceptable to the Americans, is finally written and completed, the problem of implementation remains. If, for example, there is an agreement upon whether it is a presidential or a parliamentary system of government, the immediate concern would be who would head the system: a Shi'ite President directly elected by the people, like in the US, or a Prime Minister responsible to the Parliament? The stakes are high: the Shi'ites would understandably claim that right because they are the majority, but then, nothing would be more detrimental to the system than an enshrinement of the ethnicity of the leadership position, which is a clear violation of the right of every citizen to run for office. They may also consider rotating power or a presidency by committee which would embrace the major communities. But that sort of power sharing, or power alternating, does not work effectively in a country riddled with dissensions and controversies. Yugoslavia was held together by Tito only because he was an autocrat; after his death, the attempt to establish a committee of Presidents soon collapsed and almost all of Yugoslavia's six component entities went their way and became independent states. And then the various departments of government: will they be distributed according to ascriptive identity – for example the Oil Ministry to a Kurd or a Shi'ite, who might favor the northern or southern oilfields, respectively? Will the various departments then become the private and exclusive satrapies of their heads, thus sabotaging the harmonious work of the government, and cultivating the nepotism, corruption, and inefficiency that have helped bring down Saddam's regime? The only solution is to ban ethnic or religious or tribal parties and to encourage, by various incentives, the Iraqis of all groups to enlist in parties committed to a civil program and a political platform.

Unlike the lack of experience and tradition of democracy and of elective and participatory governments in Iraq, and the Arab world for that matter, the economic reconstruction of Iraq is less ridden with political and factional controversies. True, Iraqi businessmen, either from inside the country or returning after the removal of Saddam, are not clean of personal and substantive rivalries and competition for their share in the economy. But there they also face many American competitors who were already commissioned by the American Administration to begin work, and European firms waiting for their opportunity. While there is a pretension in the American Administration regarding the political restructuring that has to be done by the Iraqis, there are no pretensions with regard to the economic reconstruction – it will be mainly contracted to Western, especially American, companies, with an emphasis on coalition members who have contributed most to the war effort, like Britain, Australia, Spain, and Poland. Following the American victory, two specialized vessels for the repair and expansion of the only deep-water port of Iraq at Umm al-Qasr, started their work of survey and dredging, one small portion of the work allotted to the Bechtel Corporation of the vast plans to rebuild Iraq. To reopen the port and clean the channel that links it to the Gulf was a priority contract, estimated to cost $680 million, because all food and heavy equipment and building materials that are to be imported must land there first and then be distributed to the various sites of reconstruction and consumption. Bechtel has also landed a contract in the restoration of the electric grid which had been badly damaged in the war. In the interim, many high-powered generators have been purchased in the region and sent to Baghdad. Those contracts, through an invitation-only bidding process that was limited to American companies, have triggered much controversy in the US, and drew the attention of thousands of sub-contractors from all over the world who are interested in part of the work.[1]

Aware of the vast scope of the work at hand, Bechtel has already launched seminars for potential sub-contractors. Though the apparent monopolization of Iraq contracts is justified by the Americans by the imperatives of speed and security, there was no doubt in anyone's mind that those who did not stick their necks out to rush to join the coalition on the road to war, much less those who opposed it and even tried to scuttle it, were excluded from the subsequent allocation of lucrative reconstruction contracts. Fluor Corporation of California formed a joint venture with the British engineering company AMEC, to seek future contracts from the US Corps of Engineers to rebuild Iraq's oil industry, to rival Halliburton where Vice-President Dick Cheney was Chief Executive from 1995 until he ran for election in 2000. Fluor and AMEC have already enjoyed a joint experience in several countries in Asia and Africa, as well as in North America. More major contracts were forthcoming from the American International Development Agency, such as restoring Iraqi economic governance, including its central bank and finance ministry, and another for monitoring the construction work, both the physical reconstruction and non-construction work like educational reform and public health services. At any rate the office responsible for monitoring the Development Agency in Iraq was already opened in Baghdad. That sort of operation is particularly needed in Iraq to monitor civil and bureaucratic integrity, because of its record of corruption and money laundering, and the added worry of acting under the continued risk of terrorism against the Americans.[2]

The New Middle East

There is little doubt that however Iraq emerges in the aftermath of the war, a new era has dawned in the Middle East, an era that one hopes is not a false dawn, as proclaimed by Shimon Peres after the Oslo Accords in 1993. In the New Middle East, the War in Iraq has had a resounding impact and influence. Countries like Syria and Iran, which shamelessly sponsor terrorism and maintain a tight grip on power, are fearful of attack and/or "regime change"; clerics are now being accused of incitement to misery and violence; terrorists who were financed, housed and maintained by sympathetic leaders are now put in the cold; and uncertainty about what the future might bring is felt by everyone. The big losers of the fallout of the Iraq War are Turkey, Saudi Arabia, Syria and the terrorist organizations (Iran can see a mixed blessing in her fortunes, having seen its enemy and neighbor, Saddam Hussein, removed from power, only to be replaced with the "Great Satan," the US). Also under threat are the regimes called "moderate" and "pro-American," such as Egypt and Jordan, which will see pressure building up against them to reform. The big winner, apart from the US, is its closest ally in the area, Israel.

For Israel, the question of defensible borders also rises in the context of the aftermath of the War in Iraq. The quest for defensible borders has been a pillar of Israeli defense policy since 1967, and this notion was incorporated in Security Council Resolution 242 and backed by successive American administrations since Reagan's in the 1980s. In the coming years, and in light of the difficulties in successfully applying the Road Map, Israel will have to assume that the Palestinian territories will not be free of terrorism, and probably even agreed-upon demilitarization will not be respected, in view of the 1990s experience, when arms were illegally imported and manufactured, and the Palestinian Authority failed to dismantle the bases of terrorism as it had previously promised. This means that the *hudna* (temporary ceasefire) that Hamas declared was breached as soon as the Palestinians were able to re-arm themselves and reconstruct the infrastructure of terrorism that Israel destroyed in its repeated incursions into Palestinian towns.

The removal of the Iraqi and the Eastern Front threat from Israel will require a new mode of strategic thinking that will re-emphasize the Palestinian threat, which is backed by Iran, Syria and Saudi Arabia (despite its protestations to the contrary), and latterly by al-Qa'ida and Hizbullah. This means that with a rearmed Palestinian entity and the renewed manufacturing of Qassam rockets, it becomes imperative for Israel to insist on defensible borders that would permit the establishment of a Palestinian state on its borders without severely compromising the security situation. A border with a Palestinian state would present Israel with a new set of security issues that it could not cope with without secure borders.[3]

Iranian operatives have been caught working with Shi'ite groups in Iraq in an attempt to build a following there from among the Shi'ites who had sought refuge in Teheran or in Qum since the rise of Saddam to power. Iran was also suspected of sending back into Iraq members of Ansar al-Islam who had infiltrated into its territory when they were bombed by the Americans during the war. The US has accused Iran of interfering in Iraq's affairs, against which Americans had repeatedly warned the Iranians due to their declared opposition to any fundamentalist Iranian-style government. Iran's government refuted these suggestions during the visit to Teheran of French Foreign Minister Dominique de Villepin. On that occasion Foreign Minister Kharrazi sarcastically said: "It is very interesting that the Americans have occupied Iraq but they accuse Iraq's neighbor of interfering in its affairs." He said that the US should recognize Iran's "positive role" rather than antagonize it. The US also claims it has evidence that some of the ferocious anti-American sentiment voiced by the Shi'ites and some Sunnites in Iraq originates from Iranian agents, members of the hardline Revolutionary Guard, and pro-Iranian Iraqis members of the Badr Brigade, who have been traveling throughout Iraq and sowing dissent against the Americans. For Kharrazi it was "natural" that the Iraqis of the Badr Brigade should be active in their country, promoting their future. He was also incensed at the American ceasefire agreement with the Mujahideen Khalq, the Iranian opposition group based in Iraq, and saw that as part of American schemes to control Iraq and the region.[4]

The US is entertaining the greatest hopes for democratization in Egypt, Syria, Jordan and the Gulf states. The latter cannot, by definition, democratize as long as a hereditary rule by autocrats hold the reins of power. But Egypt, the strongest Arab country and the leader and model of the Arabs in many ways, poses another set of problems which run counter to the democratization process. Guglielmo Ferrero established in the 1940s that legitimacy of power in the modern world stems from the democratic principle; however, it is a principle that can be manipulated fraudulently, and create distortions of the system.[5] Ferrero was thinking of totalitarian governments which sought legitimacy through a form called "revolutionary democracy," but since their regimes – whether Nazi, Marxist, Arab Socialist or Ba'ath – were inherent distortions of the democratic principle, they could never acquire legitimacy. This is precisely the plight of the autocratic, non-Islamized regimes in most Muslim countries, for the Islamized ones have obtained legitimacy by basing themselves on the Holy Scripture and Shari'a Law. Today, some of those regimes use terms like "democracy," "human rights," and "elections," in ways that do not correspond to the modern Western principles and interpretations of those principles. It is not that Muslim governments behave "fraudulently," as Ferrero would have it; rather, it is because these terms, for the Arab countries, exist in an entirely different conceptual framework – Western principles carry different meanings for them. Mubarak, for example, says that his regime is more democratic than Israel's; the Saudis claim that Islam invented the concept of democracy; Syrian officials declared the succession of Hafiz al-Assad by his son, Bashar, as "democracy in action". Such claims illustrate the very different view of democracy in the Middle East, and the difficulty America faces in trying to implement a Western democratic government.

The onus on Saudi Arabia to provide evidence of a genuine commitment to democracy and freedom is heavy, due to the Saudi origin of 15 out of 19 of the perpetrators of 9/11. It has been trying to improve its image in America with public relations campaigns. Its image was tarnished by a refusal to allow the US to launch ground attacks from Saudi territory, and its previous lack of collaboration with American investigators after the attacks on Americans in Saudi Arabia during the 1990s. The US understood that no reforms could be extorted from the Saudis, but kept silent due to their dependence on Saudi oil. Only after the victory in Iraq, which made the Saudis almost redundant economically and strategically, did the Americans dare to downgrade the privileged status of the Saudis who, though upset about their demotion, are also relieved of American pressures to conform – complying with American interests to desist from the financing of terrorism and possible reforms to their educational system to which the *ulama'* are opposed.

Egypt's lesson from the war is to preserve American economic and military aid without forfeiting its domination of the Arab League. Mubarak now realizes that while he protested against military action prior to the war, in the postwar period, which has crippled Iraq as an Arab power, his main contender for the leadership of the League is out of the way, thus presenting him with a good opportunity to regain control. Therefore he called for the overhaul of the League in such a way as to "contain conflicts at the very start of any crisis, with a modern system of Arab national security based on clear mechanisms." He said that his goal was to clear the air among Arab nations, denounce the use of force in inter-Arab tensions and promote the role of the League in the creation of an Arab common market. He asserted that if the private sector of the economy plays a greater role in developing Arab economies, their aggregate integrated economic power could be the basis for a stronger political unity, with a *Shura* Council which may develop into an Arab Parliament. Since Mubarak knows that most Arab rulers, himself included, would not want to weaken their autocratic power, it is hard to see how any of those ideas can be implemented, beyond strengthening his grip on the League.[6] Unable and unwilling to reform his own regime, but eager to show movement nevertheless, Mubarak has turned regional attention to the unlikely reform of the League.

Syria has accumulated perhaps the most incriminating material in terms of the support to terrorist organizations. During the war, it was repeatedly warned by senior American officials against letting Arab and Muslim volunteers flock to the battlefield in Iraq from Syrian territory, giving shelter to Iraqi officials, harboring terrorist organizations in Damascus or moving against the US-sponsored Road Map. The Syrians, who like to regard themselves as the champions of Arab nationalism, apparently continued their anti-American activities in secret. Their submission of intelligence about al-Qa'ida, an organization they dislike, to the CIA was not sufficient to exonerate them from American wrath. Immediately in the aftermath of the war, Secretary of State Colin Powell went to Damascus to emphasize the gravity and urgency of the American demands. The strategic situation in the New Middle East has the US as the next-door neighbor of Syria, and in an ideal position to launch a devastating strike on the regime if it fails to conform. Powell told his hosts that he expected them to shut down the HQ or terrorist organizations such as Hamas, Islamic Jihad and the Popular Front, all Palestinian rejectionist organizations sponsored by Damascus. He also demanded that Syria stop the shipments of Iranian weapons to Hizbullah in Lebanon and urged the deployment of the Lebanese army in South Lebanon as a first step to removing Syrian troops (and influence) altogether.[7]

Neighboring Lebanon is practically under Syrian occupation: Hizbullah runs its operations from Lebanon, launching cross-border attacks against Israel. The editor of a Christian daily in Lebanon questioned the validity of the independent policies of the Hizbullah in Lebanon, which actually operates as a "state within a state," under the guidance of the foreign forces of Iran and Syria. Hizbullah also jeopardizes Lebanese sovereignty by defying international public opinion and the rulings of the UN concerning the border between Israel and Lebanon, and the Security Council recommendation that Lebanon ought to deploy its forces to the south of the country in order to prevent Hizbullah's provocations against Israel. The realization that Hizbullah and Syria threaten Lebanon's existence derives directly from the Iraq War and the expectation that following Iraq, Syria and Iran's turns may come, and with them their surrogates in Lebanon. The editor warned against the Security Council adopting a resolution that Lebanon should deploy its forces in the south and take responsibility for security there, as that may give Israel the pretext to attack in order to enforce that resolution. The editor also said the earthquake that shook the Middle East following the War in Iraq threatens to topple one regime after the other and to give Israel another opportunity to evade the application of the Road Map. This awakening within Lebanon, which follows on the footsteps of the Christian demands over the past two years for the withdrawal of Syrian troops from the country, is a clear attempt by the anti-Syrian Christians to stop their country from being targeted, should the US decide to act against Syria and Hizbullah.[8]

The attack against the UN compound in Baghdad and the killing of Sergio Vieira de Mello, the Special Representative of the Secretary-General in Iraq, together with 23 other UN workers and civilians on 19 August 2003, signals a new phase in the situation in Iraq. The efforts of Paul Bremer and the IGC to normalize life in Iraq have, thus far, failed. The security situation is far from settled, with attacks against the Americans, as of October 2003, numbering nearly twenty a day. The preoccupation of the Civil Administration and the IGC with domestic security pushes down the agenda the other pressing issues of reconstruction, both economic and political, with consequences for the democracy and prosperity promised by the Americans. But a situation where 140,000 American soldiers in Iraq prove inadequate to ensure the peace and stability, even though they are reinforced by other nations and by a growing local police and armed force, and where basics such as electricity, water, telephones, medical treatment and other services are subordinate to the insoluble security needs of the population, does not augur well for the stability and a free system that the Civil Administration is working hard to implement. The attack against the UN, whose presence had been legitimized by the Security Council's 15 members 14–0 (Syria abstained) shows not only that terrorists and pro-Saddam forces are still roaming around Iraq, but they are striving to prove that the country is and will remain ungovernable from horseback. What the terrorists do not state is what kind of Iraq they want: What sort of regime, short of dictatorship, that could bring together all the ethnic, religious and tribal groups.

Notes

The New York Times is abbreviated to NYT.

2 Iraqi and Coalition War Strategies

1   For the term Islamikaze, see Raphael Israeli, *Islamikaze: Manifestations of Islamic Martyrology*, Frank Cass, London, 2003.
2   Ibid.
3   See Adam Nagourney and David Sanger, "Bush Defends the Progress of War: Privately, Republicans Fret over Uncertainties," *NYT*, April 1, 2003, B1, B3.
4   Ibid.
5   Richard Perle, a former Pentagon official and Rumsfeld associate, cited by *NYT*, April 1, 2003, B3.
6   *The New York Times*, April 1, 2003, B3.
7   See Jim Tutenberg, "Ex-Generals Defend their Blunt Comments," *NYT*, April 2, 2003, B1.
8   See J. I., Dwyer, "Sandstorm Grounds Copters," *NYT*, March 27, 2003, B5.
9   See Christopher Marquis and Nicholas Wade, "Loss of Apache in Iraq is Evidence of Vulnerability of Copters to Ground Fire," *NYT*, March 25, 2003, B3.
10 The others were the *Kitty Hawk* and the *Constellation*.
11 Lynette Clemetson, "In an F-18, Five Seconds from Deck Veiled by a Sandstorm," *NYT*, March 27, 2003, B5.
12 Eric Schmitt, "F-16's Pick off Iraqi Tanks in Kill Box near Baghdad," *NYT*, April 5, 2003, B2.
13 See Eric Schmitt, "In the Skies over Iraq, Silent Observers become Futuristic Weapons," *NYT*, April 18, 2003, B8.
14 See, e.g., stories by Iver Peterson, Marc Santora, Eric Schmitt, Adam Liptak, David Sanger, Carl Hulse and Jim Yardley in *NYT*, March 26, 2003, B7 and B11.
15 See Marc Santora, *NYT*, March 26, 2003, B7.
16 See Adam Liptak, *NYT*, March 26, 2003, B11.
17 See Emma Daly, "Five Wounded in Fighting Reach Spain for Treatment," *NYT*, March 27, 2003, B6.
18 See Jayson Blair, "Relatives of Missing Soldiers Dread Hearing Worse News," *NYT*, March 27, 2003, B13.
19 See Marc Santora, "Continued Fighting Delays Plans for Aid Distribution, Relief Workers say," *NYT*, March 25, 2003. B6.

20 Ibid.
21 David Rohde, "Kurdish Refugees Make Do, Not for the First Time," *NYT*, March 25, 2003, B7.
22 Marc Santora, "Food Arrives, but Water Supplies Cause Worry," *NYT*, March 27, 2003, B11.
23 See Felicity Barringer, "Blair and Annan Confer on UN Role in Getting Food and Water to Iraqis," *NYT*, March 28, 2003, B10.
24 For pictures of the vehicles, see *NYT*, March 26, 2003, B2.
25 See John Broder, "Far Behind the Front, But Not Out of Danger," *NYT*, March 26, 2003, B2.
26 William Broad, "Allies' Vital Supply Line Now Stretches Into Orbit," *NYT*, March 31, 2003, B10.
27 Michael Wilson, "Protecting the Rear in 100 degree Heat," *NYT*, April 6, 2003, B5.
28 Bernard Weinraub, "A Field War for Soldiers Who Face the Emotional Rigors of Combat," *NYT*, April 6, 2003, B4.
29 Ibid.

3 Shi'ites in the South

1 Amir Taheri, (a former pre-revolutionary editor of the daily *Kaihan*) *The Spirit of Allah* (in Hebrew translation), Am Oved, Tel Aviv, 1986, p. 148. See also Mahmoud Ayoub, *Redemptive Suffering in Islam*, Mouton de Gruyter, 1978, pp. 148–58; Emanuel Sivan *Muslim Radicals* (in Hebrew), Am Oved, Tel Aviv, 1985, pp. 192–5.
2 Taheri, *The Spirit of Allah*, p. 55. See also Hamid Algar, *Islam and Revolution*, University of California Press, Berkeley, 1981, pp. 329–43; and Martin Kramer (ed.), *Protest and Revolution in Shi'ite Islam* (Hebrew), Tel Aviv University, p. 29.
3 For this discussion, see Raphael Israeli, *Islamikaze: Manifestations of Islamic Martyrology*, Frank Cass, London, 2003, ch. 4.
4 This discussion is based on Moojan Momen, *An Introduction to Shi'ite Islam*, Yale University Press, 1985, pp. 261–4.
5 Ibid.
6 For some of these debates see Claude Cahen, *Islam* (Hebrew translation), Tel Aviv, Dvir, 1995, pp. 44, 117.
7 Ibid., p. 225.
8 Liora Lukitz, *Iraq: The Search for National Identity*, Frank Cass, London, 1995, pp. 15–18, 60 and 98–100.
9 The text was released by the British Embassy in Washington. *NYT*, March 25, 2003, B6.
10 *NYT*, March 26, 2003, B1–3.
11 Marc Santora, "Fear Said to Be Keeping Iraqi Dissidents from Rebelling," *NYT*, March 26, 2003, B3.
12 Craig Smith, "Basra's Defenders are Said to be Desperate and Fearful," *NYT*, April 4, 2003, B8.
13 Michael Gordon, "Basra Offers a Lesson on Taking Baghdad," *NYT*, April 7, 2003, B1.

14 Lukitz, *Iraq: The Search for National Identity*, pp. 65, 71, 133.
15 *NYT*, March 25, 2003, A1, B4.
16 Judith Miller, "US Hunts for Bio-Agents and Gas at an Iraq Depot," *NYT*, March 27, 2003, B4.
17 Steven Lee Myers, "GI's Pause on Push to Baghdad, and One Falls to a Sniper," *NYT*, March 25, 2003, B6.
18 *NYT*, March 26, 2003, B4.
19 *NYT*, March 27, 2003, A1, B4.
20 *NYT*, April 3, 2003, B8.
21 Jim Dwyer, "American Soldiers, at the Behest of an Iraqi Officer, Topple a Hussein Statue," *NYT*, April 4, 2003., B3.
22 Ibid.
23 Ibid.
24 See Momen, *An Introduction to Shi'ite Islam*, pp. 84, 91.
25 Jim Dwyer, "In Karbala, Forsaken Tanks and Pockets of Resistance," *NYT*, April 6, 2003, B4.
26 Jim Dwyer, "Tearing Loose as a New Power Arrives at the Ruins of Babylon," *NYT*, April 10, 2003, B6.
27 Ibid.
28 Judith Miller, "Hunt Finds Hint of How Iraqis Fill Power Void," *NYT*, April 10, 2003, B6.
29 See Momen, *An Introduction to Shi'ite Islam*, pp. 288–9.
30 I am indebted for this remark to my friend and colleague, Amatzia Baram, a foremost expert of Iraq.
31 Momen, *An Introduction to Shi'ite Islam*.
32 Ibid.
33 Ibid.
34 Ibid.
35 Neil Mac Farquhar, "Shi'ites, Resenting both Sides, Are Swing Groups," *NYT*, April 8, 2003, B2.
36 See ibid.
37 Craig Smith, "US-Backed Shi'ite Cleric Killed at Shrine in Najaf," *NYT*, April 11, 2003, B1–2.
38 Marc Santora, "The Tides of Revenge in Basra Rise Quickly," *NYT*, April 11, 2003, B2.
39 Marc Santora, "No More Fear that Prayer Falls on the Wrong Ears," *NYT*, April 12, 2003, B1, B4.
40 Craig Smith, "Teacher, a Survivor, Fondly Recalls Life in Hussein's Iraq," *NYT*, April 19, 2003, B 2.
41 Judith Miller, "Shi'ite Clerics Seek Control of Munitions at 2 Factories," *NYT*, April 13, 2003, B4.
42 Craig Smith, "A Long-Simmering Power Struggle Preceded Killings at an Iraqi Holy Shrine," *NYT*, April 13, 2003, B4.
43 Ibid.
44 Ibid.
45 For details, see Marc Santora, "Once Dangerous Pilgrimage is Dangerous No More," *NYT*, April 19, 2003, B1, B5.

46 Ibid.
47 Alan Feuer, "Vengeful Chaos Clouds Long-Suffering Shi'ites' New Freedom," *NYT*, April 13, 2003, B4.
48 Craig Smith, "Politics and Religion Join the Fray in Shi'ite Slum," *NYT*, April 15, 2003, B1, B7.
49 Ibid.
50 Charlie LeDuff, "Marines Ready for Anything in a Holdout City," *NYT*, April 13, 2003, B5.
51 Charlie LeDuff, "A Cleric Assumes a Bully Pulpit," *NYT*, April 19, 2003, B1, B5.
52 Ibid.
53 Ibid.

4 Kurds in the North

1 Borhanedin, Yassin, *Vision or Reality:The Kurds in the Policy of the Great Powers, 1941–47*, Lund University Press, 1995, pp. 35–7.
2 Ibid., pp. 40–3.
3 Ibid., pp. 45–51.
4 Liora Lukitz, *Iraq: The Search for National Identity*, Frank Cass, London, 1995, pp. 136–43.
5 Ibid., pp. 148–58.
6 David Rohde and C. Chivers, "US Opens Command in Northern Iraq," *NYT*, March 25, 2003, B7.
7 Ibid.
8 Charlie LeDuff, "Kurdish Hopes Fading in Light of New Moves," *NYT*, March 25, 2003, B7.
9 David Rohde, "Kurdish Refugees Make Do, Not for the First Time," *NYT*, March 25, 2003, B7.
10 David Rohde, "Kurdish Forces Prepare to Attack in Northern Iraq," *NYT*, March 26, 2003, B5.
11 *NYT*, A1 and B3.
12 Eric Schmitt and C. Chivers, "1000 Paratroopers Swoop Down on Kurdish Region to Open New Front," *NYT*, March 27, 2003, B6.
13 Charlie LeDuff and David Rohde, "Troops Won't Be Sent to Kurdish Areas, Turkish Military Chief Says," *NYT*, March 27, 2003, B6.
14 *NYT*, March 28, 2003, A1 and B4.
15 David Rohde, "Americans Protect Airstrip on the Northern Front," *The New Yorks Times*, March 28, 2003, B4.
16 C. J. Chivers, "With Militant Group Routed, American and Kurdish Forces Hunt for Clues about al-Qa'ida," *NYT*, March 31, 2003, B3.
17 David Rohde, "Scenes of the Other Iraq: Green Fields, Starry Nights, Friendly Locals," *NYT*, April 1, 2003, B10.
18 David Rohde and C. Chivers, "Iraqis Pull Back in the North; Journalist is Killed by a Mine," *NYT*, April 3, 2003, B4.
19 David Rohde, "On Pain of Death, Iraqi Soldier Kept at it," *NYT*, April 3, 2003, B5.
20 C. Chivers, "Kirkuk on the Horizon, and a Falcon and Shells Nearby," *NYT*, April 2, 2003, B6.

21 David Rohde, "10 Americans, with Help from Kurds, Stave off Iraqis," *NYT*, April 5, 2003, B4.
22 Thom Shanker and Eric Schmitt, "A Campaign Invisible, Except for the Results," *NYT*, April 6, 2003, B1, B6.
23 Ibid.
24 David Rohde, "18 Die as US Airstrike Mistakenly Hits Kurdish Force," *NYT*, April 7, 2003, B1, B3.
25 C. Chivers "While Many Islamic Fighters Surrender, Kurds Remain Wary of New Terrorist Attacks," *NYT*, April 7, 2003, B7.
26 C. Chivers, "Attention now Shifts to the Role of the Kurds," *NYT*, April 10, 2003, B5.
27 David Rohde, "View from Ancient Monastery as yet Another War Intrudes," *NYT*, April 10, 2003, B6.
28 C. Chivers, "A Sense that the Iraqi Leader is Gone Brings Joy in the North," *NYT*, April 10, 2003, B7.
29 C. Chivers, "Kirkuk's Swift Collapse Leaves a City in Chaos," *NYT*, April 11, 2003, B1.
30 Ibid., p. B4.
31 Ibid.
32 David Rohde, "As Kurds Move into Kirkuk, Arabs Fear Revenge," *NYT*, April 11, 2002, B4.
33 Frank Bruni, "Turkey Sending Military Observers to Watch Kurds; US Warns against Further Moves," *NYT*, April 11, 2003, B4.
34 "Kurds Take City in North;Grimness after Glee Elsewhere," *NYT*, April 11, 2003, A1 and B5.
35 *NYT*, April 12, 2003, B1.
36 C. Chivers, "Shaky Ground is Ahead and Behind in the North," *NYT*, ibid.
37 *NYT*, April 12, 2003, A1, B4.
38 Chivers, "Shaky Ground is Ahead," p. 4.
39 C. Chivers, "Paratroopers Find Suspicious Warheads and Rocket Parts in Kirkuk," *NYT*, April 13, 2003, pp. B1, B5.
40 David Rohde, "In Newly Occupied Mosul, US Colonel Faces 1.7 Million Added Responsibilities," *NYT*, April 13, 2003, B5.
41 Ibid.
42 C. Chivers "Groups of Kurds are Driving Arabs from Northern Villages," *NYT*, April 14, 2003, B1, B6.
43 Ibid.
44 David Rohde, "6 Iraqi Officials Offer to Surrender to US," *NYT*, April 15, 2003, B4.
45 Ibid.
46 David Rohde, "At Least 10 Iraqis Dead in Clashes in Northern Iraq," *NYT*, April 15, 2003, B3.
47 David Rohde, "Marines again Kill Iraqis in Exchange of fire in Mosul," *NYT*, April 17, 2003, B2.
48 C. Chivers, "Huge Gravesite is Found in Northern Iraq," *NYT*, April 18, 2003, B1, B3.

5 Baghdad in the Center

1 Cyril Glasse, *The Concise Encyclopedia of Islam*, Harper and Row, San Francisco, 1989, pp. 61–2.
2 Claude Cahen, *Islam* (Hebrew translation), Tel Aviv, Dvir, 1995, p. 102.
3 Ibid., pp.199–200.
4 Glasse, *The Concise Encyclopedia of Islam*, p. 62.
5 www.   Travel-guide.com/data/irq010.asp;   and www.globalsecurity.org/military/world/iraq/baghdad.htm, July 2, 2003.
6 Glasse, *The Concise Encyclopedia of Islam*.
7 http://i-cis.com/e.o/baghdad.htm, July 2, 2003
8 *NYT*, March 25, 2003, A1 and B3.
9 "The Goal is Baghdad: How Long will it Take? And at What Price?," ibid.
10 Ibid.
11 "Hussein Rallies Defenders to Stand Firm in Baghdad," *NYT*, March 25, 2003, B5.
12 Ibid.
13 Eric Schmitt, "Key to Baghdad :How Hard will Republican Guard Fight," *NYT*, March 25, 2003, B5.
14 Steven Lee Myers, "G.I.'s Pause on Push to Baghdad, and one Falls to a Sniper," *NYT*, March 25, 2003, B6.
15 *NYT*, March 25, 2003, B5.
16 *NYT*, March 26, 2003, B4.
17 Ibid., March 27, 2003, B3.
18 "Defense Minister for Iraq Vows a Fierce Fight and Predicts a Clash in Baghdad in Days," *NYT*, March 28, 2003, A1, B3.
19 "New Turns, Hard Choices: US Commanders Weigh 2 Different Strategies and a Hybrid," ibid.
20 "Heavy Strikes on Baghdad as Desert Skirmishes Go on," ibid., March 28, 2003, B7.
21 "US Troops Battle Closer to Baghdad as Clashes with Irregulars Persist in South," Ibid., April 1, 2003, B2.
22 *NYT*, April 2, 2003, A1, B5.
23 Dexter Filkins, "Onward toward the Tigris, with Iraq's Capital in Mind," *NYT*, April 2, 2003, B6.
24 Eric Schmitt and Bernard Weinraub, "Battle for Baghdad like War Plan: Kill Enemy, Limit Damage, Provide Aid," *NYT*, April 3, 2003, B1, B3.
25 Ibid.
26 Dexter Filkins, "US Force Crosses Tigris, Wondering where Republican Guards Went," *NYT*, April 3, 2003, B4.
27 Ibid.
28 *NYT*, April 3, 2003, B8.
29 Dexter Filkins, "Marines Cruising to Baghdad," *NYT*, April 4, 2003, B1, B3.
30 James Dao, "Hoping to Confuse Iraqis and Spread Panic, American Commandos Prepare to Enter Baghdad," *NYT*, April 4, 2003, B2.
31 Dexter Filkins, *NYT*, April 4, 2003.
32 "American Military Units Reach the Outskirts of a Blacked-out Baghdad," *NYT*, April 4, 2003, A1, B4.

33 "As US Tightens Noose, Troops Study Baghdad Street Maps," *NYT*, April 4, 2003, A1, B4.
34 *NYT*, April 4, 2003, B5.
35 Ibid.
36 Ibid.
37 R. Apple, "US Commander, Evoking Mc Arthur, Hops Past Cities to Baghdad," *NYT*, April 4, 2003, B8.
38 Rumsfeld's briefing at the Pentagon is cited in full in NYT, April 4, 2003, B14.
39 "For Weary US Troops, the End is Still Elusive," *NYT*, April 5, 2003, A1, B3.
40 Dexter Filkins, "Little Resistance Encountered as Troops Reach Baghdad," *NYT*, April 5, 2003, B3.
41 Ibid.
42 "The Battle for Baghdad: New Dangers in Final Push," *NYT*, April 5, 2003, A1, B5.
43 "US Military's Dash to Baghdad Leaves Debate on War in the Dust," ibid., B5.
44 "Us Troops Squeeze Baghdad in Effort to Isolate it and Ready next Step," *NYT*, April 5, 2003, A1, B5.
45 "US Tanks Make Quick Strike into the Center of Baghdad, Setting Off Firefight," *NYT*, April 6, 2003, A1, B3.
46 "Showing the Flag and Testing the Foe: Thrust Aims to Put Iraqis Off Balance," ibid., B3.
47 "Gun's Rattle Brings Ground War to Capital," *NYT*, April 7, 2003. A1, B3.
48 "US Blasts Baghdad Site, Trying to Kill Hussein," *NYT*, April 8, 2003, A1, B4. See also Steven Lee Myers,"Unguided Tour of a Lesser Palace," ibid., B6.
49 Ibid.
50 David Johnston and James Risen, "Iraqi Leaders Said to Use Civilian Areas in Baghdad," *NYT*, April 8, 2003, B5.
51 Dexter Filkins, "Some Iraqis Grateful to US but Wary of any Changes," *NYT*, April 9, 2003, B1, B9.
52 "A Section of Central Baghdad is Taken by US Forces in a Street-by-Street Fight," *NYT*, April 9, 2003, A1, B3.
53 Ibid.
54 "In a 3-Pronged Assault on Baghdad, US Seeks a Quick End," *NYT*, April 9, 2003, B4.
55 Steven Lee Myers, "Battalion Stages Assault on Iraqi Hilltop Position and Guard's Complex," *NYT*, April 9, 2003, B9.
56 Gregg Zoroya and David Lynch, "There is no Government Left, US General Says," *USA Today*, April 10, 2003, A1.
57 John Kifner, "As Tanks Move in, Young Iraqis Trek out and Take Anything not Fastened Down," *NYT*, April 10, 2003, B2.
58 James Risen and David Johnston, "Military and CIA Searching Baghdad for Hussein and his Sons or their Bodies," *NYT*, April 10, 2003, B2.
59 "Cheers, Tears and Looting in Streets of Iraqi Capital as American Troops Take Hold," *NYT*, April 10, 2003, A1, B3.
60 Ibid.
61 Dexter Filkins, "People Rise as Icons as Nations Fall Down," *NYT*, April 10, 2003, B3.

62   David Moniz and John Diamond, "Iraqi Colonel's Capture Sped up Taking the City," *USA Today*, April 10, 2003, 2A.
63   Ibid.
64   "American Forces Take Control of Baghdad; some Resistance Persists," *NYT*, April 10, 2003, A1, B4.
65   "In Baghdad Statues Fall, Vindication of American Military Strategy," *NYT*, April 10, 2003. A1, B4.
66   "Chaos Spreads in Baghdad with Widespread Looting, Arson and a Suicide Attack," *NYT*, April 11, 2003, A1, B3.
67   Ibid.
68   Dexter Filkins, "Marines Attack Baghdad Mosque Said to Have been Visited by Hussein, but Prey Slips Away," ibid., B3.
69   "Free of Hussein Forces, Baghdad is Engulfed in Looting and Mayhem," *NYT*, April 12, 2003, A1, B3.
70   Ibid.
71   "Pillagers Strip National Museum in Baghdad of its Priceless Artifacts," *The New York Times*, April 13, 2003, A1, B3. For expert discussions of the lost and missing artifacts, see: Alberto Manguel, "Our First Words, Written in Clay, in an Accountant's Hand" ; Adam Goodheart, "Missing: a Vase, a Book, a Bird and 10,000 Years of History" ; and John Tierney, "Did Lord Elgin do Something Right?," *NYT*, April 20, 2003, wk 10.
72   Ibid.
73   John Noble Wilford, "Art Experts Fear Worst in the Plunder of a Museum," *NYT*, April 13, 2003, B3.
74   "Us Troops Move to restore Order in an Edgy Baghdad," *NYT*, April 13, 2003, A1, B3.
75   *NYT*, April 15, 2003, B1.
76   "In Hussein's Hometown, His Glory Fades and Looters Romp," *NYT*, April 15, 2003, A1, B4.

6 The Hidden Agenda: Oil, Terror and WMD

1   *Al-Riyadh*, Saudi Arabia, 10 September, 2002. Cited by Nimrod Feldner, in MEMRI: Inquiry and Analysis, No. 137, 12 June, 2003, p. 1.
2   See M. Abir, "Iraq – a Source of Oil or a Quagmire for the US?" *Jerusalem Issue Brief*, Jerusalem Center for Public Affairs, Vol. 2 No. 30, June 30, 2003, pp. 1–2.
3   *Okaz*, Saudi Arabia, December 31, 2002, cited by MEMRI, see fn. 1.
4   Ibid.
5   *Al-Okaz*, April 25, 2003.
6   *Al-Sharq al-Awsat*, London, April 15, 2003. MEMRI, ibid.
7   *Al-Sharq al-Awsat*, June 1, 2003, Ibid.
8   *Al-Hayat*, London, June 3, 2003, Ibid.
9   *Reuters* from Baghdad, May 24, 2003. Cited by *Ha'aretz*, Israel, May 25, 2003, News updates, 7:41.
10   Marc Perelman, "Oil for Food Sales Seen as Iraq Tie to al-Qa'ida: US Probes Bank Network," *Forward*, June 20, 2003.
11   Ibid.

12   Ibid.
13   Neela Banerjee and Felicity Barringer, "War Fails to Halt Iraqi Oil Production, but Prompts a Debate about the Future," *NYT*, March 26, 2003, B15.
14   Ibid.
15   Charlie LeDuff and Alan Feuer, "Men from Texas, on Call in Kuwait, Cap Well Fires in Southern Iraq," *NYT*, April 1, 2003, B11.
16   Ibid.
17   Neela Banerjee, "Candidate for Production Job is a Retired Shell Executive," *NYT*, April 2, 2003, B12.
18   Felicity Barringer and Neela Banerjee, "Who'll Control Iraq's Oil? Tangled Questions Abound," *NYT*, April 9, 2003, B11.
19   Ibid.
20   Jeff Gerth, "US is Banking on Iraq Oil to Finance Reconstruction," *NYT*, April 10, 2003, B14.
21   Elizabeth Becker, "Details Given on Contract Halliburton was awarded," *NYT*, April 11, 2003, B12.
22   *NYT*, April 17, 2003, B6.
23   Neela Banerjee and Felicity Barringer, "Iraq Pipeline to Syria no Big Secret, Experts Say," *NYT*, April 17, 2003, B6.
24   C. Chivers, "Oil Fields in a Sorry State, Stripped even of the Toilets," *NYT*, April 20, 2003, B2.
25   *NYT*, April 17, 2003, B1, B6.
26   See Raphael Israeli, *Islamikaze : Manifestations of Islamic Martyrology*, Frank Cass, London, 2003, especially ch. 8 on the Western Counter-Attack Against Islamikaze terrorism.
27   The *Ahzab* Sura, Qur'an, 33:15.
28   *Al-Quds al-Arabi*, London, April 29, 2003. MEMRI, Special Dispatch No. 496, April 30, 2003.
29   *Jerusalem Post*, Jerusalem, April 29, 2003, cited by *Etoile Liante*, an internet site located in France, April 29, 2003.
30   *ABC News*, September 27, 2002.
31   *The Guardian*, London, February 14, 1999.
32   Jeffrey Goldberg, *The New Yorker*, October, 2002.
33   "Threats and Responses," *NYT*, February 6, 2003, A 19–20.
34   *The Wall Street Journal*, October 4, 1994. See also *Patterns of Global Terrorism Report*, The US Department of State, 2000.
35   *Patterns of Global Terrorism Report*, The US Department of State, 2002.
36   *The Philippine Daily Inquirer*, Manila, March 3, 2003.
37   Mansoor I'jaz, "The Clinton Intelligence Record: Deeper Failures Revealed," *National Review Online*, April 29, 2003.
38   Radio interview at *NewsMax.com*, June 23, 2003, 12:18 EDT.
39   Ibid.
40   Brian Bender, "September 11 Panel Discusses Possibility of Iraq Link: Witnesses Detail al-Qa'ida Theories," *The Boston Globe*, Boston, July 10, 2003.
41   Ibid.
42   Gilbert Merritt, "Document Links Saddam, Bin Laden," *The Tennessean*, June 25, 2003. Reproduced and distributed by Laurie Mylroie, site:

sam11@erols.com. I am indebted to Laurie for this invaluable piece of information.

43 Ibid.

44 C. Chivers, "With Militant Group Routed, American and Kurdish Forces Hunt for Clues about al-Qa'ida," *NYT*, March 31, 2003, B3.

45 See Raphael Israeli, *Islamikaze: Manifestations of Islamic Martyrology*, Frank Cass, London, 2003, especially ch. 3.

46 "Beyond Numbers, Panel on Terrorism Hears Families' Anguish," *NYT*, April 1, 2003, B15; and Robert Worth, "Terrorism Panel Hears Advice on Methods of Prevention," ibid., April 2, 2003, B15.

47 Richard Stevenson, "For Muslims, a Mixture of White House Signals," *NYT*, April 28, 2003, A13.

48 David Johnston and James Risen, "New Signs of Terror not Evident," *NYT*, April 6, 2003, B1, B14.

49 Michael Moss and Jenny Nordberg, "Imams Urged to be Alert for Suspicious Visitors," *NYT*, ibid.

50 Rachel Swarns, "Muslims Protest Month-Long Detention Without a Charge," *NYT*, April 20, 2003, A16.

51 See NYT, February 6, 2003, A1, A19–20.

52 Ibid.

53 David Sanger, "US Officials Fear Iraqis Plan to Use Gas on G.I.'s," *NYT*, March 25, 2003, B11.

54 Judith Miller, "Smoking Gun Still Proves to be Elusive for Searchers," *NYT*, April 2, 2003, B7.

55 William Broad, "Iraq May Try Defensive Use of Chemicals, Experts Warn," *NYT*, April 4, 2003, B4.

56 Nicholas Wade and Eric Schmitt, "US Use of Tear Gas Could Violate Treaty, Critics Say," *NYT*, April 5, 2003, B13.

57 Bernard Weinraub, "American Soldiers Find Drums Possibly Storing Chemical Agents," *NYT*, April 8, 2003, B1, B4.

58 William Broad, "On-Site Identification Inexact," *NYT*, ibid., B4.

59 Judith Miller, "Hunt Finds Hint of How Iraqis Fill Power Void," *NYT*, April 10, 2003, B6.

60 Judith Miller,"Hunting Weapons, a Plucky Crew Makes Do," ibid., April 12, 2003, B2.

61 Don Van Natta and David Johnston, "US Search for Illegal Arms Narrowed to about 36 Sites," *NYT*, April 14, 2003, B4.

62 Judith Miller, "US Inspectors Find no Forbidden Weapons at Iraqi Arms Plant," *NYT*, April 16, 2003, B1–2.

63 William Broad, "US Civilian Experts Say Bureaucracy and Infighting Jeopardize Search for Weapons," *NYT*, April 16, 2002, B2.

64 Ibid.

65 Judith Miller, "Illicit Arms Kept Till Eve of War, Iraqi Scientist is Said to Assert," *NYT*, April 21, 2003, cited by IMRA, April 21, 2003.

66 *The Daily Telegraph*, London, June 2, 2003.

67 *Le Monde*, Paris, May 30, 2003.

68 David Rivkin and Lee Casey, "Saddam, Nikita and Virtual Weapons of Mass Destruction: a Question of Threat Perception and Intelligence Assessment,"

The National Interest, June 11, 2003. Cited by *Updates from AIJAC*, Melbourne, June 16, 2003, pp. 2–6.

69 Robert Kagan, *The Washington Post*, June 8, 2003, B07. Cited by *Updates from AIJAC*, ibid., pp. 6–9.

70 The Associated Press (AP), June 1, 2003, cited by *Ha'aretz*, Tel Aviv, of the same day.

71 Mark Steyn, "What is Going on in those Sofa Factories," *The Jerusalem Post*, June 9, 2003. Cited by *Isranet Daily Briefing*, Montreal, June 17, 2003, pp. 2–4. See also Mona Charen, "The Nazis Again?," *The Washington Times*, June 13, 2003, cited ibid., pp. 4–5.

72 Richard Spertzel, "The Politics of Mass Destruction," *The Wall Street Journal*, June 27, 2003.

73 *AP*, June 22, 2003, cited by *Ha'aretz*, June 22, 2003.

74 Erik Schechter, "Bush May be Sitting on Iraqi WMD Evidence, FOX Analyst Says," *The Jerusalem Post*, July 11, 2003, A4.

75 For a complete version of Ekeus' comment, see Rolf Ekeus, "Iraq's Real Weapons Threat," *Washington Post*, June 29, 2003, B07.

7 Ruling From Horseback

1 Thomas Friedman, "Dear President Bush," *NYT*, April 30, 2003, A27.

2 "After the Iraq War: a GLORIA Center Roundtable Discussion," *The Middle East Review of International Affairs* (*MERIA Journal*), Vol. 7, No. 2, June 2000.

3 Ibid.

4 Alissa Rubin, "By the Snipers of Babylon," *The Jerusalem Post*, July 4, 2003, B4 (by agreement with the *Los Angeles Times*).

5 Ibid.

6 *Liberation*, Paris, Juin 16, 2003, p. 11.

7 Adrien Jaulmes, "Les Americains Traquent les Irreductibles du Baas," *Le Figaro*, Paris, Juin 13, 2003, p. 2.

8 Jacky Durand, *Liberation*, June 16, 2003, p. 12.

9 *Reuters*, London, May 25, 2003.

10 "As Hussein Faded Away, Prisoners Were Killed," *NYT*, April 28, 2003, A1, A10.

11 See photos in *NYT*, April 28, 2003, A9.

12 Jad Mouawad, "Currency In Chaos," *The Jerusalem Post*, June 13, 2003, B3.

13 Sharon Waxman, "Black and White and Read all Over," *The Jerusalem Post*, June 13, 2003, B3 (by agreement with *The Washington Post*).

14 Jane Perlez, "Veteran TV Anchors Push to Become the Voices of a New Iraq," *NYT*, April 28, 2003, A9.

15 Ibid.

16 Sabrina Tavernise, "Iraqi women Wary of New Upheavals," *NYT*, May 5, 2003, A1, A10.

17 Marc Santora "Children of Basra Face a Grim Set of Hardships," *NYT*, May 5, 2003, A11.

18 David Rhode, "Danger Lingers in Pieces of an Abandoned Arsenal," ibid.; and "Iraqis Face Dual Peril, Bombs and Cholera," *International Herald*

Tribune, citing *Reuters*, May 15, 2003, p. 3.

19 Susan Sachs, "Schools Reopen in Baghdad, but Few Students Show Up," *NYT*, May 4, 2003, A1, A27.

20 Judith Miller, "Radioactive Material Found at a Test Site near Baghdad," *NYT*, May 12, 2003, A16.

21 Michael Jansen, "Iraqi Museum Exhibit – a Public Relations Stunt," *The Jordan Times*, Amman, July 3, 2003.

22 "Cultural Catastrophe Hits Iraq," *Al-Ahram Weekly*, April 27, 2003.

23 Kanan Makiya, "Kanan Makiya's War Diary," *The New Republic*, March 29, 2003.

24 Douglas Jehl and Michael Gordon, "American Forces and Terror Group Reach Cease-Fire," *NYT*, April 29, 2003, A1, A18.

25 "In Apparent First, US Signs Cease-Fire Pact with an Iranian Terrorist Group in Iraq," *NYT*, April 29, 2003, A1; and Michael Gordon and Douglas Jehl, "On Order from Bush, US Troops in Iraq Begin Disarming Iranian Opposition Group," *NYT*, May 10, 2003, A10.

26 Glenn Simpson, "US Says it Finds Stolen Iraqi Funds," *The Wall Street Journal – Europe*, May 15, 2003, A8.

27 Betsy Pisik, "Stash of US Bills Found in Bunker," *The Washington Times*, April 22, 2003.

28 *Reuter*, London, May 25, 2003, cited by *Ha'aretz*, from the same date.

29 Edmund Andrews, "Iraq's Old Money Elite Vies for Stake in Rebuilding the Nation," *NYT*, May 10, 2003, A10.

30 Sabrina Tavernise, "Ahead of Harvest, Farm Fears Grow," *NYT*, May 12, 2003, A16.

31 Meron Benvenisti, "A War of the Early 1900's," *Ha'aretz*.

32 Jane Perlez, "Iraqis Set to Meet to Pick Transitional Government," *NYT*, April 29, 2003, A1, A18.

33 Michael Gordon, "Baghdad's Power Vacuum is Drawing only Dissent," *NYT*, April 21, 2003, A10.

34 Beatrice Lecumberri, "British Look to Tribal Leader to Restore Civilian Rule to Basra," *Agence France Presse*, cited by *Jordan Times*, April 9, 2003.

35 Zvi Bar'el, "Tribes and Shaky Allies," *Ha'aretz*, April 3, 2003.

36 Ibid.

37 Georges Malbrunot, "La Mefiance Tapageuse des Chefs de Clan Iraqiens," *Le Figaro*, Paris, June 13, 2003, p. 2.

38 Ibid.

39 Peter Finn, "New Force Moves to Gain Sway Exiles, Others Aided by US in the South," *The Washington Post*, April 12, 2003.

40 Ibid.

41 Jane Perlez, "Iraqi Family Split on Returned Exile: US Favors Him, but Who else Does?," *NYT*, ibid.

42 Adam Daifallah, "Lively Politics Start to Stir in Baghdad," *The New York Sun*, May 12, 2003.

43 "Editorial," *The New York Sun*, April 24, 2003.

44 Yochi Dreazen, "Feud Between Arabs, Kurds over Land both Call Home, is Resolved by Painful Exit," *The Wall Street Journal – Europe*, May 15, 2003, A3.

45 Peter Goodman, "Bid by Kurds for a Stake in Iraqi Oil Production is Rebuffed by US Officials," *The Wall Street Journal*, May 15, 2003, A3.
46 Jacky Durand, *Liberation*, June 16, 2003, p. 12.
47 Reuel Marc Gerecht, "How to Mix Politics with Religion," *NYT*, April 29, 2003, A29.
48 Ibid.
49 Susan Sachs, "Iraqis more Bemused than Enthused by Cleric," *NYT*, May 12, 2003, A13.
50 Matthew Gutman, "Hakim Gets Mixed Welcome in Najaf," *The Jerusalem Post*, May 13, 2003.
51 Ibid.
52 Mordechai Abir, "Iraq – a Source of Oil or a Quagmire for the US?" *Jerusalem Issue Brief*, Jerusalem Center for Public Affairs, Vol. 2, No. 30, June 30, 2003, pp. 2–3.
53 For details of the event, in which 17 Iraqi civilians met their death, see *Reuters*, April 29, 2003, cited by *Ha'aretz* of the same date.
54 For a complete transcript of Sheikh al-Nazzal's speech, see Special Dispatch No. 500, MEMRI, May 6, 2003.
55 Statement by Secretary Donald Rumsfeld, Department of Defense Briefing, April 25, 2003. http://www.defenselink.mil/trnscripts/2003/tr20030425–secdef0126.html
56 Daniel Johnson, "Don't Throw the Baby Out With the Ba'ath Water," *The Wall Street Journal*, April 24, 2003.
57 Patrick Tyler, "US–British Project: To Build a Postwar Iraqi Armed Force of 40,000 Soldiers in 3 Years," *NYT*, June 24, 2003.
58 Ibid.
59 Alisa Flatow was an American student killed in a bus bombing in the Gaza Strip in 1995. Her family was awarded $26 million in compensation, in the form of frozen Iranian funds.
60 Uriel Heilman, "Fighting for their Due," *The Jerusalem Post*, June 13, 2003, B4.
61 Bernard Weinraub, "US Seeks Solid Core to Fix Iraq's Broken Legal System," *NYT*, April 27, 2003, A24.
62 Michael Prowse, "Rival Certainties," *Financial Times*, June 20, 2003.
63 Ofra Bengio, "Reflections on the New Iraq," Paper No. 80, June 23, 2003, *The Moshe Dayan Center of Middle Eastern and African Studies*.

8 Arab and Muslim Fears: Images, Loyalties, Wishes, Delusions

1 See Raphael Israeli, *Islamikaze: Manifestations of Islamic Martyrology*, especially the Introduction and ch. 1.
2 *Al-Watan*, Kuwait, March 18, 2003. Special Dispatch, No. 481, MEMRI, March 19, 2003.
3 Dr. Turki Saqr, *Tishreen*, Syria, March 18, 2003. MEMRI, ibid.
4 *Iraqi Television*, March 21, 2003. MEMRI from the same date.
5 *Qatar Television*, March 21, 2003. Cited by MEMRI, the same date.
6 *Al-Hayat al-Jadida*, The Palestinian Authority, March 24, 2003; and *al-Quds*, also the PA, March 30, 2003. Both cited by MEMRI.

7   *Al-Hayat al-Jadida*, March 17, March 20, 2003; *Al-Quds*, March 13, 2003, March 20, 2003.

8   *Al-Quds*, March 31, 2003. MEMRI.

9   *Al Hayat al-Jadida*, March 23, 2003, March 26, 2003. *MEMRI.*

10 *Al Hayat al-Jadida*, March 26, and April 3, 2003; *Al-Ayyam*, April 2, 2003; and http://www.palestine-info.info/arabic/palestoday/dailynews/2003/ mar03/22_3/details.htm; *http://memri.org/bin/articles.cgi?Page=archives &Area=sd&ID=SP47703*; http://www.palestine-info.info/arabic/palestoday/ dailynews/2003/apr/2_4/details1.htm#8

11 Zvi Bar'el, "Solo Voices in the Arab Chorus," *Ha'aretz*, April 4, 2003.

12 Ibid.

13 *Al-Quds al-Arabi*, London, March 7, 2003; and *al-Sharq al-Awsat*, London, March 15, 2003. Both cited by MEMRI.

14 The Muslim Brothers' site in Egypt: http://www.ikhwan-info.net/news. asp?id=539, March 10, 2003; http://www/egypt-facts/org, March 11, 2003; and *al-Quds al-Arabi*, March 17, 2003. All cited by MEMRI.

15 See *al-Quds al-Arabi*, London, April 4, 2003. Ibid.

16 See *Al-Quds al-Arabi*, April 6, 2003; *Al-Hayat*, London, April 6, 2003; and http://www.albawaba.com/countries/index.ie.php3?country=egypt&lang=a, April 6, 2003.

17 Ghassan Sharbal, "Saddam Hussein: from Tikrit to the Tribunal of History," *Al-Hayat*, April 10, 2003. Cited by MEMRI.

18 *Al-Ahram*, April 10, 2003.

19 *Al-Akhbar*, April 10, 2003.

20 *Al-Hayat al-Jadida*, Palestinian Authority, April 10, 2003.

21 *Iraqi Television*, March 21, 2003. Cited by MEMRI (n.d.).

22 *Palestinian Authority Televison*, March 21, 2003. Cited by MEMRI (n.d.).

23 *IRNA*, April 9, 2003.

24 *IRNA*, April 9, 2003.

25 See *Jumhur Islami*, April 10, 2003; *IRNA* 9 and 10 April. Cited by MEMRI.

26 *Iran Daily*, April 10, 2003.

27 Editorial, *Al-Hayat*, London, March 21, 2003.

28 Hazim Saghiya, "Graves, Graves, and a Suggestion," *Al-Hayat*, London, May 25, 2003. MEMRI.

29 Abd al-Rahman al-Rashed, "Saddam was not Alone to Fall," *al-Sharq al-Awsat*, April 10, 2004.

30 Rajah al-Khuri, "But Who Will Apologize?" *Al-Nahar*, Beirut, May 20, 2003. Cited by MEMRI.

31 'Arib al-Rantawi, "The Mass Graves of Saddam," *Al-Dustur*, Jordan, May 20, 2003. Cited by MEMRI.

32 Thomas Friedman, "Amid Arab Shock, some Stirrings of Change," *The International Herald Tribune*, August 7, 2003, op. ed., page 6.

33 Editorial, *Al-Quds*, April 10, 2003.

34 Sanjay Anand, "Osama bides his Time," *The Spectator*, Britain, June 21, 2003.

35 Damien McElroy, "Al-Qa'ida Fighters Set up Base in Lebanon Refugee Camp," *Telegraph*, June 22, 2003.

36 See the text of the sermon in MEMRI, citing *Qatari Television* which broadcast it on June 13, 2003, and also its site www.qaradawi.net

9 Iraq, America and the New Middle East

1   Diana Henriques, "American Contractors Prepare to Begin the Rebuilding of Iraq" , *NYT*, April 27, 2003, A24.

2   Ibid.

3   Dore Gold, "Defensible Borders for Israel," *Jerusalem Letter/Viewpoints*, No 500, June 15–July 1, 2003.

4   Nazila Fathi, "Iran Strongly Disputes American Accusationsn of Interfering in Iraq's Affairs," *NYT*, 25 April 2003, A12.

5   Guglielmo Ferrero, *The Principles of Power*, Putnam, New York, 1942.

6   Nevine Khalil and Soha Abdelaty, "Cairo spelt out an Ambitious Plan to Reform the Arab League," *Al-Ahram Weekly*, July 4–August 4, 2003.

7   Mark Heller, "Powell in Damascus: Will Policy Change in Syria Follow Regime Change in Iraq?" Jaffe Center for Strategic Studies, *Update on Political and Strategic Developments in the Middle East*, No. 76, Tel Aviv University, May 5, 2003.

8   Jubran Tweini, "Editorial," *Al-Nahar*, August 14, 2003. MEMRI.

Bibliography

Media and Internet

ABC News
Agence France Press
Al-Ahram (Cairo)
Al-Ahram Weekly
Al-Akhbar (Cairo)
Al-Ayyam (Palestinian Authority)
Al-Dustur (Jordan)
Al-Hayat (London)
Al-Hayat al Jadida (Palestinian Authority)
Al-Nahar (Beirut)
Al-Okaz (Saudi Arabia)
Al-Quds (Palestinian Authority)
Al-Quds al Arabi (London)
Al-Riyadh (Saudi Arabia)
Al-Sharq al-Awsat (London)
Al-Watan (Kuwait)
Associated Press (AP)
The Boston Globe
The Daily Telegraph
Le Figaro (Paris)
The Financial Times
Forward
The Guardian
Ha'aretz (Israel)
IMRA (Tel Aviv)
The International Herald Tribune
Iran Daily
Iraqi Television
IRNA
Isranet Daily Briefing (Montreal)
Jerusalem Issue Brief
Jerusalem Post
The Jordan Times (Amman)
Jumhur-I-Islami (Iran)
Liberation (Paris)

The Los Angeles Times
MEMRI (Jerusalem and Washington)
MERIA Journal (Tel Aviv)
Le Monde (Paris)
The National Interest
The New Republic
National Review Online
News Max.com (Radio)
The New Yorker
The New York Sun
The New York Times (NYT)
Palestinian Authority Television
Patterns of Global Terrorism Report
The Philippine Daily Inquirer (Manila)
Qatar Television
Reuters
The Spectator (Britain)
The Tennesean
Tishreen (Syria)
Updates from AIJAC (Melbourne)
USA Today
The Wall Street Journal
The Washington Post
The Washington Times
www.Travel-guide.com./data/irq010.asp
www.globalsecurity.org/military/world/iraq/baghdad.htm, July 2, 2003
http://I-cis.com/e.o/baghdad.htm, July 2, 2003
http://www.defenselink.mil/transcripts/2003/tr20030425-secdef0126.html
http://www.palestine-info.info/arabic/palestoday/dailynews/2003/mar03/223/details.htm#3
http://memri.org/bin/articles.cgi?Page=archives&Area=sd&ID=SP47703
http://www.palestine-info.info/arabic/palestoday/dailynews/2003/apr/24/details1.htm#8
http://www.ikhwan-info.net/news.asp?id=539, March 10, 2003
http://www.egypt-facts.org, March 11, 2003
http://www.albawaba.com/countries/index.ie.php3?country=egypt&lang=a, April 6, 2003
www.qaradawi.net

Articles

Abir, M., "Iraq – a Source of Oil or a Quagmire for the US?" *Jerusalem Issue Brief*, Jerusalem Center for Public Affairs, Vol. 2, No. 30, 2003.
Anand, Sanjay, "Osama Bides his Time," *The Spectator*, June 21, 2003.
Andrews, Edmund, "Iraq's Old Money Elite Vies for Stake in Rebuilding the Nation," *NYT*, May 10, 2003, A10.
Apple, R., "US Commander, Evoking Mc Arthur, Hops Past Cities to Baghdad," *NYT*, April 4, 2003, B8.

Banerjee, Neela and Barringer, Felicity, "War Fails to Halt Iraqi Oil Production, but Prompts a Debate about the Future," *NYT*, March 26, 2003, B15.

Banerjee, Neela, "Candidate for Production Job is a Retired Shell Executive," *NYT*, April 2, 2003, B12.

Banerjee, Neela and Barringer, Felicity, "Iraq Pipeline to Syria no Big Secret, Experts Say," *NYT*, April 17, 2003, B6.

Barringer, Felicity, "Blair and Annan Confer on UN Role in Getting Food and Water to Iraqis," *NYT*, March 28, 2003, B10.

Barringer, Felicity and Banerjee, Neela, "Who will Control Iraq's Oil? Tangled Questions Abound," *NYT*, April 9, 2003, B11.

Bar'el, Zvi, "Tribes and Shaky Allies," *Ha'aretz*, April 3, 2003.

Bar'el, Zvi, "Solo Voices in the Arab Chorus," *Ha'aretz*, April 4, 2003.

Becker, Elisabeth, "Details Given on Contract Halliburton was Awarded," *NYT*, April 11, 2003, B12.

Bender, Brian, "September 11 Panel Discusses Possibility of Iraq Link: Witnesses Detail al-Qa'ida Theories," *The Boston Globe*, July 10, 2003.

Bengio, Ofra, "Reflections on the New Iraq," Paper No. 80, June 23, 2003, The Moshe Dayan Center of Middle Eastern and African Studies.

Benvenisti, Meron, "A War of the Early 1990s," *Ha'aretz*, May 5, 2003.

Blair, Jayson, "Relatives of Missing Soldiers Dread Hearing Worse News," *NYT*, March 27, 2003, B13.

Broad, William, "Allies' Vital Supply Line Now Stretches into Orbit," *NYT*, March 31, 2003, B10.

Broad, William, "Iraq May Try Defensive Use of Chemicals, Experts Warn," *NYT*, April 4, 2003, B4.

Broad, William, "On-Site Identification Inexact," *NYT*, April 8, 2003, B1, B4.

Broad, William, "US Civilian Experts Say Bureaucracy and Infighting Jeopardize Search for Weapons," *NYT*, April 16, 2003, B2.

Broder, John, "Far Behind the Front, But not out of Danger," *NYT*, March 26, 2003, B2.

Bruni, Franks, "Turkey Sending Military Observers to Watch Kurds; US Warns Against Further Moves," *NYT*, April 11, 2003 B4.

Charen, Mona, "The Nazis Again?), *The Washington Times*, June 13, 2003.

Chivers, C. J., "With Militant Group Routed, American and Kurdish Forces Hunt for Clues about al-Qa'ida," *NYT*, March 31, 2003, B3.

Chivers, C., "Kirkuk on the Horizon, and a Falcon and Shells Nearby," *NYT*, April 2, 2003, B6.

Chivers, C., "While Many Islamic Fighters Surrender, Kurds Remain Wary of New Terrorist Attacks," *NYT*, April 7, 2003, B7.

Chivers, C., "Attention now Shifts to the Role of the Kurds," *NYT*, April 10, 2003, B5.

Chivers, C., "A Sense that the Iraqi Leader is Gone Brings Joy in the North," *NYT*, April 10, 2003, B7.

Chivers, C., "Kirkuk's Swift Collapse Leaves a City in Chaos," *NYT*, April 11, 2003, B1.

Chivers, C., "Shaky Ground is Ahead and Behind in the North," *NYT*, April 12, 2003, A1, B4.

Chivers, C., "Paratroopers Find Suspicious Warheads and Rocket Parts in Kirkuk," *NYT*, April 13, 2003, B1, B5.

Chivers, C., "Groups of Kurds are Driving Arabs from Northern Villages," *NYT*, April 14, 2003, B1, B6.

Chivers, C., "Huge Gravesite is Found in Northern Iraq," *NYT*, April 18, 2003, B1, B3.

Chivers, C., "Oil Fields in a Sorry State, Stripped Even of the Toilets,"*NYT*, April 20, 2003, B2.

Clemetson, Lynette, "In an F-18, Five Seconds Before Deck Veiled by a Sandstorm," *NYT*, March 27, 2003, B5.

Daifallah, Adam, "Lively Politics Start to Stir in Baghdad," *The New York Sun*, May 12, 2003.

Daly, Emma, "Five Wounded in Fighting Reach Spain for Treatment," *NYT*, March 27, 2003, B6.

Dao, James, "Hoping to Confuse Iraqis and Spread Panic, American Commandos Prepare to Enter Baghdad," *NYT*, April 4, 2003, B2.

Dreazen, Yochi, "Feaud Between Arabs, Kurds over Land both Call Home, is Resolved by Painful Exit," *The Wall Sreet Journal – Europe*, 15 May 2003, A3.

Durand, Jacky, *Liberation*, 12, June 16, 2003, p. 16.

Dwyer, Jim, "Sandstorm Grounds Copters," *NYT*, March 27, 2003, B5.

Dwyer, Jim, "American Soldiers, at the Behest of an Iraqi Officer, Topple a Hussein Statue," *NYT*, April 4, 2003, B3.

Dwyer, Jim, "In Karbala, Forsaken Tanks and Pockets of Resistance," *NYT*, April 6, 2003, B4.

Dwyer, Jim, "Tearing Loose as a New Power Arrives at the Ruins of Babylon," *NYT*, April 10, 2003, B6.

Ekeus, Rolph, "Iraq's Real Weapons Threat," *Washington Post*, June 29, 2003, B7.

Fathi, Nazila, "Iran Strongly Disputes American Accusations of Interfering in Iraq's Affairs," *NYT*, April 25, 2003, A12.

Feldner, Nimrod, "Inquiry and Analysis," No 137, June 12, 2003, p. 1.

Feuer, Alan, "Vengeful Chaos Clouds Long-Suffering Shi'ites' New Freedom," *NYT*, April 13, 2003, B4.

Filkins, Dexter, "Onward Toward the Tigris, With Iraq's Capital in Mind," *NYT*, April 2. 2003, B6.

Filkins, Dexter, "US Force Crosses Tigris, Wondering Where Republican Guards Went," *NYT*, April 3, 2003, B4.

Filkins, Dexter, "Marines Cruising to Baghdad," *NYT*, April 4, 2003, B1, B3.

Filkins, Dexter, "Little Resistance Encountered as Troops Reach Baghdad," *NYT*, April 5, 2003, B3.

Filkins, Dexter, "Some Iraqis Grateful to US but Wary of Any Changes," *NYT*, April 9, 2003, B1, B9.

Filkins, Dexter, "People Rise Like Icons as Nations Fall Down," *NYT*, April 10, 2003, B3.

Filkins, Dexter, "Marines Attack Baghdad Mosque Said to Have Been Visited by Hussein, but Prey Slips Away," *NYT*, April 11, 2003, B3.

Finn, Peter, "New Forces Move to Gain Sway Exiles, Others Aided by US in the South," *The Washington Post*, April 12, 2003.

Friedman, Thomas, "Dear President Bush," *NYT*, April 30, 2003, A27.

Friedman, Thomas, "Amid Arab Shock, some Stirrings of Change," *The International Herald Tribune*, August 7, 2003.

Gerecht, Reuel Marc, "How to Mix Politics with Religion," *NYT*, April 29, 2003, A29.

Gerth, Jeff, "US is Banking on Iraq's Oil to Finance Reconstruction," *NYT*, April 10, 2003, B14.

Gold, Dore, "Defensible Borders for Israel," *Jerusalem Viewpoints*, No. 500, June–July 2003.

Goldberg, Jeffrey, *The New Yorker*, October, 2002.

Goodheart, Adam, "Missing: a Vase, a Book, a Bird and 10,000 Years of History," *NYT*, April 20, 2003, wk10.

Goodman, Peter, "Bid by Kurds for a Stake in Iraqi Oil Production is Rebuffed by US Officials," *The Wall Street Journal*, May 15, 2003, A3.

Gordon, Michael, "Basra Offers a Lesson on Taking Baghdad," *NYT*, April 7, 2003, B1.

Gordon, Michael, "Baghdad's Power Vacuum is Drawing only Dissent," *NYT*, April 21, 2003, A10.

Gordon, Michael and Jehl, Douglas, "On Order from Bush, US Troops in Iraq Begin Disarming Iranian Opposition Group," *NYT*, May 10, 2003, A10.

Guttman, Matthew, "Hakim Gets Mixed Welcome in Najaf," *The Jerusalem Post*, May 13, 2003.

Heilman, Uriel, "Fighting for their Due," *The Jerusalem Post*, June 13, 2003, B4.

Heller, Mark, "Powell in Damascus: Will Policy Change in Syria Follow Regime Change in Iraq?" *Update on Political and Strategic Developments in the Middle East*, No 76, Tel Aviv University, May 5, 2003.

Henriques, Diana, "American Contractors Prepare to Begin the Rebuilding of Iraq," *NYT*, April 27, 2003, A24.

I'jaz, Mansoor, "The Clinton Intelligence Record: Deeper Failures Revealed," *National Review Online*, April 29, 2003.

Jansen, Michael, "Iraqi Museum Exhibit– a Public Relations Stunt," July 3, 2003.

Jaulmes, Adrien, "Les Americains Traquent les Irreductibles du Baas," *Le Figaro*, June 13, 2003, p. 2.

Jehl, Douglas and Gordon, Michael, "American Forces and Terror Group Reach Cease-Fire," *NYT*, April 29, 2003, A1, A18.

Johnson, Daniel, "Don't Throw the Baby Out with the Bath Water," *The Wall Sreet Journal*, April 24, 2003.

Johnston, David and Risen, James, "Iraqi Leaders Said to Use Civilian Areas in Baghdad," *NYT*, April 8, 2003, B5.

Johnston, David and Risen, James, "New Signs of Terror not Evident," *NYT*, April 6, 2003, B1, B14.

Kagan, Robert, *The Washington Post*, June 8, 2003 B07. Cited by *Updates from AIJAC*, June 16, 2003.

Khalil, Nevine and Abdelaty, Soha, "Cairo Spelt out an Ambitious Plan to Reform the Arab League," *Al-Ahram Weekly*, July 4–August 4, 2003.

Khuri, Rajah, "Who Will Apologize?" *Al-Nahar*, May 20, 2003.

Kifner, John, "As Tanks Move in, Young Iraqis Trek out and Take Anything not Fastened Down," *NYT*, April 10, 2003, B2.

Lecumberri, Beatrice, "British Look to Tribal Leader to Restore Civilian Rule to Basra," *Agence France Press*, cited by *Jordan Times*, April 9, 2003.

LeDuff, Charlie, "Kurdish Hopes Fading in Light of New Moves," *NYT*, March 25, 2003, B7.

LeDuff, Charlie and Rhode, David, "Troops Won't be Sent to Kurdish Areas, Turkish Military Chief Says," *NYT*, March 27, 2003, B6.

LeDuff, Charlie and Feuer, Alan, "Men From Texas, on Call in Kuwait, Cap Well Fires in Southern Iraq, *NYT*, April 1, 2003, B11.

LeDuff, Charlie, "Marines Ready for Anything in Holdout City," *NYT*, April 13, 2003, B5.

LeDuff, Charlie, "A Cleric Assumes a Bully Pulpit," *NYT*, April 19, 2003, B1, B5.

Liptak, Adam, *NYT*, March 26, 2003, B11.

Mac Farquhar, Neil, "Shi'ites, Resenting Both Sides, are Swing Groups," *NYT*, April 8, 2003, B2.

Makiya, Kanan, "Kanan Makiya's War Diary," *The New Republic*, March 29, 2003.

Malbrunot, Georges, "La Mefiance Tapageuse des Chefs de Clan Iraquiens," *Le Figaro*, June 13, 2003, p. 2.

Manguel, Alberto, "Our First Words, Written in Clay, in an Accountant's Hand," *NYT*, April 20, 2003, wk 10.

Marquis, Christopher and Wade, Nicolas, "Loss of Apache in Iraq is Evidence of Vulnerability of Copters to Ground Fire," *NYT*, March 25, 2003, B3.

McElroy, Damien, "Al-Qa'ida Fighters Set up Base In Lebanon Refugee Camp," *The Daily Telegraph*, June 22, 2003.

Merritt, Gilbert, "Document Links Saddam, Bin Laden," *The Tennesean*, June 25, 2003.

Miller, Judith, "US Hunts for Bio-Agents and Gas at an Iraq Depot," *NYT*, March 27, 2003, B4.

Miller, Judith, "Smoking Gun Still Proves to be Elusive for Searchers," *NYT*, April 2, 2003, B7.

Miller, Judith, "Hunt Finds Hint of How Iraqis Fill Power Void," *NYT*, April 10, 2003, B6.

Miller, Judith, "Hunting Weapons, a Plucky Crew Makes Do," *NYT*, April 12, 2003, B2.

Miller, Judith, "US Inspectors Find No Forbidden Weapons at Iraqi Arms Plant," *NYT*, April 16, 2003, B1–2.

Miller, Judith, "Shi'ite Clerics Seek Control of Munitions at 2 Factories," *NYT*, April 13, 2003, B4.

Miller, Judith, "Illicit Arms Kept Till Eve of War, an Iraqi Scientist is Said to Assert," *NYT*, April 21, 2003, cited by IMRA, April 21, 2003.

Miller, Judith, "Radioactive Material Found at a Test Site Near Baghdad," *NYT*, May 12, 2003, A16.

Monitz, David and Diamond, John, "Iraqi Colonel's Capture Sped up Taking the City," *USA Today*, April 10, 2003, 2A.

Moss, Michael and Nordberg, Jenny, "Imams Urged to be Alert for Suspicious Visitors," *NYT*, April 6, 2003, B1, B14.

Mouawad, Jad, "Currency in Chaos," *The Jerusalem Post*, June 13, 2003, B3.

Myers, Steven Lee, "G.I.s Pause on Push to Baghdad, and One Falls to a Sniper," *NYT*, March 25, 2003, B6.

Myers, Steven Lee, "Battalion Stages Assault on Iraqi Hilltop Position and Guards Complex," *NYT*, April 9, 2003, B9.

Nagourney, Adam and Sanger, David, "Bush Defends the Progress of War: Privately, Republicans Fret over Uncertainties," *NYT*, 1 April 1, 2003, B1, B3.

Perelman, Marc, "Oil for Food Sales Seen as Iraq Ties to al-Qa'ida: US Probes Bank Network," *Forward*, June 20, 2003.

Perlez, Jane, "Iraqi Family Split on Returned Exile: US Favors Him, but who Else Does?" *NYT*, April 21, 2003, A10.

Perlez, Jane, "Veteran TV Anchors Push to Become the Voices of a New Iraq," *NYT*, April 28, 2003, A9.

Perlez, Jane, "Iraqis Set to Meet to Pick Transitional Government," *NYT*, April 29, 2003, A1, A18.

Peterson, Iver, Marc Santora, Eric Schmitt, Adam Liptak, David Sanger, Carl Hulse, and Jim Yardley, *NYT*, March 26, 2003, B7, B11.

Pisik, Betsy, "Stash of US Bills Found in Bunker," *The Washington Times*, April 22, 2003.

Prowse, Michael, "Rival Certanties," *The Financial Times*, June 20, 2003.

Rantawi, 'Arib, "The Mass Graves of Saddam," *Al-Dustur*, May 20, 2003.

Rashed, abd-al-Rahman, "Saddam was Not Alone to Fall," *Al-Sharq al-Awsat*, April 10, 2003.

Rhode, David, "Kurdish Refugees Make Do, Not for the First Time," *NYT*, March 25, 2003, B7.

Rhode, David and Chivers, C., "US Opens Command in Northern Iraq," *NYT*, March 25, 2003, B7.

Rhode, David, "Kurdish Forces Prepare to Attack in Northern Iraq," *NYT*, March 26, 2003, B5.

Rhode, David, "Americans Protect Airstrip on the Northern Front," *NYT*, March 28, 2003, B4.

Rhode, David, "Scenes of the Other Iraq: Green Fields, Starry Nights, Friendly Locals," *NYT*, April 1, 2003, B10.

Rhode, David and Chivers, C., "Iraqis Pull Back in the North; Journalist is Killed by a Mine,"*NYT*, April 3, 2003, B4.

Rhode, David, "On Pain of Death, Iraqi Soldier Kept at it," *NYT*, April 3, 2003, B5.

Rhode, David, "10 Americans with Help from Kurds, Stave off Iraqis," *NYT*, April 5, 2003, B4.

Rhode, David, "18 Die as US Airstrike Mistakenly Hits Kurdish Force," *NYT*, April 7, 2003, B1, B3.

Rhode, David, "View from Ancient Monastry as yet Another War Intrudes," *NYT*, April 10, 2003, B6.

Rhode, David, "As Kurds Move into Kirkuk, Arabs Fear Revenge," *NYT*, April 11, 2003, B4.

Rhode, David, "In Newly Occupied Mosul , US Colonel Faces 1.7 million Added Responsibilities," *NYT*, April 13, 2003, B5.

Rhode, David, "6 Iraqi Officials Offer to Surrender to the US," *NYT*, April 15, 2003, B4.

Rhode, David, "At Least 10 Iraqis Dead in Clashes in Northern Iraq," *NYT*, April 15, 2003, B3.

Rhode, David, "Marines Again Kill Iraqis in Exchange of Fire in Mosul," *NYT*, April 17, 2003, B2.

Rhode, David, "Danger Lingers in Pieces of an Abandoned Arsenal," *NYT*, May 5, 2003, A11.

Rhode, David, "Iraqis Face Dual Peril, Bombs and Cholera," *The International Herald Tribune*, citing *Reuters*, May 15, 2003, p. 3.

Risen, James and Johnston, David, "Military and CIA Searching Baghdad for Hussein and His Sons of their Bodies," *NYT*, April 10, 2003, B2.

Rivkin, David and Casey, Lee, "Saddam, Nikita and Virtual Weapons of Mass Destruction: a Question of Threat Perception and Intelligence Assessment," *The National Interest*, June 11, 2003. Cited by *Updates from AIJAC*, June 16, 2003, pp. 2–6.

Rubin, Alissa, "By the Snipers of Babylon," *The Jerusalem Post*, July 4, 2003, by agreement with the *Los Angeles Times.*

Sachs, Susan, "Schools Reopen in Baghdad, but Few Students Show Up," *NYT*, May 4, 2003, A1, A27.

Sachs, Susan, "Iraqis More Bemused than Enthused by Cleric," *NYT*, May 12, 2003, A13.

Saghiya, Hazem, "Graves, Graves, and a Suggestion," *Al-Hayat*, May 25, 2003.

Sanger, David, "US Officials Fear Iraqis Plan to Use Gas on G.I.s," *NYT*, March 25, 2003, B11.

Santora, Marc, "Continued Fighting Delays Plans for Air Distribution, Relief Workers Say," *NYT*, March 25, 2003, B6.

Santora, Marc, *NYT*, March 26, 2003, B7.

Santora, Marc, "Fear Said to be Keeping Iraqi Dissidents from Rebelling," *NYT*, March 26, 2003, B3.

Santora, Marc, "Food Arrives, But Water Supplies Cause Worry," *NYT*, March 27, 2003, B11.

Santora, Marc, "The Tides of Revenge in Basra Rise Quickly," *NYT*, April 11, 2003, B2.

Santora, Marc, "No More Fear that Prayer Falls on the Wrong Ears," *NYT*, April 12, 2003, B1, B4.

Santora, Marc "Once Dangerous Pilgrimage is Dangerous no More," *NYT,"* April 19, 2003, B1, B5.

Santora, Marc, "Children of Basra Face a Grim Set of Hardships," *NYT*, May 5, 2003, A11.

Saqr, Dr Turki, *Tishreen*, March 18, 2003.

Schechter, Erik, "Bush May be Sitting on Iraqi WMD Evidence, FOX Analyst Says," *The Jerusalem Post*, July 11, 2003, A4.

Schmitt, Eric, ""Key to Baghdad: How Hard Will Republican Guards Fight?" *NYT*, March 25, 2003 B5.

Schmitt, Eric and Chivers, C., "1000 Paratroopers Swoop Down on Kurdish Region to Open New Front," *NYT*, March 27, 2003, B6.

Schmitt, Eric and Weinraub, Bernard, "Battle for Baghdad Like War Plan: Kill Enemy, Limit Damage, Provide Aid," *NYT*, April 3, 2003, B1, B3.

Schmitt, Eric, "In the Skies over Iraq, Silent Observers Become Futuristic Weapons," *NYT*, April 18, 2003, B8.

Schmitt, Eric, "F-16s Pick off Iraqi Tanks in Kill Box Near Baghdad," *NYT*, April 5, 2003, B2.

Shanker, Thom and Schmitt, Eric, "A Campaign Invisible, Except for the Results," *NYT*, April 6, 2003, B1, B6.

Sharbal, Ghassan, "Saddam Hussein: From Tikrit to the Tribunal of History," *Al-Hayat*, April 10, 2003.

Simpson, Glenn, "US Says it Finds Stolen Iraqi Funds," *The Wall Street Journal – Europe*, May 15, 2003, A8.

Smith, Craig, "Basra's Defenders are Said to be Desperate and Fearful," *NYT*, April 4, 2003, B8.

Smith, Craig, "US-backed Shi'ite Cleric Killed at Shrine in Najaf," *NYT*, April 15, 2003, B 1–2.

Smith, Craig, "A Long Simmering Power Struggle Preceded Killings at an Iraqi Holy Shrine," *NYT*, April 13, 2003, B4.

Smith, Craig, "Politics and Religion Join the Fray in Shi'ite Slum," *NYT*, April 15, 2003, B1, B7.

Smith, Craig, "Teacher, a Survivor, Fondly Recalls Life in Hussein's Iraq," *NYT*, April 19, 2003, B2.

Spertzel, Richard, "The Politics of Mass Destruction," *The Wall Street Journal*, June 27, 2003.

Stevenson, Richard, "For Muslims, a Mixture of White House Signals," *NYT*, April 28, 2003, A13.

Steyn, Mark, "What is Going on in those Sofa Factories," *The Jerusalem Post*, 9 June, 2003. Cited by *Isranet Daily Briefing*, June 17, 2003, pp. 2–4.

Swarns, Rachel, "Muslims Protest Month-long Detention Without a Charge," *NYT*, April 20, 2003, A16.

Taversnise, Sabrina, "Iraqi Women Wary of New Upheavals," *NYT*, May 5, 2003, A1, A10.

Tavernise, Sabrina, "Ahead of Harvest, Farm Fears Grow," *NYT*, May 12, 2003, A16.

Tierney, John, "Did Lord Elgin do Something Right?" *NYT*, April 20, 2003, wk 10.

Tutenberg, Jim, "Ex-Generals Defend their Blunt Comments," *NYT*, April 2, 2003, B1.

Tweini, Jubran, "Editorial," *Al-Nahar*, August 14, 2003.

Tyler, Patrick, "US-British Project: To Build a Post-War Iraqi Armed Force of 40,000 soldiers in 3 Years," *NYT*, June 24, 2003.

Van Natta, Don and Johnston, David, "US for Illegal Arms Narrowed to about 36 Sites," *NYT*, April 14, 2004, B4.

Wade, Nicholas and Schmitt, Eric, "US Use of Tear Gas could Violate Treaty, Critics Say," *NYT*, April 5, 2003, B13.

Waxman, Sharon, "Black and White and Read all Over," *The Jerusalem Post*, June 13, 2003, B3, by agreement with *The Washington Post*.

Weintraub, Bernard, "A Field War for Soldiers Who Face the Emotional Rigors of Combat," *NYT*, April 6, 2003, B5.

Weinraub, Bernard, "American Soldiers Find Drums Possibly Storing Chemical Agents," *NYT*, April 8, 2003, B1, B4.

Weinraub, Bernard, "US Seeks Solid Core to Fix Iraq's Broken Legal System," *NYT*, April 27, 2003, A24.

Wilford, John Noble, "Art Experts Fear Worst in the Plunder of a Museum," *NYT*, April 13, 2003, B3.

Wilson, Michael, "Protecting the Rear in a 100 Degree Rear," *NYT*, April 6, 2003, B5.

Worth, Robert, "Terrorism Panel Hears Advise on Method of Prevention," *NYT*, April 2, 2003, B15.

Zoroya, Gregg and Lynch, David, "There is no Government Left, US General Says," *USA Today*, April 10, 2003, A1.

Auxiliary Books

Algar, Hamid, *Islam and Revolution*, UC Berkeley, 1981.

Ayoub, Mahmoud, *Redemptive Suffering in Islam*, Mouton de Gruyter, Berlin, 1978.

Cahen, Claude, *Islam* (in Hebrew translation), Dvir, Tel Aviv, 1995.

Ferrero, Guglielmo, *The Principles of Power*, Putnam, New York, 1942.

Glasse, Cyril, *The Concise Encyclopedia of Islam*, Harper and Row, San Francisco, 1989.

Israeli, Raphael, *Islamikaze: Manifestations of Islamic Martyrology*, Frank Cass, London 2003.

Kramer, Martin, *Protest and Revolution in Shi'ite Islam* (in Hebrew), Tel Aviv University.

Lukitz, Liora, *Iraq: The Search for National Identity*, Frank Cass, London, 1995.

Momen, Moojan, *An Introduction to Shi'ite Islam*, Yale University Press, 1985.

Qur'an, Suras: *al-Ahzab*.

Sivan, Emmanuel, *Muslim Radicals* (in Hebrew), Am Oved, Tel Aviv, 1985.

Taheri, Amir, *The Spirit of Allah* (in Hebrew translation), Am Oved, Tel Aviv, 1986.

Yasin, Borhanedin, *Vision or Reality: The Kurds in the Policy of the Great Powers, 1941–7*, Lund University Press, 1995.

Index

Kellog, Brown and Root Corporation,
148–9
Kelly, David, 175
see also Hutton Inquiry
Kelly, Captain Pat, 36
Khalilzad, Zalmay, 194–5
Khan, Kubilai, 178
Khanaqin, 34, 80
Kharrazi, Kamal, 238
Khatami, Muhammad, 203, 223
Khazir (Iraq), 89
Khazraji, General Nizar, 200
Khmer Rouge, 227
Khobar Towers incident, 19
Khomeini, Ayatullah, 20, 44–5, 47–9, 66,
69, 82, 202–3, 205
Iranian Revolution and, 4–5, 44, 49, 63
Khorasan (Iran), 104
Khudairy clan, 193
Khu'i, Sheikh abd-al-Majid, 65–6, 69–70
Khu'i, Grand Ayatullah, abd-al-Qassem,
48–9 65, 69, 203
Khurmal (Iraq), 85
Khurramshar, Iranian stand at, 6
Khuzistan (Iranian province), 4–5
Kifi (Iraq), 64, 88
Kim, Jong-il, 3
Kindi hospital, 131
King Abdul Aziz University, 142
Kirkpatrick, Jeanne, 143
Kirkuk, 29–31, 33–4, 78, 80–1, 84–88ff, 136,
172–3, 176–7, 182, 186, 201, 221, 233
oil in, 141ff
Komali Islami Kurdistan (Islamic group), 85
Korean War, 17
Kosovo, 232
Kubba clan, 193, 199
Kufa (*amsar*, Iraq), 51, 57, 70, 104
Kurdistan, 2, 12, 78–81, 84, 87–8, 116, 140,
150–1, 232
Democratic Party (KDP), 84, 87, 209
Patriotic Union (PUK), 84, 86, 209
Kurds
autonomy, 2, 37, 78, 80–2, 88, 91, 99
Fifth Brigade, 81
independence, 2, 13, 78, 80–3, 88, 232
in Iraq, 2, 7, 15–16, 30–4, 37–8, 49–50,
57, 77ff, 103, 126, 131, 151, 154–5,
159–60, 163, 169, 177, 186, 194, 196–8,
200ff, 206, 208–9, 211, 227, 233ff
Mountain Turks, 2
nationalism, 79–81, 83
uprising, 102
Kut, 33, 73–5, 116, 184
Kuwait, 8ff, 11, 15–17, 19, 29–31, 38–9, 51,
82, 102–3, 108, 111, 115, 120, 140, 145,
147, 154, 157, 168, 180, 212, 214, 217,
224, 226, 230

Kuwait City, 226

Latifiya (industrial plant, Baghdad), 171
League of Nations, 47, 52, 80–1
Commission, 80
Lebanon, 7, 20, 43–5, 66, 180, 192, 198,
217, 223–4, 229, 240–1
Lebensraum, Saddam's policy of, 7
Lehman, John, 157
Le Monde, 175
Lenin, Vladimir, 63
Liberation Square (Baghdad), 117
Libya, 17, 164, 169, 214, 224
Lichtenstein, 144
logistics, 32, 39ff, 51, 53, 108, 117
London, 22, 66, 70, 143, 160, 173, 219,
224–5
looting in Iraq, 86, 88, 92–9, 101, 126ff, 144,
151
Lord Hutton *see* Hutton Inquiry
Love, Sergeant, 59
Lugano (Switzerland), 145
Lynch, Private Jessica, 89

MacCaffrey, General Barry, 27
Mc Kiernan, General David, 208
Mada'in *see* Ctesiphon; Seleuceia
Mahdi, 43
Mahhod, Karim, 184
Makiya, Kanan, 200
Ma'mun, Caliph, 105
Ma'mun (Baghdad), 118
Majid, Ali Hassan (Chemical Ali), 56, 62,
131
Maliki, Abu-Imam, 154
Manchurian dynasty, 178
Mandali (Iraq), 80
Manila (Philippines), 156, 159
Mansoor, I'jaz, 155–6
Mansur, Caliph, 104
Mansur (Baghdad), 118
Maqlub mountain range, 91
Marines, 20, 29, 33, 40, 53, 56–9, 62, 72–5,
97, 100–1, 113–16ff, 127, 130, 132,
136, 177, 188, 226
24th Expeditionary Unit, 73–4
British 32
Fifth Regiment, 33
First Division, 33
First Regiment, 33–4, 114, 117ff, 129ff
Seventh Regiment, 33
Marja' Taqlid (Supreme Reference), 44, 48,
205
Maryam Bak (Iraq), 96
martyrs, 10, 13, 20, 43–7, 59, 62–3, 66, 71–4,
217
doctrine of, 43–4
see also Islamikaze

Marxism, 46, 157, 227, 238
Mashriq (the Arab East), 212
Mazyadid dynasty, 60
Mdeiras, Sheikh Ibrahim, 215, 223
Mecca, 9, 19, 63
Medes (Kurdish ancestors), 79
media, 13, 31, 34, 55, 59, 86, 92, 105, 112,
    113, 115, 117, 121–2, 154, 158, 171,
    176
    American, 19, 22–3, 25, 39, 158, 164
    Arab, 24, 31, 36, 113, 121, 130, 212ff
    electronic, 113
    "embedded", 22, 27, 115
    Iraqi, 109, 112, 158, 185, 188, 211
    Israeli, 26
    Western, 8, 27, 154, 175
    written, 113
Medina, 9, 19
Medina*, 109–11, 113, 130
Merritt, Gilbert, 157
Mesopotamia, 3, 66, 73, 104, 107, 134–5,
    194
MIAs, 36, 39, 56
Middle Ages, 105, 222
Middle East, 79–80, 100, 107, 140, 162, 180,
    194, 207, 215, 229
    American policy in, 131
    New, 11, 237ff, 240
    see also Arabs, World; Islam, World
MiG (fighter plane), 21, 166
military,
    British, 11
    Iraqi, 3–4, 10, 12, 15, 19, 56, 91–3, 106
    US, 9, 11, 19, 56
Mirage (fighter plane), 166
missiles, 8, 27, 29–30, 86–7, 113, 119, 124
    al-Sumud, 168
    ATACCM (Advanced Target
        Acquisition Counterfire), 109
    cruise, 29–30, 85
    Fatah, 168
    Hellfire, 29, 110
    Iraqi, 4, 6–7, 15–16, 30, 52, 89, 109, 113,
        124, 163, 168, 170, 207
    Javelin, 120
    Katyusha, 20, 22
    Patriot, 32
    Tomahawk, 29
missing in action (soldiers) *see* MIAs
MOAB (Massive Ordinance Air Blast)
    bomb, 14
Mobile Exploitation Team, 75,
    Alpha, 61, 170–2, 174
    Bravo, 170
Momen, Moojan, 64
Mongols, 60, 106, 153, 1768, 230–1
Morocco, 87, 160, 229–30
mortar and artillery, 86, 109, 122

mosques, 15, 45, 63, 67, 71–2 104, 132, 162,
    206
    al-Aqsa (Jerusalem), 222
    Bilal, 162
    Grand (Kut), 74
    Holy (Najaf), 69–70
    Imam al Siddiq (Basra), 67
Mosul, 12, 30, 34, 78, 80–1, 84–5, 87, 88ff
    112, 135–6, 181, 193, 196, 221, 233–4
    Airport, 97
    vilayet of 97
Mubarak, Hosni, 7–8, 161, 218, 239–40
Mufti of Jerusalem, 9
Muhammad (Prophet), 42–4, 207
Muhammad, Sheikh Khaled, 157
Muhawish (Iraq), 61, 172
mujahideen, 73, 191
    al-Khalq, 155, 190, 238
    "nuclear", 168
mujtahid (striver), 44
Mukhabarat (Iraqi intelligence/security
    apparatus), 29, 34, 50, 55, 99–100,
    102–3, 112–13, 122, 127, 154, 155–6,
    158, 165, 177, 200
Mullah, figure of, 2, 43, 45, 47–8, 67–8,
    72–3, 91
Musa, Amr, 227
Musayib complex, 167
Muslim Brotherhood, 144–5
Mu'tamad, Caliph, 105
Mu'tasam, Caliph, 105
Myers, General Richard, 29, 119, 160, 173
Mylroie, Laurie, 157

Nada, Youssef, 145
Najaf, 2, 4, 12, 32–4, 42, 47–8, 51–2, 56ff,
    61–2, 65–70, 82, 106, 108, 110, 112–13,
    120, 125, 170, 182, 195, 202–5
    custodian of the mosque in, 69–70
Najafi, Ali, 204
Nakasone, Yasuhiro, 9
Na'mani, Ali, 216
Namla, Saleh, 141
Napoleon, 127
Nasiriya, 2, 29, 33, 39, 42, 50, 56–8, 62, 65,
    73–4, 108, 110, 112, 115, 125, 184,
    194–5, 198, 204
Nasser, Gamal Abd–al, 81
Nassereddin, 145
nationalism
    Arab, 68, 97, 99, 207, 227
    Iraqi, 68, 179
    Kurdish, 79–80, 83
    National Socialism, 207
NATO, 17–18
Nazis, 20, 238
    de-Nazification, 207
    pro-Nazis, 145, 207